# INSIDERS' GUIDE® TO SAN ANTONIO

## HELP US KEEP THIS GUIDE UP TO DATE

We would love to hear from you concerning your experiences with this guide and how you feel it could be improved and kept up to date. Please send your comments and suggestions to:

editorial@GlobePequot.com

Thanks for your input, and happy travels!

INSIDERS' GUIDE® TO

# SAN ANTONIO

FIFTH EDITION

**Paris Permenter & John Bigley**

INSIDERS' GUIDE

GUILFORD, CONNECTICUT

AN IMPRINT OF GLOBE PEQUOT PRESS

All the information in this guidebook is subject to change. We recommend that you call ahead to obtain current information before traveling.

To buy books in quantity for corporate use
or incentives, call **(800) 962-0973**
or e-mail **premiums@GlobePequot.com.**

**INSIDERS' GUIDE®**



Editor: Kevin Sirois
Project Editor: Heather Santiago
Layout: Joanna Beyer
Text Design: Sheryl Kober
Maps: XNR Productions, Inc. © Morris Book Publishing, LLC

ISSN 1542-846X
ISBN 978-0-7627-7322-0

Printed in the United States of America
10 9 8 7 6 5 4 3 2 1

# CONTENTS

## Directory of Maps

# ABOUT THE AUTHORS

**Paris Permenter** and **John Bigley** are a husband-wife team of freelance writers who specialize in travel. Their work has been in numerous international, national, and statewide publications.

After their marriage in 1986, Paris and John realized they shared a talent and interest in the field of nonfiction, specifically travel. As coauthors of *Day Trips from San Antonio* and *Day Trips from Austin* (both published by Globe Pequot Press), Paris and John have covered the region extensively.

Paris and John also specialize in romantic travel around the world. The pair has authored more than two dozen guidebooks to the Caribbean islands and has visited most islands in the region. Their Caribbean guidebooks include Lovetripper.com's *Guide to Caribbean Destination Weddings,* Fodor's *In Focus Jamaica, Adventure Guide to Jamaica, Adventure Guide to the Cayman Islands, Cayman Islands Alive!, Jamaica Alive!,* and *Caribbean with Kids.*

Both Paris and John enjoy learning about a region's culture through its cuisine. They have written *Texas Barbecue, Jamaica: A Taste of the Island, Bahamas: A Taste of the Islands,* and *Gourmet Getaways: North America's Top 75 Resorts.*

Paris and John also edit Lovetripper.com Romantic Travel Guide, an online guide focusing on romantic travel and destination weddings, and TexasTripper.com, an online look at Texas travel and Texas travel news. As members of the Society of American Travel Writers, Paris and John appear frequently on local television and radio programs promoting travel. They have spoken on many of the San Antonio television affiliates.

Today Paris and John live in Cedar Park, Texas, with their dogs and cats.

# ACKNOWLEDGMENTS

To help write about San Antonio, we sought the advice of two groups: longtime San Antonians and San Antonio travelers. From both groups, we learned to love the city even more, and to both groups we say *muchas gracias.*

Our background and historical research took us throughout the city, from the public library to the resources of the San Antonio Conservation Society. We thank the librarians and volunteers who helped us search through newspaper clippings, scrapbooks, and historic documents that traced the evolution of the city's top attractions. We also relied on the San Antonio Convention and Visitors Bureau, especially Dee Dee Poteet. We'd also like to thank Geiger and Associates Public Relations for their assistance with information on San Antonio's many attractions.

As we made our way throughout the city, we talked to shopkeepers, restaurateurs, and hoteliers about their establishments. We listened to vacationers who, as the saying goes, just wanted to have fun. We talked to folks who had come back to San Antonio, some of whom had made their first visit to HemisFair decades before, as well as visitors being introduced to the city for the first time.

We depended on the people who, on a day-to-day basis, make San Antonio tourism work: the residents themselves. They share their city with an enthusiasm and friendliness that's rare these days. To all the museum docents, the bus drivers, the waiters, the ticket-takers, and the tour guides, we give our thanks.

Finally, a big thanks to Amy Permenter, who helped us fact-check this massive manuscript and keep information up-to-date in an ever-changing world.

—Paris Permenter and John Bigley

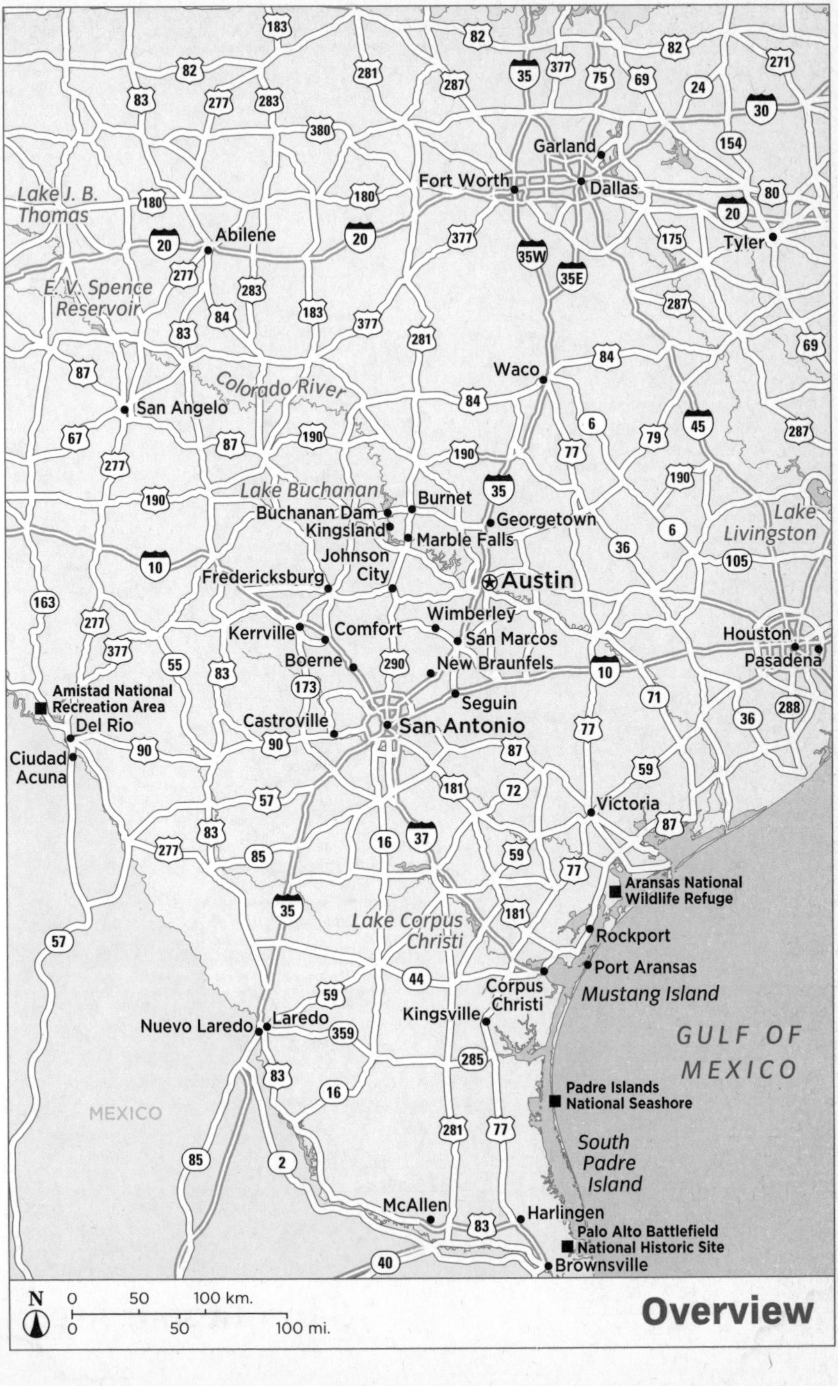

Lake J. B. Thomas
E. V. Spence Reservoir
Colorado River
Lake Buchanan
Lake Livingston
Lake Corpus Christi
Mustang Island
South Padre Island
GULF OF MEXICO
MEXICO
Garland
Dallas
Fort Worth
Tyler
Abilene
Waco
San Angelo
Burnet
Buchanan Dam
Kingsland
Marble Falls
Georgetown
Johnson City
Fredericksburg
Austin
Wimberley
Kerrville
Comfort
San Marcos
Boerne
New Braunfels
Houston
Pasadena
Amistad National Recreation Area
Del Rio
Ciudad Acuna
Castroville
San Antonio
Seguin
Victoria
Aransas National Wildlife Refuge
Rockport
Port Aransas
Corpus Christi
Kingsville
Nuevo Laredo
Laredo
Padre Islands National Seashore
McAllen
Harlingen
Palo Alto Battlefield National Historic Site
Brownsville
N
0 50 100 km.
0 50 100 mi.


## Overview

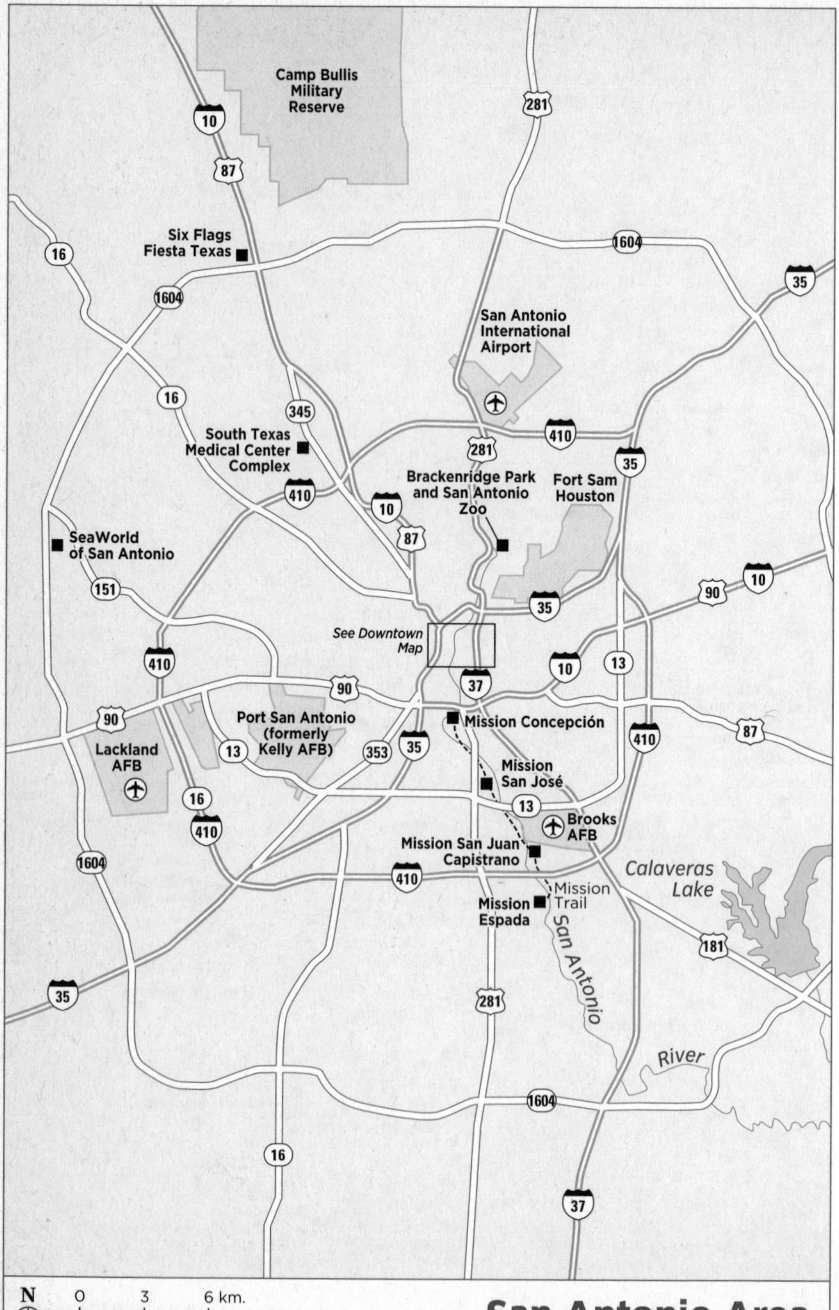


# San Antonio Area

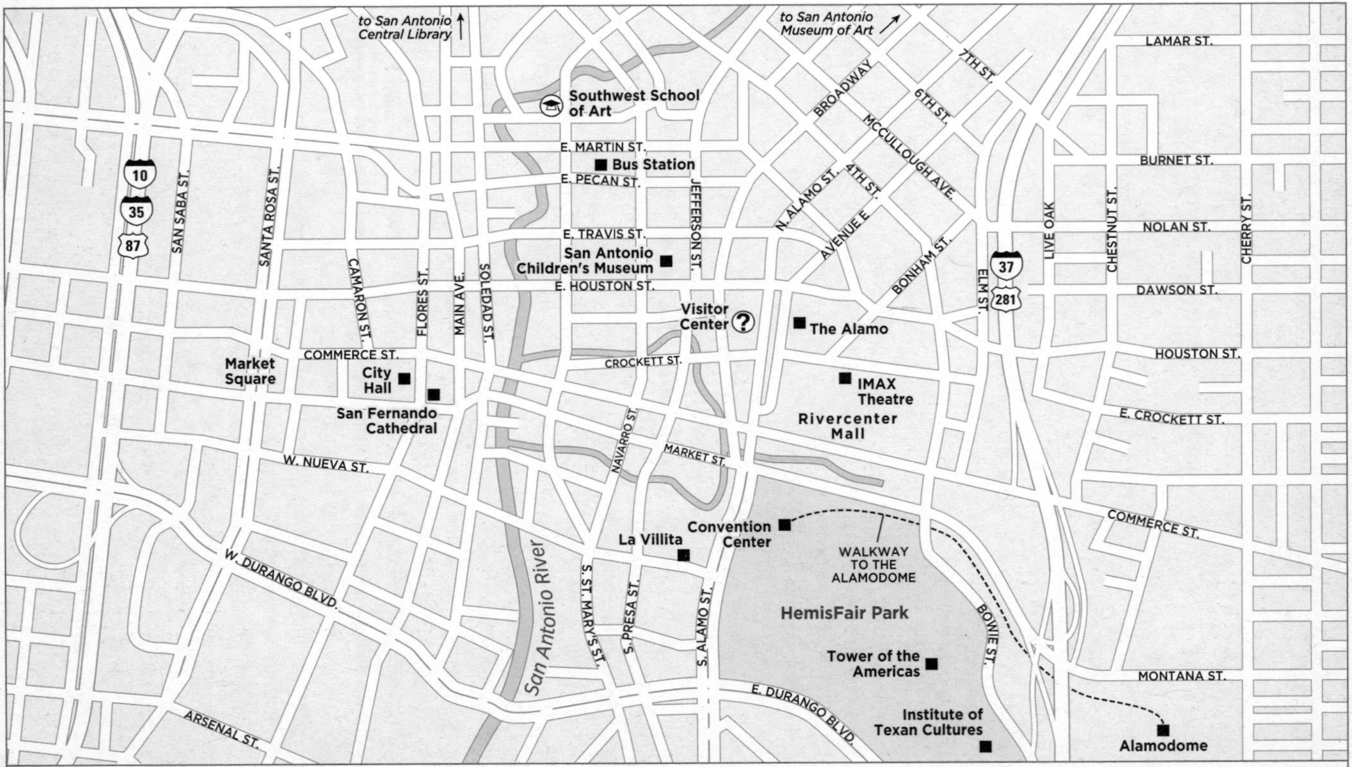
to San Antonio Central Library
to San Antonio Museum of Art
Southwest School of Art
E. MARTIN ST.
Bus Station
E. PECAN ST.
E. TRAVIS ST.
San Antonio Children's Museum
E. HOUSTON ST.
JEFFERSON ST.
Visitor Center
The Alamo
IMAX Theatre
Rivercenter Mall
BROADWAY
7TH ST.
6TH ST.
MCCULLOUGH AVE.
4TH ST.
N. ALAMO ST.
AVENUE E
BONHAM ST.
ELM ST.
LIVE OAK
CHESTNUT ST.
CHERRY ST.
LAMAR ST.
BURNET ST.
NOLAN ST.
DAWSON ST.
HOUSTON ST.
E. CROCKETT ST.
COMMERCE ST.
10
35
87
37
281
SAN SABA ST.
SANTA ROSA ST.
CAMARON ST.
FLORES ST.
MAIN AVE.
SOLEDAD ST.
COMMERCE ST.
CROCKETT ST.
Market Square
City Hall
San Fernando Cathedral
W. NUEVA ST.
NAVARRO ST.
MARKET ST.
Convention Center
La Villita
WALKWAY TO THE ALAMODOME
HemisFair Park
Tower of the Americas
Institute of Texan Cultures
Alamodome
BOWIE ST.
MONTANA ST.
W. DURANGO BLVD.
E. DURANGO BLVD.
San Antonio River
S. ST. MARY'S ST.
S. PRESA ST.
S. ALAMO ST.
ARSENAL ST.
N
0 0.2 0.4 km
0 0.2 0.4 mi.

# Downtown San Antonio

# INTRODUCTION

*Bienvenidos* to the Alamo City! Whether it's as a new home or a home away from home for a few days, you've chosen a destination that combines the best of Texas, the Southwest, and Mexico into a city that's filled with festivities, excitement, and history. Texans, whether residents of Amarillo or Zapata, have adopted San Antonio as their second hometown. When Texans think of a vacation spot in the Lone Star State, we look to the Alamo City. It brings back memories of childhood field trips to the Alamo, romantic strolls on the River Walk, Christmases beneath thousands of tiny lights, and family fun at the theme parks.

We've explored this city from end to end, mining the jewels we believe will help you make the most of your time in San Antonio, however long or abbreviated. Writing this book has given us the excuse to take the magnifying glass to our favorite Texas city and to seek out the tried-and-true as well as the often-overlooked. We've revisited some sites we had forgotten and discovered other locations that are truly Insiders' secrets. In these pages, we know you'll discover some gems as well, whatever your interests.

And, as you'll see from the size of this guide, San Antonio does boast a variety of attractions, from historic buildings to hair-raising thrill rides. San Antonio is home to 3 of the top 10 tourist attractions in the state (the Alamo, River Walk, and SeaWorld of Texas), according to the Texas Department of Transportation. But it's not just the number of attractions that draws visitors to this South Texas community, it's the atmosphere.

Will Rogers once proclaimed San Antonio "one of America's four unique cities." Wake up in the Alamo City with the scent of huevos rancheros in the air, the sound of mariachis filling the streets, and the sight of barges winding down the San Antonio River, and you'll know you're not in Kansas anymore, Dorothy. Even other Texas cities don't have San Antonio's unique spirit.

Along with a strong Hispanic influence, San Antonio brings together other cultures to create a unique identity all its own. For example, the influence of the city's early German residents can be seen on everything from architecture to menus. Families that trace their heritage back to the days of the earliest San Antonio merchants have proudly worked to conserve the history of this city and to preserve its buildings and historic sites.

While other cities may speed along in the fast lane, San Antonio prefers the scenic route, a perfect pace for the city's many tourists from around the world. Even though there are plenty of things to do, this is the kind of town where both a siesta and a museum visit are equally acceptable ways to spend an afternoon.

At the heart of the city is the San Antonio River, winding through tropical lushness and drawing residents and visitors into its current of gaiety along the riverbanks. The San Antonio River is to this city what the Seine is to Paris, the bay to San Francisco, the delta to New Orleans. It draws both residents and vacationers to its banks to enjoy a sense of place that is unrivaled anywhere else in Texas—and few places around the globe. Get to know the boutiques, stores, and restaurants located at every bend and twist in the river on the River Walk. A short walk up the steps of the outdoor Arneson River Theatre will bring you to historic La Villita, the old village of San Antonio's past. Watch artisans at work, from painters and glassblowers to candle makers, potters, weavers, and jewelers.

San Antonio is proud to be known as the "Venice of the Southwest." Once considered the "northernmost city in Mexico," San Antonio today is an exotic blend of Texas frontier and Mexican marketplace with cultural input from countries around the world. From the historic and traditional to contemporary and cutting-edge, San Antonio's attractions, arts, museums, and cuisine will take you on a sentimental journey.

An old Spanish legend says, "They who drink of the San Antonio River will return." Drink up the atmosphere, soak up the sun that filters through the cypress and banana trees, and taste the excitement. And you'll be back.

# HOW TO USE THIS BOOK

This is a book for San Antonio vacationers and conventioneers—folks looking for a good meal, a good shop, a good night's sleep, and a good time in one of the most popular vacation spots in Texas. It's also a book for city residents, especially those who have only recently made San Antonio their home. This is not an exhaustive guide to the Alamo City, but rather one that covers places that make San Antonio unique.

This guide is divided by activity. Flying in to San Antonio International Airport? Check out the Getting Here, Getting Around chapter for information on shuttles and rental cars. In this chapter, you'll also find an explanation of the boundaries we've used to divide this city into sections: downtown, inside Loop 410, between Loop 1604 and Loop 410, and beyond Loop 1604. These divisions will help you determine whether the restaurant you're eyeing is within easy driving distance of your hotel, or if you can combine two attractions in a single afternoon.

When you're ready to book a room, the extensive Accommodations chapter covers all price ranges. If you want to schedule your stay during a local festival—or during a quieter (and less expensive) period—read the Annual Events & Festivals chapter for details on the festivals and events that San Antonio throws on a scale to rival any other Texas city. Once you're settled, we'll guide you to attractions that range from museums to historic sights. The youngest travelers in the family will be especially interested in the Kidstuff chapter, with information on children's activities and museums. With San Antonio's excellent weather, you'll want to check the Parks & Recreation chapter to find places to enjoy the great outdoors. Nightlife and The Arts chapters keep you abreast of the hottest spots in town, including theaters, galleries, and nightclubs.

The unique character of San Antonio is due to more than its attractions, though; it's also a product of the city's rich history. This book includes a brief history of San Antonio, from its early mission days to its famous Alamo battle to its present role as a Texas cultural crossroads. You'll learn more about the Hispanic culture that makes San Antonio special, as well as the diversity of other cultures that call this city home. San Antonio is also closely entwined with the military world, with four military bases within its borders. We look at the role of the military in a special chapter that takes in both the historic and the present-day impact of these bases.

We've featured several unusual spots in "Close-up" stories sprinkled throughout the book. These are aimed at providing insight into the places that make the Alamo City so special. Insiders' tips (indicated by an **i**) discuss things distinctly San Antonian.

You'll also find listings accompanied by the ✻ symbol—these are our top picks for attractions, restaurants, accommodations, and everything in between that you shouldn't miss while you're in the area. You want the best this region has to offer? Go with our **Insiders' Choice.**

Finally, if you're moving to the San Antonio area or already live here, be sure to check out the blue-tabbed pages at the back of the book. There you will find the **Living Here** appendix that offers sections on relocation, media, child care, education, health care, and retirement.

No guide can be everything to every reader. Your own best judgment must prevail. Keep in mind your own limits, and make your plans accordingly. Be aware of the conditions around you, and be flexible enough to adjust to meet those conditions. For example, summer in San Antonio can be downright fiery, so you'll need to adjust your schedule to take advantage of early morning and late evening temperatures during those months.

Travel is a journey of discovery that may take you down a different—and possibly more interesting—route than the one you originally intended. For instance, if your River Walk visit coincides with the city's largest event, Fiesta, your stay will be shared with hundreds of thousands of other visitors. Things will take a little longer; your total number of stops may be fewer. But at the same time, you'll be part of a celebration that makes this city distinct.

With these tips in mind, let the trip begin. Whether you're journeying from your armchair or the driver's seat, from a rental car or a moving van, we hope the following pages will help you enjoy the Alamo City.

# AREA OVERVIEW

The term "Texas-size" is tossed around the Lone Star State to describe everything from fountain drinks to roller coasters, but it truly sums up the sprawling metropolis that is San Antonio. This city spans 417.1 square miles, an area that ranges from a dense downtown to quiet suburban neighborhoods.

But the description covers far more than geographic area; Texas-size describes everything from culture to cuisine, attractions to accommodations. Whether you're trying to decide on an afternoon activity or an afternoon meal, you'll find yourself presented with a full menu of choices. As the home of the Alamo, a symbol of Texas pride and its fight for independence, San Antonio boasts historic sites that can't be equaled. And when it's pure fun you're after—whether that translates as a museum tour or a merry-go-round—the city offers a long list of attractions that includes museums, sports, parks, children's activities, theme parks, and more.

Texas-size really describes San Antonio's true passion: fiesta. As one local resident once said, "You can't come to San Antonio without having a fiesta!" "Fiesta" encompasses all aspects of "party" but with a sizzle that only San Antonio parties can deliver. The Alamo City parties in a style like no other Texas destination, with year-round special events and festivals that incorporate foods, dances, and even special touches such as pastel streamers and cascarones, confetti-filled eggs that children (and the childlike) delight in breaking over any unsuspecting person's head.

Once a year, the fiesta spirit takes over the city with a 10-day celebration called Fiesta San Antonio. Dating back to 1891, this April celebration fills the city with parades, sporting events, live music, and a general party atmosphere.

The fiesta spirit lives year-round at the city's heart, the Paseo del Rio or River Walk. This magical place is located 20 feet below street level, nestled behind tall buildings away from street noise. With high-rise hotels and plenty of specialty shops and European-style alfresco cafes, the River Walk is easy for visitors to explore on their own. The River Walk embodies what people envision when they hear the name San Antonio: pure fun.

## LATINO INFLUENCE

San Antonio brings together the cultures of Texas and Mexico in a true melting pot, thanks not only to a shared history but also to shared family ties. Almost 62 percent of the city's residents are of Hispanic origin.

It's not surprising that practically all aspects of the city, from street names to local politics, are flavored by the cultural and historical distinctions of its dominant population.

The connection between San Antonio and Mexico is a long one; San Antonio's early history is, in fact, Mexican history. Like the rest of Texas, the city was part of Mexico until 1836. When Texas decided to break free of Mexico, several Mexican Texans took part in the historic signing of the Texas Declaration of Independence on March 2, 1836. At least seven were elected to serve at the convention; only three—José Antonio Navarro, José Francisco Ruiz, and Lorenzo de Zavala—were able to attend this historic event, one of the most important on the long road to independence. Four days later, Santa Anna's victory at the Alamo cost seven Mexican Texans their lives.

**Erasmo Seguin** and son Juan dedicated the following years, as well as their personal fortune, to the development of Texas. Erasmo Seguin became an early mayor of Bexar and worked to reinforce the relationship between Texas and Mexico. His son, Juan, had been present at the battle of the Alamo but had escaped death when he was sent out with a message calling for reinforcements. **Juan Seguin** went on to serve in the Texas Senate until 1840, the next year becoming the mayor of San Antonio.

i **Bexar County is pronounced "Bear" County.**

Hispanic involvement in Texas politics continues today. Of the five Latinos elected to the US Congress in 1994, three hailed from San Antonio. **Henry Cisneros,** a popular mayor of San Antonio in the 1980s, was named US Secretary of Housing and Urban Development by President Bill Clinton in 1993.

Throughout the city, Hispanic influences are seen in business as well. The **San Antonio Hispanic Chamber of Commerce** (www.sahcc.org) is the oldest of the 600 Hispanic chambers in the nation and now boasts 1,600 members and business associates. Originally chartered as the Mexican Chamber of Commerce in 1929, it was organized by Don Enrique Santibanez, consul general of Mexico in San Antonio and a local businessman, to promote trade, policy, and cultural harmony. While the chamber's leaders forged ahead to define modern Hispanic business, the social climate of the time posed many barriers through discrimination. Those issues prompted the chamber to alter its scope to include both social and business advocacy.

In 1987, when the Mexican Chamber of Commerce was renamed the San Antonio Hispanic Chamber of Commerce, and the organization took on a more global relationship with all of Latin America. The group helped play a role in the passage and promotion of the North American Free Trade Agreement (NAFTA). Since then, it has worked to increase the focus of small business as the backbone of the economy. Today the SAHCC is the oldest organization of its kind in the US.

Latino culture also plays an important role in the recreational side of San Antonio. The **Alameda Theatre,** constructed in the late 1940s as a movie palace, was the largest theater ever dedicated to Spanish-language entertainment. In 1998 the venue reopened following a refurbishment as a teaching facility for Latino arts and culture. Latin arts are the focus of the **Nelson A. Rockefeller Center for Latin American Art** at the San Antonio Museum of Art. Considered the most extensive collection of its kind, the center includes exhibits on Latin American folk art as well as many historic pieces. San

Antonio also is considered the birthplace of **Tejano music,** a lively combination of rock, polka, and Mexican sounds. Now enjoying a global stage, top Tejano performers are recognized at annual awards events held in San Antonio. In the film world, the **Guadalupe Cultural Arts Center** hosts an annual film festival showcasing Latino productions. In the literary world, the **San Antonio Inter-American Bookfair and Literary Festival** highlights Latino writers and books with Hispanic themes.

i The cuisine of San Antonio is inextricably tied to that of its Hispanic history. Many Mexican delights such as *aguas frescas* (fruit drinks), *buñuelos* (fried cinnamon pastries), and *raspas* (snowcones) are found at festivals throughout the city, while San Antonio eateries serve dishes such as *barbacoa* (a special type of barbecue), *cabrito* (goat), and *menudo* (tripe soup).

## AFRICAN-AMERICAN CULTURE

African Americans make up just 7 percent of the total San Antonio population, but their influence is seen throughout the city, in its festivals, its food, its booming businesses, and its appreciation of history and tradition.

The long link between the African-American community and San Antonio dates back to the 1500s, to the days when Spaniards came to establish their claim to this region. Enslaved Africans were brought by the Spaniards, and by the late 1700s many of their descendants were freed. Soon the population began to intermarry with the Spanish, Mexican, and Indian residents. In 1809 Victor Blanco, a man of mixed race, became San Antonio's first and only African-American mayor.

When Mexico won its freedom from Spain in 1821, it also won claim over the Texian territory. Under Mexican law, slavery was not permitted, although many African descendants became indentured servants. In exchange for legal papers stating their freedom, these people were paid a small sum (often only a dollar) and made indentured servants—often for their entire lives.

One such indentured servant became the subject of Texas legend. **Emily Morgan,** a mixed-race indentured servant, captured the eye of Mexican General Santa Anna, soon becoming the military leader's confidante. After gaining his trust, she learned about the general's military plans and worked as a spy, supplying the information to Sam Houston and the Texian army fighting for independence. Emily Morgan's patriotism is remembered in a song learned by all Texas schoolchildren: "The Yellow Rose of Texas."

Emily Morgan's name is well known to Texans, but the beautiful spy was only one African-American patriot in the fight for Texas independence. Several African Americans were present at the battle of the Alamo, working as slaves to the Texan settlers.

When Texas won its independence from Mexico, settlers moved to the region from throughout the South, bringing with them a number of slaves. During the Civil War, slavery was abolished throughout the country on September 22, 1862. Word of emancipation, however, did not reach Texas until June 19, 1865. That day became known as **Juneteenth,** and today it is celebrated in San Antonio and throughout the state with an annual festival.

In the years following the Civil War, the racially segregated US Army formed

African-American units. In 1867 one such unit, the Ninth Cavalry, arrived in San Antonio. Stationed along the frontier to help protect against attack, the members of this cavalry were known as the **"buffalo soldiers"** by the Native Americans because of their strength, bravery, and curly hair. Stationed at San Pedro Springs, the soldiers protected the San Antonio–El Paso mail route and were later awarded Medals of Honor. Today many of these soldiers are buried at the San Antonio National Cemetery.

Post-Reconstruction years saw a growing influence of African Americans in San Antonio as they became active in politics and gained positions in organized labor. In 1898 **St. Philip's College** was established as an industrial school for girls; in 1902 an African-American woman named **Artemisia Bowden** took leadership of the school and elevated it to a fully accredited junior college. It was the first institution of higher learning for African Americans in the San Antonio region and today is part of the **Alamo Community College District.**

Throughout the 20th century, the number of African-American businesses in San Antonio continued to rise. The Negro Chamber of Commerce was formed in 1938. It is now known as the **Alamo City Black Chamber of Commerce** (www.alamocitychamber.org) and works to assist African-American businesses. The **African American Chamber of Commerce** (www.aaccsa.com) also works for similar goals and is an affiliate of the National Association of African-American Chambers of Commerce Inc.

The influence of the African-American community also affected the city's cultural life. Many African-American nightclubs entertained local audiences with traveling headliner acts. The Library Auditorium showcased many well-known performers, and today the venue survives as the **Carver Community Cultural Center.** Performers have included Gregory Hines, Eartha Kitt, and the Dance Theatre of Harlem.

In the 1960s San Antonio residents worked to establish racial equality at a time when retail and grocery chains denied equal service to black patrons and practiced discriminatory hiring practices. Boycotts and rallies brought about integration.

Today San Antonio is home to a growing number of African-American businesses, and the African-American community is influential in fields ranging from medicine to politics.

San Antonio also welcomes a growing number of African-American travelers who come to enjoy the multicultural atmosphere of the city. Several multicultural festivals are also of special interest to African-American visitors. **Juneteenth Festival** is a day of both family celebrations and special events, including the African-American Cultural Association Juneteenth Picnic. June also brings the **Texas Folklife Festival,** when the spotlight turns to the 30-plus nationalities that helped settle this region.

In January is the annual **Martin Luther King March**—one of the largest such marches in the country—which honors the work and the life of the civil rights leader. The event takes place along a 3-mile route, which extends from the MLK Freedom Bridge to the MLK statue on the city's east side. In February the annual **African-American Harmon and Harriet Kelly Art Show** showcases the work of African-American artists; February is also the time of special productions, performances, and exhibits at the St. Philip's College Watson Fine Arts Center in observance of Black Heritage Month.

The San Antonio Convention and Visitors Bureau has mapped out a self-guided **African-American Heritage Tour** that covers 14 points of interest in the downtown area. The walk includes the Institute of Texan Cultures, where visitors can view the Black Wall, which showcases African-American contributions to the founding and building of Texas; St. Paul Square and Sunset Depot, the site of many African-American–owned businesses during times of segregation; the city cemeteries where 285 buffalo soldiers now rest; the Carver Cultural Center; St. Paul United Methodist Church, the oldest African-American church in San Antonio; and Ellis Alley, one of the first areas in the city to be settled by African Americans following the Civil War.

**i** The current estimated population of San Antonio is 2,080,311.

## MORE FACES OF SAN ANTONIO

With its strong Mexican ties, San Antonio has long had an international feel, but that cultural atmosphere reaches far beyond the Mexican borders. Since its earliest days, the city has been home to residents from around the globe. San Antonio's population of 2.1 million is approximately 62 percent Hispanic, 28 percent Anglo, and 7 percent African American, plus a smattering of other ethnic groups (Native Americans, Asians, Pacific Islanders). Census figures also report that 14 percent of San Antonians claim German ancestry, while others are of Irish (8 percent), English (8 percent), Italian (2 percent), French (2 percent), and Polish (2 percent) descent. Although lacking the extensive ethnic neighborhoods of other cities, San Antonio does have some areas that have traditionally been home to certain groups: "Southtown" remains largely Hispanic; the Alamo Heights, Olmos Park, and other communities on the city's north and northwest are mostly Anglo; and the east side is traditionally an African-American neighborhood.

## TOURISM

As the top travel destination in Texas, San Antonio's tourism business is booming; the latest figures show approximately 26 million visitors annually. With some 106,000 residents employed in the tourism business, tourism funnels in excess of $11 billion into the local economy, according to the San Antonio Area Tourism Council.

The lodging needs of visitors are met by numerous hotel rooms: nearly 12,700 in downtown alone and over 40,000 throughout the city. Nonetheless, occupancy rates average about 76 percent, above the national average. During peak periods such as Fiesta (April), Las Posadas (December), and anytime the San Antonio Spurs basketball team is playing on their home court, rooms can be at a premium.

**i** The San Antonio Convention and Visitors Bureau publishes SAVE (San Antonio Vacation Experience) coupon booklets. Representing substantial savings, the booklets include coupons for attractions and events, hotels, tours, and theme parks. You can pick up booklets at brochure racks across town; if you can't locate one, call the CVB at (800) THE-ALAMO.

## CONVENTIONS

The convention business is also booming in San Antonio. The city has answered the demand with a $193.8 million expansion of the **Henry B. Gonzales Convention Center,** now offering more than 600,000 square feet of meeting space. The expansion encouraged hotel growth; in 2008 there were over 40,000 hotel rooms, 12,700 in the downtown area alone, in nearly 200 hotels throughout the city.

San Antonio's largest meeting and exhibition facility is **The Alamodome** (www.alamodome.com), a Texas-size structure located east of the convention center. This multipurpose building can handle groups as large as 77,000; breakout meeting space totals 30,000 square feet. The **San Antonio Municipal Auditorium and Conference Center** is another popular meeting site. With a 4,982-seat auditorium, the property includes exhibit space and breakout rooms.

The River Walk is home to some of the city's top conference hotels, including the **Hyatt Regency San Antonio,** which underwent a $30 million renovation in 2010–2011; the **Marriott Riverwalk,** with 14 meeting rooms; and the **Marriott Rivercenter,** which soars up from the Rivercenter Mall and offers 60,000 square feet for meetings.

For reasons such as budget considerations, space availability, and a desire to promote group cohesiveness, meeting planners often select sites beyond the River Walk area for small to medium-size groups. Throughout the city, meeting and reception venues are available in sites of historic and cultural interest—and there are also some that are just plain fun. Market Square, Mission San José, the Lone Star Brewery, the Retama Park horse-racing track, Six Flags Fiesta Texas theme park, and SeaWorld of San Antonio are among the unusual choices available to businesses and groups that wish to hold meetings, receptions, and other special events in San Antonio.

## THINGS TO DO

Whether travelers come as part of a group or independently, they find a full array of activities in San Antonio—all of which are explored in depth throughout this book. For many, the first stop is the **Paseo del Rio—the River Walk.** The River Walk is home to high-rise hotels, shops, and European-style alfresco cafes. The best way to get an overview of the River Walk is aboard a guided river cruise; a ride on these open-air barges is a must for any first-time visitor. After a tour, stop for lunch at one of the sidewalk restaurants. San Antonio is known for its spicy Tex-Mex food, and restaurants like Michelino's and Casa Rio offer tables along the river's edge so you can watch the activity.

From the River Walk, it's a short stroll over to Texas's best-known symbol: the **Alamo.** This "Cradle of Texas Liberty" plunged into history on March 6, 1836, when 188 Texas defenders died in a battle against a large Mexican army led by General Santa Anna during the Texas Revolution. Stroll through the shrine to see artifacts and arms from the fateful battle. Just steps from the River Walk at HemisFair Plaza, the **Tower of the Americas** is a soaring reminder of the 1968 World HemisFair and is today one of San Antonio's most prominent landmarks. A one-minute elevator ride whisks you up to the observation deck at 579 feet for a great view of the city through high-powered telescopes.

Near the base of the tower stands one of the state's best museums, the **Institute of Texan Cultures.** Here you can learn about the more than 30 ethnic groups that settled Texas. Don't miss the dome slide show for a look at the many faces of the Lone Star State. Many days you'll find costumed docents moseying throughout the museum, ready to explain the role of a chuck wagon cook on a cattle drive or the rigors of life as a frontier woman. Another noteworthy San Antonio attraction lies along the oldest section of the River Walk: **La Villita.** In this "little village," nestled on the east bank of the River Walk, the focus is on history and art. Dating back to the days when the Alamo served as a military outpost, La Villita developed as a temporary village of people without land title. Today it's a National Historic District that bustles with shoppers in search of one-of-a-kind items ranging from watercolors to glass creations to handmade jewelry.

West of La Villita, and easily accessible via VIA streetcar, is **Market Square,** a shopping area that dates back to the early 1800s. The market's real claim to fame is that it was the birthplace of chili con carne, the spicy meat and bean mixture that's now the state dish of Texas. Once women known as "chili queens" sold the concoction from small stands in the market.

Today the south-of-the-border flavor of Market Square is seen in its shops and restaurants. Shop **El Mercado** for the same goods found in Mexico's mercados—but without the bargaining. When you're ready for a break, stop by **Mi Tierra,** the 24-hour restaurant that's popular with locals and visitors alike. While you wait for your Tex-Mex meal, strolling troubadours, called mariachis, take requests for Mexican ballads. Just as authentic is the adjacent *panaderia,* a Mexican bakery exuding the tasty aromas of fresh tortillas and *polvorones,* cookies topped with cinnamon and sugar.

When it's time to explore more of San Antonio's rich history, numerous options await. The Alamo may be the best-known mission in town, but it's certainly not the only one. The **San Antonio Missions National Historical Park** stretches for 9 miles along the San Antonio River and is composed of four missions constructed by the Franciscan friars in the 18th century. The missions are active parish churches today, and all are open to the public.

The chain of these historic buildings begins at **Mission Concepción,** a site that today illustrates religious life in the missions. **Mission San Juan Capistrano,** once completely self-sustaining, today explains "The Mission as an Economic Center" through interesting exhibits. The reconstructed **Mission Espada** has displays that explain vocational education at the missions.

The most active site on the mission tour is **Mission San José.** The most complete structure in the tour was once called the "Queen of the Texas Missions"; today a $9.5 million visitor center is located nearby. Save time to enjoy the mission's beautiful carvings and its restored mill with waterwheel.

Finally, for families who just want to have fun, the **Six Flags Fiesta Texas** theme park and **SeaWorld of San Antonio** are on the northwest side of town, along Loop 1604.

**i** Three of the top 10 tourist sites in Texas can be found in San Antonio. The Alamo holds the number one spot, with the River Walk in the number 6 position. SeaWorld of San Antonio is at number 8.

## INTERNATIONAL TRADE

The enactment of the North American Free Trade Alliance (NAFTA) brought major

## San Antonio Vital Statistics

**San Antonio mayor:** Julián Castro

**Texas governor:** Rick Perry

**Population: San Antonio:** 1,327,407; **Metro area:** 2,142,508; **State:** 24,782,302

**Area (square miles):** 417.1

**Nickname:** The Alamo City, River City

**Average temperatures:** July: 95 degrees; January: 62 degrees

**Average annual rain/days of sunshine:** 28 inches/300 days

**San Antonio founded:** 1718

**Texas achieved statehood:** 1845

**Major universities:** Oblate School of Theology, Our Lady of the Lake University, Palo Alto College, St. Mary's University, St. Philip's College, San Antonio College, Trinity University, Universidad Nacional Autónoma de Mexico, University of Texas at San Antonio (two campuses), University of Texas Health Science Center, University of the Incarnate Word, Wayland Baptist University–San Antonio

**Major area employers:** Public Sector—Bexar County, Brooke Army Medical Center, Brooks Air Force Base, City of San Antonio, Fort Sam Houston, North East ISD, Northside ISD, Randolph Air Force Base, San Antonio ISD, San Antonio Police Department, University Health System, University of Texas at San Antonio, University of Texas Health Science Center at San Antonio, US Postal Service

Private Sector—Caterpillar Inc., Chase Bank, Clear Channel Communications, H.E.B. Grocery Company, Kinetic Concepts, NuStar Energy, Sysco, Taco Cabana, Tesoro Petroleum Corporation, Toyota, USAA, Valero Energy Corporation, Wachovia

**Famous sons and daughters:** Carol Burnett, Henry Cisneros, Joan Crawford, Heloise, Shaquille O'Neal, George Strait

**State/city holidays:**

January 1: New Year's Day
January 19: Confederate Heroes Day
Third Monday in January: Martin Luther King Jr.'s Birthday
Third Monday in February: Presidents' Day
March 2: Texas Independence Day
March 31: César Chávez Day
March/April (varies): Good Friday
April 21: San Jacinto Day
Last Monday in May: Memorial Day
June 19: Emancipation Day (Juneteenth)
July 4: Independence Day
August 27: Lyndon B. Johnson's Birthday
First Monday in September: Labor Day

September (varies): Rosh Hashanah
October (varies): Yom Kippur
November 11: Veterans Day
Fourth Thursday in November: Thanksgiving
Friday after Thanksgiving: City Holiday Lighting and Parade
December 24–26: Christmas

**Resources and visitor centers:**

San Antonio Convention and Visitors Bureau
203 S. St. Mary's St., Suite 200
San Antonio, TX 78205
(210) 207-6700, (800) 447-3372
www.visitsanantonio.com

San Antonio Convention and Visitors Bureau Visitors Information Center
317 Alamo Plaza
(210) 207-6748, (800) 447-3372

Greater San Antonio Chamber of Commerce
602 E. Commerce St.
San Antonio, TX 78205
(210) 229-2100
www.sachamber.org

**Major airports/major interstates:** Air service is via the San Antonio International Airport. I-10, I-35, I-37, Loop 410, and Loop 1604 provide access into and across the city. At press time, numerous toll-road projects were planned for Bexar County.

**Public transportation:** San Antonio's VIA Metropolitan Transit (www.viainfo.net) serves the San Antonio area. Call (210) 362-2020 for route information. VIAtrans (210-362-2019, 210-362-2140) offers transportation for mobility-impaired riders.

**Military bases:** Brooks Air Force Base, Fort Sam Houston, Lackland Air Force Base, and Randolph Air Force Base

**Driving laws:** Seat belts must be worn in the front seats of cars and light trucks. Children under the age of 4, or less than 36 inches in height, must be secured whether they are in the front or backseat. The fine for failure to use seat belts for persons under 17 or child safety seats for younger children is $100 to $200. Proof of automobile insurance is required.

**Alcohol laws:** You must be 21 to drink in Texas. Beer and wine purchases can be made after noon on Sunday and at any time other days of the week. Liquor can be purchased between 10 a.m. and 9 p.m. Mon through Sat. Bars are open until 2 a.m. In Texas the legal limit for blood-alcohol content for drivers is 0.08.

**Daily newspapers:** *San Antonio Express-News, Daily Commercial Recorder*

**Sales tax:** A state retail tax of 6.25 percent is levied on most retail purchases except food and drugs. The City of San Antonio levies a retail sales tax of 1.125 percent on all items except groceries, prescription drugs, rent, mortgage payments, and gasoline.

growth to San Antonio industry thanks to increased trade with Mexico. In 1995, just a year after the enactment of the alliance, more than $45 billion in trade traffic flowed south from the city to Mexico. Similarly, in 1995 more than $53 billion of goods passed through San Antonio from Mexico. Half of all the US-Mexico trade travels through the city on highway and rail, according to the Chamber of Commerce.

To encourage international trade, San Antonio is also home to several foreign trade initiatives. Port San Antonio, originally Kelly Air Force Base, is one of several locations designated a Foreign Trade Zone, which offer reduced customs duties and government excise taxes for foreign merchandise. The zones are not open to the public. The **Free Trade Alliance** (203 S. St. Mary's St.; 210-229-9036; www.freetradealliance.org) operates International Business Development Center offices at Port San Antonio designed to encourage and assist foreign companies who want to do business in the US. The Port San Antonio project makes the city an inland port for international trade. The project is a joint effort of the Free Trade Alliance, the Greater San Antonio Chamber of Commerce, the City of San Antonio, the San Antonio Hispanic Chamber of Commerce, the San Antonio Economic Development Foundation, the Bexar Metropolitan Water District, and more than 600 local businesses and individual members.

Along with the Free Trade Alliance, several other international trade organizations in San Antonio work to assist in the import and export of goods. The **International Trade Center at the University of Texas at San Antonio** (210-458-2470) works to help small and medium-size businesses in the region with international trade issues. The **International Affairs Office of the City of San Antonio** (210-207-8100) assists in matching local companies with international markets. **BANCOMEXT,** the Trade Commission of Mexico (210-281-9748), works to promote investment. For San Antonio businesses interested in doing business in Mexico, and Mexican businesses interested in doing business in San Antonio, In addition to trade with Latin America, San Antonio also enjoys a growing trade with China. According to the Chamber of Commerce, more than 1,700 jobs in the city are directly related to trade in China. Among the Asian imports to San Antonio are eyewear, footwear, toys, and luggage.

**i** **Foreign currency exchange is available at Frost Bank (100 W. Houston St.). Bank of America (300 Convent St.) will exchange currency for traveler's checks only, unless you are a bank customer.**

## BIOMEDICAL INDUSTRIES

The health care industry is one of the city's top employers, bringing close to $4.2 billion into the region every year in the form of payrolls.

The **South Texas Medical Center,** located on the northwest side of the city, is one of the state's most extensive facilities, encompassing 11 hospitals, nearly 80 clinics, and many agencies.

The military health care system includes three centers: **Brooke Army Medical Center, Wilford Hall Medical Center** and the **South Texas Veterans Health Care System.** Brooke Army Medical Center is known throughout the state for its burn treatment and research facilities. Wilford Hall Medical Center is the largest medical facility under the umbrella of the US Air Force. In addition to serving military personnel, this center also provides a quarter of all the emergency health care in the city.

The South Texas Veterans Health Care System is home to acute medical, surgical, psychiatric, geriatric, and primary care services. It houses the National Institutes of Health's only sponsored research program in the Veteran's Administration. Also located here is one of 16 geriatric research, education, and clinical centers (GRECCs), which was named a Center for Excellence by the National Institute on Aging.

In addition to serving as regional hub for medical care, San Antonio is also home to a growing bioscience research industry. The combined economic impact of the health care and the bioscience research is almost $14.3 billion.

## LANGUAGE

English is the official language of San Antonio, but Spanish is spoken almost as often. Many businesses, especially in the tourism industry, have employees who speak fluent Spanish to assist the large number of tourists and business travelers who come to the city from neighboring Mexico.

## GOVERNMENT

San Antonio operates with a council-manager form of government. Eleven elected members make up the city council; this includes 10 members elected by districts and the mayor, who is elected by the city at large. City council members have two-year terms; they may serve up to two terms. The mayor also has a two-year term and may serve up to two terms.

# GETTING HERE, GETTING AROUND

San Antonio lies at the gateway to South Texas and is easily accessible from all directions by an international airport, a network of highways, and two Amtrak trains. Air travel to San Antonio is fairly simple, and nonstop flights are available to over 30 destinations ranging from Los Angeles to Newark. And, thanks to close ties with Mexico, the airport also offers numerous flights to and from destinations south of the border, including Mexico City, Monterrey, and San Luis Potosí.

If you drive to San Antonio—unless you're already familiar with the state—you'll gain a true understanding of the term "Texas-size." Just as a reference, it's 601 miles from Amarillo in the northern part of the state, called the Panhandle, to Brownsville at the coastal southern tip.

Austin lies a bit more than an hour north of San Antonio, although increasingly heavy traffic and construction along the San Antonio-to-Austin stretch of I-35 make that estimate heavily dependent on the days of the week and times of day you choose to travel. Farther north are Dallas and Fort Worth, representing a drive of about five hours. Houston, situated east of San Antonio, is about three hours away.

Getaways to the Gulf Coast from the Alamo City are an easy two-hour drive to Corpus Christi. To reach South Padre Island, renowned for its sun and sand, plan on a drive of four hours or more because it is located in the far southern reaches of the state. Another favorite getaway is Nuevo Laredo in the Mexican state of Tamaulipas, located about two hours southwest of San Antonio on I-35, which is known as the "NAFTA (North American Free Trade Agreement) Highway."

Within San Antonio itself, however, I-35 is just one of many busy roadways. And while the city has its share of snarls, San Antonio traffic in general tends to be less aggravating and more navigable than what you would find in either Dallas or Houston.

## OVERVIEW

As for finding your way through that highway system, think of San Antonio as a wagon wheel, with the downtown district at its center. Four interstate highways, five US highways, and five state highways form myriad spokes. Most of these slice through the downtown area. Two form the inner and outer rims of the wheel, however; these are the city's loops. **Loop 410** (or I-410) lassoes the prime development in town, passing the San Antonio International Airport and skirting all of the city's military bases. **Loop 1604** traces the outside perimeter of the city, forming a boundary between the city and the untamed Hill Country, where white-tailed deer still roam.

Interstate highways divide San Antonio into several areas. **I-35** runs an S-shaped curve through the city from northeast to southwest, skirting the downtown area. This mega-highway travels to Laredo at its southern end and reaches as far as Duluth, Minnesota, in its northern regions. **I-10,** which originates in Los Angeles, runs from the northwest to downtown before taking an easterly turn toward its final stop in Jacksonville, Florida. And **I-37** defines the eastern boundary of downtown before veering off to the south and down to the coastal city of Corpus Christi. (Further confusing drivers, I-37 and I-35 are the same highway in the downtown region.)

Five US highways also call on the Alamo City. **US 281,** which originates in Hansboro, North Dakota, swings through the city near the San Antonio International Airport on its way south to McAllen, Texas. **US 90,** which starts in Jacksonville, Florida, overlaps with I-10 as it approaches the city from the east and crosses the city before branching off and heading west to Van Horn, Texas. **US 87,** originating in Raton, New Mexico, also overlaps with I-10 in the western portion of the city before branching off to the east and making its way south to Port Lavaca, Texas. **US 181** (not to be confused with US 281) originates in San Antonio and travels to Corpus Christi via Beeville. Finally, **US 81** also originates in San Antonio and travels to Laredo, overlapping with I-35.

For the purposes of this guidebook, we have divided San Antonio into sections that are defined by the highways you'll encounter on your trip. Our first section is downtown, an area bounded by I-35, I-37, and I-10. This region encompasses many tourist highlights such as the Alamo, the River Walk, Market Square, HemisFair Plaza, and more.

The second section is the area inside and around Loop 410. This area takes in both sides of Loop 410 and everything inside, with the exception of the downtown area covered in the first section. In this area, you'll find Brackenridge Park, Fort Sam Houston, and the San Antonio International Airport.

The third section is the fast-growing region beyond Loop 410 and Loop 1604, including the theme parks and the outer fringes of San Antonio, where the city meets the country.

**i** **Experience the historic downtown area on a Segway, an electric-powered transportation vehicle. Three tours daily depart from SegCity (210-224-0773; www.segcity.com) headquarters at 124 Losoya St.**

## BY AIR

San Antonio doesn't rank as a hub airport (Dallas and Houston both serve as Texas hubs), but getting to the city is fairly simple, whether your chosen mode of transportation is airplane, car, bus, or train. The city is home to an international airport as well as a feeder airport.

### San Antonio International Airport

Located 13 miles from downtown San Antonio, the **San Antonio International Airport** (9800 Airport Blvd.; 210-207-3450; www.sanantonio.gov/aviation) is where most air travelers begin their visit to the city. The airport is convenient to all areas of town thanks to its location on Loop 410, which links to I-37, the direct highway into downtown.

San Antonio International Airport sees over seven million domestic passengers every year as well as nearly a quarter of a million international passengers. The number of planes coming and going is on the increase, as is the number of passengers who travel through this busy airport.

When you deplane, you'll find yourself in one of two airport terminals, each an easy walk from the other. Terminal A is home to Aeromexico Connect, Aeromar, Airtran, ASA Delta, Frontier, Skywest, Southwest, United and US Airways. Terminal B, located to the west of Terminal One, is home to American, Continental, and Continental Express.

Have questions? You can ask one of the members of the SAT Ambassadors program. These volunteers are community members who donate at least four hours of their time every week to assist passengers and to welcome them to the Alamo City. The Ambassadors are easy to spot: Look for a denim vest, a Western hat, a black or beige shirt, black or khaki pants, a name tag, and a smile. San Antonio International has more than 10,000 square feet of retail and food concession space. The area, called the "Shops at River Landing," includes local stores and national chain stores.

Traveling to San Antonio International Airport just became more convenient with the opening of a new eight-gate terminal. The $134 million Terminal B replaces the older of the airport's two terminals and caps off several years of airport renovations, which include a new long-term parking garage, bilevel roadway system, consolidated baggage handling system and new central utility plant.

### *Flight Times to San Antonio*

**From Atlanta:** 2.5 hours
**From Chicago:** 2 hours
**From Las Vegas:** 2.3 hours
**From Los Angeles:** 2.75 hours
**From Miami:** 3.5 hours
**From Nashville:** 2.5 hours
**From New Orleans:** 2.5 hours
**From New York:** 3 hours
**From Orlando:** 2.75 hours
**From St. Louis:** 2.3 hours
**From San Francisco:** 4 hours
**From Seattle:** 4.5 hours
**From Washington, D.C.:** 5 hours

Nonstop service makes the travel time much shorter to and from some cities; you can catch a nonstop flight to San Antonio from Atlanta, Chicago, Las Vegas, Los Angeles, New York, Orlando, and St. Louis.

### *Commercial Airline Telephone Reservation Numbers*

**Aeromexico Connect:** (800) 237-6639
**American:** (800) 433-7300
**America West:** (800) 235-9292
**ASA:** (800) 221-1212
**Comair:** (800) 221-1212
**Continental:** (800) 525-0280
**Continental Express:** (800) 523-3273
**Delta:** (800) 221-1212
**Mexicana:** (800) 531-7921
**Midwest:** (800) 452-2022
**Northwest:** (800) 225-2525
**Skywest:** (800) 221-1212
**Southwest:** (800) 435-9792
**Spirit Airlines:** (800) 772-7117

**Sun Country:** (800) 359-6786
**United:** (800) 241-6522

Home to both Continental and American airlines, Terminal B also has dining options from local chefs, charming shops, public art and free Wi-Fi. The flavor and decor are uniquely San Antonio. "We want people to know as soon as they step off the airplane that they are in San Antonio," says Rich Johnson, airport spokesman. Providing a taste of local cuisine are dining options such as Big'z Burger Joint, a creation of San Antonio star Chef Andrew Weissmann, and Rosario's Mexican Cafe y Cantina, an offshoot of a well-known eatery in a local historic neighborhood. Popular franchises such as Starbucks Coffee, Charley's Grilled Subs and Sbarro are also in the mix.

### *Airport Parking*

San Antonio International Airport has more than 9,000 parking spaces. Parking rates are divided into three categories: short-term, long-term, and shuttle or economy. Short-term parking costs a maximum of $24 per 24-hour day; long-term parking is a maximum of $10 per 24-hour day. The first 15 minutes of parking at all of the lots is free. Airport police patrol each of the lots and can provide free battery jumps if needed. If you are in a hurry and lock your keys in your car, they will help with that as well. Parking for drivers and passengers with disabilities is available in each of the lots. Payment for parking can be made with cash, check, or credit card; American Express, Diners Club, Discover, MasterCard, and Visa are accepted. Patrons can use Exit Express, with machines located in front of and inside both terminals, for a faster way to pay for parking.

San Antonio International Airport has placed first in two separate categories of *Airport Revenue News'* 2011 Best Concessions Poll. SAT was named the Airport with the Most Unique Services in the small airports category (four million enplanements or less) and tied for first with Edmonton International for the Airport with the Best Concessions Management Team. The award for the airport with the Most Unique Services goes to the airport that has responded best to passenger demands for convenient, high-tech business services such as high-speed fax and Internet, wireless capabilities, conference rooms, business service centers and/or other business amenities.

### *Car Rentals*

Several auto rental companies have booths at the San Antonio Airport, located near the baggage-claim area on the first level of each terminal. Restrictions vary by company, but all require a current driver's license; some have an age restriction of 25 years or older. Many companies will not allow their cars to be driven into Mexico.

Many of the companies listed offer a range of compact to luxury cars and minivans; free mileage; daily, weekly and monthly rates; and special discounts for seniors and military personnel.

**ADVANTAGE RENT A CAR**
**(210) 341-8211, (800) 777-5500**
**www.advantage.com**
This company has a site in the airport and offers free pickup service.

**AVIS RENT A CAR**
**(210) 826-6332, (800) 331-1212**
**www.avis.com**

Located at the airport and other sites in the city, Avis offers Mexican auto insurance and 24-hour emergency roadside assistance.

**DOLLAR RENT A CAR**
**(800) 800-3665**
**www.dollar.com**
Dollar offers residential pickup and return, as well as the Fast Lane express rental program.

**ENTERPRISE RENT-A-CAR**
**(210) 348-6806, (800) 736-8222**
**www.enterprise.com**
With locations throughout the region, Enterprise also has an airport location. Free pickup is available; this company also offers Mexican auto insurance.

**HERTZ**
**(210) 841-8800, (800) 654-3131**
**www.hertz.com**
Hertz offers airport terminal pickup and 24-hour emergency roadside assistance.

**NATIONAL CAR RENTAL**
**(800) CAR-RENT, (210) 824-1841**
**www.nationalcar.com**
Located at the airport, this branch of a nationwide chain offers discounts to a variety of groups.

**i** Representing an investment of $1.5 billion, San Antonio's Toyota assembly plant, the car manufacturer's sixth in the continental US, provides jobs for 1,694 workers.

**THRIFTY CAR RENTAL**
**(210) 341-4677, (800) 847-4389**
**www.thrifty.com**
Located at the airport, Thrifty offers a number of discount rates.

### *Shuttle Service*

Shuttle service is available to most areas of the city. Some hotels offer free shuttle service for their guests; the pickup location for these shuttles is just outside the baggage-claim area of each terminal. There are commercial shuttle services as well.

**AIRPORT EXPRESS**
**1731 S. San Marcos St., Building 826**
**(210) 281-9900**
**www.saairportshuttle.com**
This service provides transportation between the airport and downtown hotels. A one-way ticket is $18; a round-trip ticket can also be purchased for $32. Minibuses offer wheelchair-accessible transportation to local hotels and other area destinations.

### *Taxi Service*

Transportation into the downtown area is available by taxicabs, which offer metered service. The cost of a trip from the airport to the downtown area is about $25 to $29 plus tip; plan on about a 15-minute ride, depending on traffic. Up to four people may share a taxi.

The fee is based on a rate of $2.50 for the first mile and $2.25 for each subsequent mile during daytime hours (5 a.m. to 9 p.m.); there's an additional $1 fee at other times. There is also a minimum airport departure charge of $10.50.

If you're traveling with a large family or a group, minivans are also available for up to seven passengers.

### *General Aviation*

**STINSON MUNICIPAL AIRPORT**
**8535 Mission Rd.**
**(210) 923-4357**
**www.sanantonio.gov/aviation/stinsonairport.asp**

For most travelers arriving by private plane from US departure points, Stinson Municipal Airport is the port of entry into San Antonio. This airport is the second-oldest general-aviation airport in continuous operation in the country. Located 6 miles south of downtown on Mission Road, it is just 4 miles from the Toyota assembly plant.

The airfield has two runways. Air-traffic control is attended from 7 a.m. to 10 p.m. daily. The Stinson Field Patio Cafe is open daily except Monday for breakfast and lunch.

You might have occasion to visit Stinson even if you don't arrive by private plane. The airfield is the home of the Texas Air Museum, which traces the history of aviation in San Antonio; a rare German Folke-Wulf 190 aircraft is displayed there.

**i** Lest you be confused, San Antonio has two notable thoroughfares named "Wurzbach." One is Harry Wurzbach in the northeast area of the city; it extends from Fort Sam Houston, across Austin Highway to Loop 410 East. The other is just plain Wurzbach. This one extends from Northwest Military Highway to just behind Ingram Park Mall, where it becomes Ingram Road.

## BY LAND

Once you are in San Antonio, you have many transportation options ranging from cars to carriages. The city also offers excellent bus and trolley service. The latter is a great way to see the downtown area without the headache of finding a parking place.

Driving in San Antonio can be a challenge, especially in the downtown area, thanks to the numerous one-way streets. With some of the oldest streets in the state, San Antonio doesn't follow a grid system, but instead offers a meandering collection of byways that trace the river's passage through the city. An assortment of high-rise buildings adds to the confusion—sometimes your destination is just a block away but lies out of sight and seemingly out of reach.

What's the solution? Park and walk. Parking lots are sprinkled throughout downtown; rates are sometimes by the day and sometimes by the hour. Don't park "just for a few minutes" without paying; you will be towed.

Covered parking garages are a blessing during the hot summer months. These are more expensive but help prevent "skillet steering wheel"—a common hazard when your car sits in that blazing sun for a few hours. (A quick look around uncovered parking lots reveals that local residents use cardboard windshield shades religiously to avoid literally being in the hot seat upon their return.) You'll find covered parking garages at many of the downtown hotels (they are available to nonguests for a fee) and at sites such as Rivercenter Mall.

Once you've parked, you'll find much of downtown is easily accessible on foot. Strolling the River Walk is a real San Antonio pleasure; temperatures there are several degrees below those at street level. By walking the River Walk, you'll be able to reach the Alamo and many of the attractions found nearby. When it's time to branch out, hop aboard a trolley; the VIA San Antonio streetcars link the main tourist sites.

**Located at 13415 San Pedro Ave., the AAA North District office (210-403-5000) is open Mon through Fri from 9 a.m. until 6 p.m. and Sat from 9 a.m. until 1 p.m. For 24-hour claims reporting, call (800) 67-CLAIM.**

For all its major highways (and, occasionally, major traffic), touring San Antonio is easily accomplished because, although the city is vast, most attractions are grouped in a few areas. Downtown sightseeing starts at Alamo Plaza, home of the Alamo and birthplace not only of Texas liberty but also of San Antonio tourism. Here you can take guided tours, board a city bus or trolley, or just enjoy a stroll through the area. Behind Alamo Plaza lies the Paseo del Rio, or River Walk, one of the most-visited spots in Texas. Located below street level, the riverbanks are lined with sidewalk cafes and specialty shops.

On one edge of the River Walk rests La Villita, the "little village" that was the original settlement in Old San Antonio. Here the wares of many of the city's artisans are displayed and sold in historic structures.

La Villita sits in the shadow of the 750-foot Tower of the Americas, where you can enjoy the best view of the city from the observation deck. The tower was built as the symbol of HemisFair, the 1968 World's Fair. The tower is located in HemisFair Park. Nearby, the Henry B. Gonzales Convention Center, one of the state's busiest meeting facilities, hosts thousands of conventioneers each year. Directly south of the River Walk lies the King William Historic District, home of the city's stately mansions built during the 19th century. This area is a favorite of bed-and-breakfast lovers.

West of the River Walk area, a quick ride by trolley or car, is Market Square, the most Mexican attraction in town. Here you can shop for imports in El Mercado (the largest Mexican marketplace in the US), dine on a Tex-Mex feast, or tour some nearby historic buildings.

Along Broadway, north of downtown, lie many of San Antonio's museums and outdoor attractions. Brackenridge Park, home of the city's zoo and Japanese gardens, awaits just minutes from downtown.

If you continue north on Broadway to the intersection of Loop 410, then turn west to the intersection with US 281, you come to the San Antonio International Airport, where many visitors begin and end their stay. This also is the site of some of the city's best shopping areas, from big-name department stores such as Saks Fifth Avenue and Macy's to small import shops and art galleries.

South of downtown, the Mission Trail holds many attractions, especially for history buffs. Along this historic route, you can tour four Spanish missions, each still celebrating Sunday Mass.

On the northwest side of town, along Loop 1604, lie two of Texas's top family attractions: Six Flags Fiesta Texas and SeaWorld of San Antonio. In spring through fall these parks are filled with tourists from around the US and Mexico—and San Antonians—who come to enjoy thrill rides, musical productions, and marine animal shows.

## Trolleys

**VIA DOWNTOWN TROLLEYS**
**(210) 362-2020**
**www.viainfo.net**

Downtown trolleys, constructed like old-fashioned streetcars but with rubber tires, are a fun and inexpensive way to explore the downtown area. The red, yellow, and blue trolley lines serve four routes and stop at all major downtown attractions. The fare of $1.10 is a bargain, and you can also purchase a monthly streetcar pass for $30 if you think you'll be riding a great deal. The best deal for visitors is usually the $4 one-day pass, available at www.viaonlinestore.net. You can pay with cash, a streetcar token, or a streetcar pass. Discounts are available for seniors, children, those with impaired mobility, and Medicare recipients. Transfer slips serve as fares for equal or cheaper bus service, viable for two hours on that day's date. If you'd like to park your car and ride the trolleys, you'll find free parking at VIA's Ellis Alley Park and Ride located east of downtown at Chestnut and Ellis Alley. From the parking lot, you can take the yellow streetcar line to the downtown area.

The Blue Line travels through the southern areas of downtown. Stops include the Alamo, Blue Star Arts Complex, Central Library, Henry B. Gonzales Convention Center, HemisFair Park, the King William Historic District, La Villita, Municipal Auditorium, Rivercenter Mall, the San Antonio Information Center, and Southtown. The Blue Line runs weekdays from 7 a.m. to 9 p.m. and weekends 9 a.m. to 9 p.m.

The Yellow Line stops at the Alamodome, the Ellis Alley Park and Ride at St. Paul Square (for free parking for VIA customers), the convention center, El Mercado–Market Square, the Institute of Texan Cultures, Rivercenter Mall, St. Paul Square, Sunset Station, and the Tower of the Americas. The Yellow Line runs Mon through Fri 7 a.m. to 12:30 a.m., Sat and Sun 9 a.m. to 12:30 a.m.

Red Line stops include the Alamo, the convention center, El Mercado–Market Square, HemisFair Park, La Villita, Rivercenter Mall, and the San Antonio Information Center. Hours for this route are weekdays 7 a.m. to 10:30 p.m. and weekends 9 a.m. to 10:30 p.m.

## Buses & Shuttles

### VIA METROPOLITAN TRANSIT SERVICE
**(210) 362-2020**
**www.viainfo.net**

The metropolitan transit authority in San Antonio and Bexar County is known as VIA. Created by election in 1977, the system is funded through a 0.5 percent sales tax and spans more than 1,200 square miles.

Route 7 visits Brackenridge Park, the Japanese Tea Garden, San Antonio Botanical Garden, the San Antonio Museum of Art, San Antonio Zoo, and Witte Museum. Take Route 42 for the mIssions, Route 64 for SeaWorld of Texas or Route 94 for Six Flags Fiesta Texas.

The buses operate daily from 4 a.m. to 1 a.m., serving the region with more than 91 scheduled lines. Five service levels are available: frequent, metro, express, skip, and flex. Frequent service routes run every 15 minutes or more frequently during the day and are generally available until about 6 p.m. during general workday hours Mon through Fri. Metro service provides fixed routes operating every 30 to 60 minutes, while flex service offers transportation to outlying areas with bus service available on a call-ahead basis. Express service routes are designed for commuters because the line travels on freeways, connecting riders to employment centers directly from Park and

Rides. Skip service routes travel along major streets, skipping some bus stops to speed passengers to their destinations.

Bus fares vary by type of route. The full fare for a local or limited-stop bus is $1.10. Express-bus service is $2.50. Bus transfers are 15 cents. Reduced fares for senior citizens age 62 and over, persons with disabilities, students, and children age 5 to 11 are 35 cents per limited-stop bus ride and 75 cents per express-bus ride. Off-peak reduced fares for senior citizens and people with disabilities are available weekdays from 9 a.m. to 3 p.m. and all day on weekends; these fares are for fixed routes only.

Which bus do you want? You'll find bus information centers throughout the city. VIA's Downtown Information Center, located at 260 E. Houston St., is open daily except Sunday. Other information centers are found at the Crossroads Park and Ride, 151 Crossroads Blvd. (210-731-6616); Ingram Transit Center, 3215 Northwestern Dr. (210-521-6773); Randolph Park and Ride, 9400 I-35 North (210-564-8175); South Texas Medical Center Information Center, 7535 Merton Minter (210-614-4615); and Ellis Alley Information Center 212 Chestnut (210-299-1213).

You can also call VIAINFO at (210) 362-2020; it's an automated information system that has information in both English and Spanish. To speak to a live representative, call (210) 362-2020 or TTY (210) 362-2019. Most VIA routes and stops are accessible to people with disabilities. Additionally, VIA operates VIAtrans, a shared-ride service for residents with disabilities and their personal-care attendants. Prospective VIAtrans patrons may apply for eligibility or inquire about the service by calling (210) 362-2140. VIAtrans riders accompanied by their authorized personal-care attendants may ride the mainline bus at no charge.

If you are approved for use of a VIAtrans-type service in your home city and you're visiting San Antonio, you will qualify for use of VIAtrans; qualified visitors may use the system for up to 21 days. Call the VIA Accessible Services Office for more information.

**GREYHOUND BUS TERMINAL**
**500 N. St. Mary's St.**
**(800) 231-2222, (210) 270-5824**
**www.greyhound.com**

This bus terminal serves several commercial bus lines: Greyhound, Kerrville, and Valley Transit. Bus service throughout the state with connections around the country is available. The bus terminal includes a food-service facility that's open around the clock, a Western Union station, and shuttle service to and from the San Antonio International Airport. The terminal also has shuttle service to the city's military facilities sponsored by the military. The second-oldest terminal in the Greyhound system, the building has an interesting history. Constructed in 1945, it showcases a 40-by-8-foot mural that illustrates the Hispanic heritage of San Antonio since the 1600s. The artwork was the collaboration of the San Antonio Cultural Arts Center and the Guadalupe Cultural Arts Center.

## Taxis

Taxi service is available from the airport. Metered cab service costs $2.50 for the first mile and $2.25 for each subsequent mile. The average one-way fare from the airport to downtown hotels is about $25–$29 plus tip. Four passengers can ride for the price of one. Outside the airport, taxis can be found at most major hotels, although you may need to call for service.

**AAA TAXI SERVICE**
**(210) 599-5999**
**www.aataxi.com**

This company offers citywide pickups as well as out-of-town service. Reservations are accepted, and payment can be made by credit card.

**YELLOW CAB**
**(210) 222-2222**
**www.yellowcabsanantonio.com**

Reservations, including reservations online, are accepted by this company, which offers around-the-clock service. Four passengers ride for the price of one in all cabs; credit cards are accepted.

## Train Service

**AMTRAK**
**350 Hoefgen Ave.**
**(800) USA-RAIL**
**www.amtrak.com**

Amtrak is served by a station in St. Paul Square, located between Sunset Station and the Alamodome. This convenient location makes the train an easy way to get right to the heart of the city.

The San Antonio station is a daily stop for the Texas Eagle (www.texaseagle.com), which travels between Chicago and San Antonio; stops include Dallas and St. Louis. Several days a week, the Sunset Limited pulls into the station. This train travels between New Orleans and Los Angeles, with stops in Biloxi, Houston, El Paso, Tucson and Palm Springs.

The Texas Eagle has split-level Superliner cars. You can book a coach seat or a sleeping compartment. For the price of a sleeping compartment you also get complimentary meals served in your "room," a daily newspaper each morning, baggage assistance, turndown service, and admission to Amtrak's Metropolitan Lounge in Chicago's Union Station. The train also includes a dining car, a smoking lounge, and a lounge for sightseeing (and movies at night). Travel on Amtrak can be booked by calling the Amtrak reservation number above (you can pick up tickets at your nearest rail station or have them mailed to you), online at www.amtrak.com, or through a travel agent.

You'll find short-term and long-term parking at the Marina Parking Garage (850 E. Commerce; 210-207-7778), 4 blocks from the station. Parking costs $6 maximum, $8 flat rate.

## Limos

**AAA LIMOUSINE SERVICE**
**2668 Austin Hwy.**
**(210) 599-9999**
**www.limomax.com**

How would you like to tour San Antonio in a super-stretch Hummer? AAA has one for hire, along with classic limos, each equipped with a color TV, DVD player, CD player, fiber optics, a mirrored ceiling, neon lighting, an intercom system, privacy partitions, and a full bar. The limos are available for everything from airport transfers to wedding parties and city touring.

**ABBEY WALKER EXECUTIVE CARS & LIMOUSINES**
**1343 Hallmark Rd.**
**(210) 341-6000, (800) 341-6000**
**www.abbeywalker.com**

Owned and operated by Star Shuttle, this company has a fleet of Lincoln Town Cars and extended limousines. All drivers are uniformed professionals, and this service is a member of the National Limousine Association. City tours and airport transfers can be arranged as well as transportation for proms, weddings, anniversaries, and other special events.

**CAREY/RIVER CITY LIMO INC.**
**7701 Broadway, #203**
**(210) 824-2275, (800) 336-4646**
**www.carey.com**
San Antonio's oldest limo company has a fleet of limousines as well as sedans, mini-buses, and luxury vans.

**CORPORATE LIMOUSINE AND SEDAN SERVICE**
**651 Overhill Dr.**
**(210) 432-6193**
Affiliated with Boston Coach, this company offers airport transfers, city tours, and special-occasion transportation for weddings, proms, concerts, and more. Several employees speak Spanish.

## Water Taxis

**RIO SAN ANTONIO CRUISES**
**205 N. Presa St., Suite 201**
**(210) 244-5700, (800) 417-4139**
**www.riosanantonio.com**
Rio San Antonio Cruises operates guided cruises along the San Antonio River (see "Tours" in the Attractions chapter for more information on these pleasant excursions), but they also operate the Rio Taxi Service, a river shuttle. The shuttle is a great way for conventioneers to get to a River Walk eatery or for hotel guests on the far reaches of the River Walk to reach the more bustling areas without ever venturing up to street level. It's far more pleasant than standing on the street corner shouting "Taxi!"

The river taxis make 39 stops along the route. You can purchase a ticket from Rio San Antonio Cruises or at most of the businesses along and near the Rio Taxi stops. You'll need to buy a ticket in advance, because boat drivers cannot accept cash.

Downtown shuttle stops include the El Tropicano Riverwalk, Marriott Riverwalk, convention center, La Villita, Tower Life Building, Southwest School of Art, Buckhorn Museum and Ripley's Believe It or Not! Odditorium. On the Museum Reach, stops are the lock and dam at the Brooklyn Street Bridge, VFW Post at 10 10th St., San Antonio Museum of Art, the Grotto, and the Pearl Brewery. Rio Taxi signs identify each of the water-taxi stops.

A one-way pass on the shuttle is $5 for the downtown reach and $10 for the Museum Reach; an all-day pass (which runs through the business day, not 24 hours from purchase) costs $10. Three-day passes are available for $25. Taxis run from 9 a.m. to 9 p.m. and generally come by every 20 minutes.

## Horse-Drawn Carriages

**LONE STAR CARRIAGE**
**302 Iowa St.**
**(210) 656-7527**
**www.lonestarcarriage.com**
Lone Star Carriage picks up passengers on Crockett Street next to the Alamo and will accept reservations to pick up at certain hotels, depending on availability, for weddings and other special events. The carriages accommodate four to seven people. Cost is $40 per couple for a 20-minute tour and $75 for 60 minutes. Hours of operation can vary, depending on the weather—the service doesn't operate when the temperature is more than 95 degrees.

**YELLOW ROSE CARRIAGE**
**100 S. Alamo St.**
**(210) 225-6490**
**www.yellowrosecarriage.com**
Established in 1982, Yellow Rose Carriage provides romantic rides through the downtown district in reproduction Victorian-style carriages. Most carriages are pulled by large draft horses.

From May through Sept, the carriage typically operates from 7 p.m. to midnight; other months, rides are available from 6 p.m. to midnight. Special arrangements can be made for pickups at other times.

Prices vary by ride but start at $40 per couple for a short tour of Alamo Plaza and $80 for a tour of King William Historic District from Alamo Plaza. With each couple, one child under the age of 10 can ride free of charge.

# HISTORY

**The Spanish explorers and conquistadors who followed in the footsteps of Álvar Núñez Cabeza de Vaca had dreams of gold, of cities full of gold: enough gold to fund Spain's far-flung empire for years, enough to build Christian missions in the vast wilderness, enough to finance Spanish armies and navies. Cabeza de Vaca himself had not seen the fabled Las Siete Cuidades Doradas de Cibola (Seven Cities of Gold). Indeed, what the Spanish explorer had seen in eight years of wandering after being shipwrecked in Florida in 1528 was a land rich in mosquitoes and hostile inhabitants rather than precious metals.**

**Cabeza de Vaca and his three companions were probably the first Europeans to explore the deserts of the North American Southwest, passing through what is now Texas, New Mexico, and Arizona. The Spaniards eventually gained the trust of the natives as they undertook to heal some of the sick they encountered by invoking their faith and praying over the patients. "Our fame," he wrote, "spread throughout the area, and all the Indians who heard about it came looking for us so that we could cure them and bless their children."**

## SPANISH EXPLORERS

Cabeza de Vaca's exact route has been debated, but by some accounts, in 1535 or so he camped in a bend of the San Antonio River, where he found a friendly reception from the local inhabitants. "They indicated that they were pleased with our company and took us to their lodges . . . The merrymaking caused by our arrival lasted three days. At the end of the three days, we asked about the country ahead." Cabeza de Vaca's band eventually found their way south to Culiacán in Mexico, where they were at last reunited with their Spanish brethren. They had found no gold, but their reports led to tantalizing rumors about vast riches to the north. One of Cabeza de Vaca's three companions, Estabanico, whom he described as a "black Arab and a native of Azamor," later volunteered to guide an expedition under Marcos de Niza to search for the treasure. Cabeza de Vaca's desultory wandering had blazed a trail for several centuries of Spanish influence on the areas he visited. In some places, as in San Antonio, Hispanic influence has persisted to the present day. The Indian village where Cabeza de Vaca tarried was not identified, but it could well have been the Payaya village of Yanaguana. It was there, in 1691, that Father Damian Masanet said Mass under the cottonwood trees for the newly installed Spanish governor, Don Domingo de Teran. The spot (and the river) were renamed San Antonio de Padua in honor of St. Anthony of Padua (as this occurred on June 13, the saint's birthday).

However, the Spanish built nothing here until 1718, when Friars Antonio Olivares and Isidro Espinosa arrived to oversee the building of a new mission. It was to be named San Antonio de Valero, in honor of the Spanish viceroy of Mexico, the Marquis of Valero. At the same time, the new governor proclaimed the establishment of a new town, or villa, called San Antonio de Bexar in honor of the viceroy's brother, the Duke of Bexar, a national war hero in Spain. They chose a lovely spot, which Padre Espinosa described as "a great shady grove of very tall pecan trees, cottonwoods, elms, and clumps of mulberries, irrigated by the water of an abundant spring."

The appeal of the location was not gold, but another precious resource in a hot, dry land: water. In addition to the river, San Antonio had numerous springs that supported an abundance of trees and wildlife. These in turn attracted people to the area. A simple thing, but in the middle of dry, scrubby hills and rugged brush land, it seemed a miracle. To those early explorers, the spot was an oasis, and they resolved to claim it for church and crown. As Friar Olivares explained: "In this place of San Antonio there is a spring of water which is about three-fourths of a league from the principal river. In this location . . . it is easy to secure water, but nowhere else."

## ON A MISSION

San Antonio was founded in 1718, the same year as was New Orleans. As French activity in Louisiana threatened to intrude upon their claims in the Southwest, the Spanish began to view the area as more than just a pleasant spot. Suddenly the Spanish could no longer afford to ignore their hardscrabble claims north of "New Spain" (Mexico). A system of forts and missions was proposed by the Spanish crown to blockade the French from the east, to alleviate the threat of Indian attack, and ultimately to provide the foundations for Spanish colonization of the territory. Native tribes of the area would be instructed by the friars for conversion to Christianity, thus making them allies of the Spanish.

**i The early settlers who came to San Antonio from the US were called "Texians" by most residents as well as most Mexicans. Other names for the settlers were "Texonians," "Texasians," and "Texicans;" eventually the name was simplified to Texans.**

San Antonio's original mission, the San Antonio de Valero, has become known as the Alamo. Since its inception in 1718, the mission has been relocated and rebuilt at least twice. The moves were conducted by Father Olivares himself; around 1720 the mission was rebuilt on the other side of the river, where the soil was more fertile. After a huge storm destroyed the mission in 1724, it was again rebuilt, this time on the spot where the Alamo stands today. Although the early mission struggled, it was soon joined by several others, partly in competition, but eventually in cooperation with San Antonio de Valero. San José y San Miguel de Aguayo was founded in 1720, followed in 1731 by three others: San Juan Capistrano, San Francisco de la Espada, and Nuestra Señora de la Purisima Concepción. The latter three missions had been relocated from East Texas, too close to French Louisiana for comfort. At the same time that the missions were relocated, 56 colonists from the Canary Islands arrived to claim land offered by the Spanish

## Close-up

### San Antonio Time Line

| | |
|---|---|
| **1536** | Álvar Núñez Cabeza de Vaca explores Texas. |
| **1691** | Father Damian Masanet and Governor Don Domingo de Teran hold Mass at the Payaya village of Yanaguana, dubbing the river there San Antonio. |
| **1718** | Friars Espinosa and Olivares found the Mission San Antonio de Valero and the villa of San Antonio de Bexar. |
| **1722** | San Antonio's first permanent military accommodations, Plaza de Armes, are built by the garrison. |
| **1731** | Missions San Juan Capistrano, San Francisco de la Espada, and Nuestra Señora de la Purisima Concepción are relocated from East Texas. Fifty-six Canary Islanders arrive to colonize the area. |
| **1736** | The first bridge across San Antonio River is built, connecting San Antonio de Valero mission with the town. |
| **1773** | San Antonio de Bexar is named provincial capital. |
| **1793** | The missions are secularized by the Spanish crown. |
| **1810** | Mexican Revolution begins. |
| **1813** | San Antonio is captured by revolutionary army, then is retaken and decimated by Royalists. |
| **1819** | Major floods on the San Antonio River destroy much of the town. |
| **1820** | Moses Austin petitions governor for permission to colonize Texas. |
| **1821** | Mexico becomes independent of Spain; Austin's petition is granted by the new Mexican government. |
| **1825** | US colonists buy land and settle in Texas. |
| **1830** | Mexico closes Texas to immigration from the US. |
| **1835** | Texian army captures San Antonio; General Cos signs surrender. |
| **1836** | Santa Anna lays siege to the Alamo, which falls on March 6. |
| **1840** | Downtown San Antonio is the scene of a major battle with the Comanche; German immigration to the San Antonio area begins. |
| **1845** | Texas becomes part of the US. |
| **1848** | The Rio Grande is established as the US–Mexico border by the Treaty of Guadalupe Hidalgo, ending the Mexican War. |

government to encourage settlement. One family, it was said, was worth 100 soldiers in settling the frontier.

Despite numerous setbacks caused by inclement weather, disease, raids by the Apache and Comanche, and discord among the missions, the colonists, and the soldiers sent to protect them, the community of San Antonio began to grow on the bend of the San Antonio River. A visiting Frenchman, Monsieur Pages, wrote in 1768 that San Antonio was a town of about 200 houses, some constructed of stone, with the land "sloping gently to the river and commanding an agreeable prospect over the opposite grounds." Cut off from the rest of Hispanic America by hundreds of miles, San Antonio was forced to be self-sufficient in regard to food, shelter, and most everything else. In reality, the town was a collection of

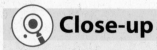

| | |
|---|---|
| **1853** | *San Antonio Zeitung,* a German-language newspaper, is first published. |
| **1861** | Confederate troops take the San Antonio army fort and control of the city. |
| **1865** | The Civil War ends; the US Army retakes the city. |
| **1876** | US Army begins work on Fort Sam Houston. |
| **1877** | The railroad comes to San Antonio. The water works are established. |
| **1886** | Geronimo and his band of Apache are imprisoned at Fort Sam Houston. |
| **1898** | Theodore Roosevelt trains Rough Riders in San Antonio. |
| **1899** | Brackenridge Park is dedicated. The first Mexican restaurant opens on Losoya Street |
| **1917** | Brooks and Kelly airbases are established. |
| **1924** | The Conservation Society is formed to preserve the city's heritage. |
| **1926** | Witte Museum is built. Flood-control projects are started downtown. |
| **1928** | The Milam Building, the world's first air-conditioned structure, opens. |
| **1930** | Randolph Field opens. |
| **1936** | The first River Parade is staged to honor the Texas Centennial. |
| **1941** | The River Walk is completed. |
| **1949** | San Antonio Municipal Airport opens. |
| **1966** | The Alamo is listed on the National Register of Historic Places. |
| **1968** | HemisFair '68 is held. |
| **1973** | The NBA San Antonio Spurs' first season begins. |
| **1987** | Pope John Paul II celebrates Mass in San Antonio. |
| **1988** | SeaWorld of Texas opens in San Antonio. |
| **1992** | Fiesta Texas opens. |
| **1993** | The Alamodome opens and hosts US Olympic Festival '93. |
| **1999** | The San Antonio Spurs win their first NBA championship. |
| **2003** | Toyota announces it will build a manufacturing plant in San Antonio. |
| **2008** | The final four NCAA teams battle to win the National Championship game during March Madness at the Alamodome. |
| **2009** | The first phase of the River Walk Expansion opens, connecting the original River Walk with the cultural attractions to the north (the Museum Reach). |
| **2010** | San Antonio is named the strongest US metropolitan area by *BusinessWeek* magazine. |

communities: the Canary Island colonists, the missions and the Indians they served, and the military contingent, each group more or less self-sufficient.

## CLASHES WITH THE COMANCHE

By the 1770s, however, a serious new threat arose to encourage the town to band closer together, at least physically. The Comanche stepped up raids on San Antonio—so effectively that they boasted that the Spanish were allowed to stay in their territory so that they could continue to raise beef and horses for their attackers. The governor complained in 1780, "There is no time day or night when reports of barbarities and disorders do not arrive from the ranches." The Comanche were skilled fighters and raiders and could not be driven out by the small troop garrisons assigned to guard the San Antonio missions, and efforts to raise more soldiers were ineffective.

## REVOLUTION IN MEXICO

In 1758 a large band of Comanche sacked the Spanish mission on the San Saba River, Santa Cruz de San Saba, killing two priests. Spanish troops pursuing the war party north were ambushed near the Red River and defeated by the Indians. The Comanche would not be pacified by payments and treaty as had the Apache; they held the upper hand on the frontier and they knew it. Yet, somehow, the town and the missions survived, and in the face of adversity, San Antonio began to develop a character all its own.

By 1800 the town's population had reached 3,000, including more than 700 soldiers. Gradually, some of the barriers between the communities within San Antonio began to dissolve, and the town's identity began to emerge: tough and self-reliant, a blend of Hispanic and Indian elements. In fact, those early inhabitants had much in common with modern-day San Antonians. But one crucial element was still missing from the melting pot, and the new century would witness another invasion from the north: the coming of the Anglos.

Ironically, this movement began far to the south, where revolution brewed after centuries of Spanish rule. A parish priest in Guanajuato, Mexico, Father Miguel Hidalgo, ignited the spark by preaching revolution from the steps of his church in 1810. A long war followed, eventually drawing in even the sleepy frontier colony of San Antonio, as Royalist forces chased revolutionaries north. One such revolutionary, Bernardo Gutierrez de Lara, succeeded in raising an army of volunteers, who took San Antonio from the Spanish government forces in 1813. The revolutionaries' triumph was short-lived, however. A few months later, an army of 2,000 Royalist troops crossed the Rio Grande and retook the town, destroying much of the rebel army and executing any townspeople suspected of siding with them. Many of the settlers fled to the US to escape the purge. San Antonio's population fell drastically once again.

Eventually, even the Royalists were forced to admit that it was necessary to repopulate the area in order to stave off attacks by the still-strong Comanche. Therefore, the Royalist government was persuaded when, in 1820, Moses Austin petitioned to colonize Texas with 300 American families. As Austin's son Stephen F. Austin recalled, "At the end of a week the governor and ayuntamiento [town or city council] of Bexar united in recommending a petition from my father to the [government] at Monterrey, asking for permission to introduce and settle three hundred families from the United States of America . . . The entering wedge was thus placed for opening a legal passage for North American immigrants into Texas."

Once the petition was granted, nothing would stop the inexorable flow of immigration into Texas, not the death of Moses Austin (his son Stephen continued the project), not even a drastic change of government in Mexico (declared independent of Spain in 1821). By the early 1830s the tidal wave of new Texians (as the early settlers were called) outnumbered Hispanics by a 10 to 1 margin. The new government in Mexico had other pressing concerns, so it allowed the Mexican colonies a high degree of self-sufficiency.

## THE ALAMO

By 1835, however, that laissez-faire attitude changed as a young firebrand named Antonio López de Santa Anna became president of Mexico. Santa Anna, who had earned a reputation as a tough military leader, established a stronger central government and curtailed many of the freedoms to which the Texians had grown accustomed. A showdown was inevitable, and it came swiftly as Santa Anna sent armies to deal with the rebellious colonists. On December 5, 1835, a large band of Texian volunteers led by Ben Milam attacked San Antonio, which was defended by a Mexican army under General Martin Perfecto de Cos. The fighting, which lasted five days, ended when the volunteers captured General Cos and forced his surrender, ending the "Battle of Bexar." The general's army was sent back to Mexico after pledging not to fight anymore on Texas soil. Shortly afterward, the Texian volunteers, believing the war over, began to disperse, leaving only a small garrison of militia to guard the town.

They had not counted on Santa Anna's resolve. When General Cos's defeated army returned to Mexico, an enraged Santa Anna took personal command and promised to avenge the defeat. "I personally assembled and organized an expeditionary army of eight thousand men in Saltillo," he wrote in his autobiography. "I took command of the campaign myself, preferring the uncertainties of war to the easy and much-coveted life of the palace."

The situation was painfully uncertain for the defenders of the Alamo, numbering at most about 150, when suddenly confronted by the might of Santa Anna's army on February 23, 1836. They grabbed what supplies and arms they could and took shelter behind the stone walls of the old mission, San Antonio de Valero, which had come to be known informally as "The Alamo." Thus began one of the most chronicled battles in history, a story to rival the Charge of the Light Brigade, Gettysburg, or Waterloo.

Due to the illness of Jim Bowie, sent to San Antonio by General Sam Houston of the Texian army, command of the Alamo's defenders fell to Lt. Col. William Barrett Travis, a 25-year-old volunteer from Alabama. To Santa Anna's demand for surrender, the young Travis replied, "I have answered the demand with a cannon shot and our flag still waves proudly from the wall. I shall never surrender or retreat." Travis and Bowie were joined by other volunteers, such as David Crockett from Tennessee, motivated by a love of liberty, and perhaps a taste for battle. When the threat facing the Texians was revealed, many of them could have escaped with their lives, but chose to stay and fight. James Bonham carried Travis's vain plea for reinforcements through the Mexican lines; after delivering his message, knowing it to be futile, he returned through the lines again to rejoin his comrades in their fight to the death.

**i** **Many first-time visitors take their image of San Antonio from the John Wayne version of the movie *The Alamo*. Remember, though, that the classic film was shot not in the Alamo City, but near Del Rio in Bracketville.**

As the third furious charge by the Mexicans at last overwhelmed the defenders, the Alamo fell at dawn on March 6, 1836. No quarter was expected by the defenders, and none was extended; Santa Anna had ordered the attack under the red flag indicating that no surrenders would be accepted.

The defenders died, the Alamo fell, and a legend was born. "Remember the Alamo!" was the battle cry a few weeks later when General Sam Houston's inspired Texian army defeated Santa Anna at the Battle of San Jacinto. San Antonio's Alamo had become a shrine of liberty in a new country: the Republic of Texas.

## THE WILD FRONTIER, STATEHOOD & IMMIGRATION

Yet even in a new country, San Antonio inhabitants suffered from old problems. The town was still very much a frontier, subject to attack by the Comanche and by Mexican troops marauding across the new border. Two such incidents illustrate the dangers faced by residents of San Antonio at the time. In 1840 a meeting between Comanche chiefs and the military of the Texas Republic deteriorated into a fierce battle in the center of town. It resulted in many deaths on both sides and further inflamed hostilities. Two years later, a Mexican army marched on the town and captured several prominent citizens, including Sam Maverick, who were taken to Mexico and imprisoned. Despite the posting of Texas Rangers to the town, these attacks unnerved residents and many moved away, reducing San Antonio's population to around 800.

With Texas statehood in 1845, however, came a new optimism, and San Antonio grew under the protection of the US military. A permanent garrison of soldiers was headquartered in barracks built by the Spanish at Military Plaza. At the western edge of the settled US, San Antonio was as strategically important at that time as it had been during the Texas Revolution. It was the beginning of a relationship between the town and the US military that continues into the present. The military's presence not only made it safer for settlers and businesses to locate in San Antonio, but also contributed to the town's growth. It had great appetites to be fed—food, supplies, services, and all the needs of a growing army base—and San Antonio's position on the frontier, long a hindrance to its development, now became a benefit as entrepreneurs, merchants, and other camp followers moved into town.

Many of the new residents were neither Hispanic nor Anglo-American but immigrants from Western Europe, particularly Germany. Due to the concerted efforts of a number of land speculators in Germany, a sizable number of German colonies were soon located in and around San Antonio. A similar immigration campaign took place in the Alsace region, and a large Alsatian community founded the town of Castroville, a few miles west of San Antonio. In the space of a few years, the demographics of San Antonio changed drastically as the German newcomers became dominant both in numbers and in influence. German, not Spanish, was the language heard on the street. Many of the Germans were skilled craftsmen and artists; others were merchants and academics. Most were well educated, hardworking, and determined to establish a good life for themselves in the New World. In this, they were mostly successful. Their drive and determination made them community leaders in San Antonio. Many built substantial homes in what is now the King William Historic District. The historic Menger Hotel was built in Alamo Plaza in 1859, the first major building to be erected there since the fall of the Alamo. It was long considered San Antonio's premier hotel, hosting such luminaries as Robert E. Lee and the poet Sidney Lanier.

The town's population swelled to more than 8,000, and San Antonio surpassed Galveston as Texas's largest city. San Antonio's fortunes began to rise on the tide of German immigration and US statehood.

## THE CIVIL WAR

Unfortunately, the town would still have to endure one more stern test: the Civil War. On February 6, 1861, General David E. Twiggs of the US Army's Second Cavalry Regiment surrendered to a secessionist force headed by Army Major Ben McCullough. On the same day, the base's inspector-general, Robert E. Lee of Virginia, was detained by secessionists who demanded that he join them or leave town immediately. Lee refused to obey "any revolutionary government of Texas" and returned to Washington. With the coming of the war, San Antonio's newfound prosperity began to wither on the vine. As Vinton James, a writer of the period, described it: "Suddenly, like a bolt of lightning from a clear sky, came the firing on Fort Sumter, which shattered all the bright prospects of San Antonio. Everything was turned to ruin and despair."

Other accounts of the time, however, indicate that the city's economy was actually in a better position than many other Southern towns. It survived partly by shipping goods to and through Mexico, thereby avoiding military blockades on the Texas coast.

Forty companies of Confederate soldiers were recruited and trained in San Antonio; most were sent to faraway battles, and some never returned. At the war's end, San Antonio was again occupied by the US Army, this time as a conquered city. Vinton James noted that after the war, "business was at its lowest ebb, there being no money to make improvements or to keep the city clean."

Fortunately, San Antonio was quick to rebound from the depression of war and reconstruction. This was partly due to its continued strategic importance to the United States' westward expansion. Army troops located here were still needed to counter the Indian threat as settlers moved farther west. San Antonio again became an important supply depot for the army.

## COWBOYS & CHILI QUEENS

Another source of wealth were the first trail drives to Kansas as entrepreneurs began to round up roaming longhorns and herd them to buyers in Abilene. The resulting influx of cowboys transformed San Antonio into a lively cow town filled with saloons and houses of ill repute, often the scene of fights and even gun battles. The rigors of months spent on the trail created in the cowboys an acute need to blow off steam while enjoying the temporary luxuries of town life. "Work hard, play hard" was their rule of living, and though the more sober townsfolk may have been shocked at their ways, the town benefited financially from the cowboys and their trade. Among the unique tradespeople of the era were the "chili queens," young women who sold hot chili stew from streetside kiosks.

San Antonio's era of the hard-riding, hard-drinking cowboys did not last very long; the invention of barbed wire in 1875 signaled the closing of the open range. Yet its wild and woolly Western legacy still claims a piece of the city's soul.

## THE GILDED AGE

In 1877 San Antonio began an unprecedented decade of growth, fueled by the coming of the railroad to town. The

Galveston, Harrisburg, and San Antonio Railroad arrived with great fanfare and celebration, carrying the luxuries of civilization and, even more important, bringing with it the optimism of an exciting, expanding nation. No more would San Antonio be an isolated outpost on the frontier. Its role as lonely oasis was over. The town's population began to expand exponentially, growing almost 70 percent between 1870 and 1880, surpassing 20,000. Most of the new arrivals were Anglo-Americans, and thus the demographic composition of the town again changed as the solid German middle class was joined by a new crop of transplants from the Southern states.

As San Antonio grew, it also rebuilt and modernized much of its infrastructure. Brick homes began to replace adobe ones in the residential areas, while downtown, new businesses sprang up almost overnight. Streets were paved (some with stone, others with blocks cut from the hardy mesquite tree), and the water supply was upgraded from dependence on open canals (the picturesque but frequently contaminated acequias) to a system of deep wells. Stable, massive iron bridges spanned the river at several crossings, and horse-powered streetcars carried citizens through the downtown area. Electric lighting and telephones were introduced in the early 1880s, and the first substantial public school system was inaugurated along with a professional police force. Santa Rosa Hospital opened its doors in 1884, and the Grand Opera House in Alamo Plaza debuted in 1886. A visiting newspaperman declared, "the magic wand of civilization has touched the city . . . In the place of the mesquite thicket, where the coyote held his nightly revels, you see fine, broad avenues, lined on either side with beautiful and stately residences, surrounded with magnificent groves of shade trees and lovely gardens of flowers."

Almost forgotten in the frantic progress of the time was the city's heritage of missions and other historic structures. But while some priceless buildings were lost to progress, many were saved, some by chance and others quite deliberately. The Alamo was preserved thanks to the efforts of Clara Driscoll and the Daughters of the Republic of Texas, who led the fight to spare it and the adjoining Long Barrack from demolition. The Daughters purchased and renovated Texas's most beloved site and have protected it up to the present day, using private funding. Despite recent controversies and challenges to their role, the Daughters' dedication has endured. A plaque on the Alamo grounds quotes Clara Driscoll, who vowed to ensure "that the sacred shrine be saved from the encroachment of commercialism and stand through eternity a monument incomparable to the immortal heroes who died that Texas might not perish."

**i The San Antonio Conservation Society Foundation Library (www.saconservation.org) is housed in the Wulff House at 107 King William St. The collection includes books, maps, photographs, oral histories, and an extensive clipping collection. The library is open to the public Mon through Thurs, 9:30 a.m. to 3:30 p.m.; for information, call (210) 224-6163.**

The Daughters were but one of many volunteer groups that sprang up in San Antonio's "Gilded Age." The German

Americans, still influential, called upon their love of music and their heritage of social clubs to build the Beethoven Maennerchor Concert Hall in 1895. The hall became the home of the city's first symphony orchestra. Another German-American club, the Turnverein, built the city's first gymnasium, Turner Halle, near the Menger Hotel. Known for its displays of athletic ability, the Turnverein also formed the basis for San Antonio's first volunteer fire department. Other societies met to discuss how best to improve various aspects of the city's cultural climate. Fiesta San Antonio and its Battle of Flowers Parade, still one of San Antonio's biggest annual events, began in 1891 as a fete for an upcoming visit by President Benjamin Harrison.

Since the days when the founding friars attempted to "civilize" the native tribes by instructing them, education has played a prominent role in San Antonio's history. Turn-of-the-20th-century San Antonio witnessed the full flowering of that tradition as the University of the Incarnate Word joined Our Lady of the Lake, St. Mary's Hall, and Ursaline Academy. It is worth noting that one local school, West Texas Military Institute, graduated its most famous alumnus, Douglas MacArthur, in 1895.

At the end of the 1800s, San Antonio saw itself poised for greatness. The largest city in Texas was renowned for its architecture, multicultural heritage, and elegant standard of living. Although much of its economic prosperity was fueled by trade and by a considerable military presence, the city's culture was much more diversified. Hispanic, European, Anglo, and many other cultural elements created a unique society that gave San Antonio a firm foundation to face the new century with optimism and pride.

## THE 20TH CENTURY

In many ways, San Antonio's evolution in the 20th century was much like that of other American cities. It experienced a burst of development in the first two decades, much like it had with the coming of the railroad. This boom, however, was sparked by other inventions in transportation: the automobile and the airplane. The latter was to transform the city. In fact, the first American military flight took place at Fort Sam Houston in March 1910. Once World War I started, San Antonio's military facilities were greatly expanded and improved. By 1930 San Antonio boasted numerous bases: Kelly Field, Brooks Field, Fort Sam Houston, and Randolph Field, which was to be known as the "West Point of the Air."

Two world wars fought by the US against Germany had a chilling effect on San Antonio's Germanic population, despite the fact that they had been Texans for more generations than many of the city's Anglo-American citizens. Street and building names were changed, and the traditional organs of German culture, the societies and their publications, were shut down. At the same time, the Hispanic population grew, fueled by refugees from the revolution in Mexico.

A catastrophic flood in 1921 destroyed much of the downtown area, initiating action to harness the San Antonio River to prevent such disasters in the future. This resulted in the building of dams to control the river and eventually in the construction of the River Walk area. Skyscrapers were constructed in the downtown area. Many of San Antonio's historical buildings were preserved, however, as by now the city was conscious of its heritage, and there were organizations such as the San Antonio Conservation Society. Historic preservation was also a by-product of the Great Depression, when the development in San Antonio, as in most American cities, stopped.

World War II pulled San Antonio out of its stagnation. The city's military bases were again enlarged, and a new base, Lackland, was constructed, eventually to train more than one-third of the air personnel serving in the war. Other research facilities sprang up: The School of Aerospace Medicine at Brooks Air Force Base opened in 1959, while the University of the Air, a college dedicated to air force personnel, opened at Randolph AFB. Trinity University relocated to San Antonio in 1942, and the University of Texas built a new campus here as well as a major medical center in the early 1970s.

In subsequent years San Antonio became more dependent on a new source of revenue: tourism. The Alamo, of course, was the main draw (it remains today the number one tourist attraction in Texas), but the city developed other attractions to increase the number of visitors, such as the River Walk, completed in 1941. This area, which remains a top tourist draw today, is a beautifully landscaped promenade along the downtown portion of the San Antonio River, flowing past alfresco restaurants, shops, and hotels. As San Antonio began to realize the potential of its unique heritage, ethnic neighborhoods such as the King William area and the old Spanish missions were beautifully restored. The missions became part of the National Park Service. Pride in the city's heritage reached full flower in 1968 with HemisFair '68, a world's fair celebrating San Antonio's 250th birthday. The fair was held near Alamo Plaza, and its symbol was the 750-foot-tall Tower of the Americas, with its revolving observation venue at the top. The Tower, as well as other fair facilities, remains today an important city landmark. Nearby, the Henry B. Gonzales Convention Center now draws more than 750,000 conference attendees annually, making this one of the most popular convention cities in the country. Another city landmark, the Alamodome, rises near HemisFair Plaza. Completed in 1993, it hosts football bowl games and special events (country musician George Strait sold out the house in 2010). The AT&T Center, formerly the SBC Center, opened in the fall of 2002 as the new home to the National Basketball Association's San Antonio Spurs.

San Antonio has emerged from the 20th century holding a special place in Texas. No longer the state's largest city, it remains, to many residents and visitors, its most charming. Although thoroughly modern, San Antonio is most proud of its past and eager to share its story with visitors.

# ACCOMMODATIONS

**Deciding where to stay in San Antonio can be difficult; the city is dotted with hotels and motels designed to appeal to all types of travelers: the leisure crowd, business travelers, and conventioneers. You'll find hotels sprinkled throughout the city, but most are clustered in a few high-demand areas: the River Walk, along I-35, and along I-10.**

**Because San Antonio has some of the highest occupancy rates in the state, obtaining a hotel room can also be a tough job, especially during peak tourist periods: the summer months, the Christmas season, Eastertime, during April's Fiesta and other festivals, and anytime the San Antonio Spurs are playing a home game. Large conventions can fill downtown and River Walk rooms at other times as well.**

**Even with the high demand, though, you can obtain choice rooms, especially if you book early. The city has more than 33,000 hotel rooms; more than 12,000 are found in the downtown area. Most of these properties are family-friendly. Some allow kids to stay free in the same room as their parents; others have children's menus at on-site restaurants. Most properties can supply cribs and additional bedding, sometimes at a surcharge.**

**The highest demand is for rooms along the River Walk, or Paseo del Rio, the city's top tourist district. Not coincidentally, these are also the city's most expensive hotel rooms. Properties such as the Hyatt Regency San Antonio, the Marriott Riverwalk, the Westin San Antonio, and La Mansión del Rio have long been favorite stops for travelers looking for luxury accommodations. These expensive hotels offer the full menu of amenities and services that you would expect to see in a first-rate property.**

## OVERVIEW

You will find a few moderately priced motels within walking distance of the River Walk, but expect to see three-figure rates at most properties any night of the week. Remember that Friday and Saturday nights are peak times in this leisure market, although weekdays can be busy as well because of the city's excellent convention facilities, located on an arm of the River Walk.

Beyond the River Walk but still within the downtown area lie some of the city's most historic and elegant properties. These historic hotels hark back to the days when the River Walk was an undeveloped and undesirable area. The Gunter Hotel and St. Anthony Hotel were preferred addresses in the city, each within walking distance of elegant theaters. Near the Alamo, the Menger Hotel has long been one of the city's most prestigious hostelries.

If you're flying into San Antonio, you'll also find a large array of hotels, motels, and extended-stay properties near the airport. Loop 410 is home to a large concentration of accommodations, many at lower prices than those found along the River Walk. Some of these properties offer shuttle service to the airport.

Many car travelers arrive in San Antonio on I-35 and I-10. Numerous motels are located on the north side of the city along I-35, one of the state's busiest thoroughfares.

All the properties listed accept major credit cards and offer a selection of nonsmoking rooms. In compliance with the Americans with Disabilities Act (ADA), all San Antonio hotels and motels have wheelchair-accessible rooms. Unless otherwise noted, the properties in this chapter do not allow pets, with the exception of service animals for guests with disabilities.

### *Price Code*

This price code is based on the price for a standard room, double occupancy, during peak season. Prices do not include hotel tax.

**$................. Less than $75**
**$$ ................. $75 to $150**
**$$$ ............... $150 to $225**
**$$$$........... More than $225**

### *Quick Index by Cost*

## HOTELS & MOTELS

### Downtown

**ALAMO TRAVELODGE** $
**405 Broadway**
**(210) 222-1000, (800) 835-2424**
**www.travelodge.com**

This simple yet comfortable hotel is conveniently located 15 minutes from the San Antonio International Airport. Close to the low-rise structure are all the exciting attractions of downtown San Antonio, including the Alamo, River Walk, Rivercenter Mall, and Henry B. Gonzales Convention Center. Alamo Travelodge offers modern-looking, air-conditioned rooms (for those hot Texas summers), a free *USA Today* every weekday, an outdoor pool, and free Wi-Fi. This is the perfect accommodation for visitors looking for a modest hotel at a great location.

**COURTYARD SAN ANTONIO DOWNTOWN/MARKET SQUARE** $$
**600 S. Santa Rosa Ave.**
**(210) 229-9449, (800) 706-0253**
**www.marriott.com**

This downtown hotel has a great location. The Alamodome, downtown San Antonio, Market Square, Rivercenter Mall, the River Walk, and the Alamo are all located within a mile. The property has an outdoor pool and whirlpool, room service, complimentary parking, express check-in and checkout, and cable TV. Each guest room has a spacious sitting area for entertaining guests or just relaxing after a long day, a desk, voice mail, phones with dataports, remote-control TV with an all-news channel, in-room movies, a newspaper delivered on weekdays, in-room coffee, an iron and ironing board, a hair dryer, and complimentary Wi-Fi. All rooms are positioned around the hotel's wonderfully landscaped courtyard. Cribs are available. This hotel has two meeting rooms and a total of 1,250 square feet of meeting space. Near the property, guests can find restaurants serving cuisines ranging from Cajun and Creole to Italian.

**CROCKETT HOTEL** $$$
**320 Bonham St.**
**(210) 225-6500, (800) 292-1050**
**http://crocketthotel.com**

Just beyond Alamo Plaza stands the Crockett Hotel, situated on grounds that were once part of the Alamo battlefield. In fact, Davy Crockett was said to have defended the southeast palisade, and the hotel is named in his honor. The original mercantile store that stood at this site was sold to the International Order of Odd Fellows, who built a lodge and hotel here in 1909. Today the 138-room hotel has been faithfully restored to its turn-of-the-20th-century grandeur. There are modern amenities as well: Guests can stay connected with free wireless Internet access.

The Crockett is the perfect place for guests who are looking for comfortable accommodations at a great location. Adjacent to the Alamo, Rivercenter Mall, and the River Walk, the hotel is within walking distance of many of San Antonio's major attractions. For active guests, golf and tennis facilities are less than 5 miles away. For business travelers, the Crockett has photocopying, Internet, fax, and printer services.

The hotel offers a restaurant and cocktail lounge, dry cleaning and laundry facilities, safe-deposit boxes, turndown service, and wake-up calls. Guests can either dine at the hotel's Landmark Restaurant or choose from any of the varied restaurants on the nearby River Walk. To finish off a busy day of shopping on the River Walk or touring the historic missions, visitors can relax in the outdoor pool or in the rooftop hot tub, which offers a beautiful view of downtown San Antonio.

**CROWNE PLAZA SAN ANTONIO RIVERWALK** **$$–$$$**
**111 E. Pecan St.**
**(210) 354-2800, (800) 972-3480**
**www.ichotelgroups.com**

A towering high-rise only steps away from the River Walk, this accommodation is perfect for visitors who plan to enjoy a lot of shopping and nightlife at the San Antonio landmark. Crowne Plaza offers visitors same-day dry cleaning and laundry services, an outdoor pool, and a gift shop featuring the work of Texas artists. Guests have access to the hotel's fully equipped health club and can enjoy a spectacular view of the River Walk from the sundeck with an outdoor pool and whirlpool. Each of the 410 rooms has a remote-control TV with ESPN, CNN, and Headline News, in-room movies, two phones, a dataport, a large desk, climate control, an iron and ironing board, electronic door locks, AM/FM clock radio, and voice mail. The 111 Bar & Grille is in the lobby, serving breakfast, lunch, and dinner. At Pecan Street Pub, guests can watch their favorite teams on wide-screen TVs.

**DOUBLETREE HOTEL SAN ANTONIO DOWNTOWN** **$$$**
**502 W. Durango Blvd.**
**(210) 224-7155, (888) 201-1718**
**http://doubletree1.hilton.com**

The Doubletree Hotel is packed with services and amenities to satisfy all types of guests, from those who are looking for rest and relaxation to those who are seeing the sights of San Antonio from morning 'til night. The Doubletree offers kid-friendly amenities, such as babysitting, and cribs, and features a children's menu. All guests enjoy the services of a concierge, a gift shop and newsstand, laundry service, and safe-deposit boxes. The hotel's outdoor pool is the perfect place to cool off; those who like to sunbathe can head for one of the lounge chairs that fill the courtyard. The exercise room is fully equipped with all types of fitness machines. Ventanas Bistro & Wine Bar dishes out distinctive bistro cuisine, and room service is available from 6 a.m. to 11 p.m. daily. The hotel is near downtown attractions such as the Alamo, the River Walk, the Henry B. Gonzales Convention Center, and the Alamodome. SeaWorld of San Antonio and Six Flags Fiesta Texas aren't far, and San

Antonio International Airport is a 15-minute drive away.

**DRURY INN & SUITES RIVERWALK $$$**
**201 N. St. Mary's St.**
**(201) 212-5200, (800) DRURY-INN**
**www.druryhotels.com**

This Drury Inn, right on the River Walk, is a historic landmark. The building was erected in the 1920s and has since been restored to its original beauty. To the delight of visitors, the period architecture of the building has been maintained. Nonetheless, the guest rooms are equipped with such modern amenities as voice mail, coffeemakers, and irons and ironing boards. Guests have access to a 24-hour business center, an exercise room, fax service, laundry services, meeting rooms, and a rooftop pool. Free hot breakfast is served every morning, and free beverages and snacks are served daily in the evenings. Hotel parking is available for a fee. The Alamodome, the Buckhorn Museum, the Children's Museum, the Henry B. Gonzales Convention Center, the Empire Theatre, La Villita, the Majestic Theatre, Market Square, the River Walk, Rivercenter Mall, and the Alamo are all within walking distance of the hotel. A Texas Land & Cattle Company Steakhouse is on the premises, and the many restaurants of the River Walk are only a few steps away.

**EMILY MORGAN $$$$**
**705 E. Houston St.**
**(210) 225-5100, (800) 824-6674**
**www.emilymorganhotel.com**

This hotel is named for the woman known in legend and song as "The Yellow Rose of Texas." General Santa Anna was enamored with Emily Morgan, a mulatto slave who acted as a spy for the Texas army. Thanks in part to her efforts, Sam Houston's troops defeated Santa Anna's men at San Jacinto on April 21, 1836, winning the Texas Revolution. Cited as one of the finest examples of Gothic Revival architecture in America, the building served for a long time as a medical arts building, and you can still see the wonderful terra-cotta gargoyles hanging over the ground-floor windows. The 177–guest room Emily Morgan offers its guests many amenities. Every room has wireless Internet, coffeemaker, hair dryer, and TV with cable. Most of the rooms also have Jacuzzis and minifridges. The hotel offers babysitting and child care services, a barber shop/salon, a fitness center, 24-hour front desk, laundry and valet services, pet-friendly services, an outdoor pool, a restaurant, room service, safe-deposit boxes, and meeting/banquet facilities.

The best feature of this hotel is its location: Literally next door to the Alamo, it is within walking distance of Rivercenter Mall, the Henry B. Gonzales Convention Center, HemisFair Park, and Market Square. Many of the guest rooms look down onto the Alamo complex. The Oro Restaurant is in the hotel.

**FAIRFIELD INN AND SUITES SAN ANTONIO DOWNTOWN $$**
**620 S. Santa Rosa Ave.**
**(210) 299-1000, (800) 228-2800**
**www.marriott.com**

Cable TV, complimentary continental breakfast, laundry facilities, and complimentary newspapers are some of the extras available at this downtown lodging place. Guests will also find an indoor heated swimming pool, exercise facilities, and in-room movies. Each of the 110 rooms offers wireless Internet, desk, dataports and telephone, and a remote-control TV with an all-news channel and in-room movies. Cribs are available on request. This Fairfield is situated near the River Walk, the Alamo, the Alamodome, Market Square, and the Henry B. Gonzales Convention Center. The hotel also has a 1,400-square-foot meeting room.

**i** To avoid the hassle of planning a wedding, couples can tie the knot in a mass wedding, held each year in San Antonio on Valentine's Day. Couples need only to show up with a marriage license, issued within 72 hours of the ceremony, to exchange vows at the San Antonio City Hall.

**THE FAIRMOUNT** **$$$**
**401 S. Alamo St.**
**(210) 224-8800, (877) 229-8808**
**www.thefairmounthotel-sanantonio.com**

This hotel calls itself "San Antonio's Little Jewel." The 37-room property pampers its guests with personal attention and style amid turn-of-the-20th-century elegance. In 1986 the hotel earned a place in the Guinness Book of World Records when the 3.2 million-pound structure became the heaviest building ever moved. The move took six days, relocating the 3-story hotel just across the street from both HemisFair Plaza and La Villita. During the excavation of the basement at the new location, artifacts from the battle of the Alamo were found. Today the site is a State Archaeological Landmark.

Each suite, salon, and junior suite is a study in European elegance, complete with antique furnishings, silk fabrics, and hand-painted tiles. For business meetings, the Director's Board Room can hold up to 44 people, and the Salon accommodates 90 guests. The 1,200-square-foot courtyard offers a serene outdoor setting with the option of a tented canopy. The Fairmount couldn't be in a better location. The Alamo is only 6 blocks away, while the River Walk is only 4. The San Antonio Art Museum, Blue Star Arts Complex, and the Alamodome are all close by.

**HAMPTON INN SAN ANTONIO—DOWNTOWN** **$$–$$$**
**414 Bowie St.**
**(210) 225-8500, (800) HAMPTON**
**http://hamptoninn1.hilton.com**

Just 2 blocks from the River Walk and Alamo, this 6-story, 169-room structure offers clean rooms, a convenient location, and numerous amenities at a reasonable price. Every room is equipped with a coffeemaker, iron, and LCD flat-screen TV with cable. Connecting rooms are available, as are cribs and hair dryers. For an additional fee, guests can use meeting and banquet facilities as well as laundry and valet services. The hotel also has free parking, pool, and free Internet access. There are several restaurants within a mile of the hotel, including Landry's Seafood House, Boudro's, Salt Grass Steakhouse, and the Hard Rock Cafe. In addition to the Alamo and River Walk, the Institute of Texan Cultures, Rivercenter Mall, the Henry B. Gonzales Convention Center, and the Tower of the Americas are within walking distance.

**HOTEL HAVANA** **$$$–$$$$**
**1015 Navarro St.**
**(210) 222-2008**
**www.havanasanantonio.com**

Built in 1914, the Hotel Havana is a state and national landmark and is listed on the National Register of Historical Places. When staying in one of its 27 rooms, you can imagine being in any exotic colonial locale from Havana to Europe to Africa. The Mediterranean Revival–style architecture, as well as the use of antiques and artifacts from around the world in the decor, adds to the mystery and romance of this eclectic hotel. Vintage furnishings, dark wood floors, and Red Flower bath products are the little touches that make this spot special, while still offering the regular amenities such as cable TV and free wireless Internet access. Located right on the River Walk, the Havana is a short walk or ride to all the downtown sights and is only 1 block from a trolley stop. The on-site Riverwalk Bar is an intimate setting, offering desserts, cigars, and cocktails.

**HOTEL INDIGO SAN ANTONIO RIVERWALK** **$$–$$$**
**830 N. St. Mary's St.**
**(210) 527-1900, (887) 846-3446**
**www.ichotelsgroup.com**

Located on a quiet stretch of the River Walk known as the Museum Reach, this upscale boutique hotel has 149 stylish guest rooms and 5 suites. The long, low-rise structure, easy to spot thanks to its reddish roof, has many rooms with balconies that overlook the River Walk.

All rooms and suites include wireless Internet access, phones with speakers and voice mail (and free local calls), cable TV with premium channels, CD players, coffeemakers, minirefrigerators, irons and ironing boards, and hair dryers. Guest accomodations and public areas sport a sleek, modern look with lots of primary colors and mininimalist appointments, with Indigo's signature murals throughout the property.

The on-site restaurant, Phi, serves breakfast from 6:30 to 10:30 a.m. Mon through Fri and 7 to 11 a.m. weekends, and dinner daily 5 to 10:30 p.m. The adjacent Phi Lounge overlooks the Riverwalk. Room service is available from 7 a.m. to 10 p.m.

The hotel has an attractive outdoor pool and a fitness center with treadmills, stationary bikes and weight machines. Business features include a meeting room seating up to 100 attendees, a boardroom and a 24-hour business center with wireless Internet, a PC and printer, and copy and fax services. The hotel also offers valet parking, laundry and dry cleaning service, and daily housekeeping. Hotel Indigo Riverwalk is extremely pet-friendly, welcoming pets without additional charges.

**i** **The third Hotel Indigo in the state, and the first in San Antonio, opened its doors in the spring of 2008. This urban retreat features 2,000 square feet of meeting space and gourmet cuisine at the Phi Restaurant and Lounge, all housed inside the Edwardian-era Gibbs Building.**

**HILTON PALACIO DEL RIO HOTEL** **$$$–$$$$**
**200 S. Alamo St.**
**(210) 222-1400, (800) HILTONS**
**www.hilton.com**

This hotel is a prefab structure, albeit a wonderfully elegant one. The property was constructed in just 202 days to be ready for HemisFair '68. Like giant children's blocks, the rooms (furnishings and all) were assembled off-site and put together here in record time. Today the hotel has a wonderful location, right in the middle of the River Walk action and just a few short steps from La Villita and HemisFair Plaza.

The Hilton has plenty of services to offer its guests. In each of its nearly 500 rooms, guests will find comfortable beds, double-line phone with voice mail and dataport, plasma screen HD television, and high-speed

Internet access. There are two restaurants on the property. The Ibiza Patio Restaurant and Bar serves Mediterranean and Texas-style foods for all three meals of the day and features live music on Friday and Saturday nights. Durty Nelly's Irish Bar allows guests to watch their favorite sports teams on TV while trying beers and appetizers. Durty Nelly's has nightly sing-alongs.

**HOLIDAY INN SAN ANTONIO RIVERWALK** **$$–$$$**
**217 N. St. Mary's St.**
**(210) 224-2500, (888) HOLIDAY**
**www.ichotelsgroup.com**
This high-rise hotel is 23 stories tall and has 313 comfortable rooms. Guest perks include a porter/bellman, dry cleaning and laundry service, free high-speed Internet access, safe-deposit boxes, wake-up calls, exercise facilities, and a pool. There is a cash machine on the property, handy for shopping expeditions on the River Walk, which is located just opposite the hotel entrance. Copying, fax, and secretarial services are offered for business travelers. Guests can stroll to many of San Antonio's main attractions. The River Walk, the Alamodome, the Tower of the Americas, Market Square, Rivercenter Mall, the Alamo, and La Villita are all less than a mile away. An on-site restaurant, Windows on the River, serves casual meals and has a view of the River Walk.

**HOLIDAY INN SAN ANTONIO DOWNTOWN (MARKET SQUARE)** **$$–$$$**
**318 W. Durango Blvd.**
**(210) 225-3211, (888) HOLIDAY**
**www.ichotelsgroup.com**
Right on Market Square, this is a great lodging place for visitors who want to see the historic sights of beautiful San Antonio. The outside of the building is styled like an old adobe mission, recalling the city's unique history. The hotel offers a pool, an exercise room, a coin-operated laundry, free Internet access, safe-deposit boxes, 6 meeting rooms for groups of up to 300 people, wake-up calls, photocopy and fax services, and complimentary parking. The on-site Madera's restaurant serves speedy breakfast, lunch, and dinner for guests who are in a hurry to see San Antonio. For guests looking to relax after a long day, there's a cocktail lounge. Less than a mile from the hotel lie Market Square, the River Walk, Rivercenter Mall, the Alamo, King William Historic District, and the Alamodome.

**HOMEWOOD SUITES BY HILTON RIVERWALK** **$$$**
**432 W. Market St.**
**(210) 222-1515, (800) CALL-HOME**
**www.homewoodsuitesriverwalk.com**
This Homewood Suites is found in the restored historic San Antonio Drug Company building, which is listed on the National Register of Historic Places. Every suite has a fully equipped kitchen and living/dining area, and guests are offered a free breakfast each morning. The hotel's Welcome Home reception, offered Mon through Thurs evenings, provides light meals and refreshments. A 24-hour Executive Business Center is equipped with a copier, color printer, fax, and Internet access. For group travelers, 1,800 square feet of meeting space is available with projection screens, private phones, audiovisual equipment, and dataports. Workout facilities include a stair climber, exercise bikes, a treadmill, and a universal-weight station. Guests can relax in the rooftop pool and hot tub and enjoy the view of downtown San Antonio. Valet parking with

## Close-up

### San Antonio Weddings

From the intimacy of a historic chapel to the opulence of a fairy-tale ballroom, the Alamo City offers an array of locales for couples celebrating a love as big as the Lone Star State.

**The Bright Shawl** (210-225-6366; www.sanantonioweddings.com) is a Texas landmark that embraces every aspect of the wedding process, from the bridal shower to the wedding reception. This cozy limestone cottage in downtown San Antonio has been a silent witness to Texas history since its construction in 1873, and today the former family residence has a new life as a special-events facility that offers a romantic locale for Texas twosomes to say "I do." Sites are available to meet the needs of the most intimate ceremony consisting of 24 people or fewer, which can take place in the Living Room, to the grandest of gatherings held at The Club, which accommodates up to 400 people.

"The Gunter Hotel, at the Center of Everything!" Bequeathed with this slogan in 1912 by the National Association of Advertising Men, the words still ring true today for the **Sheraton Gunter Hotel** (210-227-3241; www.gunterhotel.com), a historic hotel at the heart of downtown San Antonio. Located across from the Majestic and Empire Theaters, the hotel's Crystal Ballroom has hosted a number of romantic nuptials over the years. Wedding parties from 25 to 725 can be accommodated in this beautiful venue.

More than 100 couples are united in matrimony each year at **Little Church** (210-226-3593; http://lavillita.com/church/index.htm), located in La Villita. Built in 1879, this nondenominational house of worship, which still holds services twice a week, is just moments from the River Walk.

At **San Fernando Cathedral** (210-227-1297; www.sfcathedral.org) in downtown San Antonio, in the nation's oldest cathedral sanctuary, couples are pronounced husband and wife by a priest standing at a carved wooden pulpit dating back to 1874.

For the modern-minded bride, **Los Encinos Texas Hill Country Estate** (210-698-1654; www.losencinos.com) takes the worry out of wedding preparations. The catering, photography, and decorating are taken care of with the help of a wedding

unlimited in and out privileges is also available for a daily fee.

**HOTEL VALENCIA RIVERWALK** **$$$–$$$$**
**150 E. Houston St.**
**(210) 227-9700, (866) 842-0100**
**www.hotelvalencia.com**

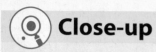

Custom designed with sleek, contemporary features for a sense of exclusiveness and luxury, this boutique hotel is right on the banks of the San Antonio River. The 213 guest suites are indisputably modern with a big-city ambience and amenities to match: twice-daily maid service, white marble bathrooms, Egyptian cotton bed linens on custom-made beds, bath amenities by Lather, hair dryers, lush waffle terry towels and robes, 42-inch color televisions with 70 cable channels and pay-per-view, coordinator who can turn any couple's dream wedding into a reality, whether they wish to release doves into the air after the ceremony or fill the night sky with fireworks. Situated on 14 oak-shaded acres on Boerne Stage Road, this secluded Texas retreat offers the perfect getaway for newlyweds, and a honeymoon suite is available on request.

Sophisticated city weddings are held at the **Omni San Antonio Hotel** (210-691-8888; www.omnihotels.com), where an on-site wedding coordinator will help with every last detail, from decorating to catering. The Grand Ballroom offers 10,000 square feet of space and can accommodate up to 650 people. Those with smaller guest lists may choose the Colonnade Ballroom, where up to 120 people can dance and dine on the 20th floor, or the La Joya Ballroom, which provides 3,000 square feet of space for up to 175 guests, who can toast the happy couple beneath the sparkle of crystal chandeliers.

Brides and grooms with a guest list of 250 or more can plan a romantic first-anniversary getaway or banish pre-wedding tension with an extended wedding package consisting of spa treatments at the **Doubletree Hotel** (210-321-4816; www.dtreeweddings.com), located on Loop 410. This elegant hotel conjures up images of a south-of-the-border romance with Spanish colonial architecture, Mexican tile, and tropical courtyards.

Native Americans once inhabited the area where **Los Patios** (210-655-6171; www.lospatios.com) now stands, and respect for nature's beauty remains at the forefront of this favored locale for unique weddings. Many couples choose to declare their love creekside beneath ancient oaks before enjoying a reception amid Spanish and Mexican accents. The venue, which has helped to join thousands of couples in marriage, can accommodate parties of up to 500 guests.

Water is often viewed as a symbol of rebirth, and what better way to begin a new life together than along the River Walk. For the largest of weddings, the **Marriott Riverwalk** (210-224-4555; www.marriott.com) offers everything you need and on-site assistance. Weddings ranging from intimate to gala events for up to 800 guests can be planned at the **Westin Riverwalk** (210-224-6500; www.starwoodhotels.com), complete with a 5,900-square-foot ballroom and several junior ballrooms that overlook the River Walk.

high-speed Internet access, minibars, plush leather chairs, free weekday newspapers, balcony and courtyard rooms, multilingual concierge staff, valet parking, same-day laundry, a fitness center and spa services. The on-site Citrus Restaurant offers the best in regional cuisine with terrace dining, while the second-floor Vbar serves cocktails and tapas and boasts breathtaking views of the River Walk. Old World meets New World in this hip yet classic hotel—a great place to stay if you want to treat yourself.

**✻HYATT REGENCY SAN ANTONIO** **$$$–$$$$**

**123 Losoya St.**

**(210) 222-1234, (800) 233-1234**

**www.hyatt.com**

Located on the bend in the river, this elegant hotel captures all the excitement of the River

Walk. Whether you enter from the street or the riverside, you'll admire the Hyatt's soaring atrium, filled with palms and the sound of falling water. The hotel added a segment to the river to divert water through the atrium and into the water gardens beyond. The water garden area now has several small bars, Jim Cullum's Jazz Club, and Shops at Pasao del Alamo. Follow the steps up the water gardens and you'll find yourself facing the Alamo.

Glass elevators whisk guests to the 632 rooms above. Each room is equipped with a TV with remote control, cable movie channels and in-room pay movies, voice mail, wireless Internet, iHome iPod alarm, in-room laptop safe, electronic door locks, an iron and ironing board, a hair dryer, a coffeemaker, and a minibar. Turndown service is available on request. The hotel also has a heated rooftop pool and whirlpool; Stay Fit health club with exercise bikes, stair climbers, and treadmills; a business center; concierge service; the Dasa Spa; laundry and dry cleaning service; room service; valet parking; and currency exchange. Hyatt Regency is right on the River Walk and a short walk from the Alamo and the Henry B. Gonzales Convention Center. On the property, Chaps Restaurant features bistro-style cuisine with a breakfast buffet, fresh salad bar, nightly dinner specials, and delicious desserts. The River Terrace Lounge is the perfect place to relax and visit with friends while enjoying cocktails and appetizers. Pets are allowed at the Hyatt; call for details.

**LA MANSIÓN DEL RIO $$$$**
**112 College St.**
**(210) 518-1000, (800) 809-OMNI**
**www.omnihotels.com**

This elegant Spanish Colonial–style structure began as St. Mary's Academy in 1854. Eventually the campus grew and was renamed St. Mary's College, and then graduated to St. Mary's University. This location served as the law school until 1966, when the campus was relocated. At that time, the building traded in blackboards for beds, desks for dressers, and started a new life as La Mansión.

Any visitor looking for a unique hotel that captures San Antonio's cultural charm will appreciate La Mansión del Rio. The building's Spanish Colonial architecture reflects San Antonio's roots, while the location, overlooking the River Walk, keeps guests in touch with the city's present-day personality. The past and present blend beautifully to offer guests a distinctive home base for their trip. Many of the 338 guest rooms have a view of the River Walk, and all offer an honor bar, remote-control cable television, evening turndown service, two-line phones, and high-speed Internet access. Around-the-clock room service and a concierge desk are available. The hotel restaurant, Las Canarias, serves up attractive meals, mixing regional fare with a twist of Texas. El Colegio, the piano bar, offers an extensive variety of Texas beers and wines as well as appetizers.

**i** **Movie buffs may recognize the large mural hanging in the lobby of the Menger Hotel as one of the props used in the 1956 epic *Giant,* starring Elizabeth Taylor, Rock Hudson, and James Dean.**

**LA QUINTA INN SAN ANTONIO CONVENTION CENTER $$$**
**303 Blum St.**
**(210) 222-9181, (800) 753-3757**
**www.lq.com**

Just a quick walk from the Henry B. Gonzales Convention Center and the River Walk, this La Quinta offers its guests numerous services and amenities. Free local telephone calls and newspapers, a free continental breakfast, premium-channel TV, high-speed Internet access, an outdoor pool, laundry facilities, a fitness center, refrigerators, AM/FM clock radios, cribs, and microwave ovens are all offered to guests, and children under 18 stay free. The property is also pet-friendly. There are 8,500 square feet of meeting space and a business center. As in all La Quinta hotels, the rooms here are clean and well equipped. Nearby, the world-famous River Walk is bustling with excitement and is ready for shopping, dining, and sightseeing.

**✷LA QUINTA SAN ANTONIO MARKET SQUARE $$**
**900 Dolorosa**
**(210) 271-0001, (800) 753-3757**
**www.lq.com**

In one of San Antonio's best districts for shopping and learning about Mexican culture, this La Quinta has a great location for seeing the city. Each of its 125 guest rooms has television with premium channels, a whirlpool bath, a safe-deposit box, free Internet access, and free local telephone calls and newspapers. Rollaway beds and cribs are available, and kids under 18 stay free. Other pluses are free continental breakfast, free parking, express check-in, a 24-hour front desk, and laundry and valet service. The accommodation also has an outdoor pool to provide relief from the hot Texas summer sun. Market Square is a few blocks from the River Walk, the Alamo, the Henry B. Gonzales Convention Center, and Rivercenter Mall. San Antonio International Airport is 9 miles from the hotel.

**MARRIOTT RIVERCENTER $$$–$$$$**
**101 Bowie St.**
**(210) 223-1000, (800) 648-4462**
**www.marriott.com**

If you want a hotel with a great location, look no further than Marriott Rivercenter. The 38-story building towers over the River Walk and dominates the San Antonio skyline. This Marriott is connected to Rivercenter Mall and opens up onto the River Walk. It is less than a mile from the Henry B. Gonzales Convention Center, HemisFair Park, Market Square, and the Alamo. The 1,000-room complex has a restaurant, 24-hour room service, a coffee shop, a cocktail lounge, laundry service and self-service laundry facilities, child care service, a gift shop, a business center, safe-deposit boxes, and a Hertz rental car desk. Each room has a desk, voice mail, telephones with dataports, high-speed Internet access, a minibar, a coffeemaker, an iron and ironing board, a hair dryer, and LCD TV with cable, an all-news channel, and in-room movies. There are several guest rooms designed specifically for business travelers and 60,000 square feet of meeting space in 36 meeting rooms. Sazo's Latin Grill serves up south-of-the-border fare for breakfast, lunch, and dinner. The hotel also has an indoor and outdoor pool, a health club, a whirlpool, and a sauna; jogging, tennis, and golfing facilities are nearby.

**MARRIOTT RIVERWALK $$$–$$$$**
**889 E. Market St.**
**(210) 224-4555, (800) 648-4462**
**www.marriott.com**

Like its sister property, Marriott Rivercenter, Marriott Riverwalk is on the famous San Antonio River Walk and near many of San Antonio's main attractions. Not quite as looming as its neighbor, this 30-story building has 507 guest rooms and 5 suites. The Henry B. Gonzales Convention Center, Rivercenter Mall, the Alamo, Market Square, and the San Antonio Zoo are all less than 5 miles from the hotel. Six Flags Fiesta Texas and SeaWorld of San Antonio are 30 and 18 miles away, respectively. Every room has a desk, voice mail, high-speed Internet access, a newspaper delivered Monday through Friday, in-room coffee, an iron and ironing board, and remote-control TV with cable, an all-news channel, and in-room movies. Cribs are available on request. The hotel has an on-site restaurant, 24-hour room service, a coffee shop, a cocktail lounge, concierge service, a gift shop, a business center, and safe-deposit boxes. There is a pool and whirlpool, a health club, and a sauna; jogging, tennis, and golf are a short hop away.

### MENGER HOTEL $$–$$$

**204 Alamo Plaza**
**(210) 223-4361, (800) 345-9285**
**http://mengerhotel.com**

The Menger Hotel is located just next door to the Alamo. This historic hotel was built in 1859 and has remained a popular stop ever since. Some of its most famous guests include Civil War generals Robert E. Lee and William Sherman, Mount Rushmore sculptor Gutzon Borglum (who had a studio at the hotel), playwright Oscar Wilde, and author William Sydney Porter (O. Henry), who mentioned the hotel in several of his short stories. Today the Menger has been restored to its Victorian splendor. The 3-story lobby features Corinthian columns, a leaded skylight, and much of its original furniture. Guests can stay in Victorian accommodations or in newer rooms. The lobby is adjacent to a tropical garden (once the home of several alligators) and shops. Directly across the street are the stores of Blum Street and the Rivercenter Mall.

The Menger prides itself on the amenities offered to guests. Among these are the full-service Alamo Plaza Spa, a Jacuzzi, the largest swimming pool in downtown San Antonio, the Colonial Room Restaurant and the famous Menger Bar. Nearby, guests will find the Alamo, River Walk, Rivercenter Mall, Henry B. Gonzales Convention Center, and Alamo Plaza.

### *MOKARA HOTEL & SPA $$$$

**212 W. Crockett St.**
**(210) 396–5800, (866) 605–1212**
**www.mokarahotels.com**

The 19th-century L. Frank Saddlery building was redesigned and opened in December 2003 as the Watermark Hotel and Spa. Now rebranded by parent company Omni Hotels & Resorts, Mokara is the first of a new product line of upscale boutique spa hotels. Many of the Watermark features, such as 12-foot ceilings, hardwood floors, and Jacuzzi tubs in guest rooms, have been retained. The 96 rooms are well-appointed with superior amenities: plush robes and toiletries, and wireless Internet access. Public areas sport wood and marble trim and exude a comfortable but luxurious feel. The centerpiece of the hotel is the on-site European-style Mokara Spa, offering massages, scrubs, soaks, and other therapies as well as a hair and nail salon that caters to both sexes. The Mokara features world-class dining at Ostra, offering fresh seafood and an oyster bar set on an exquisite terrace along the river. Fitted with every amenity imaginable and poised for impeccable service, this upscale retreat makes guests feel pampered, indulged, rejuvenated, and invigorated.

**PLAZA SAN ANTONIO MARRIOTT $$$**
**555 S. Alamo St.**
**(210) 229-1000, (800) 421-1172**
**www.marriott.com**

Adding style and atmosphere to this elegant resort are four 19th-century buildings, each listed on the National Register of Historic Places, that are located directly behind the main hotel building. The Diaz House, now used for meetings and receptions, was built around 1840. Some have pointed out the similarity of the stonework in the Diaz House to that in the outer wall of the Alamo. The health club is housed in an 1850s structure that typifies the German style so popular in San Antonio during that period. Yet another house, a Victorian cottage, is now a private dining room.

But the best known of the hotel's historic structures is the German-English School. Located next to the tennis courts, this 2-story building was originally built to teach the children of the German businessmen who lived in the affluent King William neighborhood. Now the hotel conference center, the school came to national attention in 1992 when President George H. W. Bush, Mexican President Carlos Salinas, and Canadian Prime Minister Brian Mulroney met here for the initializing ceremony of the North American Free Trade Agreement.

This Marriott property prides itself on offering guests extra amenities such as overnight professional shoeshine service, chauffeured cars to San Antonio's business district, and a full business center. In-room coffee and a free newspaper are also provided. The hotel has a health club, spa, whirlpool, and outdoor heated pool. The concierge can attend to all your needs and inquiries about the property or the city. At Anaqua, diners enjoy Mediterranean and American-style dishes while they take in the breathtaking view of the Plaza's gardens. The Palm Terrace Lounge is the perfect place to relax after a long day.

**i** **Suite 884 at the St. Anthony Hotel was renamed for actor John Wayne. The star of *The Alamo* film stayed at the hotel in 1960 and again in 1978 for the National Entertainers' Conference.**

**RESIDENCE INN ALAMO PLAZA $$–$$$**
**425 Bonham St.**
**(210) 212-5555, (800) 371-6349**
**www.marriott.com**

An outdoor pool, a fitness center, and a great location are just some of the tempting options at this all-suite property. Other pluses are dinner delivery service from some local restaurants, a complimentary breakfast buffet, safe-deposit boxes, and high-speed Internet. Each of the 220 attractively decorated suites has a desk, voice mail, telephones with dataports, cable TV with an all-news channel and in-room movies, and a full kitchen with refrigerator, coffeemaker, dishwasher, microwave and range. Rooms also feature irons and ironing boards, and hair dryers. Cribs are available on request. There are 6 meeting rooms and a total of 1,891 square feet of meeting space. The Alamo, the Henry B. Gonzales Convention Center, Market Square, Rivercenter Mall, and the River Walk are all nearby. Also close to the hotel are several golf courses, and there are plenty of restaurants to choose from on the River Walk, including a Hard Rock Cafe and Morton's of Chicago. Pets are allowed with a $100 nonrefundable fee.

**RESIDENCE INN SAN ANTONIO $$$**
**Downtown Market Square**
**628 S. Santa Rosa Ave.**
**(210) 231-6000, (888) 236-2427**
**www.marriott.com**

With only 95 suites, this smaller hotel provides a more intimate feeling for its guests. Each spacious suite has separate living and sleeping areas, a desk, a phone with voice mail and dataports, wireless Internet, remote-control TV with an all-news channel and in-room movies, a full kitchen with a refrigerator and microwave, a coffeemaker, and an iron and ironing board. Cribs are available on request. The property offers a complimentary continental breakfast; laundry service as well as self-service laundry facilities; fax, printer, and copy machine access; secretarial services; safe-deposit boxes; and dinner delivery from some local restaurants. For guests looking for something active to do, there is an outdoor pool, an exercise room, and a whirlpool on-site, and golfing nearby. Pets are allowed with a nonrefundable sanitation fee ($100). For meals, the numerous restaurants of the River Walk are only a half-mile away. Also close by are the Alamo, Market Square, the Alamodome, the Henry B. Gonzales Convention Center, and the San Antonio Zoo.

**RIVERWALK PLAZA RESORT HOTEL & SUITES $$**
**100 Villita St.**
**(210) 225-1234, (800) 554-4678**
**www.riverwalkplaza.com**

Just steps from the River Walk, Market Square, La Villita, the Alamo, King William Historic District, the Henry B. Gonzales Convention Center, and the Alamodome, this hotel prides itself on its personal touches and amenities. The heated swimming pool is surrounded by a tropical courtyard where guests can enjoy cocktails or cold drinks. There is a 24-hour fitness center with the latest exercise equipment. Each of the 129 rooms and suites features either a king-size or full bed, remote-control TV with HBO and Showtime, a hair dryer, an AM/FM clock radio, coffeemaker, and complimentary high-speed Internet. A 24-hour business center offers a full range of services including copying and faxing, courier services, notary services and office supplies. The on-site restaurant, Signature Tapas, serves a large array of different tapas as well as sandwiches, salads, pasta, and pizzas, while the Bar-Salona cocktail lounge specializes in martinis and homemade sangria.

**ST. ANTHONY RIVERWALK WYNDHAM HOTEL $$–$$$**
**300 E. Travis St.**
**(210) 227-4392, (877) 999-3223**
**www.wyndham.com**

A part of the Wyndham Historic Hotel group, the St. Anthony has certainly seen its share of history and probably even made some at the same time. Construction began on the hotel in 1909, when San Antonio was just a Texas cow town. Soon after its opening, it was rated in the same category as New York City's Waldorf-Astoria by some visitors. The property was bought in 1935 by entrepreneur Ralph W. Morrison, who initiated many changes, including the addition of a 10-story tower and air-conditioning. Since 1909, the St. Anthony has been the place for celebrities and dignitaries to stay while in the Alamo City. First Lady Eleanor Roosevelt stopped here, as did General Douglas MacArthur, President Dwight D. Eisenhower, Prince Rainier and Princess Grace of Monaco,

Judy Garland, Lucille Ball, Fred Astaire, John Wayne, Gregory Peck, and Rock Hudson. More recently, Bruce Willis, George Clooney, and many others have stayed at this elegant lodging place.

The St. Anthony pampers all its guests—famous or not. Each room is equipped with a work desk, hair dryer, coffeemaker, telephone with dataport and voice mail, high-speed Internet access, and iron and ironing board. Children under 18 stay free. The 24-hour business center has copy, binding, shipping, laser printing, and secretarial services, as well as rental computers and cellular phones. The hotel is a short walk from the River Walk, the Alamo, the Henry B. Gonzales Convention Center, La Villita, the Alamodome, San Antonio Children's Museum, and HemisFair Park. If you'd like to dine where the stars eat, look no further than the Madrid Room, found on the grounds of the St. Anthony. The Madrid Room serves breakfast, lunch, and dinner in an Old World Spanish atmosphere and features Italian cuisine with a Southwestern twist. Also on the property, Castiza offers guests drinks and light meals. The hotel also offers room service daily from 6 am to midnight.

**SHERATON GUNTER** **$$$$**
**205 E. Houston St.**
**(210) 227-3241, (800) 325-3535**
**www.starwoodhotels.com**

Back in 1909, Jot Gunter turned the Frontier Hotel into the Gunter Hotel with the aim of creating the definitive lodging place for the booming city of San Antonio. In the year 2000 the Gunter celebrated its 91st anniversary with a rededication ceremony and an $8 million renovation project. The guest rooms, lobby, and meeting areas have all been beautifully restored.

Guests will find many extras here. A fitness center, an outdoor heated pool, 24-hour room service, a pub with a big-screen TV and a whirlpool are all on-site, as is Barron's Restaurant, which serves breakfast, lunch, and dinner every day. Barron's well-known pasta bar is open for lunch during the week. The Sheraton Gunter Bakery bakes mouthwatering treats for guests and visitors. Breads, pastries, cookies, cheesecake, and delicious chocolate-covered strawberries are among the selections found here.

Gunter's hospitality continues into the guest rooms, where visitors will find comfortable appointments and generous amenities. Every room has an alarm clock; voice mail; private bath; remote-control television with 35 channels, pay-per-view movies, and video games; iron and ironing board; and vintage-style furniture. For guests looking for extra room, Sheraton Gunter suites have the same amenities as the guest rooms but include a separate parlor. The Sheraton Gunter is a pet-friendly property.

**THE WESTIN RIVERWALK** **$$$–$$$$**
**420 W. Market St.**
**(210) 224-6500, (800) 937-8461**
**www.starwoodhotels.com**

Looking for a hotel that has as much to offer as San Antonio itself? Then head to the Westin Riverwalk. Each of the 473 guest rooms and 66 suites has two-line telephones with voice mail, a hair dryer, an iron and ironing board, a coffeemaker with Starbucks coffee, hypoallergenic pillows, an in-room safe, and a remote-control color TV with in-room movies and on-command video. The Westin boasts "The Heavenly Bed," with cozy down bedding that is sure to satisfy any fatigued guest. The hotel also features 24-hour room service, concierge service, safe-deposit boxes, wake-up calls, a business center, a health club, sauna, spa services, and an outdoor heated swimming pool,. The hotel accepts pets with a nonrefundable charge of $125. The hotel's ZOCCA restaurant is open for breakfast, lunch and dinner, serving Italian fare in an ideal environment for a romantic dinner or for relaxing and conversing with friends. The lobby-level Cafecity serves coffee, pastries, and other light fare till 5 p.m. This property is the perfect choice for travelers who want to make their accommodations another attraction on their trip.

## Inside & Along Loop 410

### BEST WESTERN POSADA ANA INN–AIRPORT $$

**8600 Jones Maltsberger Rd.**
**(210) 342-1400, (866) 642-1400**
**www.bestwestern.com**

Less than a mile from San Antonio International Airport, this Best Western property treats its guests like family. Every morning a complimentary, cooked-to-order full breakfast is served, and in the evening, popcorn and cookies are available in the lobby. Other extras include an outdoor pool, free local telephone calls, free wireless Internet, an airport courtesy van, fax services, and guest laundry facilities. Pets are welcome with some restrictions (call for details). For business guests, there are meeting rooms on-site. Many of San Antonio's top attractions are very close to this inn. The Alamo, Alamodome, River Walk, and Henry B. Gonzales Convention Center are 6 miles away; the San Antonio Zoo, Quarry Market, Quarry Golf Course, and North Star Mall lie closer still. Six Flags Fiesta Texas is 10 miles away, and SeaWorld of San Antonio is only a 14-mile drive. There are several dining options within a block of the property, including Applebee's Neighborhood Grill & Bar and Texas Land & Cattle Steakhouse. This is a good choice for families who want a good location, but not a high price.

### COMFORT INN & SUITES AIRPORT $$

**8640 Crownhill Blvd.**
**(210) 249-2000, (877) 424-6423**
**www.comfortinn.com**

With only 100 guest rooms, this Comfort Suites provides guests with an intimate atmosphere in the middle of a bustling, fast-paced city. A mile from San Antonio International Airport, the hotel is less than 15 miles from the Alamodome, Six Flags Fiesta Texas, HemisFair Plaza, and the Alamo. Cascade Caverns, Natural Bridge Caverns, and SeaWorld of San Antonio are less than 20 miles away. In addition to its great location, this property offers an array of services and amenities. Every room has free high-speed Internet, refrigerator, microwave, coffeemaker, an iron and ironing board, hair dryer, free local phone calls, remote-control cable TV with free movies, and voice mail. The hotel also offers its guests free airport and mall shuttles, a free full breakfast, an exercise room, a business center, fax and copy machines, lighted parking areas, an outdoor heated pool and Jacuzzi, safe-deposit boxes, guest laundry facilities, valet cleaning service, and a gift shop. Pets are accepted for a fee ($25).

### COURTYARD BY MARRIOTT SAN ANTONIO AIRPORT $$

**8615 Broadway**
**(210) 828-7200, (800) 706-0241**
**www.marriott.com**

This reasonably priced hotel takes care of all a traveler's needs. The on-site restaurant is open for breakfast, and there's also complimentary coffee in the lobby. Other conveniences include laundry service and guest laundry facilities, free parking, fax and copy services, and safe-deposit boxes available at the front desk. Each of the 145 comfortable rooms and suites has a desk with a lamp, voice mail, telephones with dataports, high-speed Internet access, remote-control cable TV with an all-news channel and in-room movies, a coffeemaker, an iron and ironing board, and a hair dryer. Each room also has a spacious sitting area that provides guests with the perfect setting for chatting with friends and relaxing following a day of sightseeing. Cribs are available on request. For more active guests, this Courtyard has an outdoor pool, fitness center, and a whirlpool, and jogging, tennis, squash, and golf are close by.

**CROWNE PLAZA SAN ANTONIO AIRPORT HOTEL $$**
**1111 NE Loop 410**
**(210) 828-9031, (800) 972-3480**
**www.ichotelsgroup.com**

This Crowne Plaza, with its tall palm trees and high-rise structure, is reminiscent of a classic Las Vegas hotel in the 1950s. Luckily for San Antonio visitors, it isn't found in Nevada, but in the Lone Star State, only a few minutes from San Antonio International Airport. Nearly all of the 224 units here have cable TV with premium channels such as HBO, CNN, and ESPN; wireless Internet access; electronic locks; iron and ironing board; telephone with voice mail; a desk; coffeemaker; and full kitchen with refrigerator and microwave. Open for every meal, the hotel's restaurant, Cilantro Oven, serves pizzas and Southwestern cuisine, while the Cilantro! Bar in the lobby serves wine and cocktails. Room service is available from 6:30 a.m. to 10 p.m. Golf, bowling, jogging, basketball, a walking track, and tennis courts are all only 5 miles away, and there is a 24-hour fitness center, whirlpool and outdoor pool on the property. Many of the sights of San Antonio are close by, too.

**DAYS INN COLISEUM/ AT&T CENTER $–$$**
**3443 I-35 North**
**(210) 225-4040, (800) 548-2626**
**www.daysinnsanantonio.com**

This two-story structure has basic, functional guest rooms and suites, each opening onto exterior corridors for easier access. Every standard room at this Days Inn has a king-size or double bed, free local telephone calls, free wireless Internet and cable TV with HBO. Pets are allowed at the rate of $25 per day. The Executive King Suites and Family Suites have a living room, sleeper sofa, and private bedroom. The Honeymoon Suite, the perfect place for a romantic evening, has a king-size bed, heart-shaped Jacuzzi, and sleeper sofa. All suites have a refrigerator, microwave, coffeemaker, hair dryer, and Jacuzzi tub. The River Walk (the perfect place for a night on the town or a day of shopping), the Alamo (a good place to visit for a history lesson), and Six Flags Fiesta Texas and SeaWorld of San Antonio (for lots of family fun) are all only a few miles away.

**DOUBLETREE HOTEL SAN ANTONIO AIRPORT $$–$$$**
**37 NE Loop 410**
**(210) 366-2424, (800) 222-TREE**
**www.doubletree.com**

Only 5 minutes from San Antonio International Airport, this hotel, built in 2000, has an abundance of amenities to offer its guests. The exterior is Spanish Colonial in style, while inside, traditional Texas hospitality reigns. The hotel's 290 guest rooms have 24-hour housekeeping; clock radios; hair dryers; electronic locks with a secondary lock; irons and ironing boards; telephones with auto wake-up, voice mail, and dataports; adjustable thermostats; desks; air-conditioning; cable TV with HBO, CNN, ESPN, and Pay-Per-View; coffeemakers; Internet access; and a free *USA Today* Mon through Fri. Some rooms also have balconies and a sofa bed. The business center offers a full range of services, and the property also boasts a fitness center with hot tub, sauna and pool. The hotel's Cascabel Restaurant, the seven-time winner of the AAA Four Diamond Award, serves Southwestern fare in a comfortable atmosphere. The Cascabel Bar is a great place to have a quiet drink, and limited room service is available from 11 a.m. to 1 a.m.

**FAIRFIELD INN AND SUITES SAN ANTONIO AIRPORT $$**
**88 NE Loop 410**
**(210) 530-9899, (888) 236-2427**
**www.marriott.com**

The friendly attitude of the staff is one of the highlights of this 85-room, 35-suite hotel. Guests here are met with a smile and a hospitable atmosphere. Each guest room has a desk with a lamp, wireless and wired Internet access, and cable TV with in-room movies and premium channels. Other conveniences include minirefrigerators, microwaves, free local calls, self-service laundry facilities, fax and copy services, and safe-deposit boxes. Complimentary continental breakfast is yet another plus. Active guests can take advantage of the hotel's indoor pool, whirlpool and fitness center. Pappadeaux's, the hotel's on-site restaurant, offers Cajun cuisine for lunch and dinner, and the hotel also offers dinner delivery service from area restaurants. For guests who want to eat out, Applebee's Neighborhood Grill & Bar, TGI Friday's, and Texas Land & Cattle Steakhouse are close by and serve lunch and dinner. Pets are allowed only as service animals for guests with disabilities.

**HAMPTON INN SAN ANTONIO AIRPORT $$**
**8902 Jones Maltsberger Rd.**
**(210) 558-3999, (800) HAMPTON**
**http://hamptoninn.hilton.com**

Have tickets to a San Antonio Spurs game? This hotel is 7 miles from the AT&T Center. Looking for a good restaurant that won't drain your budget? Jason's Deli and Chick-Fil-A are a short drive away. What about a place for a nice romantic or business dinner? Ruth's Chris Steak House and Texas Land & Cattle are both a quick drive from the hotel. The hotel has a pool, and every room has remote-control television with premium cable, high-speed Internet, a hair dryer, and an iron and ironing board. Cribs are available on request, and for an extra charge, guests can use the meeting and banquet facilities and laundry services. The complimentary hot breakfast gets your day off to a good start.

**HILTON SAN ANTONIO AIRPORT $$–$$$**
**611 NW Loop 410**
**(210) 340-6060, (800) HILTONS**
**www.hilton.com**

Each of the 384 guest rooms at this posh hotel has a Texas theme, perfect for visitors who want to immerse themselves in the rich history and culture of the Lone Star State. Amenities include 24-hour housekeeping, the Hilton Serenity bed, a newspaper delivered Mon through Fri, cable TV with premium channels such as HBO, CNN, and ESPN, a telephone with dataport, high-speed Internet access, a coffeemaker, and a desk with lamp. Guests on the Executive Level receive a daily newspaper, complimentary breakfast, and bathrobes to use during their stay. The hotel has a fitness center, an indoor pool, a putting green, and a video arcade, as well as complimentary airport shuttle service. For business travelers and groups, there are 6,336 square feet of exhibit space, including 2 ballrooms. Tex's Grill offers all-day dining, while Tex's Sports Bar has several televisions broadcasting games via satellite while serving guests drinks and dinner from a full menu. One of the property's prime assets is its location, not only close to the airport but also within a 5-minute drive of North Star Mall. In less than 20 minutes, guests can find themselves at a golf course, driving range, bowling alley, playground, basketball court, or tennis court.

**HOLIDAY INN SELECT SAN ANTONIO INTERNATIONAL AIRPORT $$–$$$**
**77 NE Loop 410**
**(210) 349-9900, (800) 972-3480 or (888) HOLIDAY**
**www.holidayinn.com**

Like most hotels in the Holiday Inn chain, this one offers guests tidy, efficient rooms at a good price. Also on the premises are 2 restaurants, a cocktail lounge, a gift shop, guest laundry facilities, an outdoor pool, and a cash machine. The full business center has copy and fax machines as well as PCs and printers, and wireless Internet access. The hotel also has over 10,000 square feet of meeting space and 12 meeting rooms. For guests with shopping on the agenda, North Star Mall is just a quick walk away.

**HOMEGATE STUDIOS & SUITES SAN ANTONIO AIRPORT $$**
**11221 San Pedro Ave.**
**(210) 342-4800**
**www.homegatesuitessa.com**

The 115 roomy suites here are equipped with full-size kitchens with most appliances, remote-control TV with HBO and Showtime, two telephone lines with voice mail, and irons and ironing boards. Guests can enjoy the pool and spa, or work out at the on-site fitness center. Guest laundry and valet services are available.

**HYATT PLACE SAN ANTONIO AIRPORT/ NORTH STAR MALL $$**
**7615 Jones Maltsberger Rd.**
**(210) 930-2333, (888) 492-8847**
**www.sanantonioairport.place.hyatt.com**

Only 2.5 miles from San Antonio International Airport, this nice hotel offers many amenities. Each of the 128 colorful suites offers such conveniences as an iron and ironing board, a hair dryer, a refrigerator, a microwave, a wet bar, a coffeemaker, a 42-inch flat-panel HDTV with on-command movies, telephones with dataports and voice mail, and wireless Internet access. Other extras: complimentary breakfast buffet, self-service check-in/check-out kiosks, laundry facilities, valet service, a free daily newspaper, a Stay Fit fitness center, free local transportation, an outdoor heated pool, complimentary parking and an "e-room" with complimentary public computers and printer. There are 2 meeting rooms on the property, totaling 1,056 square feet; facilities can accommodate up to 50 people.

### LA QUINTA INN & SUITES SAN ANTONIO AIRPORT $$

**850 Halm Blvd.**
**(210) 342-3738, (800) 753-3757**
**www.lq.com**

This La Quinta Inn & Suites is conveniently located less than 1 mile south of San Antonio International Airport and only minutes from downtown. Amenities include a daily complimentary continental breakfast, free local calls, a fitness center, pool, and a washer and dryer. All rooms feature a 25-inch television, in-room coffee, voice mail, free high-speed Internet access, iron, ironing board, and hair dryer. Inexpensive food options abound in the surrounding area, including McDonald's, Whataburger, and Jim's Restaurant, with finer dining options at the North Star Mall just around the corner.

### MICROTEL INN & SUITES $

**1025 S. Frio St.**
**(210) 226-8666, (800) 337-0044**
**www.microtelinn.com**

This is a good home base for visitors who want to pack in all of the San Antonio sights in just a few short days. Market Square, the Alamo, the River Walk, Rivercenter Mall, and the Henry B. Gonzales Convention Center are all nearby. SeaWorld of San Antonio is 15 miles away, as is San Antonio International Airport, and Six Flags Fiesta Texas is 20 miles from the hotel. Every room is equipped with a remote-control TV with premium channels such as ESPN, CNN, and HBO. There is also a pool and free continental breakfast every morning as well as free local and long distance calls within the continental US. Several fast-food chain restaurants are nearby—great for families with young kids and visitors looking to maximize their sightseeing time.

**i** TripAdvisor has included San Antonio in its Travelers' Choice Destinations for 2010. Winners were based on reviews and opinions from travelers on TripAdvisor.com.

### RED ROOF INN SAN ANTONIO $$

**4403 I-10 East**
**(210) 333-9430, (800) REDROOF**
**www.redroof.com**

Formerly a Comfort Inn, this member of the reliable Red Roof chain is located within 2 miles of the AT&T Center. Free continental breakfast, a fitness center, an outdoor seasonal pool, safe-deposit boxes, copy- and fax-machine access, and guest laundry facilities are available. Each guest room has a refrigerator, iron with ironing board, AM/FM radio, free Wi-Fi and cable TV with free movies. Children under 17 stay free with accompanying adult. Pets also stay free. Near the hotel are a beauty shop, a car rental company, a convenience store, a barber shop, fishing, a gift shop, a golf course, and shopping. Nearby restaurants include Denny's, Olive Garden, and Red Lobster.

### RESIDENCE INN SAN ANTONIO AIRPORT $$–$$$

**1014 NE Loop 410**
**(210) 805-8118, (800) 368-6105**
**www.marriott.com**

Each of the 120 one- and two-bedroom suites at this 3-story Residence Inn has a full kitchen—complete with refrigerator, microwave, and coffeemaker—and separate living and sleeping areas furnished with a desk, remote-control cable TV with premium channels, telephone with voice mail, and iron and ironing board. All rooms and public areas have wireless Internet. Parking and a daily breakfast buffet are free, and guest laundry facilities, fax and copy services, and safe-deposit boxes are available. The hotel has an outdoor pool, exercise room, and whirlpool, and there are 4 golf courses within a 10-mile radius. Pets are allowed with a $100 fee. There are several restaurants nearby, including Chili's and Formosa Garden (Chinese).

**RODEWAY INN DOWNTOWN** **$**
**900 N. Main Ave.**
**(210) 223-2951, (877) 424-6423**
**www.rodewayinn.com**

The best thing about this Rodeway Inn is its location. The Alamodome, the Alamo, San Antonio Botanical Garden, HemisFair Park, the IMAX Theatre, the Japanese Sunken Gardens, Brackenridge Park, Market Square, Rivercenter Mall, the River Walk, San Antonio Zoo, and Splashtown are all within a 5-mile radius, and San Antonio International Airport is just 7 miles away. The modest property has a multilingual staff, an outdoor pool, and an on-site restaurant, and it offers the usual services and amenities: free continental breakfast, free local calls, wake-up service, access to a fax machine, laundry service, and safe-deposit boxes. Most of the 120 rooms have a coffeemaker, full-length mirror, alarm clock, and cable TV. Free high-speed Internet is available in the lobby, and parking is also free. Pets are welcome with a $10 surcharge per night.

**SAN ANTONIO AIRPORT PEAR TREE INN** **$$**
**143 NE Loop 410**
**(210) 366-9300, (800) 282-8733**
**www.druryhotels.com**

Right in the heart of San Antonio's business district, this hotel has 124 clean rooms and affordable prices, making it a good choice for business travelers. It's also handy for shoppers and golfers: North Star Mall is only 2 blocks away, and the Quarry Golf Course is just a mile down the road. The property also boasts friendly, helpful staff members and a number of perks: free continental breakfast, free evening drinks daily from 5:30 to 7 p.m., free local telephone calls (and 60 minutes of free long distance calls), free parking, and a complimentary airport shuttle. Guests also have access to an outdoor pool, fax services, laundry facilities, and on-site meeting rooms. Pets are allowed. Several restaurants are only a short walk away.

## Beyond Loop 410

**COMFORT SUITES** **$$–$$$**
**6350 I-35 North**
**(210) 646-6600, (877) 424-6423**
**www.comfortsuites.com**

Recently renovated, this Comfort Suites offers quite an array of guest amenities. The suites are reasonably priced and accommodate several people quite comfortably. Each has free high-speed Internet access, remote-control cable TV, coffeemaker, refrigerator, microwave, and iron and ironing board. Other services include a free breakfast, free newspaper on weekdays, outdoor parking, free local telephone calls, a newsstand, an outdoor pool and a whirlpool. Market Square, La Villita, and the River Walk are all 6 miles away.

**i** Most corporate-lodging hotels have a minimum-stay requirement. If you're thinking of renting an apartment at one of these facilities, make sure that the minimum stay isn't longer than your trip!

**DAYS INN SAN ANTONIO** **$**
**9401 I-35 North**
**(210) 650-9779, (888) 440-2021**
**www.daysinn.com**

Built in 1996, this motel is only 5 miles from the airport and offers simple but comfortable rooms and moderate rates. Each of the 60 units is furnished with either a king-size or double bed, remote-control cable TV with HBO, coffeemaker, AM/FM clock radio, and free wireless Internet; rollaway beds and cribs are available on request. The property also features an outdoor pool and offers free continental breakfast, express checkout, free parking with space for RVs, free local phone calls, a 24-hour front desk, guest laundry services, and fax and copy services. It's a good choice for families on a budget.

**EMBASSY SUITES SAN ANTONIO INTERNATIONAL AIRPORT** **$$–$$$**
**10110 US 281 North**
**(210) 525-9999, (800) EMBASSY**
**http://embassysuites1.hilton.com**

The major advantage of this comfortable hotel is its location near the airport. Hotel facilities include a pool, whirlpool, Ellington's Restaurant and Lounge, a game room, an exercise room, meeting rooms, and laundry facilities; guests may also use a microwave and a refrigerator. Each room comes equipped with a coffeemaker, hair dryer, iron and ironing board, and cable TV with premium channels and on-command movies; cribs are available on request. Other amenities include high-speed Internet access, complimentary hot breakfast, free newspapers, a free airport shuttle, room service (evenings), safe-deposit boxes, voice mail, and a gift shop.

**HOWARD JOHNSON INN AND SUITES SAN ANTONIO** **$–$$**
**3817 I-35 North**
**(210) 224-3030, (800) 230-4134**
**www.hojo.com**

One of the highlights of this property is its landscaped pool area; the many large palm trees and other tropical plants create a relaxing and exotic atmosphere. The hotel offers numerous extras, including an outdoor spa, free deluxe continental breakfast, and rooms equipped with a microwave, refrigerator, coffeemaker, air-conditioning, and cable TV with ESPN. Free local calls, high-speed Internet access and a business center are also available. Conveniently located 0.2 mile from Splashtown and 2.5 miles from the downtown area.

**KNIGHTS INN SAN ANTONIO/ MEDICAL CENTER/ FIESTA AREA** **$–$$**
**9447 I-10 West**
**(210) 558-9070**
**www.knightsinn.com**

Rooms at Knights Inn properties can be rented by the day or for extended stays. Each of the rooms at this property has a microwave, refrigerator, hair dryer, iron and ironing board, and television with satellite programming. A pool cools guests off in the hot Texas summers, and a heated spa warms when the weather cools. The front desk is available around the clock to take care of any needs that guests may have, and coin-operated laundry facilities can be found on-site. The property serves a free continental breakfast daily from 6:30 to 9:30 a.m., and high-speed Internet access is available. Pets are welcome for a $10 fee. Knights Inn has free parking.

**SUPER 8 SAN ANTONIO AIRPORT $**
**11355 San Pedro Ave.**
**(210) 342-8488, (800) 800-8000**
**www.airportsuper8.com**

Not the most elegant lodging place in town, but certainly not the shabbiest, this modest motel offers guests clean rooms for a good price. Extras include an outdoor pool, cable TV, complimentary continental breakfast, in-room safes, free local telephone calls, wireless Internet access, and laundry facilities. There is also a business center, and a fax machine is available. The hotel has a well-documented pet-friendly policy, charging $15 nightly for each pet. San Antonio International Airport is very close to this property, and all of the excitement of downtown San Antonio and the River Walk is a short drive away.

## EXTENDED-STAY ACCOMMODATIONS

Are you staying in San Antonio for more than a week or two? Or are you traveling with children and in need of more space than the average hotel room provides? If so, you may want to look into business lodging hotels. These are properties that provide fully furnished and equipped apartments to guests who are planning a long stay, whether they are vacationing, relocating to the area, or in town on business.

**CANDLEWOOD SUITES SAN ANTONIO NORTHWEST/MEDICAL CENTER $$**
**9350 I-10 West**
**(210) 615-0550, (800) 972-3480**
**www.ichotelsgroup.com**

This home away from home, conveniently located close to Lackland Air Force Base, USAA, and the Medical Center, provides a bilingual staff that welcomes guests staying overnight or for an extended visit. Business travelers will appreciate their suite's work desk, two phone lines with voice mail, free high-speed Internet access, and the hotel's meeting room, which accommodates up to 15 people, while vacationers enjoy the outdoor pool, gym, and free video and CD library. A full kitchen features a microwave, refrigerator, coffeemaker, and pots and pans, and the 24-hour in-house eatery, Candlewood Cupboard, offers snacks and frozen entrees. For those looking to dine out, Pappasito's, SaltGrass Steakhouse, and the County Line Smokehouse and Grill are nearby. Pets are allowed for a modest daily surcharge.

**EXTENDED STAY DELUXE SAN ANTONIO—COLONNADE $**
**4331 Spectrum One Rd.**
**(210) 694-1229**
**www.extendedstayhotels.com**

Offering all the comforts of home, each studio is equipped with a kitchen complete with a refrigerator, stovetop, and microwave. For the business traveler, Wi-Fi is available, as are personalized voice mail, a computer dataport, and unlimited local calls. Guests can stay active at the on-site fitness center and pool. Allowed one per room, faithful furry friends are accommodated for a $25 per day cleaning fee. Guests staying at least one full week are allotted one full housekeeping service.

**HOMESTEAD STUDIO SUITES SAN ANTONIO—AIRPORT $–$$**
**1015 Central Pkwy. South**
**(210) 491-9009**
**www.homesteadhotels.com**

Only 3 miles from the San Antonio International Airport, business travelers will find themselves less than 1 mile from such high-power companies as Symantec and IBM, while vacationers are conveniently close to the North Star and Central Park Malls. To please every palate, a plethora of restaurants is nearby, including Chili's, Denny's, and Olive Garden; or guests can concoct a meal in their studio suite's full kitchen. On the hotel's official website, potential guests can view a virtual tour of both studio suite and deluxe studio suite rooms. Patrons staying 7 nights or more are provided with a full housekeeping service that includes vacuuming, dusting, emptying trash, cleaning bathroom and kitchen, changing linens and towels, and replenishing soap and toilet articles. Pets are allowed for a $25 daily fee.

**RESIDENCE INN SAN ANTONIO DOWNTOWN/ALAMO PLAZA $$$**
**425 Bonham St.**
**(210) 212-5555, (800) 371-6349**
**www.marriott.com**

Guests looking out the windows of this 220-suite hotel, located in the heart of the city, are afforded a view of the River Walk. For the business traveler, 6 meeting rooms offer 1,891 square feet of space, and overnight delivery/pickup, fax, and copy services are available. Families will appreciate the proximity of other top attractions, including the San Antonio Children's Museum and the San Antonio Zoo. On-site amenities include a heated outdoor pool, whirlpool, fitness center, self-service laundry facilities, high-speed Internet, and cable TV with premium channels and pay-per-view movies. Each suite is equipped with a full kitchen, which includes an oven, stovetop, refrigerator, microwave, and dishwasher. A complimentary breakfast buffet is served daily. Pets are allowed with a $100 sanitation fee.

**RESIDENCE INN SAN ANTONIO NORTHWEST/MEDICAL CENTER $$**
**4041 Bluemel Rd.**
**(210) 561-9660, (800) 228-9290**
**www.marriott.com**

Guests at this 128-suite retreat can start the day with a complimentary buffet breakfast or a hot cup of coffee brewed in the coffeemaker found alongside the stove, refrigerator, and microwave in each room's fully equipped kitchen. Located just a short distance from Kiddie Park, Malibu Castle, and the San Antonio Children's Museum, the hotel has an outdoor swimming pool, whirlpool, and sport court. A fitness room featuring cardiovascular equipment is available to guests, and Gold's Gym is only 1 mile away. Guest rooms include free Wi-Fi, cable TV, and pay-per-view movies. Guests can add a touch of luxury to their stay by requesting a suite with a fireplace. Pets are allowed with a $100 sanitation fee.

**STAYBRIDGE SUITES SAN ANTONIO AIRPORT $$–$$$**
**66 NE Loop 410**
**(210) 341-3220, (877) 238-8889**
**www.ichotelsgroup.com**

Just 1 mile from the San Antonio International Airport and only 0.5 mile from the North Star Mall, this extended stay retreat offers guests a complimentary full breakfast buffet and evening sundowner reception with appetizers and drinks. Or guests can whip up a meal with items purchased at the in-house 24-hour BridgeMart convenience store in a kitchen furnished with a microwave, refrigerator, toaster, cooking utensils, plates, and dishwasher. For those who want to dine out, Pappadeaux and Texas Land & Cattle Steak restaurants are located next door. Guests can enjoy an outdoor pool, whirlpool, and 24-hour exercise center, or simply relax and watch cable TV or an in-room movie, or surf the web via the high-speed Internet connection.

**STAYBRIDGE SUITES SAN ANTONIO NW NEAR SIX FLAGS FIESTA $–$$**
**6919 N. Loop 1604 West**
**(210) 691-3443, (877) 238-8889**
**www.ichotelsgroup.com**

After a day browsing for bargains at the Rim Shopping and Entertainment Center, guests at Staybridge Suites can watch a blockbuster at the hotel's on-site movie theater. Fitness buffs can work out at the 500-square-foot health and fitness center, with weight machines, treadmills, stair climber, and elliptical bike, or swim laps in the outdoor pool. Business travelers can take advantage of the hotel's business services, which include copying, high-speed Internet access, wireless data connection, and even a private limousine. Dining options include creating meals in a fully equipped kitchen, cooking on a barbecue grill, or dining out at Pizza Hut, TGI Friday's, or Red Lobster, all of which are within a 5-mile radius. The hotel allows pets with a nonrefundable $150 deposit.

**STAYBRIDGE SAN ANTONIO NORTHWEST COLONNADE $$**
**4320 Spectrum One Rd.**
**(210) 558-9009, (800) 972-3480**
**www.ichotelsgroup.com**

A convenient locale for visiting parents of University of Texas at San Antonio students, this member of the Staybridge chain offers studio, 1-bedroom, and 2-bedroom accommodations, complete with a full kitchen. Rooms boast phones with voice mail, wireless Internet access hair dryer, and cable TV plus DVD player. You'll also find a pool and a recreation and sports court, and a fitness center on-site. A business center with a printer, fax, and high-speed Internet access is available for the business traveler. A complimentary breakfast is served daily, and nearby restaurants include Saltgrass Steak House and Romano's Macaroni Grill. A convenience store, the 24-hour BridgeMart, is located on the property. Pets are allowed for a modest daily fee.

**STAYBRIDGE SUITES DOWNTOWN AT SUNSET STATION $$–$$$**
**123 Hoefgen Ave.**
**(210) 444-2700, (877) 238-8889**
**www.ichotelsgroup.com**

Located downtown at the lively Sunset Station entertainment complex, this 138–guest room retreat, which opened in August 2007, offers a kitchen complete with stove, refrigerator equipped with an icemaker, toaster, microwave, cooking utensils, and dishwasher. A complimentary hot breakfast buffet is offered every morning, and guests can order from a Mexican-inspired menu at Aldaco's restaurant, which is conveniently located across the street from the hotel. Staying in close proximity to the Alamodome, Rivercenter Mall, and the Alamo, hotel guests can come back to a guaranteed free parking space in the lot by the hotel. On-site, guests can swim in the outdoor pool, work out in the 24-hour fitness center, join an evening sundowner reception, or simply stay in their suite and watch their favorite shows on a 32-inch HD plasma TV. This hotel welcomes pets for a modest ($10–$15) daily fee.

## RESORTS

### HYATT REGENCY HILL COUNTRY RESORT AND SPA $$$$

**9800 Hyatt Resort Dr.**
**(210) 647-1234, (800) 633-7313**
**www.hillcountry.hyatt.com**

This elegant resort is situated in the rolling hills of the beautiful Texas Hill Country. The ranch house–style property's exposed wood beams and wooden porches with breathtaking views of the Hill Country give it a homey feel. The resort offers a wide range of recreational facilities, but it is an especially great choice for golf lovers. Hyatt Hill Country's 27-hole championship course has been rated the best in Texas by *Condé Nast Traveler* magazine. Private lessons are available for guests. Three tennis courts also are available for guest use, and a tennis pro is on hand for lessons or just a few tips. Guests can rent equipment from the pro shop. Table tennis, volleyball, croquet, and horseshoes can all be played at the health club, which also features the latest exercise equipment. Guests can pamper themselves with a variety of services at the Windflower spa, including massages, scrubs, wraps, facials, manicures, and pedicures. Check out the SPAhhhT, a spa designed for kids offering youth-oriented services.

Guests of all ages love Hyatt Hill Country's Ramblin' River, a 950-foot landscaped river where swimmers and floaters can drift along and enjoy the sun. Near the Ramblin' River are 2 swimming pools separated by a waterfall. Little guests will also enjoy Camp Hyatt, open to children between the ages of 3 and 12; kids can participate in games, nature walks, and other activities.

The resort has several categories of rooms. Each of the 500 guest rooms offers cable TV with in-room movies, high-speed Internet access, telephones with voice mail and computer hookup, video checkout, climate control, electronic door locks, an iron and ironing board, an AM/FM clock radio, a hair dryer, a refrigerator, and a coffeemaker. Suites offer an additional room, a dining table and chairs, and a sofa bed, while VIP suites have 2 bedrooms and 2 bathrooms. Some of the suites are decorated in a Texas or Old West theme, with leather armchairs and Texas artwork.

Several restaurants on the property offer a range of cuisines. The spacious Antlers Lodge, given a Four Diamond rating by AAA, offers a complete menu of Texas cuisine with creative touches, served with style and accompanied by an impressive wine selection, while the casual Springhouse Cafe serves up a buffet and a la carte menu with local specialties. Don't miss the Hill Country Quesadillas—Texas favorites, they are flour tortillas filled with beef, chicken, or chorizo. The Cactus Oak Tavern serves grilled burgers, salads, and sandwiches at the clubhouse, where there's a pool table and the 2 TVs are always tuned to sports channels Pets are allowed at the resort; call for details.

**i** **Mirroring the bevy of blooms that beautify the state's highways each spring, the guest rooms at the Hyatt Regency Hill Country Resort and Spa feature English Axminster wool carpets decorated with a wildflower print, just one of the improvements in the hotel's $10 million facelift.**

### JW MARRIOTT SAN ANTONIO HILL COUNTRY RESORT & SPA $$$–$$$$

**23808 Resort Pkwy.**
**(210) 276-2500, (866) 882-4420**
**www.marriott.com**

Opening in 2010 as the world's largest JW Marriott, this Texas-size resort features over 1,000 guest rooms in a hacienda setting. With rolling grounds dotted by live oaks, this expansive property maintains a Hill Country atmosphere, even down to its guest rooms and suites. Each room is painted a soothing sunset tint with furnishings and accessories reflecting a rustic yet refined Texas style. All guest rooms are smoke free.

The centerpiece of the resort is the 26,000-square-foot Lantana Spa, which features treatments ranging from body scrubs and wraps to massages and paraffin hand treatments. Massage lessons are also available. The spa features 30 treatment rooms, including 3 couples' treatment suites and 2 outdoor private treatment rooms. The facility includes a complete fitness center with a range of equipment as well as exercise, yoga, and fitness classes. The spa also features a private, lagoon-like spa pool. The Replenish Spa Bistro offers healthy options created in partnership with local artisan and organic farmers.

Along with the Replenish Spa Bistro, the resort features numerous dining choices. The main restaurant is the Cibolo Moon, offering Southwestern (yes, even Texas barbecue) and Mexican-inspired dishes for breakfast, lunch, and dinner. For a Texas-style steak, 18 Oaks (located in the TPC San Antonio Clubhouse) offers an array of aged steaks as well as fresh seafood and poultry dishes along with paired wines; it's a favorite for Sunday brunch. High Velocity is the resort's sports bar, serving American favorites, while the Rivertop Bar and Grill also features American favorites with local specialties such as chili. The Crooked Branch, the lobby bar, serves cocktails as well as barbecue, Tex-Mex dishes, and more.

The resort is also a favorite with golfers thanks to its 2 Tournament Players Club golf courses. The Pete Dye–designed AT&T Canyons Course and the Greg Norman–designed AT&T Oaks Course challenge golfers from around the world. The courses also draw many groups, with over 140,000 square feet of meeting space at the facility.

**i** **In March 2011 NBC's *Today Show* highlighted the JW Marriott San Antonio Hill Country Resort and Spa as a top "Spring Break Family Getaway." The property, the world's largest JW Marriott resort, is ranked by *Travel + Leisure* as one of the top 500 hotels in the world.**

***WESTIN LA CANTERA $$$–$$$$**
**16641 La Cantera Pkwy.**
**(210) 558-6500, (800) WESTIN-1**
**www.westinlacantera.com**

Guests will find just about everything they could ever want in a resort at this 300-acre, $115 million property on the northwest side of San Antonio. Thirty-six holes of golf, 6 swimming pools, 3 hot tubs, spa services, a full fitness center, a kids' club, great restaurants, and magnificent views of the Texas Hill Country are all part of the package here.

The Traditional Rooms offer 2 double beds or 1 king-size bed with all the standard amenities: a large desk, 2 telephones with voice mail, modem jacks, an in-room safe, 2 closets, a coffeemaker, a minifridge, cable TV with in-room movies, an iron with a full-size ironing board, a hair dryer, and a makeup mirror. Deluxe Rooms offer the same features as Traditional Rooms but with a view of the Hill Country, the pool, or the city; some have balconies or patios. Deluxe Rooms on the

Royal Hacienda Level offer such additional perks as concierge service, evening cocktails, continental breakfast, and access to the club lounge with beautiful views of the natural Texas landscape. Junior Suites have a separate sitting area with a sleep sofa for extra guests. The top-of-the-line Executive Suites are more than 1,000 square feet. The main feature of these suites is a parlor area equipped with a wet bar, entertainment center, foldout couch, and coffee table. A balcony presents amazing views of the city.

Among the many restaurants on property, Francesca's at Sunset offers gourmet Southwestern fare, accompanied by a gorgeous view. The La Cantera Grille serves three meals a day; steak is the specialty of the house, but fish and chicken dishes are also popular choices. The Gantry is at the Lost Quarry Pools, and guests can eat while lounging in the sun; seasonal Texas-style cookouts here are not to be missed. A fun and easygoing atmosphere makes Brannon's Cafe a popular choice for meals. The menu is varied and the views are remarkable. For in-room dining, room service is offered around the clock. Looking for a place to unwind after a long day? Stop in at Tio's Lobby Lounge or Steinheimer's Bar. The facilities at La Cantera are outstanding. Castle Rock Health Club provides guests with a wide range of spa services, including pedicures, manicures, facials, and many types of massages. Enchanted Rock Kids' Club, for guests between the ages of 5 and 12, offers organized activities such as arts and crafts, outdoor sports like volleyball and swimming, games—and a chance to play with other kids. Rates for Enchanted Rock Kids' Club vary, so check with the resort.

The health club, numerous dining options, and the kids' activities all may sound wonderful, but the pride of this resort is the golf. Two 18-hole golf courses make up the property's backyard. The Resort Course at La Cantera was designed by golf course architect Jay Morrish and PGA Tour pro Tom Weiskopf. The Palmer Course at La Cantera was developed by Arnold Palmer, his first in the area.

## BED-AND-BREAKFASTS

The capital of San Antonio's bed-and-breakfast world is the King William Historic District. This region, located on a quiet bend of the river, is a far cry from the bustling River Walk but still within easy walking distance of the restaurants and shops of the tourist area. Rich in 19th-century atmosphere, King William is dotted with historic homes that have been transformed into unique accommodations.

You'll also find bed-and-breakfast properties in some of San Antonio's other exclusive neighborhoods, such as Monte Vista, a historic district that was first granted by King Philip of Spain as public land.

### A BECKMANN INN AND CARRIAGE HOUSE $$

**222 E. Guenther St.**
**(210) 229-1449, (800) 945-1449**
**www.beckmanninn.com**

Built in 1886 by Albert Beckmann for his bride, this Greek Revival home stayed in the Beckmann family for 70 years. The beautiful house is now owned by Paula and Charles Stallcup, who run this elegant bed-and-breakfast inn. The wraparound porch invites guests to enjoy its shade, and the house's other porch is furnished with wicker chairs and love seats, so guests can unwind and enjoy complimentary chocolates, cookies, and tea.

The interior is decorated with Victorian-style furniture that gives the house a dignified, elegant atmosphere. Each of the 5 spacious guest rooms has its own bathroom and a colorful floral decor, and is equipped with a ceiling fan, a television, a phone, a refrigerator, armchairs, and a desk. Rooms also have irons, ironing boards, and hair dryers. The focal point of each room is an elaborately carved, queen-size Victorian bed. Adjacent to the main house, the Carriage House has been converted from the Beckmanns' maid's quarters and horse and carriage shelter into 2 minisuites for guests seeking more privacy. They feature shuttered windows, gardens, balconies, and colorful flowers.

Guests are served a gourmet two-course breakfast every morning in the house's formal dining room. Fresh-ground coffee, teas, juices, fresh fruit, muffins, pastries, and a main entree are served at tables set with china, crystal, and silver. Paula and Charles guarantee that no guest will be served the same breakfast twice during their stay.

**i** **Some bed-and-breakfasts can be entirely rented by groups, such as people attending a reunion or wedding. Arrangements for such a takeover must be made many months in advance.**

**ALAMO STREET VICTORIAN INN** **$$–$$$**
**951 S. Alamo St.**
**(210) 212-5533, (800) 630-3722**
**www.alamostreetvictorianinn.com**

The cheerful yellow facade of this lovingly restored Gilded Age beauty is a ray of sunshine in the heart of the King William Historic District. The legendary Mexican revolutionary Pancho Villa, who frequented the former home in years gone by, would feel at home today in one of the inn's 6 guest rooms, each furnished with period antiques such as English armoires, Italian marble–topped side tables, and vintage French bedspreads, adjoined by a Victorian-style private bathroom stocked with Bath and Body Works products. Those looking for a romantic getaway may want to choose either the Starlight Suite, which is decorated with a mural of the Texas Hill Country, or the Grand Victorian, which offers a whirlpool tub. Those in the city for business can conduct meetings in the King William Room, with table seating for 35 and a 90-foot-long veranda that offers a view of the Tower of the Americas. While the inn caters to an adult-only clientele, children age 12 or over are allowed to stay in the main house, and families with young ones and pets can book the guest house on the premises.

After a light breakfast served between 7 and 10 a.m., guests can embark on a shopping spree along the River Walk by hopping aboard a trolley that conveniently stops on the street across from the inn. To unwind after a day of sightseeing, guests can indulge in a variety of spa treatments offered at the inn, including hot stone massage and Swedish massage.

**ARBOR HOUSE SUITES BED AND BREAKFAST** **$$–$$$**
**109 Arciniega**
**(210) 472-2005, (888) 272-6700**
**www.arborhouse.com**

A sense of Texas pride pervades this series of houses, with each of the modern-decorated suites named after one of the men who died a hero's death at the Alamo. It is located near many of San Antonio's main attractions,

## Close-up

### B&Bs Mean Business

Many companies are finding that bed-and-breakfast inns make excellent meeting sites, offering employees the chance to bond in a family atmosphere. Individual business travelers are also turning to these homey properties. At the end of another long day on the road, they are happy to enjoy an evening at "home," reading magazines or watching TV in a comfortable living room, enjoying some friendly conversation, or perhaps sitting out on the front porch sipping a glass of wine or iced tea.

As B&Bs have become more aware of the business traveler's needs, they have added features such as separate phone lines for individual rooms, fax machines, photocopying service, Internet access, and desks in guest rooms. It's a trend that's taking place nationwide. The Professional Association of Innkeepers International (PAII) reports that 93 percent offer free wireless Internet, 45 percent of its members offer blackboards and flip charts, 42 percent have meeting rooms, 32 percent own audiovisual equipment, 77 percent offer fax services, and 50 percent offer copying services.

Business travelers are turning to these nontraditional accommodations for several reasons. "First, B&Bs are getting more accommodating to the needs of the business traveler. They're getting adequate phone service, they're serving early breakfast, they're doing the things business travelers want them to do," explains Pat Hardy, co-executive director of PAII. "Second, they're becoming more mainstream. You can find B&Bs in big cities as well as small towns."

But for many business travelers, it's the chance to be recognized as an individual that makes the B&B increasingly attractive. "Anyone who's on the road a long time gets tired of seeing the same room and of being a number," explains Hardy. "The

including HemisFair Plaza, the Botanical Garden, the River Walk, and the Alamo. After a day of sightseeing, visitors can take a break from the hustle and bustle in the verdant courtyard, which is embellished with a serene fountain. Newlyweds should ask for the Honeymoon Special, which offers three nights in the Pecos House honeymoon suite.

**i** Jerry Karkoska, the manager of Arbor House Suites Bed and Breakfast, is a direct descendant of James George, one of the valiant men who live on in Texas history as defenders of the Alamo.

**✻THE BONNER GARDEN $$–$$$**
**145 E. Agarita Ave.**
**(210) 733-4222, (800) 396-4222**
**www.bonnergarden.com**

Located in what is now San Antonio's Monte Vista neighborhood, the Bonner Garden was built in 1910 by architect Atlee Ayers for Louisiana aristocrat Mary Bonner. Bonner's four previous homes all burnt down, so Ayers answered her concerns by erecting a 4,000-square-foot concrete Italian villa, reinforced with steel, cast in iron, and cased in stucco. Bonner became famous for her artwork, much of which is now displayed in the house.

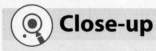

opportunity to be a human being and not someone's number is one of the big draws of the B&B."

The corporate world is also turning to B&Bs as meeting sites. For some groups, the added security of a B&B is a plus. By renting the entire inn, meetings can be held without security worries that might be faced in a hotel, whether those worries take the form of corporate espionage or simple eavesdropping.

Security is an asset that draws individual business travelers as well. Since resident innkeepers know who is supposed to be on property and who is not, some people feel safer staying in a B&B.

Here are some tips for business travelers considering a stay at a San Antonio bed-and-breakfast:

- Look into the phone service. Is phone service available in all guest rooms? Do the guest rooms each have separate lines?
- Confirm mealtimes. Breakfast at B&Bs may range from a simple continental buffet to a massive sit-down feast. Some innkeepers put out the food for guests to enjoy at their leisure; others stick to a set mealtime. Check to see if the inn serves early breakfast so you can get out and on the road.
- Check fax availability.
- Ask if the rooms are computer-friendly. More and more B&Bs are providing modem hookups, but check first. Also, see if the guest rooms include a work space, either a table or a desk.
- Recognize that B&Bs are not hotels. Don't look for 24-hour room service, laundry service, and twice-a-day maid service.

Each of the 6 guest rooms at the Bonner Garden has its own style and atmosphere, and some rooms feature either a computer or Internet access. Guests looking for privacy and seclusion should reserve The Studio. The original studio of Mary Bonner, this stone-walled building is detached from the main house. Guests can relax in its queen-size canopy bed and Mexican-imported furniture. The Studio has modern amenities, too, including a television and DVD player, a telephone, and a private bathroom. The popular Ivy Room features a queen-size sleigh bed, a Louis XVI armoire, English bedside tables, and a colonial-era writing desk. The bathroom has both a bathtub and a shower, and the imported tile floor gives it a certain flair. For honeymoon couples, the Bridal Suite is the obvious choice. It features a blue porcelain tile fireplace, a Louis XVI armoire, and a queen-size mahogany canopy bed. A two-person Jacuzzi bathtub is the highlight of the private bath.

The upstairs Garden Suite overlooks the property's gardens and swimming pool. Guests can lounge on the love seat by a sizable fireplace or rest in the room's king-size four-poster bed. The bathroom has a Jacuzzi tub for relaxing after a long day of sightseeing or shopping. The Portico Room has its own entrance to the pool and gardens, making it a good choice for guests who want to get some sun or who just like a little extra privacy. The focal point of this room is the hand-painted, imported porcelain fireplace, though the mural on the ceiling by San Antonio artist John Crawford certainly deserves attention, too. The private bath has a shower and a mosaic tile floor.

**i** For a full listing of B&Bs and inns in San Antonio, check out the website of the San Antonio Bed and Breakfast Association, www.sanantoniobb.org. It compares amenities and prices for all the top B&B properties and even has a listing of events happening around town.

**BRACKENRIDGE HOUSE** **$$–$$$**
**230 Madison**
**(210) 271-3442, (877) 271-3442**
**www.brackenridgehouse.com**

This intimate inn is decorated with comfortable antiques and quilts to make guests feel right at home. Each of the 5 guest rooms comes equipped with a king- or queen-size bed, wireless Internet, cable TV with premium movie channels, a coffeemaker, a mini-fridge, a private telephone, and a microwave. Each also has a private bath with a claw-foot tub. A heated pool and hot tub in the garden area behind the house make a perfect retreat.

The Wren's Nest Suite, done in rose colors, has a sitting area and kitchenette. It opens onto the front porch near the wicker swing and rocking chairs that allow guests to relax and enjoy the beautiful King William neighborhood. Decorated in shades of red, the Cardinal Room features a queen-size brass bed and a garden entrance only a short distance from the hot tub. Similar to the Wren's Nest Suite is the Bluebird Suite, but its color scheme is mauve and blue. The Eastlake bed is covered in a beautiful turn-of-the-20th-century patchwork quilt. A quilt and crocheted bedspread cover a beautiful iron king-size bed in the Hummingbird Room,, whose predominant color is a soft teal. Honeymoon or anniversary couples will feel at home in the Mockingbird Suite, on the second story of the house. The private veranda overlooking the garden and hot tub is just the spot for a romantic tête-à-tête. Decorated in shades of white, and with a king-size bed and lovely Victorian love seat, this room is the perfect place for couples who want to get away for a weekend.

**BULLIS HOUSE** **$–$$**
**621 Pierce St.**
**(210) 223-9426, (877) 477-4100**
**www.bullishouseinn.com**

Across the street from Fort Sam Houston in the Government Hill Historic District, the Bullis House is a state historic landmark. Built between 1906 and 1909 by noted architect Harvey Page, the house was designed for General John Lapham Bullis and his family. Bullis was a frontiersman famous for his role in capturing Apache chief Geronimo. After his capture, Geronimo and his warriors were imprisoned at the fort, and legend holds that his spirit still roams the Fort Sam Houston grounds.

This unique part of San Antonio's past is now a bed-and-breakfast inn, featuring comfortable guest rooms with antique furnishings, 14-foot ceilings with plaster medallions, chandeliers, and French windows. Room amenities include cable TV, clock radios, and air-conditioning. Some boast marble wood-burning fireplaces with mirrored mantles. The inn's location makes it convenient for exploring historic Fort Sam Houston and the Government Hill area. Guests are served an expansive continental breakfast menu daily and may take their breakfast in the inn's dining room or on the large front porch.

**GARDENIA INN** **$$**
**307 Beauregard St.**
**(210) 223-5875, (800) 356-1605**
**www.gardenia-inn.com**

In the very heart of the King William Historic District lies this romantic antebellum abode, where guests can relax on the expansive front porch, on the second-story veranda, or in the garden gazebo after a leisurely stroll along the River Walk nearby. Continuing the Gardenia Inn's flower theme, each guest room is named after a fragrant blossom. Those looking for Lone Star–inspired accommodations should choose the Bluebonnet Room, where guests can view the Tower of the Americas through the room's bay windows. The Western-tinged Desert Bloom Suite offers 2 connected bedrooms and a living room, while feminine touches abound in the Lily Room; the Lavender Room, which offers a two-seat swing on a private veranda; and the Magnolia room, which has a shared second floor veranda. Free high-speed Internet access in each room provides a harmonious blend of antiquity and modernity.

A light breakfast is served between 8:30 and 9:30 a.m. on weekdays, and 9 to 10 a.m. on weekends, and several dining establishments are within walking distance, including BJ's Tacos, for a taste of true Mexican cuisine, and La Focaccia, for Italian fare.

**THE KING WILLIAM MANOR** **$$–$$$**
**1037 S. Alamo St.**
**(210) 222-0144, (800) 405-0367**
**www.kingwilliammanor.com**

Majestic Corinthian columns stand like silent sentinels as guests step onto the front porch of this 1892 Greek Revival inn. A time capsule of days gone by, the inn features period furnishings and faithful Victorian-era reproductions that blend harmoniously in the kitchen, where a gourmet breakfast is served each morning, and in each of the bedrooms in both the main house and the guest house.

A leisurely walk from the AAA Four-Diamond bed-and-breakfast leads to several of San Antonio's tourist treasures, including La Villita, the River Walk, and the Alamo, and guests who stay in the Verandah room—a sanctuary featuring an antique claw-foot bathtub and a brass four-poster queen-size bed—can plan their day as they stand on the second-floor balcony and look out on the downtown area.

In addition to the 3 bedrooms in the main house, the Guest House contains 9 more rooms, decorated in a variety of themes from Gulf Coast casual to the stately Amelia Island room, with gas fireplace and Jacuzzi. The Guest House also has a common room furnished with books, magazines, games, and a computer for guest use.

**1908 AYRES INN** **$$**
**124 W. Woodlawn Ave.**
**(210) 736-4232**
**www.1908ayresinn.com**

Located in the historic Monte Vista neighborhood, the 1908 Ayres Inn is San Antonio's only four-star bed-and-breakfast. The inn's 5 guest rooms are named for heros of the

## Close-up

### Historic Lambermont

While serving as ambassador plenipotentiary to Belgium under President Benjamin Harrison, Edwin Terrell saw many grand European castles, and when he returned home to San Antonio in 1894, he had his own built on a 1-acre site and named it **Lambermont** in honor of a business associate. Hard to miss, this grand mansion operated as the Terrell Castle B&B for many years. The mansion (950 E. Grayson St.; 210-271-9145, 800-481-9732; www.lambermontevents.com) is now a unique venue for weddings and other special events.

Lambermont's main floor boasts amazing architectural details. Much of the library is in its original state, including the cabinetwork. The library's fireplace is the best of the 9 in the house and features unique molded brickwork. The French chandelier in the parlor accents the magnificent round front window, the highlight of the room. The formal dining room still maintains the original detailed woodwork. The impressive curved windows at one end of the room even feature curved glass. Be sure to note the unusual design of the original border of the floor. The Central Hall features the remarkable main staircase, with carved, rounded newel posts.

Groups retaining the property for an event have the option of staying overnight in some of Lambermont's historic bedrooms, including the Honeymoon Suite, which features a private veranda.

Alamo and boast hardwood floors, rich wood paneling, and crown moldings to impart the spirit of the city's opulent past. However, along with the old-fashioned atmosphere, the inn offers modern conveniences such as flat-screen TVs with digital cable, Blu-Ray players, complimentary cell phones and Wi-Fi, modernized bath rooms with whirlpool baths, and iPod and iPhone docking stations. All rooms are air-conditioned. The house is surrounded by porches and landscaped gardens with a goldfish pond. A full continental breakfast is served daily in the dining room, which overlooks the gardens. A gated parking area is provided for all guests.

**i** **The VIA trolley is an excellent way for bed-and-breakfast guests in the King William Historic District to reach major tourist attractions without the hassle of driving and parking.**

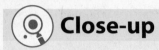

**THE OGÉ HOUSE ON THE RIVERWALK** **$$$–$$$$**
**209 Washington St.**
**(210) 223-2353, (800) 242-2770**
**www.ogeinn.com**

Guests staying at the Ogé House (pronounced "OH-jhay") are sure to be impressed by all the work that owners Liesl and Don Noble have done to restore this pre–Civil War home. Set on 1.5 acres in the King William Historic District and overlooking the River Walk, the house was built in 1857 by Texas ranger and cattle rancher Louis Ogé. It has 10 guest rooms and suites furnished with early American Victorian furniture yet offering all of today's conveniences, including a flat-panel TV with cable and a DVD player, a telephone with voice mail, and a minifridge. Every room here has something special to offer, but guests looking for a great view should stay on the third floor, where each suite has access to the veranda or a private balcony. Liesl and Don provide guests with a full breakfast served in the formal dining room or on the veranda.

**A YELLOW ROSE** **$$**
**229 Madison St.**
**(210) 229-9903, (800) 950-9903**
**www.ayellowrose.com**

Tucked away in the quiet King William Historic District, this elegant B&B is in a 130-year-old Victorian structure. Innkeepers Deb and Kit Walker have attended to every detail in an effort to make each guest's stay as comfortable and memorable as possible. Each of the 5 spacious guest rooms is decorated with art and fresh flowers. There are beverages in the refrigerator, and as an added bonus, Godiva chocolates find their way onto the pillows at night. A private entrance and porch, an en suite bath, and a queen-size bed, as well as traditional amenities such as a radio, premium cable TV, a hair dryer, and an iron and ironing board, make these rooms even more tempting.

Deb and Kit do everything they can to make sure your stay at A Yellow Rose is memorable, whether you're celebrating a special occasion such as a birthday or anniversary, or just out for a relaxing weekend. For a small additional fee, guests can arrange to have a bouquet of roses or a basket filled with goodies like champagne or chocolate waiting in their room upon arrival. The Walkers also offer special weekend packages that include such extras as massages and flowers. They'll even work with you to create a custom package—one that will surely make your visit unforgettable.

# RESTAURANTS

**While Easterners were sitting down to meals seasoned with imported spices and served on fine china, Texas was still a frontier. Throughout much of its history as part of Mexico, then as an independent republic, and finally as a state, Texas remained a vast land sparsely populated by cowboys and hardy pioneer types who learned to cook using the ingredients they had at hand, including prickly pear pads and rangy beef that was as tough as shoe leather.**

**Today San Antonio boasts some restaurants whose haute cuisine and continental fare have been lauded by national publications. But many people think the best food in San Antonio is served up at the small diners, the neighborhood cafes, and the smoky barbecue pits across the city. That's where you'll find reminders of that frontier ingenuity in dishes like fajitas and chicken-fried steak, plus ethnic favorites such as German sausage and Tex-Mex tacos and enchiladas.**

## OVERVIEW

Our restaurant listings are arranged by cuisine. We haven't included chain restaurants as a rule except for those properties that are especially unique or those chains that are headquartered near San Antonio.

Most restaurants are open for lunch and dinner and remain open between meals; we've indicated if restaurants deviate from this practice. You'll find that the majority of restaurants in San Antonio don't serve into the wee hours. Most close up around 10 p.m.

Thanks to the ADA, restaurants are wheelchair accessible for the most part. A city ordinance bans smoking unless the proprietor has made certain alterations to enclose a smoking area. Many, however, have outdoor patios.

Some larger restaurants accept (and encourage) reservations; we've indicated these in the listings. Often, however, you'll just need to show up and get your name on the waiting list, especially at River Walk area restaurants. Waiting time varies, but expect long waits on Friday and Saturday evenings. Outdoor tables are especially popular any time the mercury dips below the mid-90s during summer months and any time winter days are sunny and clear. Most River Walk restaurants also have indoor seating, popular with those in search of a little air-conditioned relief.

Most restaurants accept major credit cards; we've indicated those that deviate from this practice.

### *Price Code*

The price key symbol found in each listing is the approximate price for a meal for two including an entree and nonalcoholic beverage as well as appetizer and dessert. Some restaurants have a wide variety of entrees, so some listings have a price range.

**$................. Less than $20**
**$$ .................. $20 to $40**
**$$$ ................. $40 to $60**
**$$$$ ........... More than $60**

***Quick Index by Name***

## AMERICAN

### BLUE STAR BREWING COMPANY $$–$$$

**1414 S. Alamo St., #105**
**(210) 212-5506**
**www.bluestarbrewing.com**

Located in the Blue Star Arts Complex in the King William Historic District, this was the city's first full-scale brewpub. Owned and operated by Joey and Maggie Villarreal, it stands across from Pioneer Flour Mill on a quiet stretch of the river. Although it may be San Antonio's first brewpub, the structure has a long history with hops: It first served as a beer warehouse.

Patrons can dine inside or on the outside deck and beer garden. The menu is extensive. Lunch specialties include burgers, soups, and salads as well as many deli sandwiches; dinner options include fresh catch of the day, chicken-fried chicken breast, chicken fajita plate, jerk chicken, and often a mixed grill. Vegetarians find plenty of options as well—a tasty black bean soup, veggie burgers, and more. Appropriately, a "blue-plate special" is popular here. And what other pub do you know that has its own pastry chef? All this is served up with the real specialty of the house: beer. Among the brews on tap are Texican Lager, King William Ale, Tower Stout,Black IPA, and others. The pub is open 7 days a week for lunch and dinner.

**DEWESE'S TIP TOP CAFE** **$**
**2814 Fredericksburg Rd.**
**(210) 732-0191**
**www.tiptopcafe.com**

If good comfort food is your goal, a trip to the Tip Top is a must. Often voted tops in the "home-cooking" category, DeWese's is famous for its huge but tender chicken-fried steaks, onion rings piled sky-high on a plate, chili, and desserts like your mama made. This is a popular place, so you may want to arrive a bit early to avoid a wait. Once settled, however, you're in for a fine—albeit fattening—meal. Think *Father Knows Best* or *The Life of Riley.* Even the decor is nostalgic (although that may not be intentional), with its knotty pine walls, mounted deer heads and fish, and worn Formica-topped tables. The cafe is open from 11 a.m. to 8 p.m. Tues through Sat, and 11 a.m. to 7 p.m. Sun.

**DICK'S LAST RESORT** **$$–$$$**
**406 Navarro St.**
**(210) 224-0026**
**www.dickslastresort.com**

Dick's is known as the most wisecracking restaurant and bar on the river. The waiters and waitresses like to make jokes and toss out matchbooks decorated with old photos of topless women, and the ladies' room has vending machines offering fluorescent condoms. The restaurant offers both inside and outside seating. If you dine inside, you'll sit at huge communal tables and enjoy R&B, funk, and contemporary music played by some of the area's finest musicians. The menu here leans toward barbecue but includes choices from burgers at lunch to chicken to shrimp. Everything is served in small tin buckets on a table covered with white butcher paper. Main dishes arrive with a bucket of french fries and bread. Save room for the desserts: cheesecake and peanut butter pie.

**✳GAZEBO AT LOS PATIOS** **$$–$$$**
**2015 NE Loop 410**
**(210) 655-6171**
**www.lospatios.com**

For more than 3 decades, this northside restaurant just 5 minutes from the San Antonio International Airport has served diners. The restaurant lies just below the traffic of Loop 410, offering a quiet retreat in the heart of the hustle and bustle of the Loop. Gazebo is located in the heart of a 20-acre open-air mall filled with specialty shops.

The menu offers light fare, primarily salads, chicken, and shrimp. But the real charm of Gazebo lies in its lushly green setting. Located on the banks of Salado Creek, the restaurant is nestled among majestic live oaks and exotic plants. Open for lunch only from 11:30 a.m. to 2:30 p.m., and Sunday buffet 11 a.m. to 2:30 p.m. Want to do lunch with your dog? Los Patios was issued San Antonio's first dog-friendly permit; diners with their well-behaved canines are welcomed in a special outdoor courtyard of the Gazebo.

**HARD ROCK CAFE SAN ANTONIO $$–$$$**
**111 W. Crockett St.**
**(210) 224-7625**
**www.hardrockcafe.com**

Part of the South Bank development project, the Hard Rock Cafe offers rock 'n' roll memorabilia, good old American food, and, of course, the Hard Rock Cafe gift shop selling the requisite T-shirts. This popular restaurant has both indoor and River Walk dining (our favorite); the outdoor tables are nestled beneath shade trees so it's not too toasty even on summer days. But even if you eat outside, save time for a peek at the indoor collection of rock 'n' roll artifacts; Sotheby's says that Hard Rock Cafe has the most extensive collection of rock memorabilia in the world.

**JIM'S RESTAURANT $$**
**4108 Broadway and numerous other locations**
**(210) 828-5120**
**www.jimsrestaurants.com**

Texans know Jim's, but they may not be familiar with the success story that lies behind this popular chain of family restaurants. Jim Hasslocher began his entrepreneurial endeavors by renting bikes and selling watermelon slices in Brackenridge Park in 1947. A few years later, he opened the Frontier Drive-In, with carhops dressed like cowgirls.

Today the cowboy remains on the Jim's Restaurant logo, one that's seen in 15 locations in San Antonio alone. Started in 1963, the popular chain serves excellent breakfasts—everything from traditional eggs and bacon to an array of waffles—as well as lunch and dinner. Most of the locations are open around the clock and appeal to travelers as well as families and shift workers.

After Jim's took off, Jim Hasslocher branched out, opening other San Antonio eateries. The Magic Time Machine Restaurant, popular with kids of all ages, was founded by Hasslocher, past president of the National Restaurant Association. The entrepreneur also started the Biloxi Belle Casino Resort.

**i** During Culinaria Restaurant Week, San Antonio diners can sample cuisine as dozens of area restaurants present prix fixe menus at special rates. Restaurant Week (www.culinariasa.org) is held each summer.

**MAGIC TIME MACHINE RESTAURANT $$–$$$**
**902 NE Loop 410**
**(210) 828-1470**
**www.magictimemachine.com**

Started in 1973, this fun-loving restaurant offers more than a meal: It's an experience. Start with the waitstaff dressed as cartoon and movie characters: You might be seated by Captain Jack Sparrow or Dora the Explorer—it's just the luck of the draw. And the seat you'll receive is no Formica table or corner booth, either. You might be assigned the Jail Cell, the Orgy Pit, or the Mine Shaft, depending on the crowd that night. You'll serve yourself from the salad bar, set in an authentic 1953 MG Roadster.

The brainchild of Jim and Veva Hasslocher (who also founded the Jim's Restaurants), this unique eatery has spawned similar restaurants in Dallas. The menu features a mix of seafood, steaks, and grilled items, but the highlight is the Roman Orgy, a massive meal consisting of brisket, chicken, corn on the cob, and more. This restaurant is open daily for dinner only, except on Saturday and Sunday, when it also serves lunch.

**MALT HOUSE** **$**
**115 S. Zarzamora St.**
**(210) 433-8441**

The Malt House has been a San Antonio institution for more than half a century, serving up classic dishes like the quarter-pound Fat Boy burger with the obligatory order of fries. Other options include enchiladas and fried fish. But the real centerpiece of the Malt House menu is, predictably, its malts. Save room for one of these creamy creations (chocolate is an all-time favorite) and enjoy a taste of the 1950s, San Antonio style. This restaurant is often selected by San Antonians as a favorite for budget watchers, a place where you can dine for less than $2 per person. It's open daily for breakfast, lunch, and dinner. It also offers curb service, along with inside eating.

**MR. AND MRS. G'S HOME COOKING** **$**
**2222 W.W. White Rd. South**
**(210) 359-0002**

Call it soul food or call it food like your grandmother used to cook, but you will definitely call it good. Mr. and Mrs. G's is a plain-Jane establishment that pours all its effort into the comfort food served there. All-time favorites include fried pork chops, smothered steak, and fried chicken, although the meat loaf and pot roast are delicious, too. The side dishes range from greens to fried okra to sweet potatoes, and the desserts are legendary. Most popular are the peach cobbler and the banana pudding. Service is cafeteria style, and the clientele includes servicemen and -women, neighborhood locals, and businesspeople from all over. Located in a sprawling old house, Mr. and Mrs. G's has been around for almost 20 years, and patrons hope it will go on forever. Less than $10 will buy you a heaping plate with two meats, two side dishes, bread, iced tea, and dessert. There's no better deal anywhere. The Garners serve their food from 11 a.m. to 6 p.m. on weekdays only.

**OLMOS BHARMACY/PATTY LOU'S RESTAURANT** **$$**
**3902 McCullough Ave.**
**(210) 822-1188, (210) 706-9855**
**www.olmosbharmacy.com,**
**www.pattylousrestaurant.com**

Until 2005, this art-deco landmark operated as Olmos Pharmacy, a drugstore with a luncheonette and an old-fashioned drugstore soda fountain. It was a great place to drink in gobs of nostalgia along with your chocolate malt. Now reborn as Olmos Bharmacy ("Your Neighborhood Bhar"), it has retained both the look and feel of the old pharmacy, with its iconic neon signage and historic soda fountain, which now serves wine and beer along with malts and milk shakes. The specialty of the house is—what else?—the Beer Milk Shake. Patty Lou's Restaurant handles the food service, serving breakfast (til 3 p.m.!), lunch, and dinner, featuring a wide assortment of burgers, soups, and salads as well as chicken-fried steak and seafood. At night, the Bharmacy features live music. It's still a great place to grab a burger and drink in the Old San Antonio vibe.

**PAM'S PATIO KITCHEN** **$-$$**
**11826 Wurzbach Rd.**
**(210) 492-1359**
**www.pamspatio.com**

Homemade soups, sandwiches, and desserts—all made with TLC—are the delightful fare at Pam's Patio Kitchen, a bright little spot located in the Elms neighborhood shopping area. Proprietress Pam Strain uses half-and-half or sour cream in the cream soups she serves (cream of asparagus is fabulous!), fresh-squeezes her lemonade (it comes in mango and strawberry variations), and makes mouth-watering desserts like praline cake and blueberry pie from scratch. Among the favorite salads here are Thai beef and the spinach-strawberry-pecan. You can dine indoors or on the patio from 11 a.m. to 3 p.m. Tues through Sat and from 6 to 9:30 p.m. on Thurs, Fri, and Sat.

## ASIAN

**FUJIYA JAPANESE GARDEN** **$$**
**9030 Wurzbach Rd.**
**(210) 615-7553**
**http://fujiyajapanesegarden.com**
Located between I-10 West and Fredericksburg Road, this eatery holds the title as San Antonio's oldest authentic Japanese restaurant. You'll feel like you've taken a quick trip to Japan in the authentic tatami dining room with seating on mats, although seating options also include tables and chairs. The restaurant serves favorites such as *sukiyaki,* along with numerous seafood, vegetarian, and noodle dishes; more than 50 varieties of sushi are also available. Open daily for lunch and dinner.

**i** San Antonio Citysearch (http://sanantonio.citysearch.com) offers many restaurant reviews online as well as news of new restaurant openings.

**HUNAN RIVER GARDEN** **$$**
**506 River Walk**
**(210) 222-0808**
Located right on the River Walk, this long-time local eatery offers up traditional Chinese fare, from sweet-and-sour pork to Kung Pao chicken, with a view that's definitely nontraditional. Szechuan, Hunan, and Cantonese cuisines are featured. This is the only Chinese restaurant on the River Walk and, as such, is always crowded. Daily lunch specials draw many office workers in the area as well as tourists. Entrees range between $7.95 and $14.95. Open daily for lunch and dinner.

**i** River Walk restaurants can get very crowded on weekends and during peak tourist season. Not all restaurants take reservations, but some do; call ahead to make the best use of your time.

**KABUKI JAPANESE RESTAURANT** **$$**
**15909 San Pedro Ave.**
**(210) 545-5151**
This restaurant is located in the Galleria Oaks Shopping Center, just off US 281 North at the Thousand Oaks exit. The elegant eatery features teppanyaki hibachi cooking as well as the creations of a Japanese sushi chef. Popular menu selections include sashimi, *chirashi, sukiyaki* for two, *shabu-shabu* for two, tempura, teriyaki chicken, and teriyaki beef. The restaurant offers a happy hour special on Tues, Wed, Thurs, and Sun from 5 to 7 p.m. with $1 sushi. Open Tues through Fri for lunch and dinner (closing between 2 and 5 p.m.) and weekends for dinner only.

## BARBECUE

### BILL MILLER BAR-B-Q $

**2750 Bill Miller Lane**
**(210) 533-5143**
**www.billmillerbbq.com**

The largest barbecue chain in the nation is headquartered in San Antonio. Bill Miller Bar-B-Q has more than three dozen locations in San Antonio alone. It might be considered the fast-food version of barbecue spots, with a product milder and more geared to family tastes than some of its competitors. Nevertheless, the offerings here are plentiful and inexpensive. Take the whole family and order anything on the menu—brisket, chicken, sausage, or ham followed by an excellent slice of homemade pie—and you still won't break the family budget.

### BUN 'N' BARREL $

**1150 Austin Hwy.**
**(210) 828-2820**
**www.bunnbarrel.com**

If you're nostalgic for the 1950s, visit the Bun 'n' Barrel. Founded in 1950, this diner is a genuine product of those happy days, complete with carhops, frothy malts, and a lunch counter. The walls are dotted with photos of classic cars, and a bulletin board by the cash register is dotted with ads offering classic cars and parts for sale.

But the best reason to visit the Bun 'n' Barrel is the barbecue—and the buns. Order the chopped beef sandwich, a finely chopped mixture devoid of fat, seasoned with tangy sauce. It's served up on a homemade braided roll dotted with poppy seeds. If you're in the mood for something other than beef, try the pork ribs, beef sausage, ham, or turkey breast served with potato salad and ranch-style beans.

### COUNTY LINE SMOKEHOUSE AND GRILL $$–$$$

**111 W. Crockett St.**
**(210) 229-1941**
**www.countyline.com**

The County Line is an institution among Texas barbecue lovers—folks who know good barbecue. With locations around the state, this restaurant is a step above the usual barbecue restaurant; it's the kind of place where you might go to celebrate a special event with some special food.

This River Walk location is tucked next door to the Hard Rock Cafe in the South Bank Complex and offers indoor and outside dining. The restaurant has a roadhouse atmosphere, casual and fun. Like the other locations, this County Line specializes in slow-cooked barbecue. Have your table order the all-you-can-eat extravaganza and you'll feast on beef ribs, brisket, and sausage served family style, with huge bowls of sour cream potato salad, crunchy coleslaw, and tasty pintos. The side dishes are made from scratch daily. There's even homemade bread that rises twice before baking.

One extra this location offers that other County Lines can't boast is its party barges. Call to reserve a private barge if you'd like to take your barbecue and beer cruising on the river.

The other San Antonio County Line is located just 3 miles from Fiesta Texas (10101 I-10 West, 210-641-1998). With its position right on the edge of the Hill Country, this location has a genuine country atmosphere, complete with a big breezy country porch and a landscaped patio. Like the chain's other locations, this restaurant serves up barbecue in the finest Texas tradition. Open for lunch and dinner daily.

## Close-up

### Texas Barbecue

Barbecue is big business here. At last count there were more than 90 smokin' pits across San Antonio. The state itself boasts about 1,300 barbecue joints, but that statistic only hints at the seriousness with which Texans take their task. The business of barbecue rings up over a half-billion dollars annually, a cobweb of commerce that connects an otherwise diverse, sprawling state with a common mission: Go forth, Texans, to cook and consume good barbecue.

Beef rules most of the Texas barbecue pits in the form of brisket, ribs, sausage, and chopped beef. But you'll find plenty of chicken and pork, plus an occasional offering of mutton.

Every Texas barbecue joint, whether the jukebox is playing cowboy or *conjunto* tunes, features **beef brisket.** Following the brisket, menus might involve some regional variation. *Cabrito* (barbecued goat) is often spotted in the western portion of the state, while lamb is a more common offering in East Texas. Cooking styles can vary as well.

Barbecue got its start in this region in the meat markets and butcher shops. These pioneer merchants were determined to find a use for cuts that weren't selling. On the weekends, they began smoking those quickly aging meats, hoping to make them more palatable with an infusion of smoke. It worked. Soon the smell of barbecue permeated the small towns and captured the attention of those doing their Saturday marketing. Farmers and ranchers in town for weekend trading came by the meat market and found an inexpensive lunch served up on the only plate a butcher had on hand: butcher paper.

Eventually, farm and ranch families began making the meat market a regular weekend stop, dining off the backs of their wagons. Soon some meat markets began to put up a few picnic tables for customers. Today the best joints still have a picnic table or two. Some still serve their product on butcher paper.

The rules of Texas barbecue are few, whether produced in a smoky restaurant, a backyard cooker, or a mobile rig.

1. **Take your time.** Professional pitmasters spend as long as 18 to 20 hours to cook a brisket to smoky perfection, even when thermometers outside top 100 degrees. Cookoff competitors are known to stay up through the night stoking their smokers.

2. **Texan barbecue is always smoked, never grilled.** True Texas barbecue is accomplished in a closed smoker, a treasure chest that seals in the meats

**FATSO'S SPORTS GARDEN** $$
**1704 Bandera Rd.**
**(210) 432-0121**
**www.fatsossportsgarden.com**

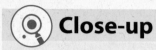

Known primarily as a sports bar and restaurant, this eatery serves up lots of barbecue in the form of mesquite-smoked chopped or sliced brisket, baby back ribs, smoked sausage, and grilled chicken. You

with the smoke to ensure the union of the two. (Just how the smoker should be arranged, however, is the topic of yet another 'cue controversy. In the community of Llano, north of San Antonio, pitmasters use an indirect barbecuing method. Wood, primarily mesquite, is placed in the firebox and allowed to burn down to coals; then it's transferred to the main section of the pit beneath the meat. Here it flavors and cooks the meat to perfection, imparting a delicate smoky taste that is subtler than that achieved through ordinary smoking.)

But with those ground rules in place, it's a cook's free-for-all when it comes to the preparation and presentation of the meal. In researching barbecue across this vast state, we also saw myriad ingredients tossed into rubs and sauces. Beer, cider vinegar, mustard, Worcestershire, brown sugar, Chinese chili oil, celery seed, white vinegar, soy sauce, pancake syrup, honey, apple jelly, gin, rum, Creole mustard, cayenne pepper, molasses, chipotles, Jamaican PickaPeppa sauce, orange juice, and even cranberry sauce have made appearances in Texas barbecue sauces and marinades. One pitmaster explained his varying recipe by saying, "It depends what I've got on hand," while another said his recipe "depends on how much beer I've had to drink that day."

One point that cooks will agree on, however, is that the barbecue sauce should be held back until the last stages of barbecuing to prevent burning. Although many cooks continue to mop the meat with a spicy marinade during the smoking process, the actual barbecue sauce sees the meat only during its final minutes in the flames, if at all. Instead, cooks baste the meat with flavorful marinades to keep it moist in its trial by fire and to impart a unique taste. Many barbecue joints dish up their meat right off the smoker, sans sauce, with the tomato-based concoction served on the side, usually accompanied by a shaker of hot peppers soaking in vinegar to add a tangy kick to the meal. Rub recipes are similarly eclectic. These mixtures of dry ingredients, often heavy with garlic powder, chili powder, and black pepper, complement the meat's tastes without overpowering it.

Wood is another matter of personal choice—and controversy. Oak, hickory, pecan, and mesquite chips are the choices of many Texas pitmasters, often in combination.

Barbecue ranks with state politics when it comes to provoking heated discussion between Texans. One barbecue joint has a sign over its counter that says it best: "Bar-b-que, sex and death are subjects that provoke intense speculation in most Texans. Out of the three, probably bar-b-que is taken most seriously."

can order the meat alone or with sides of homemade potato salad, baked potatoes, or beans. Appetizers include hot wings served with celery and chunky blue-cheese dressing, potato skins and bacon, or nachos. Chalupas are also available, filled with brisket or chicken. The atmosphere here is pure fun, with volleyball courts, pool tables, and 8 big-screen televisions. The restaurant is open for lunch and dinner nightly.

## Close-up

### Glossary of Texas Barbecue

**Baby back ribs**—Ribs from a young hog; usually the most tender of the rib cuts.
***Barbacoa***—The Spanish took the Indian word *barbacoa,* the basis for our own word *barbecue,* to describe this smoky meat. You will find *barbacoa* on the menu in many South Texas restaurants, especially Tex-Mex. It refers to a special type of barbecue: the head of a cow wrapped in cheesecloth and burlap, slow-smoked in a pit.
**Beef clod**—Part of the shoulder or the neck near the shoulder; used like brisket.
**Brisket**—Chest muscle of a cow. This typically tough cut requires a long, slow cooking period to break down the fibrous meat. When many Texans say they're eating barbecue, they mean brisket. Every joint probably serves up this barbecue dish of Texas.
***Cabrito***—Young goat.
**Country-style pork ribs**—Backbone of a hog. These ribs contain large chunks of meat and sometimes resemble a pork chop.
**Marinade**—A seasoned liquid mixture in which meat is soaked prior to cooking. Acidic marinades such as those containing lime juice help tenderize meat. (Note: Acidic marinades should never be used in aluminum containers.)
**Rub**—Dry ingredients rubbed onto meat to season it during cooking.
**Sauce**—The flavored liquid used as a condiment after the meat has cooked. In Texas, most sauces are tomato-based.
**Skirt steak**—Diaphragm muscle of a cow. This tough cut is usually used for fajitas after marinating.
**Slab of ribs**—A whole side of the rib cage.
**Smoke ring**—The telltale pink ring in meat that authenticates it as barbecue.
**Sop**—A basting sauce applied during the barbecuing process.
**Spare ribs**—The lower portion of a hog's ribs.
**Texas hibachi**—A used 55-gallon drum used as a barbecue cooker.

**GRADY'S BAR-B-QUE** $
**4109 Fredericksburg Rd.**
**(210) 732-3636**
**www.gradysbbq.com**

Grady's restaurants have been keeping the folks in San Antonio happy with big plates of barbecue since 1948. The restaurants serve up some of the most inexpensive offerings in the region in large, comfortable dining rooms decorated with cowboy art. You can choose from beef, sausage, ham, or rib plates. We opted for brisket and ribs and couldn't have been happier. The brisket was tender and thinly sliced, served with a tangy sauce. The ribs were also cooked to tender perfection. All the plates arrive with a corn muffin plus a choice of two side dishes. Additional San Antonio locations are at 7400 Bandera Rd. (210-684-2899); 3619 I-35 North (210-343-8050); 327 Nakoma St. (210-343-8070); and 6510 San Pedro Rd. (210-805-8036).

**MARY ANN'S PIG STAND** $
**1508 Broadway**
**(210) 222-9923**
**www.maryannspigstand.com**

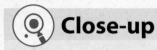

Once a chain of coffee shops, Pig Stands rose to prominence in the 1930s, billed as the "world's first drive-in." The first location was in Dallas, built in 1921, and the San Antonio site opened shortly afterward on Broadway. When the highway interchange project took place awhile back, the original building was condemned and the restaurant was moved a few hundred yards away. Now the nationwide chain is no more but the San Antonio Broadway restaurant has survived, thanks to longtime Pig Stand waitress Mary Ann Hill, who purchased the place in 2007 and now operates it as Mary Ann's Pig Stand. Other than the name, not much has changed; it still serves up the pig sandwiches, burgers, and malts that made them famous, along with chicken-fried steak, breakfast dishes, barbecue, sandwiches, salads, and soups. The original Pig Stand neon signs proudly hang and the parking lot still serves as a gathering place for classic-car owners every Friday night. On Fri and Sat nights it's open til 2 a.m.; other nights open til 11 p.m.

**RUDY'S COUNTRY STORE AND BAR-B-Q** **$–$$**
**24152 I-10 West, Leon Springs at Boerne Stage Road**
**(210) 698-2141**
**http://rudysbbq.com**

Rudy's calls itself "the worst bar-b-q in Texas." You sure wouldn't know that from the taste of the product, or from the crowds that flock to Rudy's, especially the original sprawling joint just north of San Antonio in Leon Springs. Mention barbecue in the Alamo City and you'll hear Rudy's name. Once you arrive, you'll find an old-fashioned meat market with indoor seating plus an always-packed outdoor area filled with picnic tables holding bottles of vinegar and sauce. (If Rudy's "Bar-B-Q Sause" is too spicy for you, ask for the "Sissy Sause.") Rudy's has an extensive menu: pork, baby back, St. Louis, and beef short ribs, plus chicken, prime rib, pork loin, chopped beef, sausage, turkey, and even rainbow trout. Side dishes are good, too, especially the creamed corn. Additional San Antonio locations are at 10623 Westover Hills Blvd. (210-520-5552) and 15560 I-35 North, Selma (210-653-RUDY).

## BREAKFAST & BRUNCH

**EARL ABEL'S** **$**
**1201 Austin Hwy., Suite 175**
**Terrell Plaza Shopping Center**
**(210) 822-3358**
**www.earlabelssa.com**

The location has changed, but the regulars who used to grab a booth at 4210 Broadway still enjoy the same decor, good service, and their favorite menu choices at the new home of this San Antonio landmark. Curly, the maitre d'mannequin, still greets customers as they come inside and order a good old-fashioned scrambled egg and pancake breakfast or a burger, chicken-fried steak, fried chicken, or made-from-scratch daily specials. Meals are topped off with desserts sure to blow any diet—like triple-layer German cake and coconut cake, to name just two. Kids eat free all day Tues and from 5 to 8 p.m. Mon, Wed, and Thurs. Along with in-house dining, the restaurant offers food to go; for orders, call (210) 822-7333. Open for breakfast, lunch, and dinner daily.

**GUENTHER HOUSE RESTAURANT** **$$–$$$**
**205 E. Guenther St.**
**(210) 227-1061, (800)-235-8186**
**www.guentherhouse.com**

Located in the elegant former home of Carl Guenther, founder of Pioneer Flour, this restaurant features, not too surprisingly, plenty of biscuits and gravy, sweet cream waffles, and pancakes. The coffee is wonderful. After a morning of looking at King William's elegant homes, you can stop here to enjoy a light lunch of salad, a sandwich, or soup. There are outdoor tables, cooled by misters, and an elegant but small dining room. This eatery is very popular with San Antonians who work nearby, and gets busy during the lunch hour and weekend brunch.

**JOSEPH'S STOREHOUSE RESTAURANT & BAKERY** **$–$$**
**3420 N. St. Mary's St.**
**(210) 737-3430**
**www.josephs-storehouse.net**

Joseph's is open for breakfast and lunch but the breakfasts are especially pleasant. Wonderful pastries and muffins are available as well as huge plates of bacon, eggs, and toast. The bowls of gourmet oatmeal and fresh fruit are tasty for folks with less cholesterol in mind. The restaurant is large and airy, with old tables and chairs scattered throughout, as well as photos of the owner's family. Lunch can be light, with sandwiches, soups, and quiche, or more substantial with entrees like King Ranch chicken and spaghetti. Still another bonus is the in-house bakery, which makes the place smell heavenly and supplies a lovely array of cakes and pastries.

**MAGNOLIA PANCAKE HAUS** **$**
**606 Embassy Oaks, Suite 100**
**(210) 496-0828**
**www.magnoliapancakehaus.com**

If you don't have the time or inclination to get up in the morning and make a big breakfast, then just head to the Magnolia Pancake Haus. Just about everything, from the pancakes to the sausage to the corned-beef hash, is made from scratch. Specialties of the house include the Munich apple *pfannekuchen* and the omelet Monterrey. This smoke-free restaurant offers a children's menu as well as take-out service. Open for breakfast 7 days a week and for lunch Mon through Sat.

## CAJUN & CREOLE

**ACADIANA CAFE OF SAN ANTONIO** **$–$$**
**1289 SW Loop 410**
**(210) 674-0019**
**www.acadianacafe.com**

When you enter Acadiana, you enter Cajun country. Catfish and crawfish abound in this huge (seats up to 300) cedar building. You can start out with appetizers of Cajun popcorn (fried crawfish tails), alligator nuggets, or fried dill pickles. Moving on to the main course, you can order a number of Cajun and seafood specialties or opt for the less spicy chicken-fried steak. Of note, they offer a Cajun sampler that includes everything from crawfish étouffée to red beans and rice, and a country platter that serves up selections like chicken and dumplings and sliced tomatoes. There is a good selection of vegetables and country-style cooking. This is a casual, kid-friendly place fairly close to SeaWorld. Open daily for lunch and dinner.

## COFFEEHOUSES

**CANDLELIGHT COFFEEHOUSE** **$–$$**
**3011 N. St. Mary's St.**
**(210) 738-0099**
**www.candlelightsa.com**

Found on the St. Mary's Strip, this cafe is one of the most popular coffeehouses in San Antonio, offering free Wi-Fi along with an arty ambience. A cup of joe here promises to be rich and not too strong. Candlelight Coffeehouse also is known for its lunch and dinner menu. Insiders like to design their own sandwiches, selecting from the variety of gourmet breads and fillings. Other light fare such as soups and pastas is also served, along with substantial dinner entrees like pasta bakes and Moroccan chicken. A large variety of wines rounds out the menu. This favorite hangout is open from 11 a.m. to midnight Tues through Sat, with Sunday brunch offered from 10 a.m. to 2 p.m.

**ESPUMA COFFEE AND TEA EMPORIUM** **$$**
**928 S. Alamo St.**
**(210) 226-1912**

In the elegant King William Historic District, Espuma Coffee and Tea Emporium is one of San Antonio's favorite coffeehouses. Folks come from all around the city to enjoy the good drinks and the casual atmosphere that's reminiscent of the 1930s. If you want a little food to go with your coffee, you're in luck. Espuma serves light fare such as soups and sandwiches with a special twist (don't miss the tomato, mozzarella, and pesto sandwich). Gracing the brightly painted walls is original art by local artists. There is live music here on most Friday nights, so call ahead to see if you'll be able to catch an act. Espuma closes at 6 p.m. Mon through Thurs. Weekend hours vary, so call ahead. A location inside San Fernando Cathedral's City Centre, 115 Main Plaza, Building #2, also serves breakfast tacos.

**GRACE COFFEE CAFE** **$–$$**
**3233 N. St. Mary's St.**
**(210) 736-6576**
**www.gracecoffeecafe.com**

Coffee lovers, if you're looking to spend some quality time with your beans, you can't go wrong at the Grace Coffee Cafe. Housed in a former Albertson's grocery market near the Tri-Point YMCA on St. Mary's, the cafe is a spacious, friendly place to nurse a latte or cappucino while playing card or board games (provided) or using their free Wi-Fi. A full range of coffee-centric beverages is offered as well as tea, cocoa, and smoothies. Food items include pastries, home-baked cookies, and a generous array of sandwich choices. The Grace Coffee Cafe is operated by the Trinity Baptist Church, and the profits support the church's ministry and San Antonio community services. The cafe is open daily for breakfast and lunch and serves dinner Mon through Fri. If you like to linger over your cuppa, this is your place, but they do have a drive-through if you are in a hurry.

**MADHATTER'S TEA HOUSE & CAFE** **$$**
**320 Beauregard St.**
**(210) 212-4832**
**www.madhatterstea.com**

Located in a rambling old house in the heart of the King William Historic District, Madhatter's Tea Cafe is a charming establishment featuring more than two dozen teas and an eclectic menu. Best known for its breakfasts—a popular choice is the eggs Benedict, which they call "Benny's"—it also has tasty and unusual sandwiches and gorgeous pastries. This tearoom/cafe has some good choices for vegetarians, too, and is within walking distance of the River Walk. If you have little girls in your party, you'll want to know that Madhatter's enjoys having kids in for tea parties. Open Mon through Fri from 7 a.m. to 9 p.m., Sat from 8 a.m. to 9 p.m., and Sun from 9 a.m. to 3 p.m.

## CONTINENTAL

### FIG TREE RESTAURANT $$$$

**515 Villita St.**
**(210) 224-1976**
**www.figtreerestaurant.com**

One of the most elegant and pricey restaurants at La Villita, and indeed in the city, is the Fig Tree, where continental cuisine is the order of the day. Dining here is by candlelight at linen-topped tables set with china and crystal.

Fig Tree Restaurant has been the recipient of the DiRoNA (Distinguished Restaurants of North America) Award every year since 1998. It has long been considered a place to celebrate special occasions. The restaurant is housed in one of the last private buildings in La Villita—the building was purchased in 1970 by the Phelps family as a residence, but the family opened it as a restaurant one year later. The menu here reflects the elegant style of the dining room, starting with appetizers such as *pâté de campagne* and roasted Texas Hill Country quail. Entrees include wild Tasmanian salmon, cold-water Australian lobster tail, braised duck breast, rack of lamb, beef Wellington, and filet mignon. Desserts are equally impressive: A delicate crème brûlée with seasonal fruit, Bananas Foster flamed table-side, and baked Alaska are among the choices. This restaurant is open for dinner only, and reservations are recommended. Dress is business casual.

## DELIS

### JASON'S DELI $$

**25 NE Loop 410**
**(210) 524-9288**
**www.jasonsdeli.com**

This dependable nationwide deli chain at 4 locations offers a diverse menu with plates to satisfy any palate. For the health-conscious eater there are several heart-smart choices, including the turkey wrap, a spinach veggie wrap, and a turkey Reuben, while vegetarians can sample a grilled portobello wrapini or a garden po'boy. Hungry youngsters can order such childhood classics as a PB&J, a grilled cheese sandwich, or macaroni and cheese. Three other San Antonio locations are at 9933 I-10 West (210-690-3354); 5819 NW Loop 410, Exchange Plaza (210-647-5000); and 1141 N. FM 1604 East, #108 (210-545-6888).

### SCHILO'S DELICATESSEN $

**424 E. Commerce St.**
**(210) 223-6692**
**www.schilos.com**

Schilo's (pronounced "SHE-lows") is a San Antonio favorite, and what it lacks in atmosphere, it definitely makes up for in history. The deli was founded by Papa Fritz Schilo, a German immigrant. He opened a saloon in 1917, but when Prohibition came along, he converted the operation to a deli. It was a lucky break for diners—mere suds could never match the subs and sandwiches that keep this deli packed with locals. Try a Reuben or a ham and cheese, or go all out for dinner with entrees like Wiener schnitzel or bratwurst. The homemade root beer is a must, as is the pot pie on days when they serve it. Open for breakfast, lunch, and dinner Mon through Sat.

## FRENCH

**BISTRO VATEL** **$$$**
**218 E. Olmos Ave.**
**(210) 828-3141**
**www.bistrovatel.com**

Its location in a small Olmos Park strip center belies the sophistication of this Parisian-style restaurant, which offers diners a fine coq au vin, steamed mussels with cream sauce, duck breast with rhubarb, and a prix fixe menu that's quite a bargain. Sauces and dressings are excellent, and the food is served with flair. Lunch is served Tues through Fri, and dinner is served Tues through Sat. Dress is business casual.

**RESTAURANT LE REVE** **$$$**
**152 E. Pecan St. at N. St. Mary's Street**
**(210) 212-2221**
**www.restaurantlereve.com**

San Antonio's own Andrew Weissman has drawn national attention—including a spot on the list of the nation's 50 best restaurants from *Gourmet* magazine—with Le Reve, his contemporary French restaurant on the San Antonio River. A small, intimate establishment located in the lower level of the Exchange Building, Le Reve maintains a friendly but formal ambience for serving specialties such as the much-acclaimed onion tart, scallops with caviar beurre blanc, or lamb on couscous. The restaurant also presents an impressive wine list. Open for dinner Thurs through Sat. Reservations are recommended.

## GREEK

**DEMO'S GREEK FOOD** **$-$$**
**7115 Blanco Rd.**
**(210) 342-2772**
**www.demosgreekfood.com**

Demo's has more than just good food—it also offers a crash course in Greek culture. On the first Saturday of each month, Demo's fills with music and dance as a Greek band cuts loose and diners find themselves in the right frame of mind to enjoy the family-like atmosphere. Don't worry if you don't know how; there's always someone around who wants to teach you. Hopefully, you will have enjoyed dinner beforehand and sampled the gyro plates or souvlaki plate with chicken. At lunchtime, there's always the special featuring a gyro, fries, and a small Greek salad that's very satisfying, but—alas!—no dancing. Demo's is open for lunch and dinner 7 days a week. Two other San Antoino locations are at 2501 N. St. Mary's St. (210-732-7777) and 1205 N. Loop 1604 West (210-798-3840).

**KOSTAS' GREEK FOOD** **$**
**12606 Nacogdoches Rd.**
**(210) 590-6969**

Decorated with posters of Greek villages, this cafe is nothing fancy but nevertheless fun. Greek dishes are the order of the day, ranging from the traditional gyro, made with strips of lamb and beef rolled in tender pita bread, to *spanakopita* (spinach pie). Meals are accompanied by Greek salads topped with feta cheese. Be sure to save room for the real showstopper: the homemade baklava, a honey and nut creation that's the perfect complement to the spiciness of the main dishes. For even greater decadence, Kostas' frequently prepares a chocolate chip–filled baklava.

**MINA AND DIMI'S GREEK HOUSE** **$**
**7159 US 90 West**
**(210) 674-3464**
**www.agreekhouse.com**

A mural of a whitewashed Greek village sets the scene at this popular Greek restaurant. Casual and fun, the eatery offers gyro sandwiches in chicken, beef, or lamb. A specialty of the house is the *dolmades,* seasoned beef and rice in rolled grape leaves. Meat lovers often select the lamb chop platter, featuring charbroiled lamb chops with pita bread, fried okra, oven-baked potatoes, and a Greek salad. Others opt for moussaka, a Greek eggplant casserole with potatoes and seasoned ground beef with bechamel sauce. The restaurant, located in Gateway Plaza, also hosts special events, including a wine tasting on the first Thursday of every month. Friday and Saturday nights bring belly dancing to the family-friendly place. Open for lunch and dinner Mon through Sat.

## INDIAN

**INDIA PALACE RESTAURANT $$**
**8440 Fredericksburg Rd.**
**(210) 692-5262**
**www.indiapalacesa.com**

While this family-owned dining establishment offers an array of lamb and chicken entrees, the vegetarian dishes, which include eggplant sautéed with herbs and spices, a sautéed spinach dish topped with cheese, and fried Indian bread, will be a hit. The restaurants also offer 4 catering options for both their vegetarian and meat-loving patrons. Be sure to print out the online coupons found on their website for extra savings on your meal.

**SIMI'S INDIA CUISINE $$**
**4535 Fredericksburg Rd., #109**
**(210) 737-3166**

This modest restaurant is a hidden treasure in a strip center across from Crossroads Mall. Simi's has a daily lunch buffet that is a veritable feast featuring tandoori chicken, *sag paneer* (a creamed spinach and cheese dish that even spinach-haters will love), a wonderful rice pudding, and several other dishes. During the dinner hour, one of the most popular orders is the Empire Dinner for two, which includes an array of dishes such as tandoori chicken and shrimp, *seekh kebab, tekka masal,* lamb *shahi korma,* and much more. Wine and Indian beer are available, and the cooks will prepare your order to specifications: spicy, medium, or mild. Open daily for lunch and dinner.

## ITALIAN

**ALDO'S RISTORANTE ITALIANO $$$**
**8539 Fredericksburg Rd.**
**(210) 696-2536**
**www.aldos.us**

Located in a century-old house, this Italian eatery is a favorite for romantic occasions. Decorated with antiques, the restaurant is filled with the soft sounds of live piano music on weekend evenings. The menu offers a wide variety of Italian dishes such as *trota alla ariglia* (trout served with pasta and roasted vegetables) and chicken gorgonzola. A good wine list offers plenty of selections to accompany your meal. Aldo's is open for lunch on weekdays and for dinner nightly.

**MICHELINO'S RISTORANTE ITALIANO $$**
**521 River Walk**
**(210) 223-2939**
**www.michelinos.us**

The taste of Italy, from calamari to capellini with shrimp and scallops, comes to the River Walk at this popular eatery. Pasta dishes and pizzas are offered along with more elegant fare, such as grilled pork tenderloin with focaccia and fine wine. The outdoor tables, sheltered and shady, are the most popular but well worth the wait. Open daily for lunch and dinner.

**OLIVE GARDEN** **$$**
**13730 San Pedro**
**(210) 494-3411**
**www.olivegarden.com**

With 6 locations in the city, this popular nationwide chain provides reliable service and a menu that caters to individualized needs. For the weight-conscious diner, several low-fat delicacies are on the menu, such as linguine alla marinara, capellini pomodoro, and chicken giardino. For those watching their carb intake, grilled entrees can be served alongside fresh vegetables. Check out their website for additional San Antonio locations.

**PAESANOS** **$$–$$$**
**555 E. Basse Rd.**
**(210) 828-5191**
**www.paesanos.com**

**PAESANOS RIVER WALK** **$$–$$$**
**111 W. Crockett St.**
**(210) 227-2782**
**http://paesanosriverwalk.com**

**PAESANOS 1604** **$$–$$$**
**3622 Paesano Pkwy.**
**(210) 493-1604**
**www.paesanos1604.com**

This restaurant has 3 locations: The River Walk location is tops with tourists, locals tend to gravitate to the Basse Road location, which overlooks the Quarry golf course, and diners who wish to enjoy the sights of the Hill Country congregate at the venue on Paesano Parkway. The restaurants are well known for the signature dish: shrimp *paesano,* a delicate blend of angel-hair pasta and seasoned shrimp. But if you don't like seafood, don't despair—plenty of other options await. First-course selections include steak *churrasco* with herb vinaigrette and field greens, and Parmesan-crusted artichoke hearts with basil aioli. Main courses range from pizza (the Margherita with cheese and fresh basil is tough to beat) to chicken parmigiana with spaghetti, tomato, and mozzarella.

The downtown location is considered to have one of the River Walk's most extensive wine lists. You'll also find an extensive martini menu at all 3 locations, which are open for lunch and dinner daily.

**ROME'S PIZZA** **$**
**Post Office Center**
**5999 De Zavala Dr.**
**(210) 691-2070**

Consistently listed in the *San Antonio Express-News* Readers' Choice Awards as the best in local pizzerias, this Italian eatery offers not only traditional and exotic-style pizzas, but also oven-toasted sandwiches, Mediterranean-influenced *dolmas* and *homus,* calzones, and pastas. A special kids' menu is available.

**TRE TRATTORIA DOWNTOWN** **$$$**
**401 S. Alamo St. at the Fairmount Hotel**
**(210) 223-0401**
**www.thefairmounthotel-sanantonio.com**

Rightly dubbed the Jewel of San Antonio, the Fairmount Hotel offers an Italian eatery that adds extra sparkle to any dining experience. Tre Trattoria is an authentic Tuscan restaurant in the heart of San Antonio. The creation of Chef Jason Dady, Tre Trattoria

## Close-up

### Edible Texas Traditions

Texas specialties have two things in common. First, most Texas dishes can trace their roots to harder times, when it was a necessity to use every cut of meat, even some that more gentrified diners might consider scrap.

Another characteristic that Texas dishes have in common (along with enough cholesterol to harden any artery) is a reliance on beef. Cattle ranching is king here, and beef makes an appearance on every menu and at every backyard cookout.

Those early cowboy cooks knew that not all meat was steak; some of it was tough and even stringy. They used Western ingenuity to turn what could have been waste into dishes that award-winning restaurants are now proud to serve. **Chicken-fried steak** is such a dish, using one of the toughest cuts of meat: the round steak. It's tenderized (the cook just beats the meat into submission), then dipped in an egg-and-milk batter, floured, and fried to a golden crispiness. The chicken-fried steak is the equivalent of white bread in Texas cuisine. Folks feel comfortable with chicken-fried steak. It's not spicy, so even those who can't handle the fiery heat of other local dishes love this one.

When you're ready for something spicier, order up the state dish of Texas: **chili.** More than a century ago, young women known as "chili queens" sold chili con carne from kiosks in San Antonio's Market Square. When the dish went to the Chicago World's Fair in 1893, chili caught on, and the rest, as they say, is history. For all its variety, San Antonio's best-loved cuisine remains **Tex-Mex.** While you will find delightful dishes from the interior of Mexico on some menus, the standard enchilada, tamale, and taco offerings of the Tex-Mex restaurant rule. This cuisine was imported from the Monterrey region of Mexico, an area rich with cattle. Tex-Mex favorites feature lots of beef and plenty of cheese. Side dishes of refried (pinto) beans and Spanish rice are standard, along with hot tortillas, either corn or flour. Baskets of fried tortilla chips accompanied by hot sauce (which is either green or red and can range from mild to fiery) are also standard fare.

**Fajitas** are a favorite "trash to treasure" Tex-Mex treat. Fajitas were a brainstorm of chuck wagon cooks who learned that marinating the tough skirt steak in lime

offers generous portions of antipasti, house-cured salami, hand-made pasta, and pizzas, as well as scenic views of Hemisfair Park and San Antonio's Tower of the Americas. The restaurant is open 11 a.m. to 10 p.m. Mon through Fri, 10 a.m. to 10 p.m. Sat and Sun, with a weekend brunch served 10 a.m. to 3 p.m.

**THE VINEYARDS RESTAURANT $$$**
**27315 FM 3009, 1.5 miles past Natural Bridge Caverns**
**(830) 980-8033**
**www.thevineyards.org**

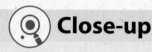

Tucked away amid the junipers and limestone ledges of the beautiful Texas Hill Country, the Vineyards Restaurant is quiet and romantic. You can dine in the candlelit wine cellar or overlooking the vineyards and rose garden. Among the chef's specials are juice broke down the meat into chewable consistency. Sliced in narrow strips and grilled, the meat is now served with cheese, salsa, and guacamole and rolled into a flour tortilla.

You can find great chicken enchiladas with a flavorful verde tomatillo sauce, as well as vegetarian dishes or even shrimp enchiladas. But the real Tex-Mex favorite, known affectionately as **Regular Plate No. 1,** is an order of beef enchiladas, refried beans, and Spanish rice. If you're lucky, *leche quemada,* a sugary pecan praline, will be brought out with your check.

**Tamales,** both mild and spicy varieties, are also found on every Tex-Mex menu, but they're most popular during the Christmas season. Stores sell tamales by the thousands during the holidays, when it's popular to bring them to office parties and home get-togethers.

As you venture farther south in Texas, you'll find a larger variety of Tex-Mex dishes, including some that are sold primarily in Hispanic neighborhoods. One of these dishes is *cabrito,* tender young goat usually cooked over an open flame on a spit. Cabrito is a common dish in border towns, where you can often see it hanging on spits in market windows.

Although San Antonio's cuisine borrows heavily from the Mexican culture, it also draws from other ethnic groups that settled this land. People of more than 30 nationalities, from Alsatians to Czechs to Poles, settled communities throughout Texas, bringing their own culinary styles and adjusting them to fit the food supply they found on the frontier.

The Germans, one of the city's largest immigrant groups, settled the area northwest of San Antonio and founded the towns of New Braunfels and Fredericksburg. A New Braunfels museum explains that when German farmers butchered a pig, they "used everything but the squeal." Some shoppers preferred not to see all those pig parts looking back at them across a meat counter, so the German meat markets used whatever didn't sell to make sausage. Today the central Texas town of Elgin is the capital of the sausage world. Barbecue joints throughout the state sell **Elgin sausage,** a spicy, greasy concoction that's now all beef.

chicken florentine, a boneless chicken breast stuffed with spinach and prosciutto rolled and covered with a spicy Alfredo sauce and served over a bed of pasta; and mesquite-smoked peppered prime rib, 12 ounces of trimmed prime rib coated with crushed black peppercorns and accompanied by sautéed wild mushrooms. The Vineyards offers a variety of wines, including its Vineyards Signature Cuvee produced by Becker Vineyards in nearby Fredericksburg, using the very grapes you see on the premises. A popular place for weddings, the Vineyards is open for dinner 7 days a week and for lunch on Fri, Sat, and Sun. See the website for a map.

## NEW AMERICAN & ECLECTIC

**ANAQUA ROOM** **$$–$$$**
**555 S. Alamo St.**
**(210) 353-8042**
**www.marriott.com**

The Marriott Plaza San Antonio is home to this often-lauded restaurant. Located just off the lobby, the sunny eatery has indoor and outdoor seating. The cool Saltillo tile floor lends a colorful accent to the outdoor seating area (where you may be joined by Chinese pheasants that roam the grounds). It's shaded and cooled by surrounding tropical foliage and ivy-covered columns. The menu features New American cuisine, ranging from Mediterranean-influenced pastas to Tex-Mex selections to Pacific Rim infusion dishes. Innovative presentations make for an adventurous experience with creative dishes such as masa-battered shrimp and orange-jicama salad. Open for breakfast, lunch, and dinner (closed between lunch and dinner).

**i** **Restaurant reviewers at the *San Antonio Express-News* have voted Biga's "Best Brunch in the Alamo City."**

***BIGA'S ON THE BANKS** **$$$**
**203 S. St. Mary's St.**
**(210) 225-0722**
**www.biga.com**

Biga's chef and owner, Bruce J. Auden, has been nominated for the James Beard Foundation Award, one of the dining world's highest honors. One of San Antonio's most lauded restaurants, Biga's was also named one of "America's Best Restaurants" by *Gourmet* magazine. These recognitions come as no surprise to San Antonio residents, who have long enjoyed the elegant eatery's innovative fare and events.

Located on the River Walk at street level, the contemporary-style restaurant boasts natural lighting, river views, and a sophisticated loftlike atmosphere.

An eclectic menu awaits diners, who find that the New American cuisine of Biga's reflects the flavors of both Mexico and Asia. The menu changes daily. Typical appetizers include Bibb and radicchio game packets with Asian chili sauces; duck confit bao buns with Chinese barbecue and chili orange–dressed pea tendrils; and tempura Gulf shrimp served with chili-lime noodles, watermelon, peanuts, and mint. Entree selections might include seared red grouper and chipotle grits with yard long beans and fruit pico; Hunan barbecued red grouper with young greens, winter vegetables, and crispy noodle net; spiced Texas Hill Country Axis venison chops and grilled quail with potato puree and chestnuts; and smoke-roasted pork tenderloin with potato rosti, juniper-braised cabbage, maple sour cream, and Riesling apple sauce.

One of Biga's most innovative concepts is its Table 31. Situated with a view of the kitchen, this table is available for parties of 6 to 8 guests, who enjoy a prix fixe tasting menu. Participants select a menu of 6, 7, or 8 courses, paired with wine. Don't have 6 or 8 people in your party? Tables of 2 can also be accommodated at a private screened table. Reservations are required for Table 31, which is offered every evening. The restaurant also offers many special events throughout the year, from jazz brunches to international tastings. Reservations are recommended for all dining. You can call the restaurant, or reserve online at www.biga.com/reservations.html. Biga's is open for dinner nightly.

## SEAFOOD

**SEA ISLAND SHRIMP HOUSE** **$–$$**
**322 W. Rector St.**
**(210) 342-7771**
**www.shrimphouse.com**

Operating since 1965, the original locale on West Rector has become a San Antonio institution. The family-owned establishments, many offering both a patio and a children's play area, feature a menu filled with seafood favorites such as charbroiled shrimp and shrimp salad. Together, the restaurants serve about 13 million premium Texas Gulf shrimp a year, hand-peeling each one. And don't leave without sampling the baked-from-scratch Key lime pie. Check out their website for information on other San Antonio locations and sign up online for news regarding special offers.

## SOUTHWESTERN & LATIN

***ANTLERS LODGE $$$**
**9800 Hyatt Hill Country Resort Dr.**
**(210) 520-4001**
**www.hillcountry.hyatt.com**

The Hill Country Golf Club, located at the Hyatt Hill Country Resort near SeaWorld, is home to Antlers Lodge, a restaurant featuring Southwestern cuisine that boasts an atmosphere casual enough to enjoy after a day of sightseeing in downtown San Antonio but special enough to celebrate a birthday, anniversary, or other occasion. The restaurant, with views of the greens, is lit by giant chandeliers made from deer antlers, appropriately enough, and the warm woodsy colors further enhance the lodge atmosphere. The eclectic menu offers some unique items such as South Texas wild boar chops. Tamer fare, including steaks and Chilean sea bass, rounds out the options. Antlers Lodge is open for dinner Mon through Sat. Reservatons are suggested.

**AZUCA NUEVO LATINO $$$**
**713 S. Alamo St.**
**(210) 225-5550**
**www.azuca.net**

Azuca is festive in both attitude and flavor. Diners will find themselves surrounded in bright colors and boldly hued, hand-blown light fixtures when they arrive at this establishment at the entrance to the King William Historic District in downtown San Antonio. This establishment is housed in a two-building complex that dates back to 1909. The cuisine (and atmosphere) shows the influence of Caribbean and Central and South American tastes. Specialties include pasta paella Latina, linguini pasta with chicken, sausage, pork ribs, seafood, and vegetables in a tasty saffron broth; and salmon *jibaro,* a fresh fillet crusted with thin plantain strips and served with cilantro crab butter, baby carrots, and chayote. And don't pass on the house corn bread—it's fabulous. Parents will be pleased to see a children's menu serving grilled cheese and chicken tenders.

Azuca has a full bar and offers a wide variety of Latin cocktail concoctions. If you're into the salsa, merengue, or flamenco scene, you're in luck. There's live music and dancing 2 nights a week. Call for a schedule. The restaurant is open Mon through Sat for lunch and dinner and for dinner on Sun from 5 to 9:30 p.m., and a happy hour is scheduled from 4 to 7 p.m. Mon through Fri.

**BOUDRO'S $$$–$$$$**
**421 E. Commerce**
**(210) 224-8484**
**www.boudros.com**

Located right on the River Walk between the Hyatt and the Hilton hotels, this steak and seafood restaurant is always packed.

It offers the finest in Southwestern cuisine, usually with a twist that makes it unique even among San Antonio's plethora of excellent eateries. Start with a cactus margarita, a frozen concoction with a jolt of red cactus liqueur. Follow that eye-opener with an appetizer of Gulf Coast crab seacakes with corn and jicama slaw or chili-fried oysters on yucca chips. Save room, though, for Boudro's specialties—coconut shrimp, pecan-grilled fish fillet, or the specialty of the house, blackened prime rib. Seating is available on the River Walk or in the dining room. Boudro's is open daily for lunch and dinner.

**FRANCESCA'S AT SUNSET** **$$$$**
**16641 La Cantera Pkwy.**
**(210) 558-6500**
**www.westinlacantera.com**
With a spectacular sunset view of the San Antonio city lights, Francesca's at Sunset has all the right ingredients for romantic dining. Located on the third floor of the Citadel at the Westin La Cantera Resort, this elegant venue bills its cuisine as "farm-to-table," presenting a South Texas–centric approach with a Southwestern flair. More than 80 percent of products (from beef and game to produce and wine) are from South Texas ranchers, farmers, and vintners. Favorite entrees include corn crepe–lobster enchilada, a lobster-filled crepe with shallots, potatoes, and cilantro covered with roasted poblano sauce, or the Broken Arrow Ranch wild boar from Ingram, Texas, served with a caramelized wedge of sweet pumpkin and Shiner Bock chili. Recommended appetizers include the quail croquette served with butternet squash salsa or the sweet corn–dusted crab cake with chipotle aioli. Open daily for dinner. Appropriate attire is business to dressy. Reservations are recommended.

**ZUNI GRILL** **$$$**
**223 Losoya St.**
**(210) 227-0864**
**www.zunigrill.com**
Part of the Paesanos family of local restaurants, Zuni Grill is a cut above typical Tex-Mex. Instead, this River Walk restaurant beside historic Hugman Bridge serves Southwestern cuisine, with selections that start with blue corn nachos and cilantro crabmeat croquettes and then progress to specials such as blue corn chicken enchiladas and spicy fajitas served with black beans. The bar pours several specialty drinks, both alcoholic and non; don't miss the cactus pear margaritas. Zuni Grill is open daily for breakfast, lunch, and dinner.

## STEAKHOUSES

**BOHANAN'S** **$$$–$$$$**
**219 E. Houston St., #275**
**(210) 472-2600**
**www.bohanans.com**
This romantic steak and seafood place offers lunchtime dishes—such as a 10-ounce prime rib au jus with horseradish crème fraîche and a house slaw—as elegant as its evening fare. Head chef and owner Mark Bohanan prepares all of the food, from the duck confit egg rolls to the venison tenderloin with five-spice rub and Texas gold sauce to the Madagascar vanilla crème brûlée. The restaurant's beautiful dining room and the attentive service make a meal here a truly enjoyable experience. Located across the street from the historic Majestic Theatre, Bohanan's is open for lunch and dinner Mon through Fri and for dinner only on the weekend. Reservations are accepted, and dress is business casual to dressy.

**GREY MOSS INN** **$$$–$$$$**
**19010 Scenic Loop Rd., Helotes**
**(210) 695-8301**
**www.grey-moss-inn.com**

This steak house began as a tearoom in 1929. Located 12 minutes from Six Flags Fiesta Texas on Scenic Loop Road, the restaurant is about a 45-minute drive from downtown San Antonio, but well worth the trip, thanks to its romantic candlelight atmosphere and excellent food. You can choose from indoor or patio seating. Along with a full selection of mesquite-grilled steaks, the Grey Moss Inn also serves non-beef dishes such as mesquite-grilled Pacific salmon and lamb chops with fresh rosemary cabernet sauce. The extensive list of over 500 wines has been cited by *Wine Spectator* magazine.

The Grey Moss Inn is one of San Antonio's favorite wedding spots. The entire property and beautiful grounds are available for rent, or smaller groups can be accommodated in the 1929 cottage on the property; the inn's Garden Room, with its wood-burning stove; or the Veranda Room, which has a fireplace. Reservations are recommended at this popular restaurant, which is open for dinner nightly.

**i** **The Grey Moss Inn was immortalized on the silver screen in the 1993 biopic *8 Seconds,* in which actor Luke Perry portrayed the life of bull-riding champion Lane Frost.**

**LITTLE RHEIN STEAK HOUSE** **$$$**
**231 S. Alamo St.**
**(210) 225-2111**
**www.littlerheinsteakhouse.com**

Serious beef lovers should make plans to dine at the Little Rhein Steak House. Located where La Villita meets the River Walk near the Arneson River Theatre, this restaurant offers an excellent selection of fine steaks served on terraces overlooking the river. On less pleasant days, you may choose to dine inside the historic Bombach House, built in 1847, which witnessed the development of San Antonio under six flags. In later years, the neighborhood was called the Little Rhein District because of its many German immigrants, and the restaurant took its name from that early title. In 1967 Frank W. Phelps (also the owner of the Fig Tree Restaurant) opened the Little Rhein Steak House, filling it with collectibles such as a 1907 bar and a light fixture that once illuminated President Theodore Roosevelt's Pullman car.

The extensive menu offers all types of beef, from T-bones to rib eye to porterhouse steak, all served with asparagus, sauteed wild mushrooms, and au gratin potatoes. The restaurant attracts a young professional crowd. Dress is business casual, and reservations are recommended. The restaurant is open daily for dinner only.

**MORTON'S OF CHICAGO STEAKHOUSE** **$$$$**
**303 E. Crockett St.**
**(210) 228-0700**
**www.mortons.com**

Located in the Rivercenter Mall, this steak house is part of the Morton's of Chicago chain of elegant eateries. The restaurant specializes in USDA prime aged beef as well as fish, lobster, lamb, and chicken entrees. The house specialty is a 24-ounce porterhouse; other top choices are the 20-ounce New York sirloin and a 14-ounce double-cut filet. The restaurant is open for dinner only; reservations are recommended.

### TEXAS LAND & CATTLE STEAK HOUSE $$$

**60 NE Loop 410**
**(210) 342-4477**
**www.texaslandandcattle.com**

Serving up rib-sticking portions of such Lone Star staples as smoked sirloin nachos, carne and enchiladas, Texas rib eye, and baby back ribs, Texas Land & Cattle Steak House has grown into a franchise with 28 locations across the country. Open Sun through Thurs from 11 a.m. to 10 p.m. and Fri and Sat from 11 a.m. to 11 p.m., menus are available in both English and Spanish. A gluten-free menu is also available. Additional San Antonio locations are at 9911 I-10 West (210-699-8744) and 201 N. St. Mary's St. (210-222-2263).

## TEXAS CUISINE

### LONE STAR CAFE $–$$

**237 Losoya St.**
**(210) 281-1292**
**www.lonestarcafe.us**

This popular River Walk restaurant serves up plenty of good old-fashioned country cooking. Look here for chicken-fried steaks, fried chicken, and seafood. A kids' menu offers hot dogs, chicken fingers, and mac and cheese. The restaurant is located at street level, above the pedestrian traffic on the River Walk, so it's a little away from the hustle and bustle. The tables on the porch, nestled under tall cypress trees, are a great place for people-watching. Open 7 days a week for lunch and dinner.

### REPUBLIC OF TEXAS $–$$

**526 River Walk**
**(210) 226-6256**
**www.therepublicoftexasrestaurant.com**

Search for the table umbrellas that look like the Lone Star flag, and you'll have found the Republic of Texas. This restaurant serves up a little of everything, from fajitas to catfish to burgers, in a building that was once the office of River Walk architect Robert H. H. Hugman. The building still bears his name, and the title "Architect" still appears on the former river-level office. Hugman once wrote, "As soon as the river walkway was finished, I opened my office at water level. When I did this, people said, in essence, 'I knew you were a dreamer, but now I know you are also a fool. You'll be drowned like a rat in your own hole.'" Open daily for breakfast, lunch, and dinner.

## TEX-MEX

### ALAMO CAFE $–$$

**14250 US 281 North**
**(210) 495-2233**
**www.alamocafe.com**

Since 1981 this restaurant has been a favorite of many San Antonio residents. Although the name might make you think it would offer traditional Texas food, don't look for barbecue or chicken-fried steak here: This is the land of enchiladas, tacos, and tortillas. The restaurant also has several specialties, including *carne guisada* (a stew of beef, chili peppers, and tomato), fajitas, and that winter favorite, tortilla soup. A children's menu includes tacos and nachos, as well as hamburgers and chicken nuggets. Open daily for lunch and dinner. A second location is at 10060 I-10 West (210-691-8827).

### CAFE OLE! $$

**521 River Walk**
**(210) 281-1292**
**www.cafeole.us**

Located one level up from pedestrian traffic, this restaurant is right on the banks of the River Walk. From the covered porch you can watch the continual conga line of sidewalk activity that parades through this stretch of the walk—all while you've got your hands wrapped around a frozen margarita or a sizzling fajita. Other Tex-Mex favorites are served here, too. Cafe Ole! is open daily for lunch and dinner.

**✻CASA RIO** **$**
**430 E. Commerce St.**
**(210) 225-6718**
**www.casa-rio.com**

For more than 60 years, this restaurant has been best known as a tourist stop catering to folks eager to try some traditional Tex-Mex right on the banks of the river. But, hey, what's wrong with being popular with the tourist trade? Sure, your fellow diners may say "jal-a-peeno" instead of "hal-a-pen-yo" or (shudder) "fa-ji-tas" instead of "fa-hee-tas," but even diners brand-new to Tex-Mex soon learn what tastes good. There's a real reason behind Casa Rio's long-running popularity—the food. The green enchiladas with chicken and cheese are especially tasty, both served with sides of good ol' cholesterol-laden beans, rice, chips, and tortillas.

The choicest tables at Casa Rio are at riverside, and you may have to wait awhile for one of these seats. It's worth the wait. With tables right on the edge of the river (many of the River Walk restaurants are located about 10 feet from the water's edge), you'll have an unbeatable view of the action up and down the river. This restaurant dates back to 1946, when it was built by Alfred F. Beyer on land first granted title in 1777 by the King of Spain. A hacienda was built here during the city's Spanish colonial period, and today it remains the core of the restaurant; cedar doors, cedar window lintels, a fireplace, and thick limestone walls are evidence of that early dwelling.

This restaurant was the first business in San Antonio to take advantage of its setting on the River Walk. The owner used canoes, gondolas, and paddleboats, which eventually evolved into tours and dinner boats, San Antonio's first river cruises.

Even the menu is historic. The Regular Plate—a combo that includes a cheese enchilada, tamale, chili con carne, rice, and beans—was introduced in San Antonio in the 1800s and has been appearing on Casa Rio's menu since 1946. Today it's joined by the Deluxe Dinner, which adds a crispy beef taco and guacamole to the mix. Lighter eaters might prefer the El Rio, a plate with one cheese enchilada, one taco, guacamole, chili con carne, rice, and beans. On cooler days,tortilla soup, a combination of poblano peppers, corn, tomatoes, and chicken, is a flavorful choice. Any time of year, the Casarita, a 20-ounce margarita, is a popular drink. Casa Rio is open for lunch and dinner daily.

**EL MIRADOR** **$–$$**
**722 S. St. Mary's St.**
**(210) 225-9444**
**www.elmiradorrestaurant.com**

A local favorite, El Mirador may be best known for its soup—especially the tortilla soup and the *sopa Azteca*—but the other entrees are tasty in their own right. El Mirador is located a stone's throw from downtown in a terra-cotta–hued stucco building. On the inside, Saltillo tiles cover the floor, and a few art prints and painted Mexican plates hang on the brightly colored walls. A covered patio outside provides more space and is a pleasant place to eat in mild weather. The restaurant serves 3 meals a day, offering the Mexican standards (enchilada plates, etc.) as well as more sophisticated dishes such as filet poblano or *lomo de puerco,* especially at dinnertime. A recently added lounge pours margaritas and other libations with a happy hour from 5 to 6:30 p.m. daily. Dress is casual. El Mirador opens daily at 6:30 a.m.

**JACALA MEXICAN RESTAURANT** **$**
**606 West Ave.**
**(210) 732-5222**
**http://jacala.com**

This restaurant, located on the north side of San Antonio about 12 minutes from downtown, holds the distinction of being the oldest originally owned Mexican restaurant in San Antonio. Since 1949 the Quinones family has owned and operated this popular eatery.

The restaurant offers a weekday lunch special that includes an enchilada, a taco, rice, beans, and iced tea. Although the enchiladas and tacos are local favorites, the restaurant is also known for its *caldo* (chicken soup) as well as its *menudo* (tripe soup) and tortilla soup. Other options include chile rellenos, chicken molé, chalupas, tamales, and more. You can dine indoors or outside in the courtyard. If you want to take a taste of San Antonio home with you, purchase a jar of Jacala's salsas or its jalapeño jelly (ask the staff how to use the jelly). The restaurant is open daily for lunch and dinner, and meals are also available to go.

**LA MARGARITA MEXICAN RESTAURANT AND OYSTER BAR** **$–$$**
**120 Produce Row**
**(210) 227-7140**
**www.lamargarita.com**

Just around the corner from Mi Tierra (see below) is its sister restaurant, La Margarita. This place was established to accommodate the huge overflow of Mi Tierra customers, but today it draws a regular clientele of its own. Styled like a New Orleans restaurant with outdoor patios, the often-noisy eatery has a definite Mexican feel, thanks not only to the food but also to wandering mariachi musicians. Gulf oysters are served 3 ways: cocktail-style with shrimp, baked with Jack cheese, and on the half-shell. Fajitas are another specialty of the house, and they're served with spicy pico de gallo, a mixture of chopped onions, cilantro, and peppers strong enough to wake up any palate. If you choose alfresco dining, you can enjoy watching shoppers stroll among the many specialty shops and vendor carts. The restaurant is open for lunch and dinner daily.

**LOS BARRIOS** **$$**
**4223 Blanco Rd.**
**(210) 732-6071**
**www.losbarrios1.com**

If you fall in love with the food at Los Barrios, you're in luck! That's because you can purchase the *Los Barrios Family Cookbook* to replicate many—but not all—of the recipes at home. The food at this San Antonio favorite is cooked *casero* style (homemade), whether the dish is a Tex-Mex or interior Mexico recipe. One of the most popular dishes is a classic enchilada assortment featuring 3 types of enchiladas. Open from 10 a.m. to 11 p.m. Mon through Sat and from 9 a.m. to 11 p.m. Sun, Los Barrios attracts a clientele from across the city. This establishment, located in a hacienda-style building, is fairly large, so reservations are unnecessary except for large groups.

## Close-up

### A Tex-Mex Primer

Here are some traditional Tex-Mex dishes that you're sure to see on San Antonio restaurant menus.

***Botanas***—Appetizers.
***Buñuelos***—Cinnamon crisps served as a dessert.
***Cabrito***—Young, tender goat.
***Cerveza***—Beer.
**Chalupa**—Fried, flat corn tortilla spread with refried beans and topped with meat, lettuce, tomatoes, and cheese; an open-faced taco.
***Chicarrones***—Fried pork cracklings.
**Chile rellenos**—Stuffed peppers.
**Chorizo**—Spicy pork sausage.
**Enchilada**—Corn or flour tortilla wrapped around a filling and covered with a hot or mild sauce; varieties include beef, chicken, cheese, sour cream, and shrimp.
**Fajita** (pronounced fa-hee-ta)—Grilled skirt steak strips, wrapped in a flour tortilla and usually served still sizzling on a metal platter with condiments (pico de gallo, sour cream, cheese) on the side.
**Flan**—Baked, sweetened custard.
**Flauta**—Corn tortilla wrapped around beef, chicken, or pork and fried until crispy; may be an appetizer or an entree.
***Frijoles refritos***—Refried beans.
**Guacamole**—Avocado dip spiced with chopped onions, peppers, and herbs.
**Huevos rancheros**—Ranch-style eggs, spicy and made with tomatoes and chiles.
***Leche quemada***—A pecan praline made with burnt sugar; the number one dessert in Tex-Mex restaurants.
**Margarita**—Popular tequila and lime drink, served in a salted glass either over ice or frozen.
***Menudo***—Soup made from tripe.
***Migas***—Eggs scrambled with torn strips of corn tortillas.
***Molé*** (pronounced mole-ay)—A sauce made with nuts, spices, and unsweetened chocolate; served over chicken enchiladas.
**Picante sauce**—Red sauce made from tomatoes, peppers, and onions and used as a dip for tortilla chips; ranges from mild to very hot.
**Pico de gallo**—Hot sauce made of tomatoes, chopped onions, peppers, and cilantro.
**Quesadilla** (pronounced kay-sa-dee-ya)—Tortilla covered with cheese and baked.
**Salsa verde**—Green sauce made with tomatillos, green chiles, garlic, and cilantro; used as a dip or on enchiladas.
**Sopapilla**—Fried pastry dessert served with honey.
**Tamale**—Corn dough filled with chopped pork, rolled in a corn husk, and steamed; served with or without chile sauce.
**Tomatillo**—A small, green, tomato-like fruit used in Mexican cooking.
**Tortilla** (pronounced tor-tee-ya)—Flat breadlike disc made of flour or corn; used to make many main dishes, and also served as an accompaniment to the meal, with or without butter.
**Tostada**—Fried tortilla.

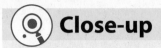

**✻MI TIERRA CAFE AND BAKERY $**
**218 Produce Row**
**(210) 225-1262**
**www.mitierracafe.com**

This restaurant never sleeps. This San Antonio institution serves up some of the city's best Tex-Mex fare 24 hours a day, 365 days a year. No matter when you visit, Mi Tierra is packed with locals and visitors. They crowd into the festive eatery, into booths garnished year-round with Christmas decorations, to enjoy Tex-Mex specialties.

Breakfast is a busy time, and locals start their day here with huevos rancheros, *chiliquiles* (scrambled eggs mixed with cheese, onions, and strips of corn tortillas, served with refried beans), or breakfast tacos. All feature the best tortillas in San Antonio. For lunch and dinner, Tex-Mex delights include enchiladas, *carne asada* (grilled beef prepared with an olive oil and garlic rub), and quesadillas. Strolling mariachis take requests for Mexican ballads and give the restaurant a truly authentic air. Just as authentic is the adjacent *panadería,* a Mexican bakery exuding its own tasty aromas: fresh tortillas and *polvorones,* cookies topped with cinnamon and sugar. Mi Tierra is open 24 hours daily.

**ROSARIO'S CAFE Y CANTINA $–$$**
**910 S. Alamo St.**
**(210) 223-1806**
**www.rosariossa.com**

This cafe and cantina is popular with the arts community in King William, but it's also known for its specialties: tortilla soup, enchiladas de molé, chile rellenos, and carne de puerco cascabel (pork tips in red chile sauce). Decorated with original art and lots of terra-cotta pots, this funky restaurant offers live music on the weekends. It's open for lunch and dinner seven days a week.

**TOMATILLOS CAFE Y CANTINA $–$$**
**3210 Broadway**
**(210) 824-3005**
**www.tomatillos.com**

This casual and family-friendly restaurant serves up grande proportions of Tex-Mex favorites. Start with quesadillas, marinated beef fajita taquitos, or nachos topped with beef or chicken fajita strips. The restaurant has several specialties, including the puffy taco (like the name says, puffed tortillas filled with spicy beef or chicken). An original dish is Tomatillos's Mexican-style spare ribs marinated in tequila, cilantro, citrus, and jalapeño. This restaurant is open daily for lunch and dinner.

# NIGHTLIFE

From clubs where you can wear your boots and learn to line dance to places where you can sip a martini in a quiet corner and enjoy the smooth sounds of a jazz ensemble, San Antonio has a varied nightlife scene. This chapter covers the highlights, including some of the city's best nightspots and some of our personal favorites. Although not every nightclub in San Antonio is listed, it is a pretty good start.

There are a few things you should know before venturing out into the night in San Antonio. Some places, especially those that offer live music, have a cover charge. This is only the fee for getting through the door—drinks or meals are not included. Cover charges can vary greatly from place to place, but the typical cover runs from $3 to $8. If a big-name musician is playing at the club, the fee may be higher, and in some cases, tickets may need to be bought in advance.

Most San Antonio bars and clubs close at 2 a.m. on the weekends and earlier on weekdays. Every joint has its own hours, so if you're planning on hitting the town, call ahead to find out the closing times and plan your evening accordingly. Lastly, most of the places in this chapter are 21-and-over bars. The legal drinking age in Texas is 21, and minors are not even allowed in most places. If a bar or club admits those who are 18 and over, or is an all-ages spot, this information is included in the listing. In other words, if our listing doesn't mention a minimum age, assume that it is only for those 21 and older.

Unlike some Texas cities such as Austin, where liquor cannot be carried off premises, San Antonio does allow open containers of alcohol to be taken out of bars. Many sidewalk cafes along the River Walk sell margaritas, cold beer, and piña coladas to go.

## BARS

**BOMBAY BICYCLE CLUB**
**3506 N. St. Mary's St.**
**(210) 737-2411**
**http://bombaybicycleclubsa.com**

Located on the edge of Brackenridge Park, the Bombay Bicycle Club is part restaurant, part funky college singles bar. Starting with the colorful mural on the side of the building, the space is filled with collectibles and kooky junk that give it a fun and inviting feel. Students from the nearby Trinity University linger here on the weekends, as it's a lively place to grab a bite and have a few drinks with friends. The indoor bar boasts an awesome jukebox and 3 pool tables, while the restaurant has nice, park-lined outdoor seating. The club is open 11 a.m. to 2 a.m. Mon through Sat, and Sun noon to midnight, with one of the longest happy hours in town (11 a.m. to 7 p.m. daily).

## Close-up

### San Antonio Icehouses

Everyone knows what an icehouse is. It is (or was) a place to get ice, right? Not necessarily, if you are in San Antonio. Here, the term has a much more specific meaning, encompassing more than obtaining frozen water. True, San Antonio icehouses did begin as ice supply depots, back in the 1920s when the icebox, not the refrigerator, was the kitchen standard. Gradually these ice depots, usually rather rough, utilitarian structures made of tin siding, began selling not only blocks of ice but also cold watermelons, a few groceries, soft drinks, and eventually beer. Over time these icehouses became familiar places to hang out, drink a cold one, and shoot the breeze over a game of dominoes. In other words, they became part general store, part tavern, and part neighborhood community center. Now most of San Antonio's original icehouses have given way to the modern convenience store, and San Antonians find haven in other venues. The few that remain, such as Hills & Dales, have modernized and expanded to stay competitive. Newer establishments around town also have appropriated the icehouse moniker and strive to re-create that old-timey icehouse experience, modified to appeal to a modern crowd. The old and the new both deserve credit for trying to keep the San Antonio icehouse tradition alive for a new generation.

**CADILLAC BAR RESTAURANT**
**212 S. Flores St.**
**(210) 223-5533**
**www.sawhost.com/cadillac**

The restaurant part of the Cadillac Bar Restaurant serves full meals on a quaint outdoor patio, but the real attraction here is the bar and dance floor. Because of its close proximity to Bexar County Courthouse and San Antonio City Hall, you may find this place full of lawyers and city officials during the week—it's a favorite after-work spot for folks who work in those buildings. On the weekends, though, the place is hopping with local 30-somethings out for a good time. On Wednesday and Saturday nights, a DJ provides the music, but on Friday it's all live. Local groups with sounds ranging from soul to modern rock play at the Cadillac.

**COYOTE UGLY**
**409 E. Commerce St.**
**(210) 465-UGLY**
**www.coyoteuglysaloon.com**

Located near the Rivercenter Mall, this branch of the popular chain offers the same raucous service that was immortalized on the big screen in the 2000 movie named after the nationwide bars, launched in New York in 1993. It is open 7 days a week from 11 a.m. to 2 a.m. Join the Coyote Ugly girls each day from 4 to 8 p.m. for happy hour as they mix strong spirits with tabletop dancing. There is also a substantial food menu to help you keep your strength up.

***HILLS & DALES ICE HOUSE**
**15403 White Fawn Dr.**
**(210) 695-2307**

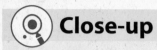

In the old days, Hills & Dales used to be an icehouse in the woods with a reputation for selling an unusual selection of beer. Even though it's off the beaten track on Loop 1604, once the University of Texas at San Antonio moved into the neighborhood, business took off, and it officially became more of a bar than a convenience store. The single-room establishment is lined with long picnic tables and still has a huge selection of beer with more than 80 varieties ranging from Abita to Shiner. Suck down a few over a game of pool while tapping toes to the latest hits on the jukebox.

**LIBERTY BAR AT THE CONVENT**
**1111 S. Alamo St.**
**(210) 227-1187**
**www.liberty-bar.com**

For years the Liberty Bar resided in an off-kilter frame building north of downtown (a site now occupied by Boehler's Bar & Grille). Now located in another historic structure, a former home for Benedictine Sisters dating from 1883, the bar operates as the Liberty Bar at the Convent. It still attracts a young-ish, hip clientele attracted by its upscale restaurant as well as by its libations. It's still a civilized place to have a few drinks and enjoy conversation without being bothered by loud music. If you stop in, be sure to order up some of their fresh-baked bread and olive oil. Open 7 days a week.

**✳THE MENGER BAR**
**204 Alamo Plaza**
**(210) 223-4361**
**www.mengerhotel.com**

The historic bar at the Menger Hotel has witnessed many famous figures who have stayed here while visiting the Alamo City. Based on the design of the House of Lords Pub in London, this softly lit retreat pours your favorite cocktail as well as ales and beers. In 1898, then-Colonel Teddy Roosevelt enlisted some of his Rough Riders in this very bar before leading them into battle during the Spanish-American War. The cherrywood ceilings and decorative glass cabinets provide an elegant atmosphere, perfect for socializing with friends.

**MIX NIGHT CLUB**
**2423 N. St. Mary's St.**
**(210) 735-1313**

This is definitely a place for a younger bunch, or for older folks who don't mind mixing with the pierced and tattooed crowd. That's not to say that the Mix isn't a fun place to be. The loud music and pool tables keep the fans coming, especially those who attend the nearby San Antonio College. Cheap drinks are probably the main appeal of the bar, but whatever it is, it works. The Mix is nearly always packed, especially on the weekends.

**PAT O'BRIEN'S SAN ANTONIO**
**121 Alamo Plaza**
**(210) 220-1076**
**www.patobriens.com**

A franchised replica of the New Orleans original, the home of the rum Hurricane, has made its mark on San Antonio's night-life. Just like the original, there is a lush patio with a flaming fountain for folks to enjoy the evening air and some authentic Big Easy specialties, such as muffaletta sandwiches and bowls of jambalaya. Downstairs there is a swinging piano bar for sing-along types, and the upstairs main bar makes for a memorable place to order specialty drinks such as the mint julep or the Cyclone. Later in the evenings the main bar pumps out DJ-powered music for your dancing pleasure.

**REBAR**
**8134 Broadway**
**(210) 320-4091**
**www.rebarsatx.com**
One of the hippest places in town, Rebar is the place for the young and stylish. Located in the upscale neighborhood of Alamo Heights, Rebar is host to live music every night and has a TV bar inside and an outdoor seating area out back. San Antonio's 20-something set lines up to get in here on Saturday nights, though every night seems to be happening at this neighborhood favorite.

**RIVERWALK BAR**
**1015 Navarro St.**
**(210) 222-2008**
**www.havanasanantonio.com**
If you're looking for a spot with a little romance, try the cozy bar at the Hotel Havana. Located in one of San Antonio's hippest hotels, it's a nice respite from the typical hotel atmosphere. Located in the hotel's basement, this Latin-themed lounge features premium rums and mescal along with mojitos, margaritas, Cuban coffee, and desserts. It's also a great place for wine, fabulous finger food, and intimate conversation. The decor suggests another time, and the music sets the stage for love, but mind the price tag. Those on a cheap date should look elsewhere.

**SWIG**
**111 W. Crockett St., #205**
**(210) 476-0005**
**www.swigmartini.com**
Though the clientele is mostly in their 20s, Swig is more upscale than some of its River Walk neighbors. A "1940s-style contemporary bar," Swig specializes in martinis and live jazz 6 nights a week for the more sophisticated of the younger set. Outdoor seating on the river is complemented by a nice menu of fine draft beers and a medley of cocktails and spirits, from the Swig Martini to scotch whiskey. Sit back, have a cognac, smoke a cigar, and enjoy the atmosphere while rubbing shoulders with some of San Antonio's hippest trendsetters.

**ZINC CHAMPAGNE & WINE BAR**
**207 N. Presa St.**
**(210) 224-2900**
**http://zincwine.com**
This is not a place to go if you're pinching pennies, but if you want to experience a real upscale bar in San Antonio, this is your spot. The drink list here isn't limited to wine and champagne, but they are the most popular choices. A metal bar area gives the place a modern look and feel. A small menu of snacks offers escargot, pâté, and the like. There are televisions in the bar, but an adjoining room provides a TV-free environment.

## BREWPUBS

***BLUE STAR BREWING COMPANY RESTAURANT & BAR**
**1414 S. Alamo St. at the Blue Star Arts Complex**
**(210) 212-5506**
**www.bluestarbrewing.com**
Toward the back of the Blue Star Arts Complex sits the funky building that houses Blue Star Brewing Company. This is a real brewpub that makes its own beer—to the delight of patrons. It's a very popular place and draws an eclectic crowd. Students from the University of Texas at San Antonio and customers of the adjoining arts complex all

come here to have a good meal and an even better beer. Blue Star Brewing Company is a great place to spend a Saturday night, and you can make an evening of it by visiting the mixture of art galleries and shops in the rest of the complex.

### FREETAIL BREWING COMPANY
**4035 N. Loop 1604 West**
**(210) 395-4974**
**www.freetailbrewing.com**

Located on Loop 1604 West, this new brewpub takes its name from the Mexican freetail bat, "the official Texas flying mammal." It pumps out a huge array of craft brews to go with a food menu offering artisan pizzas, sandwiches, salads, appetizers, and desserts. Its signature brew, Freetail Ale, is a copper-hued draught balancing caramel overtones with a bitter finish. You can sample the wares, which vary by season, or try beers produced by other Texas microbreweries in the taproom or out on the large outdoor patio. Freetail offers free tours of its brewery each Saturday at noon. Happy hour is held Mon through Fri, 3 p.m. to 7 p.m., and Tues evening is Pint Night.

## COMEDY CLUBS

### LAUGH OUT LOUD COMEDY CLUB
**618 NW Loop 410, Suite 312**
**(210) 541-8805**
**www.lolsanantonio.com**

Located near San Antonio International Airport on Loop 410, LOL is the kid brother of Rivercenter Comedy Club and offers a similar comedy experience. It features a full bar with silly-named drinks, such as the Fifty-Seven Chevy and the Alien Secretion, as well as a restaurant serving burgers, salads, and steak entrees. Unlike Rivercenter, LOL is a totally smoke-free venue. The club is dark most Mondays, while Tuesday features free open mic shows at 8 p.m. Showtimes are 8 p.m. Wed and Thurs, 8 and 10:15 p.m. Fri and Sat (with an occasional midnight show), and 8 p.m. Sun. Regular show prices are $15. And like its big-brother club, LOL has a 2-item minimum per person. As they say, "You have to buy something!"

### THE RIVERCENTER COMEDY CLUB
**849 E. Commerce St. at Rivercenter Mall**
**(210) 229-1420**
**www.rivercentercomedyclub.com**

On the top floor of the Rivercenter Mall, this club is the best place in town for live comedy and is one of the hottest tickets on the River Walk. A-list performers featured on HBO, Showtime, *The Tonight Show with Jay Leno*, and *The David Letterman Show* come here to show off their funny bones; headliners have included A. Whitney Brown, Carlos Mencia, and Rodney Carrington. Showtimes are usually at 8:30 p.m. Sun through Thurs, 8:30 and 10:30 p.m. Fri, and Sat at 8:30 and 10:30 p.m., with Midnight Madness at 12:30 a.m. The box office is at the top of the escalators in the mall. Make sure to call ahead to confirm times, performers, and prices, because they can change. The club also serves up great munchies and a good variety of dinner choices.

Along with featuring headliners, the club hosts several regular shows. The Oxymorons perform every Tuesday, rising regional comics star in the Comedy All-Stars show at 8:30 p.m. most Mondays, and an adult-oriented late-night revue, After Midnight Madness, is scheduled for Saturday nights starting about 12:30 a.m. and running until 2 a.m.

Reservations for all shows are suggested; call the number above. Ticket prices are $15 for most acts.

## CONCERTS

### AT&T CENTER

**1 AT&T Center Pkwy.**
**(210) 444-5000**
**www.attcenter.com**

Not just the home of the Spurs and the San Antonio Stock Show and Rodeo, the AT&T Center is also the place to see big-ticket stadium acts like Lady Gaga, Justin Timberlake, Dixie Chicks, and Christina Aguilera, as well as old favorites such as the Rolling Stones, Placido Domingo, and George Strait. Whatever hot act is on a national tour, they are sure to swing by for a gig. Ticket and parking prices vary, so check the website for prices and advance purchasing options. The stadium features premium seating for that extra-special someone if you have money to burn, as well as wheelchair-accessible seating.

### THE ALAMODOME

**100 Montana St.**
**(210) 207-3663**
**www.alamodome.com**

The Alamodome's striking facade, with its cable-suspension roof, has become as much a part of the San Antonio skyline as the Tower of the Americas. It's probably best known as the one-time home court for the San Antonio Spurs and the site of the Valero Alamo Bowl, a major NCAA football game held annually near New Year's Day. In recent years the Dallas Cowboys have held their training camp here as well. The facility is much more than a sporting venue, however. Built with flexibility in mind, it accommodates various conventions, conferences, and trade shows and has hosted a variety of entertainment events, such as the Ringling Brothers and Barnum & Bailey Circus, Disney on Ice, and concerts, such as one by country music superstar George Strait in 2010 that set an attendance record, drawing over 55,000 fans.

## COUNTRY & WESTERN CLUBS

### MIDNIGHT RODEO

**12260 Nacogdoches Rd.**
**(210) 655-0040**
**www.midnightrodeosanantonio.com**

You saw all the movies before you came to San Antonio, and now you're wondering: Where are all the cowboys? They're here. So dust off the boots and break out the Stetson—at Midnight Rodeo, you can learn the latest line dances and sip a beer by the jukebox that blares country music nonstop. Dinner is served at a small buffet, but the main attraction is the bar, especially on Wednesday, when all drinks are $1.50. There's live music on the weekends. Open Wed through Sun from 7 p.m. to 2 a.m., except on Friday, when doors open 2 hours earlier.

## DANCE CLUBS

### BONHAM EXCHANGE

**411 Bonham St.**
**(210) 271-3811**
**www.bonhamexchange.net**

Housed in a building that during World War II was the USO, today the Bonham Exchange is one of San Antonio's hottest 18-and-over nightspots. Popular with the gay crowd, this isn't just a club; it's a dance experience. Five bars and 3 dance floors let patrons get loose and boogie, with theme nights like "Saturday Night Live," and go-go boys. Sometimes the place doesn't get hopping until past midnight, so don't be in a rush to get there. This is a great spot that shouldn't be missed by anyone who enjoys the dance club scene.

**ACAPULCO SAM'S**
**212 College St.**
**(210) 220-1972**
**www.acapulcosamssa.com**

You can take your pick at Acapulco Sam's, a two-story dance club located on the River Walk: Downstairs the Latin-themed Ultra Lounge pulses out DJ-powered dance hits, fusion, and clean hip-hop while go-go dancers strut their stuff. Upstairs it's always spring break at Sam's Beach Club, as you relax with a mojito or margarita while lounging on a beach chair in a cabana. Either way, you'll find a fun atmosphere. Bar dancing is de rigueur here, especially on one of the frequent special theme nights, such as Retro '80s Night each Friday, Bikini Nights, or Pajama Parties, or during holidays such as Halloween and New Year's Eve, and during Fiesta. Acapulco Sam's also offers VIP seating near the dance floor, a cigar bar, and an extensive beer list.

**THE SAINT**
**1430 N. Main Ave.**
**(210) 225-7330**
**www.thesaint-satx.com**

If your idea of a good time involves drag shows and dancing iron men in Speedos, then The Saint is the perfect place for you. Mostly attracting men in their 20s (some in drag, some not), this club always provides a good time. The decor here is all about fun. The walls are painted with depictions of angels and fairies (perhaps not the kind for children's eyes), and balloons hang from the ceiling, giving the whole place a New Year's party feeling. Tuesday nights bring the Amateur Drag Show, and there are male dancers on Wednesday and Saturday nights. There is no cover at The Saint before 11 p.m.

## LIVE MUSIC

**JOHN T. FLOORE'S COUNTRY STORE**
**14492 Old Bandera Rd., Helotes**
**(210) 695-8827**
**www.liveatfloores.com**

Serving up country music for more than 60 years, John T. Floore's Country Store is one of the last true Texas honky-tonks. The list of performers who have graced its stage is long and prestigious: Willie Nelson, Patsy Cline, Hank Williams, Elvis Presley, Bob Dylan, and Merle Haggard, to name just a few. The inside is decorated with autographed photos, Christmas lights, antique memorabilia, and all the original oak fixtures, while outside are the dance floor and stage where most concerts happen. A dance hall and cafe, Floore's serves up great barbecue that you can eat outside at picnic tables while you enjoy the show.

**i** More than a mere dance hall, Club Rio, located at 13307-A San Pedro Ave., frequently hosts concerts by Top 40 Latin pop, rock, and hip-hop entertainers. Past performers have included Alejandra Guzman, La Ley, Ivy Queen, and Juanes. To find out which award-winning acts are scheduled to play, visit the event calendar at www.club-rio.net or call (210) 403-2582.

***GRUENE HALL**
**1281 Gruene Rd., New Braunfels**
**(830) 606-1281**
**www.gruenehall.com**

North of San Antonio, on the north side of New Braunfels in a former ghost town called Gruene, a 46-star US flag hangs over a steamy dance hall. Advertisements from the 1930s decorate the walls, and the only air-conditioning is a breeze through the wide front door. Burlap bags, suspended from the ceiling, dampen the sounds of shuffling feet and country and western bands.

Although it may sound like another Hollywood version of small-town life in Texas, this is Gruene Hall, the oldest dance hall in the Lone Star State. Since 1878 this joint has shook to the sounds of Texas music—from gutbucket country to folk to blues. Over the years the dance and music styles may have changed, but Gruene Hall, like a good pair of boots, is as dependable as ever. The place has rocked to all sorts of music performed by a variety of both locally and nationally known artists, including Guy Clark, the Fabulous Thunderbirds, Joe Ely, Nanci Griffith, Jimmy Gilmore, John Hiatt, Tish Hinojosa, Townes Van Zandt, and many more.

The dance hall is also home to one of Texas's most unique events: Gospel Brunch with a Texas Twist in Gruene Hall. Like a New Orleans–style gospel brunch, this special event fills the historic hall with the sounds of gospel, served up with an expansive buffet. The brunch is scheduled for the second Sunday of the month throughout the year. During the holiday season, there are also special performances featuring traditional, cowboy, and Christmas gospel tunes. Dress is as casual or as nice as you'd like it to be.

All ages are welcomed at the dance hall. Tickets for concerts and special events can be purchased by phone, online, or at the dance hall. Ticket prices vary by performer. Seating is at large tables for parties of 12.

**i** **Bar and dance club visitors under age 21 may be branded with a permanent-marker "X" on their hand, signifying that they may not purchase alcohol. Other clubs will not allow entry by anyone below the legal drinking age.**

**JIM CULLUM'S LANDING**
**123 Losoya St.**
**(210) 223-7266**
**www.landing.com**

Established in 1963, Jim Cullum's Landing is the place to be for jazz on the River Walk. Located at the Hyatt Regency, this is a casual and fun spot to have a drink and hear some great music by the Jim Cullum Jazz Band. Bandleader Jim Cullum and his crew are well known in San Antonio, delighting crowds with jazz primarily from the World War II era. The sounds of Jelly Roll Morton, Louis Armstrong, and other jazz greats often fill the air of the Paseo del Rio. Band members play vintage instruments in keeping with their historic sound; Cullum plays a 1927 Conn Victor model cornet.

Each circular table here is made to look like a classic LP, and hanging from the umbrellas atop the tables are trumpets, saxophones, and other instruments.

If you enjoy the sounds of The Landing and want to hear more, tune in to Riverwalk Jazz, a weekly radio series cohosted by Cullum. Since 1988 the series has been bringing the sound of jazz across the country via Public Radio International. The show is heard on more than 150 US radio stations; for a list of the stations, see www.riverwalkjazz.org. Cullum and his crew have also appeared on the big screen in *Still Breathing,* a 1996 film in which they play themselves. Their music can also be heard on the soundtrack of *The Newton Boys,* a 1997 movie shot in San Antonio and Austin. Live jazz music is featured every night of the week at The Landing, which is also open for lunch and dinner serving Tex-Mex fare; wines, liquors, beers, and coffee drinks are available at the bar. The Landing also offers special jazz cruises on the river for a minimum of 15 people.

**SALUTE INTERNATIONAL BAR**
**2801 N. St. Mary's St.**
**(210) 732-5307**
Any kind of live music you could imagine can be heard at Salute International Bar. Local and regional bands play everything from heavy metal to blues to alternative rock at this dive. It's a local favorite, so be prepared for big crowds packed into a very small space, especially on Thursday. The cheerfully painted walls invite patrons to relax and enjoy the show. The club is only open Thurs through Sat nights from 8 p.m. until 2 a.m.

***SAN ANTONE CAFE**
**1150 S. Alamo St.**
**(210) 271-7791**
**www.casbeers.com**
A local institution (as Casbeers, then as Casbeers at the Church) since the 1930s, this establishment now has a new address and a modified name to boot, but it's still a San Antonio music must-see. From a stage in a former Methodist church south of downtown, it hosts some of the most popular local and regional bands, playing music ranging from rock to bluegrass. The food is almost as legendary as the music. Heaping portions of enchiladas, burgers, and chili are available Tuesday through Saturday, though one Sunday a month the place opens up for the famous Gospel Brunch, where for the small price of $12 you are treated to an unlimited buffet and a gospel set.

**WHITE RABBIT**
**2410 N. St. Mary's St.**
**(210) 737-2221**
**www.sawhiterabbit.com**
Appealing mostly to the younger crowd, this is a great place to hear live music, if you prefer hard rock and the like. This all-ages club attracts touring and local bands that love to play loud and fast. Try to show up early, because the place can get crowded and seats are scarce. Despite the packed room, the sound system here is hard to beat, though you may lose your hearing from the volume. Call ahead to find out who is playing if you don't want to get stuck listening to some local teenagers pound out hard-rock riffs.

## MOVIE THEATERS

Catching a movie in San Antonio is a nice way to beat the summer heat or cozy up on those long winter nights. The Alamo City boasts numerous movie theaters, most of which show first-run films. There are four major chains in the city: AMC, Cinemark, Regal, and Santikos (including a handful of specialty and discount theaters). Ticket prices may vary, but first-run shows will be around $5 for matinee shows (movies before 6 p.m.) and $8 for evening shows. There are discounts for children, students, and seniors at most locations. The numbers in the movie theater names indicate the number of screens.

### AMC Theaters

There are two AMC Theater locations in San Antonio, each offering stadium-style seating and high-tech sound systems. Tickets are available at the box office, by phone, or online at www.moviewatcher.com.

**AMC HUEBNER OAKS 24**
**11075 I-10 West at Huebner Oaks Shopping Center**
**(210) 558-3490**

**AMC RIVERCENTER 9**
**849 E. Commerce St. at Rivercenter Mall**
**(210) 228-0351**

## Cinemark Theaters

There are two Cinemark Theaters in San Antonio, one specializing in second-run movies at a discounted price. Movies are only $1 for the first matinee of the day. Later matinee prices (til 6 p.m.) are $1.50; evening shows cost $1.75, except on Friday and Saturday, when they're $2.25. The McCreless Market location shows first-run movies at regular prices.

Call ahead or check www.cinemark.com for movies and times.

**CINEMARK DOLLAR MOVIES 16**
**5063 NW Loop 410**
**(210) 523-1294**

**CINEMARK MCCRELESS MARKET**
**4224 S. New Braunfels St.**
**(210) 532-4459**

## Regal Cinemas

All Regal Cinemas offer stadium seating, and the Fiesta 16 specializes in mainstream as well as art-house fare. Tickets are available at the box office, by phone, or online at www.fandango.com.

**REGAL ALAMO QUARRY STADIUM 16**
**255 E. Basse Rd.**
**(210) 804-1115**

**REGAL CIELO VISTA STADIUM 18**
**2828 Cinema Ridge**
**(210) 680-1125**

**REGAL FIESTA 16 STADIUM THEATRE**
**12631 Vance Jackson Rd.**
**(210) 641-6906**

**REGAL LIVE OAK STADIUM 18**
**7901 Pat Booker Rd.**
**(210) 657-4480**

**REGAL NORTHWOODS STADIUM 14**
**17640 Henderson Pass**
**(210) 402-6839**

## *Santikos Theaters

All theaters offer stadium seating, and tickets are available at the box office, by phone, or online at www.santikos.com.

**SANTIKOS EMBASSY 14**
**13707 Embassy Rd.**
**(210) 496-4957**

**SANTIKOS MAYAN PALACE 14**
**1918 SW Military Dr.**
**(210) 923-5531**

**SANTIKOS NORTHWEST 14**
**7600 I-10 West**
**(210) 349-6514**

**SANTIKOS THE RIALTO**
**2938 NE Loop 410**
**(210) 967-7648**

**SANTIKOS SILVERADO 16**
**11505 W. FM 1604 North at Bandera Road**
**(210) 695-5279**

## Special Movie Theaters

You can always see a movie at home, so why do it on vacation? San Antonio has three unique theaters that you can't find anywhere else.

**SANTIKOS BIJOU CINEMA BISTRO**
**4522 Fredericksburg Rd.**
**(210) 734-4552**
**www.santikos.com/bijouex.php**

Also a member of the Santikos Theater family, San Antonio's only art-house theater specializes in independent, classic, and foreign films. Playing on the theme of dinner and a movie, the theater also has a full-service cafe, and beer and wine are served and can be enjoyed during the film. The menu includes sandwiches, gourmet pizza, hors d'oeuvres, coffee, and desserts. The Bijou offers a unique moviegoing experience for folks who want to leave the kids at home and enjoy a civilized evening out. Tickets for this 6-screen theater are $7 before 6 p.m. and $9 after 6 p.m. and are available at the box office, by phone, or online at www.santikos.com.

## San Antonio on the Big Screen

Since the first flickering images were shown on the big screen, the beauty of the Alamo City has captivated moviegoers. Here are just a handful of Hollywood hits filmed, at least in part, in San Antonio:

*Ace Ventura: When Nature Calls* (1995)

*All The Pretty Horses* (2000)

*The Big Parade* (1925)

*Miss Congeniality* (2000)

*Selena* (1997)

*Spy Kids* (2001)

**SANTIKOS PALLADIUM THEATER**
**17703 I-10 West**
**(210) 798-9949**
**www.santikos.com**

San Antonio's second IMAX theater, this Greek-inspired gathering place offers a movie experience with a touch of elegance. Adults can enjoy a glass of wine or beer along with a meal at the Agora Bar or sip an espresso from Starbucks while adolescents test their skills on the latest arcade games before the lights go down in the 19 stadium-seat auditoriums.

**✳SAN ANTONIO IMAX ALAMO THEATRE AT RIVERCENTER MALL**
**849 E. Commerce St. in Rivercenter Mall**
**(210) 247-4629**
**www.imax-sa.com**

This 6-story theater is home to *Alamo: The Price of Freedom,* one of the best accounts on film of the fateful battle for Texas independence. This film, which premiered in 1988, never ceases to please moviegoers. The theater also shows 2- and 3-D IMAX features, which usually run about one hour. Occasionally, the theater shows first-run films that are particularly thrilling and thus well suited to the extra-big screen (for example, *Pirates of the Caribbean: On Stranger Tides* and *Tron: Legacy*).

## PIANO BARS

**HOWL AT THE MOON**
**111 W. Crockett St.**
**(210) 212-4770**
**www.howlatthemoon.com**

Probably the most popular piano bar on the River Walk, Howl at the Moon is a San Antonio institution. Two bars serve patrons while a pianist plays old favorites and invites the audience to sing along. The piano players take requests, for an extra "tip." Musicians at Howl at the Moon have been known to drag unsuspecting patrons to the piano, creating a slightly embarrassing situation, but it's all in good fun. Even if piano bars aren't usually your cup of tea, Howl at the Moon is worth a stop just so you can see a classic one in full swing.

## PUBS

### DURTY NELLY'S IRISH PUB

**200 S. Alamo St.**
**(210) 222-1400**
**www1.hilton.com**

A major hot spot on the River Walk, Durty Nelly's features a lively pub environment as well as ice-cold beer. Located at the Hilton Palacio del Rio hotel, the floor is covered in peanut shells, and the Irish decor rules. Truly a place to kick back and have fun, there is live piano music every night (with an Irish theme) that includes requests and sing-alongs, as well as one of the best beer selections in town. Locals and tourists alike flock here to soak in the authentic Irish flavor. Open Mon through Sat 11:30 a.m. to 2 a.m., and Sun noon to 2 a.m.

### THE IRISH PUB

**9726 Datapoint Rd.**
**(210) 692-7620**
**www.theirishpubsa.com**

Deemed the top live music venue by sanantonio.citysearch.com, the Irish Pub pours draft beer and domestic longnecks 7 days a week from 2 p.m. to 2 a.m. Happy hour is daily from 2 to 8 p.m. There are daily drink specials, dartboards, free Wi-Fi, and karaoke contests on Saturday nights.

### THE LION & ROSE BRITISH RESTAURANT & PUB

**5148 Broadway**
**(210) 822-7673**
**www.thelionandrose.com**

Sample the spirits of jolly old England at a faithfully reproduced pub with a menu featuring such UK standards as shepherd's pie, bangers in a blanket, and Scotch eggs. Plasma and flat-screen tellys broadcast sporting events, and patrons can test their aim during a game of darts. Additional San Antonio locations are at 842 NW Loop 410, Park North Shopping Center (210-798-4154); 700 E. Sonterra Blvd., #318 (210-798-5466); and 8211 Agora Pkwy., #112 (210-547-3000).

## SPORTS BARS

### FATSO'S SPORTS GARDEN

**1704 Bandera Rd.**
**(210) 432-0121**
**www.fatsossportsgarden.com**

Beer, food, and TVs everywhere! What more does the sports nut need? Twenty-one satellite receivers, eight 61-inch big screens, and a beach volleyball court out back make this the ultimate mecca for the San Antonio sports enthusiast. Fatso's shows all the big games in hockey, baseball, and basketball and touts itself as the "only sports bar in San Antonio to show all NFL games at one time." There's even Friday- and Saturday-night karaoke. Happy hour runs every day from 11 a.m. to 7 p.m., and indoor/outdoor seating as well as a wide menu of barbecue and burgers round out the Fatso's experience. A second San Antonio location is at 15630 Henderson Pass (210-404-0121; www.fsgnorth.com).

### O'MALLEY'S SPORTS AND SPIRITS

**8637 Fredericksburg Rd.**

**(210) 561-9665**

This no-nonsense neighborhood pub offers up a pleasant environment to watch the game while sipping a draft Shiner Bock or a thickheaded pint of "the dark stuff." A very Irish pub ripe with regulars, the drink specials differ from night to night, and you can watch the big game on 1 or all of 4 TVs, including 1 big screen. When your team is losing, you can medicate the pain with a round of darts, pool, or the ever-popular video golf.

**i** The late Selena Quintanilla Perez was known as the Queen of Tejano music. Her legacy lives on in both the movie of her life, starring Jennifer Lopez, and in her music. More than a decade after her death, hits such as "Amor Prohibido" and "Como La Flor" are still staples on Tejano radio stations and in Tejano nightclubs.

## TEJANO CLUBS

### GRAHAM CENTRAL STATION

**4902 Fredericksburg Rd.**

**(210) 979-9303**

**www.grahamcentralstationsanantonio.com**

Six nightclubs at the same venue offer music for any mood, and while club hoppers dance to hip-hop and house at Vertigo and South Beach, partiers with a preference for Cumbias, Norteno, and Tejano tunes can head to T2001 and Arriba del Norte. Tejano musical acts take the stage every Friday night. Open Wed through Sat evening until 2 a.m.

# SHOPPING

San Antonio has been a shopping destination since its founding as a Spanish outpost. Along with the missionaries, soldiers, and colonists came the traders and merchants, determined to sell their products for the best price. During the Civil War, San Antonio became a center of commerce with Mexico, a distinction it still enjoys. El Mercado on Produce Row is the largest Mexican market north of the border and has operated on the same site for more than 100 years. Although the "chili queens" no longer sell their wares from rudimentary carts in Haymarket Square and Military Plaza, you can still eat a good meal there when you are tired from shopping. Much of San Antonio's shopping now takes place in that modern marketplace, the mall, and the city has a great many from which to choose, in all parts of town. But it's not all modern glitz. Strip shopping centers and mom-and-pop establishments make up a large percentage of San Antonio retail space. A little dated, these may not be the hippest places to shop, but they are comfortable and somehow reassuring, just like the city itself.

## MALLS & SHOPPING AREAS

### ALAMO QUARRY MARKET

**255 E. Basse Rd.**
**Alamo Heights**
**(210) 824-8885**
**www.quarrymarket.com**

Alamo Quarry is definitely an upscale shopping destination. Located in the ritzy Alamo Heights area, it is built on the site of an old cement factory. In fact, the original cement plant's smokestacks still remain, lending character to the mall's steel-and-glass exterior. Inside you'll find the usual array of mall shops (Banana Republic, Old Navy, Whole Foods Market), eating establishments, and the Regal 16-Plex Cinemas. There is also a Bally's Health Club here and a Starbucks.

### CRAFTIQUES MALL

**6751 Bandera Rd.**
**(210) 523-0232, (888) 272-3847**
**http://craftiquesmall.com**

A hodgepodge of handmade items, collectibles, and antiques, there's something for everyone at these stores. Collectors can rummage for finds 7 days a week: Mon through Sat from 10 a.m. to 6 p.m. and Sun from noon to 6 p.m. A second Craftiques is at 2375 NW Military Hwy. (210-541-9960, 888-272-3847).

### THE FORUM

**8320 Agora Pkwy., Selma**
**(210) 566-7604**
**http://theforum-sa.com**

The Forum is a Texas-size outdoor mall with several major stores such as Best Buy, Target, and Home Depot. There are a number of chain eateries, too, including Chili's, Outback Steakhouse, IHOP, and Romano's Macaroni Grill. Selma is directly north of San Antonio on I-35.

**HUEBNER OAKS**
**11745 I-10 West**
**http://shophuebneroaks.com**

This is another large outdoor shopping center with several national chain stores, such as Old Navy, Eddie Bauer, Talbot's, and Banana Republic. It also has an admirable slate of restaurants, including La Madeleine and the Saltgrass Steakhouse. A 24-screen AMC movie theater shows first-run releases.

**INGRAM PARK MALL**
**6301 NW Loop 410**
**(210) 523-1228**
**www.simon.com**

Located on the city's northwest side, this mall has all the offerings one expects from a large, modern mall: large anchors (Dillard's, JCPenney, Sears), chain specialty shops (Victoria's Secret, Bealls, Gap), and restaurants such as Chick-Fil-A and Luby's Cafeteria.

***LA VILLITA**
**Historic Arts Village**
**South Alamo at Nueva or River Walk at the Arneson Theatre**
**(210) 207-8610**
**http://lavillita.com**

Though this may be a major shopping area today, La Villita has an extensive history. It was the site of some of the first houses the Spanish built after they discovered the area; the earliest were erected circa 1722. A few years later, colonists from the Canary Islands resided here. The area also marks the spot where General Cos of the Mexican Army surrendered his army in 1835 and ceded independence to the colonizing Texans, an emancipation soon revoked with a vengeance by Mexican President Santa Anna with his attack on the nearby Alamo. Eventually the historic area fell into disrepair and ruin as the town grew in other directions. It remained a slum area until 1939, when a city ordinance called for its restoration. As a result it became a center for crafts and recreation as part of the National Youth Administration Program. In 1972, 27 structures here were added to the National Register of Historic Places. Each year, La Villita is the scene of one of the city's biggest celebrations, Night in Old San Antonio. During the day, the picturesque area is filled with shoppers looking for handicrafts and artwork.

**LOS PATIOS**
**2015 NE Loop 410**
**(210) 655-6171**
**www.lospatios.com**

Los Patios is a quiet retreat in the heart of the hustle and bustle of the Loop. This 20-acre open-air mall is filled with specialty shops. The shopping area also has several indoor/outdoor restaurants. But, as excellent as its shopping is, the real charm of Los Patios lies in its setting. Located on the banks of Salado Creek, the retail area is nestled among majestic live oaks and exotic plants, making for a pleasant shopping experience—whether you buy something or not.

**i** **In December 2010, Forbes.com included San Antonio among its Top 10 cities in two lists: Best Shopping Cities in America and America's Best Cities for Young Adults.**

**NORTH STAR MALL**
**7400 San Pedro Ave. and Loop 410**
**(210) 340-6627**
**www.northstarmall.com**

Shopping is more cosmopolitan at this, the priciest mall in town. With anchor stores such as Saks Fifth Avenue, Dillard's, and Macy's, you'll find the best money can buy here. North Star Mall is easy to spot on the Loop—just look for the boots. The 40-foot-tall pair of cowboy footwear was the creation of sculptor Robert Wade.

**RIVERCENTER MALL**
**849 E. Commerce St.**
**(210) 225-0000**
**www.shoprivercenter.com**

This popular mall contains more than 125 specialty shops and big-name department stores, as well as many restaurants. The Marriott Rivercenter hotel soars from one arm of the structure. One of the most attractive shopping malls in the nation, Rivercenter has more than 1 million square feet of retail space encased in aqua-colored glass, giving shoppers a lovely view of the River Walk. Although the shopping is nice, the real attraction here is the river. A new branch of the San Antonio River was actually dug so that the river and the River Walk could be brought right into the U-shaped mall. The two sides of the mall are connected by the Bridge Market. Modeled after Italy's Ponte Vecchio in Florence, this area of the complex is filled with artisans selling their work.

Entertainment takes place throughout the day at the mall's outdoor performance island. As river taxis lazily cruise past, singers and dancers entertain shoppers and diners. On weekends, visitors can look forward to anything from lively mariachi music to singers performing rousing Texas tunes to Peruvian flute music.

i Membership in the Rivercenter Concierge Club is free to visitors from out of town, who need only show a hotel room key or out-of-town ID upon application at the mall. Members receive a free gift as well as special offers at mall shops.

**WONDERLAND OF THE AMERICAS MALL**
**Loop 410 and I-10 at Fredericksburg Road**
**(210) 785-3500**
**http://wonderlandamericas.com**

This westside property houses more than 70 shops, including major retailers such as the Burlington Coat Factory and Stein Mart. It also boasts a Bijou Cinema Bistro theater with 6 screens, with some dedicated to art and foreign films.

## ANTIQUES & FINE ART

**AVALON-RIFKIN ANTIQUES AND ESTATES**
**3601 Broadway**
**(210) 222-0265**
**www.avalon-riklin.com**

From a Lladro vase to elegant Tiffany boxes, this antiques gallery showcases items from around the globe. Family heirlooms and estate sale finds can be appraised online, for a fee.

**CHARLOTT'S ANTIQUES AND CLOCKS**
**2023 Austin Hwy.**
**(210) 653-3672**
**http://charlottsantiqueshop.blogspot.com**

This antiques shop has such a variety of items and collectibles that nearly every shopper will find something he or she likes. From fine china to pottery to jewelry, Charlott's has it all. If you'll be in San Antonio for a while, try to make a few trips to this store—they get new items in every week.

### GALERIA ORTIZ
**102 Concho St. in Market Square**
**(210) 225-0731**

This unique gallery specializes in contemporary Southwestern art by local and international artists. Folk art, silver jewelry, sculptures, paintings, gifts, and more are exhibited. Specialty items include handcrafted Southwestern jewelry—silver and gold with indigenous stone. With a focus on Southwestern art, Galeria Ortiz represents regional and nationally recognized artists such as Miguel Martinez, Alberto Saucedo, Orlando Agudelo-Botero, Robert Ytuarte, Philomene Bennett, Nivia Gonzalez, Rolando Garza, and Celina Hinujusa. Galeria Ortiz ships fine art to clients throughout the world and is a great place for finding unique decorative items, vases, and folk art as well as fine art.

### GALLERIA II
**418 Villita Building, #500, La Villita**
**(210) 227-0527**

This artists' cooperative is housed in a Victorian building that dates back to 1873. You'll see artists at work creating pottery, stained glass, and watercolor paintings.

### MARSHALL'S BROCANTE
**8507 McCullough, Suite B1**
**(210) 829-5752**
**www.marshallsbrocante.com**

Furniture from Europe and America, silver, and fine art can all be found at Marshall's Brocante. If you're looking for Western or Texas art, then this is your place, too. Louis and Beth Marshall have set up a nice store that has an amazing variety of antiques and collectibles.

### RIVER ART GROUP GALLERY
**418 Villita St., Suite 1400, La Villita**
**(210) 226-8752**
**www.riverartgroup.com**

Located next to the Little Church, the River Art Group Gallery represents over 350 artists and craftspeople. The River Art Group was founded in 1947, making it the city's oldest art group. Its members sponsor the annual River Art Show in October and another show during San Antonio's Fiesta celebration in April. The artists display their works year-round in the gallery, which is open daily. If you're looking for a watercolor of the Paseo del Rio, you'll find one here.

## BOOKSTORES

### BARNES AND NOBLE BOOKSELLERS
**11711 Bandera Rd.**
**(210) 521-9784**
**www.barnesandnoble.com**

This chain bookstore has 5 locations in San Antonio. Offering a very large selection of books and magazines, these stores are good places to find what you're looking for and curl up on a comfortable chair to read. Each also has a full-service coffee bar and a wide variety of compact discs for sale. Additional locations are at 18030 US 281 North (210-490-0411); 15900 La Centera Pkwy. (210-558-2078); 321 NW Loop 410 (210-342-0008); and 6065 NW Loop 410 (210-522-1340).

## The Alamo in Film

History buffs will find plenty of movies featuring the story of the Alamo. *The Alamo,* starring Dennis Quaid, Billy Bob Thornton, and Jason Patric was the latest (2004) cinematic rendition of the 13-day siege. Although a defeat at the box office, the movie is notable for its depiction of the numerous stages of the battle and, many say, one of the most balanced views. *Alamo: 13 Days to Glory* (1987), a production that starred James Arness and Brian Keith, was less known and featured a young Alec Baldwin. The 1988 *Alamo: The Price of Freedom* still shows at the Rivercenter IMAX; watch for Don Swayze, brother of Patrick, in the 42-minute docu-drama. The best known, however, remains the 1960 John Wayne classic *The Alamo.*

**HALF PRICE BOOKS**
**3207 Broadway**
**(210) 822-4597**
**www.halfpricebooks.com**

Half Price Books is a uniquely Texas institution that began in Dallas back in the counterculture days of 1972. Since then the stores have spread to 16 states, but the basic idea remains the same: They sell used books at (approximately) half their cover price. And they will buy almost any books you bring in, though you may not always get as much for them as you hoped. Most of the stores are located in retail storefronts that were designed for other businesses, so each Half Price store is funkily different from the others. Additional San Antonio locations are at 11654 Bandera Rd. (210-647-1103); 11255 Hoebner Rd., #208 (210-558-3247); and 125 NW Loop 410 (210-349-1429).

**L&M BOOKSTORE**
**1716 N. Main Ave.**
**(210) 222-1323**
**www.lm-bookstore.com**

This is a great spot to find college textbooks for those heading back to school. L&M has new and used textbooks, educational software for good prices, and an especially good selection of nursing texts and reference books and contractor code books. School supplies are also sold. A second location is at 15503 Babcock Rd. (210-695-8872).

**LIFEWAY CHRISTIAN STORES**
**17802 La Cantera Pkwy., Suite 115**
**(210) 694-2995**
**www.lifewaystores.com**

Christian materials such as Bibles, inspirational books, and music can all be found here. Whether it's for a gift or for yourself, if you're looking for religious gifts and products, you'll probably find something suitable here.

**MEXICAN-AMERICAN CULTURAL CENTER BOOKSTORE AND GIFT SHOP**
**3115 W. Ashby Place**
**(210) 732-2156**
**www.maccsa.org**

The Mexican-American Cultural Center Bookstore and Gift Shop has a variety of books, videos, and gifts that reflect the cultural diversity of the city of San Antonio. This is the place to buy bilingual (Spanish/English) religious materials, videos, and language-education books. The store will place special orders for customers who can't find exactly what they're looking for.

## BOUTIQUES & GIFT SHOPS

### BLESS YOUR HEART GIFT SHOP

**18771 FM 2252, at Bracken Village**
**(210) 651-1000**
**www.brackenvillagesa.com**
**www.shoppingismycardio.com**

This quaint shop has many gifts that will delight you or your friends and family. Items from Mary Engelbreit and Vera Bradley line the shelves, along with greeting cards, novelty bath products, and good-smelling candles. There is a variety of jewelry, too.

### COLLECTOR'S GALLERY

**13500 West Ave.**
**(210) 497-2525**
**www.colgal.com**

This gallery calls itself the "area's largest and finest gift shop" with good reason. The large shop has collectibles from such names as Dept. 56, Radko, M.I. Hummel, Swarovski, and David Winter. Boyds Bears, Precious Moments, Fenton Glass, Cherished Teddies, and other collectible lines also can be found here.

### THE PINK GIRAFFE

**250 E. Houston St.**
**(210) 227-8851**

The Pink Giraffe has a varied selection of collectibles and figurines, greeting cards for any occasion, many types of candy, and lots of other gifts. You can't miss this gift shop—it's on Houston Street by the famous Majestic Theatre.

## COMIC BOOKS & COLLECTIBLES

### ALIEN WORLDS

**6412 Bandera Rd.**
**(210) 826-3800**

This comic-book store has much more than just comics. Alien Worlds is a great source for role-playing games, collectible card games, action figures, and collectible cards. It also carries rare and not-so-rare Star Wars, GI Joe, Pokémon, Yu-gi-oh, and Transformers figurines. An additional San Antonio location is at 3333 Wurzbach Rd. (210-681-0701).

### COLLECTORS AUTHORITY

**1534 SE Military Drive**
**(210) 977-8818**
**www.collectorsauthority.com**

Offering over 2 decades of knowledge in the field of comic books, owner Pedro Contero Jr. can help customers find that elusive issue of *Spider-Man* or *The Incredible Hulk* or lead collectors to the latest Captain America statue or Balrog bust. Open Sun and Mon from noon to 6 p.m. and Wed through Sun from 10 a.m. to 7 p.m.

> ### Chimaeracon
>
> Video game and CCG enthusiasts gather annually at the San Pedro Village Event Center, at 9926 San Pedro Ave., for **Chimaeracon** (www.chimaeracon.com), a South Texas gaming and more festival. While teens check out the latest games and collectibles on the market at vendor booths, parents and kids can play classic board games like Monopoly or Battleship or cheer on the contestants who show off their anime-inspired wardrobe during a costume contest.

### DRAGON'S LAIR COMICS & FANTASY

**7959 Fredericksburg Rd.**
**(210) 615-1229**
**http://dlair.net**

Here you'll find a good selection of old and new comic books and collectibles as well as other toys, games, models, collectible cards, and Japanese anime. There are also game rooms available for rent. Open Mon and Tues 10 a.m. to midnight; Wed and Thurs 10 a.m. to 9 p.m.; Fri and Sat 10 a.m. to 10 p.m.; Sun noon to 6 p.m.

**HEROES AND FANTASIES**
**4945 NW Loop 410**
**(210) 340-0074**
**www.heroesandfantasies.com**
This store claims to have more than a million comic books, and once you step inside, you may not doubt it. In addition to new and used comics, Heroes and Fantasies also stocks a variety of role-playing games, card games, action figures, sports memorabilia, posters, T-shirts, gifts, and models. Collectors of Japanese anime or Pokémon, Dragonball, Star Wars, Archie, Yu-gi-oh, or Spider-Man stuff will be happy here. A second location is at 914 Pat Booker Rd. (210-945-4376).

## FLEA MARKETS

**BUSSEY'S FLEA MARKET**
**18738 I-35 North, Schertz**
**(210) 651-6830**
**http://busseysfm.com**
This flea market is located 6 miles north of San Antonio, almost to the town of New Braunfels. Situated on more than 20 acres, Bussey's has more than 500 dealer spaces. Buyers will find items here to add to their antiques collections or to begin new collections. Bussey's is open Sat and Sun only, 7 a.m. to 5 p.m.

**EISENHAUER MARKET CENTER**
**3903 Eisenhauer Rd.**
**(210) 653-7592**
**www.eisenhauermarket.com**
Eisenhauer Market Center is one of the largest indoor flea markets in America, making it a must for flea-market aficionados. A wide variety of antiques and collectibles is available. Admission to the market and parking are both free. Note that the market is closed on Monday and Tuesday.

**MISSION OPEN AIR FLEA MARKET**
**707 Moursund Blvd.**
**(210) 923-8131**
Operating for over 20 years, this market has hundreds of sellers on 45 acres of space. Whether you're looking for antiques or new merchandise, this is a worthwhile place to check out. An enormous variety of items makes this a great spot to poke and browse. Mission Open Air Flea Market is open only on Wed, Sat, and Sun, 6 a.m. to 5 p.m.

## CLOTHING

### Kids' Clothing

**BEST FRIENDS KIDS BOUTIQUE**
**923 N. Loop 1604 East**
**(210) 349-9233**
Featuring specialty clothing for boys and girls of all ages, this place is sure to have something unique for your little ones. If you're planning on visiting the store on Sunday, make sure to call first and make an appointment.

### THE CHILDREN'S PLACE
**4224 S. New Braunfels Blvd.**
**(210) 534-4102**
**Parkway**
**(210) 877-2901**
**www.childrensplace.com**

A dependable chain of 892 children's clothing stores around the US and Canada, the San Antonio locations offer attire and accessories for sizes 0–14, in a kid-friendly atmosphere. Check out their website for additional area location information.

## Men's Clothing

### CASUAL MALE XL
**7334 San Pedro Ave.**
**(210) 344-6409**
**www.casualmale.com**

As the name might suggest, Casual Male XL is a great stop if you're looking for nice clothing for a big and/or tall man. The store carries sizes 1X to 6X and XLT to 5XLT. If you need large shoes to go with your new big-guy clothes, they've got those, too. Sizes 11 to 16W are carried here in many major brand names. The staff is friendly and ready to answer your questions. Additional San Antonio locations are at 11075 I-10 West, Suite 302 (210-696-3460); 8251 Agora Pkwy., Selma (210-590-0686); and 5755 NW Loop 410, Suite 103 (210-521-8904).

### PENNER'S
**311 W. Commerce St.**
**(210) 226-2487**
**www.pennersinc.com**

Boasting the largest supply of Mexican *guayaberas* in the world, Penner's also carries a range of shoes, retro wear, Hawaiian-style shirts, accessories, and wedding apparel.

### SATEL'S
**5100 Broadway, at Alamo Heights**
**(210) 822-3376**
**www.satels.com**

Clothing with recognizable names like Oxxford, Hickey-Freeman, Tommy Bahama, and Zanella can be found at this men's store. Satel's has a wide selection of designer clothing and a knowledgeable staff to make sure you get the clothes that fit you best. They also offer custom-made clothing.

## Women's Clothing

### ADELANTE BOUTIQUE
**200 E. Grayson**
**(210) 826-6770**
**www.adelanteboutique.com**

The thatched roofs may give you the impression that you're entering an imports store, and in a way you are. Adelante Boutique features the latest trends, which are inspired by cultures all over the globe. In business in San Antonio for over 30 years, this shop provides Alamo City women with comfortable clothes that look great and don't put a big dent in their bank accounts. Women of all ages flock here in search of the latest trends, and they find them—and not just the ones that look good only on 15-year-old girls. Make sure to check out the sales rack; good deals can almost always be found.

### KATHLEEN SOMMERS RETAIL STORE
**2417 N. Main Ave.**
**(210) 732-2207**
**www.kathleensommers.com**

As the name suggests, this shop specializes in Kathleen Sommers clothing. The relaxed yet trendy nature of the Sommers line is a big hit with San Antonio women. In addition, the shop features an array of accessories:

Bath products with relaxing scents can be found throughout the store, as can purses, shoes, and books.

## IMPORTS & HANDICRAFTS

### ANGELITA

**418 Villita St., Building #300**
**La Villita**
**(210) 224-8362**

Angelita is the oldest import boutique in the city, offering a mixture of clothing and jewelry from Mexico, Guatemala, and several other Central American countries. The shop is housed in an adobe building that dates back to the mid-1800s (watch out for the low doorway!).

### CASA MANOS ALEGRES

**418 Villita St., Building #600**
**La Villita**
**(210) 224-5107**

This import gallery, located near Angelita, features Latin American folk art, from tin art to *milagros* (miracle charms) to Nativity sets.

### THE VILLAGE GALLERY

**502 Villita St.**
**La Villita**
**(210) 226-0404**

This shop specializes in handblown glass, plus stoneware and pottery, most crafted by owners Walt and Cynthia Glass.

### VILLAGE WEAVERS

**418 Villita St., Building #800**
**La Villita**
**(210) 222-0776**

Handwoven clothing, placemats, rugs, and other textile items are the specialties of the Village Weavers. This shop handles the work of artists from both San Antonio and many Latin American countries. Blankets, skirts, sweaters, and more abound in this interesting shop.

### VILLITA STAINED GLASS

**418 Villita St., Building #100**
**La Villita**
**(210) 223-4480**

Original designs in stained glass and glass ornaments are featured in this shop. Visitors are invited to watch the craftspeople at work.

## MEXICAN MERCADO

### ✱MARKET SQUARE

**514–612 W. Commerce St.**
**(210) 207-8600**
**www.sanantonio.gov/dtops/marketsquare**

One of the neatest things about shopping in San Antonio is the opportunity to buy great Mexican-made items. Although scores of small boutiques and shops throughout the city sell Mexican goods, there's one place where virtually every conceivable kind of Mexican handicraft is represented. It's the largest Mexican market in the US, known variously as El Mercado or Market Square. A few blocks from downtown, this market is where generations of San Antonians have come to buy and sell everything under the sun: vegetables and meats, hay and firewood, clothing, hammocks, chess sets, musical instruments—you name it.

Clothing, leather purses, and textiles are always best sellers at El Mercado. The traditional Mexican dress, complete with an embroidered bodice and short sleeves, starts at about $35. To make sure you're getting a high-quality garment, look for tight embroidery stitches. Men's shirts, called *guayaberas,* are found in many stores as well. These solid-color, short-sleeved shirts, decorated with pleating and stitching, are worn outside the pants.

Blankets are another popular item. Many stores sell striped ones in a variety of sizes and colors, most made from a wool blend. A 5-by-7-foot blanket typically costs $8 to $10; ponchos and hoodies sell for $12 to $17.

Piñatas are found throughout Market Square. At Mexican birthday parties, one of these colorful paper creations is filled with candy and hung from a tree. Blindfolded children take turns swinging at the piñata with a stick until someone finally breaks it and the loot spills all over the ground. Look for piñatas in the shapes of watermelons, clowns, donkeys, and even parrots.

*Cascarones,* dyed eggshells filled with paper confetti and covered with tissue paper, are sold in many stores. They're especially popular during the annual Fiesta, when children break them over the heads of their friends (or sometimes complete strangers).

## MUSIC STORES

**CD EXCHANGE**
**9861 I-10 West**
**(210) 641-1600**
At any of the many CD Exchange locations, you'll find a good selection of music for good prices. Mostly used CDs are sold, but they tend to be in very good condition. If you've got some old albums that you'd like to get off your hands, bring them down and they'll pay you for them.

**FLIP SIDE RECORD PARLOR**
**1445 SW Military Dr.**
**(210) 923-7811**
Flip Side is a one-stop record shop. In addition to a wide selection of domestic and imported albums in LP, CD, and cassette format, there is a variety of videos, T-shirts, stickers, and jewelry.

**HOGWILD RECORDS TAPES AND CDS**
**1824 N. Main Ave.**
**(210) 733-5354**
This record shop specializes in Texas music, heavy metal, reggae, blues, dance music, and imports. In addition to a large selection of music, it stocks music paraphernalia like T-shirts and posters. It also buys used records and CDs.

## OUTLET SHOPPING

**NEW BRAUNFELS MARKETPLACE**
**651 I-35 North**
**New Braunfels**
**(830) 620-7475**
**www.nbmarketplace.com**
What started out as a factory store for West Point Pepperell has become a destination for busloads of shoppers from Houston and Dallas. The stores, which often sell new product lines, are owned by the factories, but unlike some factory outlets, this mall does not feature second or discounted merchandise. Open daily.

**SAN MARCOS PREMIUM OUTLETS**
**3939 I-35 South**
**San Marcos**
**(512) 396-2200**
**www.premiumoutlets.com**
This open-air mall features more than 140 shops that sell direct from the factory. Luggage, shoes, leather goods, outdoor gear, china, kitchen goods, and other specialty items are available. Along with stores,

shoppers find plenty of special features: a food court, a children's playground, free stroller and wheelchair loans, and tourist information. Chartered buses from as far away as Dallas and Houston stop here regularly. San Marcos is a 45-minute drive north of San Antonio.

**TANGER OUTLET CENTER**
**4015 I-35 South**
**San Marcos**
**(512) 396-7446**
**www.tangeroutlet.com**

Just south of San Marcos Premium Outlets lies the expansive Tanger Factory Outlet Center. Here you can shop for name-brand goods ranging from housewares and footwear to home furnishings and fine perfumes. More than 100 shops are located in this open-air mall.

## SPECIALTY FOOD STORES

**ALI BABA INTERNATIONAL FOOD MARKET**
**9307 Wurzbach Rd.**
**(210) 691-1111**

Ali Baba is a family-owned specialty shop featuring exotic food items from around the world. Middle Eastern, Indian, Eastern European and Turkish, Iranian, and Pakistani food items make up most of the food section. This is the only pita bread bakery in San Antonio. The store is especially known for its wonderful grocery items. Check out its huge selection of spices—which range from curry and saffron to turmeric—or grab Ali Baba's house brand Seven Spices, which combines seven popular seasonings for poultry and other meats. The meat market prides itself on the fresh goat and lamb (halal). The store carries fresh Mediterranean cucumbers, fresh chestnuts, and other specialty fruits when they're in season. Tea lovers have a huge selection of 72 teas, from Russian and Polish to Arab and Indian. Chocolate lovers can feast on favorite international sweets.

## SPORTING GOODS

**A-1 SPORTS CENTER**
**1027 Bandera Rd.**
**(210) 433-1246**
**www.a1sportstx.com**

A-1 Sports Center carries everything you might need to join the team. Whether you play basketball, baseball, football, or soccer, A-1 has the uniforms, jackets, caps, and equipment you'll be wanting. They can also do custom silk-screening and computerized monogramming so you can personalize your purchases. Open Mon through Sat.

**GASSMAN'S ARCHERY AND AIR RIFLE**
**102 Jackson Keller Rd.**
**(210) 822-7131**

This is San Antonio's hunting supplies store. Gassman's carries a good selection of bows (including crossbows) and arrows and bow accessories. It also stocks air guns from America and Europe, blow guns, camouflage clothing, and game calls.

**RACQUETBALL PROS OF SAN ANTONIO**
**5504 Bandera Rd.**
**(210) 680-8800**

This is the place to shop in San Antonio when you're looking for racquetball supplies. Here you'll find racquets, eyeguards, gloves, and shoes that could help improve your game. The store carries such brand names as Head, Wilson, and E-Force, to name a few.

It also offers services like racquet regripping and restringing.

**SOCCER LOCKER USA**
**6487 Blanco Rd.**
**(210) 349-5021**
**www.soccerlockerusa.net**

Many kids today are involved in team soccer, and Soccer Locker USA has the supplies they need for the coming season. The store has a large selection of soccer balls, shin guards, and cleats. It offers team discounts, takes special orders, and even does printing and silk-screening to personalize the equipment.

**SOCCER WORLD**
**3949 Fredericksburg Rd.**
**(210) 734-7906**
**www.soccerworldtx.com**

Soccer World calls itself "The Most Complete Soccer Store In Town" with good reason. They have a huge selection of practically anything connected with the sport, including uniforms and equipment. Soccer World also offers team discounts and in-house monogramming. This is a great place to shop for anything soccer.

## THRIFT STORES & RESALE SHOPS

**GOODWILL STORES**
**727 NW Loop 410**
**(210) 924-8581**
**www.goodwillsa.org**

Goodwill has several locations in the San Antonio area, and all of them have the same low prices. At most stores, you'll be able to find blouses for under $5, jeans for under $6, and dresses for under $10. Look for sale signs around the store to get up to 50 percent off on certain items. Check out their website for additional area location information. A second location is at Highway 281 at Evans Road.

**TEXAS THRIFT STORE**
**7500 I-35 North**
**(210) 654-7222**

With 4 locations in the San Antonio area, Texas Thrift Store claims to have some 4,000 new items every day. Leave a generous amount of time to explore these stores, because there is a lot to sort through. Additional locations are at 6776 Ingram Rd. (210-521-3336); 3606 Fredericksburg Rd. (210-733-1707); and 6708 S. Flores St. (210-921-2300).

## WESTERN GEAR

**BOOT HILL**
**849 E. Commerce St. at Rivercenter Mall**
**(210) 223-6634**

If you want to outfit the whole family to look like John Wayne, then you'll want to make a stop here. Jeans from Wrangler and other Western brands can be found, as can tops and shirts. The prices at Boot Hill are reasonable.

**CAVENDER'S BOOT CITY**
**5075 NW Loop 410**
**(210) 520-2668**
**www.cavenders.com**

Cavender's Boot City sells name-brand clothing at good prices. There is a large selection here, so if you're looking for jeans, boots, or cowboy hats, head on over. The sales staff is always knowledgeable and friendly. Two additional San Antonio locations are at 303 NW Loop 410 (210-377-4241) and 8640 Four Winds Dr. (210-590-2668).

**GIL'S BOOTS & WESTERN WEAR**
**4803 Rigsby**
**(210) 333-3203**
**www.gilsboots.com**

Family-owned and -operated since 1984, the 10,000-square-foot store is stacked with cowboy-style attire for the entire family, from Stetson hats and Wrangler shirts to Tony Lama boots and belt buckles emblazoned with the Texas seal.

**LUCCHESE BOOT COMPANY**
**255 E. Basse Rd.**
**(210) 828-9419, (800) 548-9755**
**www.lucchese.com**

Every cowboy needs boots, and this shop has been making Western boots for more than a century. Many are made with exotic leathers such as alligator and ostrich.

**PARIS HATTERS**
**119 N. Broadway**
**(210) 223-3453**
**www.parishatters.com**

If you want to look like a real cowboy, you'll need a Western hat. Since 1917 Paris Hatters has outfitted cowboys and cowboy wannabes with Stetsons and other authentic headgear. Notable customers have included Pope John Paul II; Johnny Cash; Paul McCartney; US Presidents Lyndon Johnson, Dwight Eisenhower, Harry Truman, and George W. Bush; King Juan Carlos of Spain; and Sammy Davis Jr.

# ATTRACTIONS

**Want to follow the conquistadors who came here in search of gold? Splash in a Texas-shaped swimming pool, or get almost as wet watching an acrobatic killer whale leap and dive in a seven million–gallon tank? Perhaps you'd like to view some of the nation's finest Latin-American art? Or maybe your taste runs to touring elegant Victorian homes built by German immigrants in the mid-1800s.**

**If ever there was a destination with something for everyone, it's San Antonio. Regardless of age, gender, or nationality, you will find attractions here that pique your interest or provide a feast for the eyes. Others will inspire you, and some are just plain fun.**

**The first attraction most people associate with San Antonio is the Alamo. The former mission is surrounded by Alamo Plaza, a site that is historic and hysterical, the ultimate shrine to Texas history alongside shrines to the Texas tourist. The Alamo, the mission that represents the fight for freedom and the spirit of Texas, is a place where tones are hushed and respectful, a destination to which every true Texan makes a pilgrimage at least once in his or her life. In juxtaposition, Alamo Plaza is the home of the city's most tourist-oriented businesses: souvenir stands, a wax museum, and a bounty of tour companies. But both solemnity and souvenirs somehow work together to create a memorable destination.**

## OVERVIEW

To help you maneuver through the many attractions of San Antonio, we've divided this chapter into sections: Downtown, In and Around Loop 410, San Antonio Missions, Outside Loop 410, Historic Districts, and Tours.

You'll find that these attractions—and the city itself—are most crowded in the summer months. Other peak times are in April during Fiesta and at Christmastime. In planning your itinerary during a summer visit to San Antonio, keep the heat in mind. Do what residents do: Plan outdoor and strenuous excursions in the morning hours, then head for indoor or shady attractions during the heat of the day.

From the cypress-lined River Walk to beautiful Brackenridge Park, San Antonio has plenty of destinations for a shady stroll. Don't miss our chapter on Parks and Recreation, which lists lots of options for everything from a jog to a picnic. You'll also find more things to see and do in the chapters covering Nightlife, Kidstuff, The Arts, Spectator Sports, and the Military.

***Price Code***

The price ratings below are for one adult admission fee during the summer high season. Keep in mind that many attractions offer significant discounts for children, seniors, and military personnel. Additionally, many have discount coupons on their websites.

**$..................Less than $5**
**$$ ....................$5 to $10**
**$$$ ................. $10 to $20**
**$$$$............ More than $20**

## DOWNTOWN

**✳ALAMO** **FREE**
**300 Alamo Plaza**
**(210) 225-1391**
**www.thealamo.org**

If you visit only one San Antonio attraction, make it the Alamo. The most famous sight in Texas, this former mission is a symbol of the fight for freedom in the battle for independence from Mexico. It's often referred to as the "cradle of Texas liberty," and even today, men remove their hats and photography is prohibited. It stands as a reminder of the Spanish colonization of this area and of the bloody battle that was fought so valiantly.

Although today it is primarily known as the Alamo, the mission was originally called San Antonio de Valero. The mission was closed in 1793, and the buildings began to fall to ruin. Troops from San José y Santiago del Alamo Parras in northern Mexico converted the building into a fort in 1801, and the structure took the name of the troops' hometown. Since that moniker was a real mouthful, the name was later shortened to simply "El Alamo." And just what is the English translation of Alamo? Cottonwood.

The Alamo was originally a large compound. Today all that remains of the mission is the original church and the Long Barrack. When you enter the Alamo, you'll be struck by the quietness of the complex. It retains a chapel-like atmosphere despite the hundreds of thousands of visitors who tour it each year. The Alamo operates under the care of the Daughters of the Republic of Texas, a conservation group that protects and guards the mission, many say, as fiercely as the Texian troops did a century and a half ago.

First-time visitors should budget about two hours for a look at the chapel and its displays, the barrack, and the film that tells the story of the historic battle. Gardens behind the chapel are also well worth a visit.

The story of the Alamo is a tale taught to every young Texan: It's the account of fewer than 200 brave volunteers who faced nearly 10 times as many Mexican troops in a battle whose outcome was predetermined. To further the cause of Texas independence, they gave their lives but won a place in the history of the Lone Star State.

The battle of the Alamo was preceded by battles in Gonzales, Goliad, and San Antonio itself. Mexican troops led by General Martin Perfecto de Cos had taken refuge in the Alamo and surrendered in early December. The surrender had angered Mexican President Antonio López de Santa Anna. He vowed to get rid of the Anglos and to punish the Tejanos, the Mexicans living in Texas who had taken part in the battle.

After the surrender by General Cos, the Texas army floundered without a leader for several months, and its numbers dwindled. Simultaneously, Santa Anna was rallying his troops for the long journey from Mexico City to San Antonio.

Texas troops still occupied the Alamo, joined by volunteers such as Davy Crockett from Tennessee. The troops believed they would be joined by reinforcements before Santa Anna would arrive, but they were wrong. Santa Anna's advance troops first arrived in San Antonio on February 23, 1836. The revolutionaries scrambled inside the protective walls of the mission, bringing along cattle and supplies that commander William Travis thought could sustain them until help arrived.

Travis quickly made another appeal for more troops, knowing that the brunt of Santa Anna's army was only days away. On March 3, after the help so desperately needed failed to arrive, Travis allegedly drew a line in the earth with his sword. All men who wanted to stay and defend the Alamo were to cross the line—showing their dedication to independence even at the cost of battling an enemy that vastly outnumbered them. Only one man did not cross the line.

The battle began with bombardments from Mexican cannons, but the real surge took place at about 5:30 a.m. on March 6. Perhaps as many as 1,800 Mexican soldiers stormed the mission, fighting first with guns and finally hand to hand as they progressed up the walls. By 7 a.m., the battle was over. All the Texas revolutionaries died or were executed, but Santa Anna's troops permitted several women and a slave of William Travis's to live. The most famous survivors were Suzanna Dickinson and her daughter, Angelina, the family of an Alamo officer. They were left to spread the word of the Alamo defeat. And spread the word they did. "Remember the Alamo!" became a battle cry. Months later, the Texans defeated Santa Anna at the Battle of San Jacinto, and Texas became an independent republic.

Visitors who are in San Antonio on March 6 can watch an early-morning reenactment of the fateful battle. Taking the official tour can give you a better understanding of that event.

The Alamo is open Mon through Sat from 9 a.m. to 5:30 p.m. and Sun from 10 a.m. to 5:30 p.m. The facility is closed December 24 and 25.

**ALAMO CENOTAPH** **FREE**
**Alamo Plaza**

Directly in front of the Alamo stands the Alamo Cenotaph, a memorial to the men who lost their lives in the battle. The marble monument, designed by Italian-born and Texas-adopted sculptor Pompeo Coppini, was erected in 1939 by the Texas Centennial Commission and includes the names of all the Alamo defenders. Vehicles are no longer permitted in this area, a gesture of respect for the Native Americans buried in a cemetery found in front of the church.

**PEARL BREWERY** **FREE**
**200 E. Grayson**
**(210) 212-7260**
**www.atpearl.com**

The birthplace of Pearl Beer, this longtime staple of the San Antonio skyline is being redeveloped into an art-filled urban village next to the River Walk's Museum Reach. The transformation, which began in 2009, has been undertaken with the goal of preserving the old brewery's historic character while incorporating modern, eco-friendly technology, including solar power. Once completed, the Pearl site will include loft living spaces, retail space, and entertainment venues in a unique gathering spot for the city. Already in place are eateries including Il Sogno Osteria, featuring Italian specialties; La Gloria Ice House, serving upscale interior Mexican dishes; and the Sandbar

Fish House and Market, offering fresh oysters and seafood from a perch overlooking the river. Eclectic shopping opportunities abound, and the Pearl Farmers' Market offers fresh seasonal fruits, vegetables, cheeses, and meats, as well as live entertainment in a street market setting on Wednesday and Friday. The Culinary Institute of America recently opened its newest campus here, offering cooking classes as well as a 30-week culinary arts certificate program for emerging chefs. The campus includes a demonstration kitchen, 7 cooking areas, and a Latin American outdoor cooking space, as well as classrooms and presentation venues. Other attractions at Pearl include an Aveda Institute and spa; a Synergy Studio, offering exercise and yoga classes; and the Twig Bookshop, featuring children's literature and story times. Pearl Park is a quiet retreat on the river with picnic tables, an amphitheater seating 1,000, and a stop where you can catch a river taxi.

**BOLIVAR HALL** **FREE**
**418 La Villita St., La Villita**
**(210) 224-6163**

Operated by the San Antonio Conservation Society, this museum contains exhibits on the society's work as well as its Night in Old San Antonio (NIOSA) annual event. Photographs trace the evolution of this annual event and of Fiesta. The exhibit is open daily from 10 a.m. to 5 p.m.

**BUCKHORN SALOON AND MUSEUM** **$$$**
**318 E. Houston St.**
**(210) 247-4000**
**www.buckhornmuseum.com**

In 1881 the Buckhorn Saloon opened as a Texas watering hole. Soon hunters and trappers were stopping by eager for a cold brew, so they traded in furs and horns. Owner Albert Friedrich collected the horns, some of which his father made into horn chairs. Today you can see the heads, hides, and horns on a guided tour of the Buckhorn Hall of Horns, one of four unusual museums housed here. The tour also includes the Buckhorn Hall of Fins (marine trophies and fishing lures) and the Buckhorn Hall of Feathers (mounted birds).

A recent addition is the Texas Ranger Museum, highlighting the history of the famous lawmen. Exhibits include an extensive collection of firearms, historic photographs, and "Ranger Town," a walk-through re-creation of San Antonio during the Wild West days with a jail, shops, and saloon. Buckhorn Saloon and Museum is open daily. Hours vary by season.

**CASA NAVARRO STATE HISTORIC SITE** **$**
**228 S. Laredo St.**
**(210) 226-4801**
**www.visitcasanavarro.com**

This small home was once the residence of Jose Antonio Navarro (1795–1871), a signer of the Texas Declaration of Independence. The adobe and limestone structure includes an office used by Navarro, who was one of the first major cattlemen here. Navarro was a member of the Texas legislature under Mexico, the Republic of Texas, and the US. His father served as a mayor of San Antonio. This home is considered one of the few remaining dwellings that provides a picture of what residences were like during the years of independence. Casa Navarro is open Tues through Sun from 9 a.m. to 4 p.m.

**IMAX THEATRE AT RIVERCENTER MALL** **$$$**
**849 E. Commerce St.,**
**(210) 247-4629, (800) 354-4629**
**www.imax-sa.com**

Located at the Crockett Street entrance of Rivercenter Mall, this IMAX theater is the home of *Alamo: The Price of Freedom.* The story of the fall of the Alamo comes to life on this 6-story screen several times daily. The 45-minute docudrama is one of the best film versions of the 13-day siege, giving viewers a real sense of participation in the action. The film was produced at Alamo Village in the West Texas town of Brackettville, using a replica of the Alamo built for the John Wayne film of the same name. From a rolling thunderstorm over the rugged Texas landscape to the daybreak siege by Santa Anna's troops, this movie makes viewers feel as if they are witnessing the fateful battle and the days leading up to it. When not running *The Price of Freedom,* the IMAX Theatre shows other films produced especially for the big screen.

**✻INSTITUTE OF TEXAN CULTURES** **$$**
**801 E. Durango Blvd.**
**(210) 458-2300**
**www.texancultures.utsa.edu**

Operated by the University of Texas at San Antonio, the Institute of Texan Cultures offers cultural history, science, and technology and their influence on the people of Texas. You'll find hands-on exhibits and presentations by trained docents, in addition to the schedule of festivals and major exhibits.

The biggest event by far is the Texas Folklife Festival, held every June on the spacious grounds of the institute. More than 10,000 statewide participants stage the 3 days of colorful events—music, food, dance, crafts, and traditions representing about 45 different cultures from 60 counties—for 70,000 to 100,000 visitors. This event is a real gem. (Get more information in the Annual Events & Festivals chapter.)

The exhibit floor features a dome theater that displays a variety of shows throughout the day. The Solar Power Plant adds modern technology to the historical interpretive area on "the Back 40." Museum hours are 9 a.m. to 5 p.m. Mon through Sat and noon to 5 p.m. Sun. Hours may vary with special programs and holidays. (See the Kidstuff chapter for additional information.)

**MARKET SQUARE** **FREE**
**514–612 W. Commerce St.**
**(210) 207-8600**
**www.sanantonio.gov/dtops/marketsquare**

Bounded by I-35 and Santa Rosa, Dolorosa, and Commerce Streets, this 2-block area embraces 3 special shopping centers: Farmer's Market Plaza, a renovated former produce market now ripe with crafts and imports after a $2.1 million renovation; an open-air consortium of specialty boutiques; and El Mercado, the largest Mexican market in the US.

The history of Market Square dates back to the early 1800s, to a time when Mexico ruled the settlement of San Antonio de Bejar. The market's biggest claim to fame lies in the fact that it was the birthplace of chili con carne, the spicy meat and bean mixture now considered the state dish of Texas. In the early 1800s young girls known as "chili queens" sold the concoction from small stands in the market.

El Mercado offers the kinds of items that shoppers typically find in a Mexican border town. Styled after a traditional Mexican *mercado* (market), albeit one that is enclosed and air-conditioned, El Mercado has merchandise piled to the ceiling. Look for onyx chess sets, ashtrays, painted pottery, silver jewelry, sombreros, and charro hats. The prices here are slightly higher than those found in Mexican border towns, and unlike the fare offered in traditional mercados, the merchandise carries set prices. Prices vary from store to store within the market, and most shops accept major credit cards. (For more on Market Square, see the Shopping chapter.)

The stores of Market Square are open 10 a.m. to 8 p.m. during the summer months, closing at 6 p.m. during the winter. Restaurants keep longer hours. Expect most stores to be closed Thanksgiving, Christmas, New Year's Day, and Easter.

**MUSEO ALAMEDA** **$**
**101 S. Santa Rosa**
**(210) 299-4300**
**www.thealameda.org**

Housed in a 1940s movie palace next to Market Square, Museo Alameda showcases the history of the Hispanic community in the US. In honor of the venue's heyday, posters, photos, and other memorabilia showcase Alameda's cinematic origins, while an ever-changing array of exhibitions celebrates the artistic achievements and vibrant Latino culture. Open to the public Tues through Sun from noon to 6 p.m. Admission is $4 for adults, $2 for seniors, and $2 for students with ID and children between the ages of 5 and 17; on Tuesday, admission is free.

**LOUIS TUSSAUD'S WAXWORKS** **$$$**
**301 Alamo Plaza**
**(210) 224-9299**
**http://sanantonio.ripleys.com**

This museum depicts the famous, from Jesus to John Wayne, reproduced in wax. The sculptures are well done, and many are displayed in elaborate sets depicting movie scenes. Alamo visitors will appreciate the "Heroes of the Lone Star" exhibits on the fateful battle. See the Kidstuff chapter for more details.

The museum is open from 10 a.m. to 10 p.m. Sun through Thurs and 10 a.m. to 11 p.m. Fri and Sat. The ticket box office closes one hour prior to closing time.

**BELIEVE IT OR NOT! ODDITORIUM** **$$$**
**301 Alamo Plaza**
**(210) 224-9299**
**http://sanantonio.ripleys.com**

Located in the same facility as Louis Tussaud's Waxworks, the Believe It or Not! Odditorium houses more than 500 oddities, including freaks of nature and miniatures. It's the largest Ripley's museum in the United States. The collection is open daily; hours vary by season, so call ahead. See the Kidstuff chapter for more details.

**RIVER WALK (PASEO DEL RIO)** **FREE**
**Downtown**
**(210) 227-4262**
**www.thesanantonioriverwalk.com**

The Paseo del Rio, or River Walk, is a magical place 20 feet below street level. Nestled behind tall buildings, away from traffic and street noise, the River Walk is the most popular spot in town, lined with specialty shops and alfresco cafes. Visitors stroll the walkways that follow the winding river. Some sections throng with shoulder-to-shoulder crowds; others have a quiet, almost parklike atmosphere.

The River Walk is the heart of the city. Tourists from around the world pack the hotels here. Military personnel from San Antonio's five military bases enjoy a few hours off duty at the outdoor cafes. And locals come to the area to enjoy a respite from the hustle and bustle of the city.

But the popularity of this riverside goes back long before the days when people came here for sizzling fajitas and frozen margaritas. Payaya Indians called this river Yanaguana, or "refreshing waters." It also had a less elegant nickname that meant "a drunken old man going home at night"—a reference to its numerous twists and turns. Indians camped along the riverbanks and hunted on the rich land nearby.

On June 13, 1691, the feast day of San Antonio de Padua, the Spanish renamed the Yanaguana. The change was just a hint of the many transformations the river would soon witness as Spanish domination came to the area.

In the early 1700s the Spaniards constructed several missions on the river's bends. The northernmost one was built first: San Antonio de Valero, later known as the Alamo. It was followed by four other missions to the south. The Indians who lived in the missions dug ditches or acequias from the river to their fields to irrigate crops of beans and corn.

Soon settlement began on the riverbanks. When the missions were secularized and later occupied by military troops, camp followers and tradesmen built temporary houses near the river to serve those stationed at the Alamo. After Texas became a republic, permanent settlements developed on the riverbanks. As the population rose, bathhouses sprang up along the water's edge.

Eventually the condition of the river declined, and for many residents its only characteristics were bad ones. The river was untamed, and it wreaked havoc in the downtown area after heavy rains. In 1921 a devastating flood killed 50 people, and talk was that the river should be covered with concrete and converted to a storm sewer. But on March 22, 1924, the San Antonio Conservation Society stepped in.

The river was saved with a puppet show called "The Goose That Laid the Golden Egg." Cloth puppets resembling city officials dramatized the tale and helped San Antonians realize that their river really could be an attribute to the city. A flood-control program was started, and dams were built to protect the horseshoe bend during floods.

Though the river was saved, the real gold came later, thanks to a visionary named Robert H. H. Hugman. As part of a WPA program, Hugman was commissioned to develop the scenic walkway. He pictured a festive area he called "The Shops of Aragon and Romula," named for the cities of Old Spain. The project, which was formally named the River Walk, was completed in 1941.

Unfortunately, development along the River Walk remained minimal until the World HemisFair in the late 1960s. As it prepared for global visitors to the fair, the city beautified the park, investors opened businesses along the walkways, and the River Walk, as visitors today now know and love it, was born.

No matter what day of the week, no matter what time of the year, activity abounds along the River Walk. This is where city residents come to party, where conventioneers come to meet, and where vacationers come to taste the flavor that is San Antonio. The River Walk is especially beautiful at Christmas, when all the trees are laden with bright lights that reflect in the water below. (See the Holiday River Parade and Lighting Ceremony in the Annual Events & Festivals chapter.)

The original River Walk spans from Municipal Auditorium to the north to the King William Historic District to the south. The Museum Reach expansion, completed in 2009, added 1.3 miles to the original River Walk, linking it with several museums, the historic Pearl Brewery, and other San Antonio cultural attractions. Work on this historic attraction—both restoration and expansion—continues today. For the best overview, take a river cruise, a narrated tour that provides a look at stretches most pedestrians never see. (See "Rio San Antonio" in the Tours section.)

**SAN FERNANDO CATHEDRAL FREE**
**115 Main Plaza**
**(210) 227-1297**
**www.sfcathedral.org**

San Fernando has long occupied a unique position for the city and for the thousands of visitors who come each year. Founded on March 9, 1731, by the original 16 families from the Canary Islands, the cathedral played a vital role in San Antonio history.

During the Texas war for independence from Mexico, General Santa Anna raised his flag of "no quarter"—signifying to the Texians that he would take no prisoners—from the church. Many years later, folks believed San Fernando was the final resting place for the Alamo defenders because of entombed ashes discovered during a construction project. Although that tomb holds the remains of some unknown soldiers, modern historians do not believe they were the Alamo defenders because evidence of military uniforms—never worn by the Texians—has turned up among the remains.

Today San Fernando is home to many public rituals and celebrations of the Mexican Catholic faith. One, a Flamenco Mass, is performed every year for Good Friday and Easter Vigil. Holy Week also includes a reenactment of the Passion of Jesus Christ and other popular religious commemorations (funeral procession and the burial of Jesus, and *pesame,* or condolences to the Virgin).

In 2003 the cathedral finished a $5.5 million restoration. Visitors should note the 3 *retablos.* The center screen, which depicts Christ, features workmanship in 24-carat gold. The cathedral is open to its congregation and visitors alike.

**i** More than 4,000 people congregate each weekend for Mass at San Fernando Cathedral, a house of worship that was honored with a visit by Pope John Paul II on September 13, 1987.

**SOUTHWEST SCHOOL OF ART FREE**
**300 Augusta St.**
**(210) 224-1848**
**www.swschool.org**

The Southwest School of Art offers a good overview of the San Antonio artistic scene. The school is housed in the former Ursuline Academy, which in 1851 became the first girls' school in the city. The long halls of the one-time dormitory are now lined with art, and a gallery is open across the street. The Gallery Shop sells handcrafted items, including contemporary jewelry, pottery, and other artworks. Grab a sandwich or salad at the on-site Copper Kitchen. The school is open to visitors Mon through Sat 10 a.m. to 5 p.m., and Sun 11 a.m. to 4 p.m. For additional details, see The Arts chapter.

**SPANISH GOVERNOR'S PALACE** **$**
**105 Military Plaza**
**(210) 224-0601**
**www.spanishgovernorspalace.org**
Located just down the street from Market Square, this historic site was once the home of the officials of the Spanish Province of Texas. Today it's the only remaining example in Texas of an early aristocratic Spanish home. Completed in 1749, the structure is now open for self-guided tours of its antiques-furnished rooms and cobblestone patio.

Don't expect a palace in the usual sense of the word—turrets and towers are replaced by a simple patio and courtyard here. Remember, this building dates back to the early 18th century, a time when the area was wild and unsettled, and this house was considered quite ornate, comparatively speaking. The palace is open Tues through Sat from 9 a.m. to 5 p.m. and Sun from 10 a.m. to 5 p.m.

**i** The Spanish Governor's Palace offers a glimpse into its past on the final Sunday of each month as La Compania de Cavalleria del Real Presidio de Bexar, a troupe of re-enactors, don the regalia of the men who once guarded the Alamo and its encompassing colony. The living history group walks the grounds from 10 a.m. to 5 p.m.

**TOWER OF THE AMERICAS** **$$**
**600 HemisFair Park**
**(210) 223-3101**
**www.toweroftheamericas.com**
Talk about a room with a view! This symbol of the 1968 World HemisFair remains a landmark for downtown San Antonio. Visitors get a 360-degree view of the city from the observation deck at 579 feet. Four decades after its construction, this is still one of the tallest free-standing structures in the Western Hemisphere—87 feet taller than the Seattle Space Needle and 67 feet higher than the Washington Monument.

Since its construction, the Tower and its grounds have undergone many changes. In April 1988 HemisFair Park was rededicated after a $12 million renovation of the grounds. In March 1990 a $1.2 million restoration was completed on the Tower. Following its 2006 renovation, you can now enjoy a one-minute elevator ride (traveling 7 miles per hour) to the observation deck, where high-powered telescopes provide a bird's-eye view of the city's sights. Eight panoramic photo panels help visitors locate major attractions. There are both enclosed and open-air observation decks, and at night the view is especially breathtaking. Top off your visit by taking in the sights of the Lone Star State in the Skies Over Texas 4-D theater ride, which is included in the price of a Tower ticket.

## IN & AROUND LOOP 410

**BRACKENRIDGE PARK** **FREE**
**3910 N. St. Mary's St.**
**(210) 207-7275**
The largest park in the city, Brackenridge sprawls across 343 acres shaded by majestic oaks. A popular picnic destination, the park is also home to the San Antonio Zoo (see

listing), housed in a former rock quarry. Nearby, the Japanese Tea Gardens (see listing) showcases lush flowers, climbing vines, and tall palms alongside many koi-filled ponds. For more details on the park, see the Parks & Recreation chapter.

**JAPANESE TEA GARDEN FREE**
**3853 N. St. Mary's St.**
**(210) 207-7275**

San Antonio's semitropical climate encourages the lush flowers, climbing vines, and tall palms found inside this quiet, serene place, part of the San Antonio Zoo. The ponds, with beautiful rock bridges and walkways, are home to koi (large goldfish).

This limestone quarry was transformed into a garden with fish ponds and a palm-thatched arbor in 1918. Later, a pagoda was added, and a Japanese-American couple operated a tearoom nearby. During World War II, public pressure forced the family to move; when the tearoom was taken over by a Chinese family, the attraction was renamed the Chinese Tea Garden. Later, descendants of the original owners of the tearoom, along with the Japanese ambassador to the US, were in attendance when the garden was officially renamed the Japanese Tea Garden. Recent renovations upgraded the garden's infrastructure, including its 60-foot waterfall. The garden is open daily from dawn to dusk.

**MARION KOOGLER MCNAY ART MUSEUM $$**
**6000 N. New Braunfels Ave.**
**(210) 824-5368**
**www.mcnayart.org**

This Spanish Colonial Revival–style mansion (designed by Atlee B. and Robert M. Ayres in 1926 and remodeled in 1954) was the home of the late art collector Marion Koogler McNay, heiress to an oil fortune and an artist herself. The 24-room house, which was converted to a museum in the 1950s, is now home to a collection of European and American art. Works of Picasso, Van Gogh, Matisse, and Gauguin are found in the permanent collection. After a look at the impressive artwork, visitors can stroll the palm-shaded grounds, popular with picnickers. The museum is open Tues, Wed, and Fri from 10 a.m. to 4 p.m., Thurs from 10 a.m. to 9 p.m., Sat from 10 a.m. to 5 p.m., and Sun noon to 5 p.m. General admission is free on Thursday nights and the first Sunday of each month. For additional details, see The Arts chapter.

***SAN ANTONIO BOTANICAL GARDEN $$**
**555 Funston Place**
**(210) 207-3250**
**www.sabot.org**

Separate gardens for roses, herbs, and native plants are found within these 33-acre gardens. The centerpiece here is the Lucile Halsell Conservatory, designed by Emilio Ambasz, formerly curator of design at New York's Museum of Modern Art. To take advantage of the cooling effect of the earth during hot Texas summers, the greenhouse is built 16 feet underground. Separate structures showcase palm trees from around the world, desert plants, and tropical foliage. The garden is open daily except Thanksgiving, Christmas and New Year's Day. Hours are 9 a.m. to 5 p.m. For additional details, see the Parks & Recreation chapter.

**SAN ANTONIO MUSEUM OF ART $$**
**200 W. Jones Ave.**
**(210) 978-8100**
**www.samuseum.org**

This expansive museum is housed in the buildings of the former Lone Star Brewery and maintains its factory feel with skywalks and glass elevators. Collections include Egyptian, Greek, and Roman antiquities; Asian art; and 18th-, 19th-, and 20th-century American work. The museum offers the 3-story Nelson A. Rockefeller Center for Latin American Art, considered one of the nation's best collections of Latin American art. For additional details, see the museum's entry in The Arts chapter. The museum is open Tues 10 a.m. to 9 p.m., Wed through Sat 10 a.m. to 5 p.m., and Sun noon to 6 p.m. Admission is free Tues from 4 to 9 p.m.

**SAN ANTONIO ZOO $$$**
**3903 N. St. Mary's St.**
**(210) 734-7184**
**www.sa-zoo.org**

Widely considered one of the best zoos in the nation, the San Antonio Zoo is located at the headwaters of the San Antonio River. Surrounded by limestone cliffs (this was once a rock quarry) and plenty of shade, the exhibits include animals from habitats around the world.

The zoo is best known for its excellent collection of African antelopes and other hoofed species. You'll find many other interesting creatures, too, including African lions and Asian elephants, snow leopards, and the elusive okapi. More than 3,500 animals representing 600 species live here. Birds, including many housed in open-air exhibits, make up a large part of the collection. Other notable accomplishments include the first Caribbean flamingos hatched and reared in a zoo, the first white rhino born in North America, and a breeding program for the rare snow leopard. The zoo also includes an aquarium that exhibits species ranging from tiny seahorses to deadly red piranha. The zoo is open 365 days a year, 9 a.m. to 6 p.m.

**SPLASHTOWN $$$$**
**3600 I-35 North**
**(210) 227-1400**
**www.splashtownsa.com**

San Antonio's closest water park lies on the north side of the city and provides cool relief on hot summer days. Spanning 20 acres, this park offers a variety of rides whose pace varies from relaxing to thrilling. For more information on this park, see the Kidstuff chapter.

**TEXAS AIR MUSEUM—STINSON CHAPTER $**
**1234 99th St.**
**(210) 977-9885**
**www.texasairmuseum.org**

If you're a private pilot, you're probably familiar with Stinson Field, the country's second-oldest continuously used airfield. Other visitors to the city might be more familiar with Stinson as the home of this museum, which features the early aviation history of San Antonio. The display includes Katherine Stinson's original engine on a replica of a 1914 Bleriot-type aircraft, a 1927 WACO 10 with OX-6 engine, a World War II German Focke-Wulf 190, an astronaut rotational simulator built and used at Brooks Air Force Base, a replica of a 1914 Curtiss Pusher, and a 1940 Bucker Jungemeister, plus numerous WWI and WWII artifacts. The museum is open Tues through Sat 10 a.m. to 5 p.m.

**TEXAS HIGHWAY PATROL MUSEUM $**
**812 S. Alamo St.**
**(210) 231-6030**
**www.thpa.org**

One of San Antonio's small treasures, this often-overlooked museum honors the highway patrol officers who have fallen in the line of duty. Some of the first officers to lose their lives were those shot by bank robbers Bonnie Parker and Clyde Barrow. Additional exhibits are concerned with motor safety. The museum is open Tues through Fri 10 a.m. to 4 p.m.

**TEXAS TRANSPORTATION MUSEUM** **$$**
**11731 Wetmore Rd. at McAllister Park**
**(210) 490-3554**
**www.txtransportationmuseum.org**

Train and antique-car buffs enjoy this museum, whose exhibits include antique pedicabs, horse-drawn vehicles, model railroads, and more. Train rides are offered every 60 minutes on Sat and Sun from 10:30 a.m. to 4:30 p.m. The exhibits are open Fri from 9 a.m. to 3 p.m. and on Sat and Sun from 10 a.m. to 5 p.m.

**✷WITTE MUSEUM** **$$**
**3801 Broadway**
**(210) 357-1900**
**www.wittemuseum.org**

This exciting interactive museum covers all things Texan, from the area's early dinosaur inhabitants to the white-tailed deer that roam the region today.

The museum collection is extensive. One of the best exhibits is "Texas Wild: Ecology Illustrated," a look at the ecology of this diverse state. Nearby, a display takes a look at the ancient Texans who roamed the region as hunter-gatherers more than 8,000 years ago. The Witte also features several changing exhibits.

After a look around the museum, step out back to see the historic homes that have been relocated to the courtyard. Here you'll also find the H-E-B Science Treehouse, a 4-story collection of interactive exhibits on science concepts. Perched in concrete "trees," this museum is a favorite with children. (For more details, see the Kidstuff chapter.)

The museum is open 7 days a week, but hours vary, so call ahead. Admission is free on Tues from 3 to 8 p.m.

**YTURRI-EDMUNDS HISTORIC SITE** **$**
**128 Mission Rd.**
**(210) 534-8237**
**www.saconservation.org**

When the missions were secularized, this land was granted to Manuel Yturri-Castillo, and he built an adobe-block home here in the mid-1800s. It was later given to the San Antonio Conservation Society by his granddaughter, Ernestine E. Edmunds. Today you can tour the residence and its shady grounds and have a look at the working mill and the acequia (aqueduct), the only one of its kind still in use in the country. The site is open by appointment only.

## SAN ANTONIO MISSIONS

Many don't realize it, but the Alamo—originally San Antonio de Valero—was a Catholic mission long before history made it a symbol of Texas's fight for independence. The Alamo was, in fact, one in a chain of missions built by the Spanish to convert Indians to Catholicism. But the Spanish had political as well as religious reasons for building the missions: They wanted to stake a claim on lands in which their rival, France, was showing interest.

While the Alamo is fascinating for its heroic story, visiting the **San Antonio Missions National Historical Park** is a better way to get a full picture of the roles missions played in this area. Once these missions—Concepción, San José, San Juan Capistrano, and Espada—covered many acres, land that was irrigated with an acequia (a type of irrigation ditch) fed by the San Antonio River.

The first San Antonio mission, the **Alamo,** was built to serve as a way station between missions in East Texas and those in Mexico City. Two years later, **San José y San Miguel de Aguayo Mission** was built south of the Alamo. Three other missions in East Texas subsequently proved unsuccessful, due to the French influence in Louisiana and the widespread malaria that resulted from settling in the swampy woodlands. As a result, in 1731 three missions were relocated to San Antonio, forming the densest concentration of Spanish missions in the New World.

The Indians who would live in the missions were Coahuiltecan, hunter-gatherers from South Texas and northeastern Mexico. Because European diseases brought by the Spanish had taken their toll on the native population and hostile Apache were a constant danger, the Indians allowed themselves to be recruited by the friars. By the late 1700s, however, the missions became secularized, and the Indians moved to neighboring land. Many of the mission buildings began to fall to ruin.

In the 1920s the San Antonio Conservation Society and the federal government began to preserve the deteriorating structures; then in 1978 the San Antonio Missions National Historical Park was established to protect and operate the four sites. (The Alamo is a separate entity, operated by the Daughters of the Republic of Texas.) The cooperative effort between the Park Service, the San Antonio Conservation Society, the State of Texas, the City of San Antonio, and Bexar County also included a cooperative agreement with the Archdiocese of San Antonio that keeps the mission churches open for regular religious services.

Today each of the missions is open to the public free of charge, with a suggested donation from visitors. When planning your visit, remember that these are active parish churches (unlike the Alamo). Services are conducted every Sunday, and respectful visitors are welcome. Mission San José has a Mariachi Mass every Sun at 12:30 p.m., as does Mission Concepción (at noon). These bilingual services are very popular with visitors.

A free National Park Service brochure with a map showing all sites and how to get to them is available at the **San Antonio Missions National Historical Park Visitors Center at Mission San José** (6701 San Jose Dr.). The map also may be downloaded in PDF format at www.nps.gov/saan.

Even with the map, getting to the missions can be a little tricky (the National Park Service brochure warns that "the route that connects the four missions can be confusing for visitors"). The way is marked with brown National Park signs, but it twists and turns among residential neighborhoods and parks. Further complicating matters, during heavy rains, two low-water crossings are closed, necessitating an alternate route. The National Park Service brochure outlines both the traditional Mission Trail as well as alternate routes to take during inclement weather.

For your tour of the missions, be sure that you wear some type of sturdy walking shoes. All the sites have irregular staircases and stone walkways that are especially slippery on rainy days. The missions are open daily 9 a.m. to 5 p.m. but are closed Thanksgiving, Christmas, and New Year's Day.

## MISSION CONCEPCIÓN

**807 Mission Rd., at Felisa Street**

Mission Concepción, the first stop for most travelers, is located south of the I-10 overpass on Mission Road. The drive from downtown to the Mission Concepción (pronounced "con-cep-see-OWN") takes about 15 minutes. This site is tucked into a quiet residential neighborhood, far different from the bustling Alamo area. The parish was moved here in 1731. Its full name is a mouthful: Mission Nuestra Señora de la Purisma Concepción de Acuna.

Displays at each of the 4 missions illustrate different aspects of mission life. At Concepción, the theme is "The Mission as a Religious Center," appropriate for one of the oldest unrestored stone churches, and the oldest unrestored Catholic church, in the nation.

Mission Concepción is especially notable for its wall paintings. Geometric and religious symbols in ochre, blue, and brown decorate the ceilings and walls of several rooms. The most striking is the *Eye of the God,* a face emanating rays of light.

Like the Alamo just over 2 miles to the north, Mission Concepción has seen some bloodshed. On October 28, 1835, Colonel James Bowie and 20 Texans were surprised by a detachment of the Mexican army. They fought well and forced the Mexicans, with 14 dead and 40 wounded, to retreat. The Texians only suffered one loss, further bolstering their spirits. Less than five months later, however, Bowie and his men would again fight the Mexican army, with far less success.

**i** **In 1777 Mission San José was dubbed the "Queen of the Missions" by Fray Juan Augustin Morfi, known as the first historian of Texas.**

## *MISSION SAN JOSÉ

**6701 San Jose Dr.**

**www.nps.gov/saan**

The second stop on the mission trail is the grandest in terms of size and architectural detail, so much so, in fact, that more than 200 years ago it was termed "Queen of the Missions." Founded in 1720 by Fray Antonio Margil de Jesus, in its heyday Mission San José boasted 300 residents, a granary that held 5,000 bushels of corn, and elaborate ornamentation. Its full name is Mission San José y Miguel de Aguayo, named for the governor of Coahuila at that time.

You may find yourself humming "Do You Know the Way to San Jose?" while making your way to this second site. The route mapped by the Park Service is the most scenic but not the most direct. Just follow the signs and be patient; San José is worth the effort. Thanks to an extensive renovation in 1936 for the Texas Centennial, this mission is in spectacular condition. The elegant structure echoes with reminders of an earlier time, when Texas was a frontier and this mission was a haven in an unsettled land. The most famous detail here is the rose window (*La Ventana de Rosa*). Legend has it that an architect named Pedro Huizar created the window for his lost love, Rosa. (When you're downtown, look at Dillard's exterior window displays at the Rivercenter Mall. These are copies of "Rosa's Window.")

Begin your visit with a stop at the modern visitor center adjacent to Mission San José to pick up a free Park Service brochure (a necessity for driving the Mission Trail); then start your self-guided tour of the chapel. The flagstone floor has borne thousands of worshippers, from barefooted Native Americans two centuries ago to tennis-shoed tourists today.

Walk around the grounds to get an idea of the size of this former community. Indians lived in rooms along the outside wall, and the priests lived in the 2-story *convento*. The land in the quadrangle was used for crops. The theme of San José's exhibits is "The Mission as Social Center and a Center for Defense." Displays show that Indian residents were instructed in the use of guns and lances to help defend the mission against Apache and Comanche raiders. The mission also shows a 23-minute film about early mission life.

**MISSION SAN JUAN CAPISTRANO**
**9101 Graf Rd.**
The theme for San Juan's exhibits is "The Mission as an Economic Center." This mission, like the others, was once completely self-sustaining. San Juan grew enough crops to help meet the needs of other communities in the area. Skilled artisans made ironwork and leather goods and wove cloth in the mission workshops.

To appreciate the natural richness of this area, take a hike on the San Juan Woodlands Trail. In about a third of a mile, the trail winds along the low river-bottom land and gives you a look at many of the indigenous plants used by the mission.

The chapel, with its bell tower and elaborate altar, was destroyed by a storm in 1886. In 1909 the building was repaired, and in the 1960s it underwent an extensive renovation. Today it is an active parish church and a good example of how San Antonio continues to use its historic structures both for tourists and for the local community.

San Juan also has a small museum featuring items found at the site and artifacts typically used by missionaries in Texas.

**MISSION ESPADA**
**10040 Espada Rd.**
From Mission San José, head west on Mission Road to Ashley, turn left, then right on Espada Road. This will take you to the most remote spot on the route, Mission Espada. Located about 9 miles from the downtown area, this mission was named for St. Francis of Assisi, founder of the monastic order of Franciscans. The mission's full name is Mission San Francisco de la Espada (de la Espada means "of the sword," referring to St. Francis's decision to be a "soldier of God").

This mission's theme is "The Mission as a Vocational Education Center," and its displays focus on how the local Indians were educated in blacksmithing, woodworking, and other vocational areas.

The park opens Rancho de las Cabras, located near the town of Floresville, at 10 a.m. on the first Saturday of each month. This addition to the parks system once served as a ranch that supported the residents of Mission Espada. If you would be interested in visiting Rancho de las Cabras, call (210) 932-1001 for information and reservations.

## OUTSIDE LOOP 410

**NATURAL BRIDGE CAVERNS $$$–$$$$**
**26495 Natural Bridge Caverns Rd., at exit 175 on I-35**
**(210) 651-6101**
**www.naturalbridgecaverns.com**
The largest cave in Central and South Texas is Natural Bridge Caverns, which takes its name from a rock bridge between two sinkholes, the original entrance to the mouth of the cavern. Local residents had known of the sinkholes since the 19th century, but there is evidence of much earlier visitors. Bones of an American black bear at least

8,000 years old have been discovered, as well as human bones, stone weapons, and other Indian artifacts. Don't expect Natural Bridge Caverns to be cool inside—it's actually warm and humid. Today the cave offers 5 tours. The Discovery Tour is the traditional guided tour; it departs at least every 40 minutes and lasts about 75 minutes. The tour takes visitors through enormous rooms that look like the playing fields of prehistoric dinosaurs. The rooms have been given fanciful names like The Castle of the White Giants. The Illuminations Tour leads visitors through 2 enormous chambers full of rare formations such as "soda straw" stalactites and waves of "cave ribbon." The natural magnificence of the formations is enhanced by dramatic lighting.

In 2 separate Adventure Tours, participants are outfitted in spelunking gear. The mile-long excursions descend to a depth of 230 feet below the surface and are rated moderate to hard in terms of difficulty. Activities include crawling through passageways to view rarely seen cave features. You'll need to make reservations for these tours.

The Lantern Tour takes visitors armed with powerful flashlights 120 feet below the surface to the newest area for exploration. Aboveground, Natural Bridge offers a 50-foot climbing tower with two 350-foot zip lines and a "mining company" that allows guests to pan for gems and minerals.

There are different prices for the various tours, the zip line, and mining experience, so call ahead or visit their website for details.

**NATURAL BRIDGE WILDLIFE RANCH** **$$$**
**26515 Natural Bridge Caverns Rd.**
**(830) 438-7400**
**www.wildliferanchtexas.com**

Located next to the Natural Bridge Caverns, this ranch holds the title of Texas's most-visited safari park (and the state's oldest). Established on a family's century-old ranch, the park boasts species from around the globe; more than 50 species of animals roam these fields. You'll receive a bucket of food when you arrive, and the animals come right up to the car to greet their guests—and get a bite to eat. Don't miss "Lemur Island," a new attraction of the park featuring lemurs from Madagasgar. The park is open daily, although hours change seasonally.

**SCHLITTERBAHN WATERPARK RESORT** **$$$$**
**305 W. Austin St.**
**New Braunfels**
**(830) 608-8532**
**www.schlitterbahn.com**

Texas's largest water park is located just about a half-hour north of San Antonio in a natural setting on the clear Comal River. This family-oriented park is not just a leader in the world of Texas parks but also a worldwide innovator with numerous water park products. The winner of numerous industry awards, including "most beautiful water park," Schlitterbahn ("slippery road") offers 1- and 2-day passes, which offers a hint at the size and incredible number of rides in this expansive park. The park has an excellent website that offers extensive information on the park and the resorts associated with it, as well as invaluable tips for your visit. Included are practical things ranging from advice on wearing glasses at the park to the availability of life vests. This place is plenty of fun for adults and kids. You can find additional information in the Kidstuff chapter.

## Close-up

### Haunted San Antonio

Behind a San Antonio home built more than 200 years ago, a night watchman hears the sound of a woman's cries coming from the depths of a sealed well. Elsewhere in the city, a museum's deceased curator still roams his former place of employment. And in an art center, a photographer feels a hand on his shoulder and turns to see a dark shadow in the room with him.

These are just a few examples of the spirited encounters that are said to have occurred in San Antonio and the nearby area. "San Antonio is a very haunted city," says Docia Williams, an author specializing in the eerie side of the Alamo City. Williams has interviewed police officers, night guards, and residents of private homes throughout the city and searched the library's archives in the process of gathering material for seven ghostly tomes, among them *Spirits of San Antonio* and *South Texas and Ghosts Along the Texas Coast.*

One of San Antonio's oldest buildings, the **Alamo** is also reported to be one of the most haunted. Today's night watchmen have heard unexplained sounds in the old mission, but the hauntings date back to the days of the historic battle. Following the battle, Mexican soldiers were said to have run from the Alamo shouting "diablos" (devils). The reference could have been to their opponents—or to some other presence in the mission.

Another Alamo ghost story concerns the order that was issued to burn the fort following the Battle of San Jacinto. Soldiers entered the old building but soon fled, refusing to carry out their mission. It is said that when their leader entered the building, he was met by six ghosts holding swords of fire—rumored to be the ghosts of the Spanish priests who built the Alamo.

The priests who haunt the Alamo are in the company of nuns not far away at the **Southwest School of Art,** according to Williams. Today a gallery and working studio for many San Antonio craftspeople, the building was once a girls' school run by cloistered nuns. "The only men ever allowed here were the doctor, if someone were very ill, and the parish priest who said the mass on Sunday," says Williams. "No other men were allowed. Now there are all these male teachers and security guards.

"The photography teacher was in the darkroom not too long ago, and he came out and felt a hand on his shoulder kind of shoving him," says the author. "He turned around and there was nothing but a dark shadow. About a month or so later, the same thing happened to him, but this time it was a misty white shadow."

Several San Antonio museums are also rumored to be haunted. The **Institute of Texan Cultures** is supposedly haunted by the ghost of its former director, a pipe smoker. Williams says late-night employees still report smelling his tobacco smoke. And when night guards make their rounds, they often find the doors of the hearse in the Castroville exhibit mysteriously open. They close the hearse doors, make their rounds, and return to find them open once again.

Another allegedly haunted museum is the **Jose Navarro house** at 228 S. Laredo, home of one of the signers of the Texas Declaration of Independence. Located next to the jail, the home is said to have cold spots, rocking chairs that move without human help, and furniture that rearranges itself. Not far away, the **Spanish Governor's Palace,** built in 1749, is supposedly haunted by the spirit of a former servant in the home. The woman was killed by robbers, and her body was thrown into a well behind the home. Today the well is capped, but night guards still report hearing her moans, says Williams.

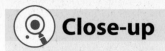

## SEAWORLD OF SAN ANTONIO $$$$

**10500 SeaWorld Dr.**

**(210) 523-3611, (800) 700-7786**

**www.seaworld.com**

Located 16 miles northwest of downtown, this 250-acre park is the largest marine-life adventure park in the world. Displays and shows featuring killer whales, dolphins, sea lions, and otters are featured, along with an enjoyable amusement and water park. The star of SeaWorld is Shamu, the 2.5-ton killer whale who engages in graceful swimming exercises with his human partners. There's room for 3,800 onlookers in this stadium, and most of the seats are safe from the huge splashes that Shamu produces as he leaps and dives in his 5 million–gallon tank. An impressive 300,000-gallon coral reef display contains the world's largest collection of Indo-Pacific fishes in a simulated coral reef environment.

SeaWorld also offers numerous rides, including 2 roller coasters and several cool (literally) water rides. More than 25 shows, rides, and animal attractions keep families happy. Lost Lagoon water park is one of SeaWorld's most popular spots on hot summer days (see the Kidstuff chapter for details). Shamu's Happy Harbor adventure play area is tops with younger visitors. The park's newest attraction, Sesame Street Bay of Play, features children's rides and opportunities to meet some beloved characters.

The park is open daily from early Mar through Dec. Hours and days of operation vary.

**i** **Traveling with your dog? Check with Six Flags Fiesta Texas and SeaWorld to arrange kennel space during your visit.**

## SIX FLAGS FIESTA TEXAS $$$$

**17000 I-10 West**

**(210) 697-5050**

**www.sixflags.com/fiestaTexas**

Fiesta Texas is a great day of entertainment for adults and kids alike. Located in a former limestone quarry in the La Cantera (that's Spanish for "quarry") development near I-10 and Loop 1604, it includes a water park, games, music, the antics of Looney Toons characters, plus rides for thrill-seekers and small fry.

Except for the water park, Fiesta Texas is divided into areas representing the area's German and Mexican heritages, the Texas coast, 1950s USA, and the Old West. Each area features food, building design, games, and rides that reflect the theme, and the park's workers—students, mostly—dress in colorful lederhosen, poodle skirts, or other bright-colored garb.

The park also features several theaters for live shows and concerts, earning frequent Golden Ticket Awards for "best theme park shows in the country."

Another favorite at the park is, of course, the rides. One of Fiesta Texas's claims to fame is the "Rattler," one of the world's tallest wooden roller coasters. Another crowd-pleaser is the "Superman Krypton Coaster," one of the largest steel coasters and the only floorless coaster in the Southwest. This one takes riders through 400-plus feet of spiral loops and corkscrew turns at a speed of more than 70 mph.

Be aware that the rides, including those in the water park, sometimes have height restrictions. Fortunately, there's a menu of rides for the younger crowd, too. (For more information on attractions for the little guys, see the Kidstuff chapter.)

During the summer, lots of visitors plan to visit the water park, with its 11 water rides and attractions, during the afternoon hours to cool off. Some families—especially those with smaller children—opt to leave the park entirely for lunch and a nap before returning in the evening for more rides and the end-of-the-day laser light show. This Texas-flavored show uses the former quarry's tall limestone cliffs as a dramatic backdrop.

Of note, this park is a perennial favorite of local junior-high-age kids, who generally buy season tickets and meet their friends there on a regular basis. Fiesta Texas is open on weekends beginning in March, for several consecutive days over spring break, and daily during the summer beginning at 10 a.m. In the fall, Fiesta Texas stays open on weekends through the middle of November.

## HISTORIC DISTRICTS

### Dignowity Hill Historic District

Located on the east side of town, north of Commerce Street, this historic neighborhood is named for Michael Dignowity, a Czechoslovakian immigrant. Dignowity served as a medical doctor in San Antonio after his arrival in the mid-1800s. The doctor had to flee the city for his life because of his outspoken views against secession; he didn't return until 1869 and at that time set about trying to recover his property, which at one time extended for blocks. Much of the surrounding land had been sold to German businessmen, and the neighborhood quickly became a wealthy enclave. The neighborhood is known for its numerous cemeteries. More than 30 dot the historic district, one of the densest collections of cemeteries in the US. It's also the site of the Hays Street Bridge, a whipple-style iron-truss bridge brought here from Louisiana between 1908 and 1910.

> **Armchair Traveler**
>
> San Antonio's many districts and neighborhoods each have their own unique style, feel, and offerings. You can check out some of these fascinating parts of town through an interactive neighborhood tour website, **www.saculturaltours.com,** an easy-to-use guide to the city's many lesser-known treasures. Whether you want to explore the westside, eastside, or downtown/River North neighborhoods, this interactive website will seamlessly guide you to the best places to eat, shop, catch a show, meet interesting people, and more. You can uncover many of the city's artists and entrepreneurs, musicians and authors; find such quirky stops as the childhood home of Carol Burnett; and immerse yourself in a fantastic array of bold and inspiring murals. It's San Antonio like you've never seen it before—through an intimate and off-the-beaten path lens.

### Ellis Alley

Located east of I-35 just beyond the Alamodome on Chestnut Street, this section of the city was one of the first to be settled by African Americans following the Civil War. Today it's primarily a residential neighborhood, but the area was once best known for its live entertainment. The focal point of the district was an auditorium that first opened in 1905 as the Colored Community House, serving as a library for the African-American population of the area. A new building was constructed in 1930 and named the Colored Library Auditorium; it soon grew to host graduations, live concerts, and debutante balls. During its peak years, Ella Fitzgerald, Duke Ellington, Nat King Cole, Paul Robeson, and many other nationally known performers appeared here. The auditorium later was renamed the Carver Library Auditorium in honor of Dr. George Washington Carver. Following desegregation, use of the auditorium declined, and eventually the facility was abandoned and slated to be demolished. Local community activist Norva Hill lay in the path of the bulldozers and stopped the destruction of the historic landmark. The auditorium was saved, and Hill was awarded the lease on the facility. In 1977 the building reopened as the Carver Cultural Community Center and is today known for its art galleries and diverse performances. (See The Arts chapter for details.)

## Government Hill

Located on the north side of town just west of I-35 around Fort Sam Houston, Government Hill is one of the most historic neighborhoods in the city. Approximately 27 percent of the neighborhood contains historic buildings.

The site is rich with military history and is known as the home of the "soldier medic." Military medical personnel from more than 30 countries around the globe train at Fort Sam Houston, which is the world's clearinghouse for military combat medicine. The base is adjacent to the original site of the West Texas Military Academy, established in 1893. The academy's most famous graduate was General Douglas MacArthur in 1897.

One of the most unique historic buildings on Government Hill is Lambermont, built in 1894. Previously known as Terrell Castle, the mansion looks out at what was once called General's Row, a street lined with the elegant homes of the fort's military leaders.

## King William Historic District

If there's a preferred address in San Antonio, it's most likely in the King William Historic District. Just a stone's throw south of the River Walk, this neighborhood boasts elegant homes, stately shade trees, and an atmosphere of grace and gentility.

Its status as a superior neighborhood goes back to the mid-1800s, when this district was populated by the Alamo City's most successful businessmen and their families. Many of these frontier citizens were German immigrants with names like Guenther, Wulff, and Heusinger. With their wealth gained in merchandising and investing, they set about building the most lavish homes in the city, most in the grand Victorian style. One of the most opulent of these residences is the Steves Homestead, positioned right on the banks of the river. Besides a natatorium (indoor swimming pool) and a carriage house, the home also boasted the finest furnishings and detail work of its era. Today it's open for public tours, as is the Guenther House, next to Pioneer Flour Mills (see below for details on both). The old mill still churns out some of the best flour gravy mix found on grocery shelves, along with corn bread, pancake, and other mixes. The San Antonio Art League Museum is also located in a historic home in this district (see below). Other historic homes in King William are privately owned, but residents are accustomed to tour buses and pedestrians sightseeing in the area. You can enjoy a self-guided tour by picking up a brochure ("King William Area—A Walking Tour") in front of the San Antonio Conservation Society headquarters in the Anton Wulff House at 107 King William St. (210-224-6163) or at a visitor center in town. The walk takes you past more than three dozen stately homes.

**EDWARD STEVES HOMESTEAD $$**
**509 King William St.**
**(210) 225-5924**
**www.saconservation.org**

On a walking or driving tour of King William, you may wonder just what the inside of these mansions is like. Satisfy your curiosity with a tour of the Steves Homestead. Once the home of German immigrant Edward Steves, founder of Steves Lumber Company, today the grand house is owned by the San Antonio Conservation Society.

The home is an example of Victorian French Second Empire style and is furnished with late 19th-century antiques. At Christmastime the house is decorated in the holiday style popular in that era. One unique feature of the property is the River House, a 1-story brick building at the rear of the mansion, which contained a natatorium—San Antonio's first indoor swimming pool. Today flooring has been laid over the pool, and the building is used as a meeting space for the San Antonio Conservation Society.

Even older than the home is its Carriage House, built a year before the grand residence. This 2-story building was later used for storage. The year after the home's completion, servants' quarters were added. Today these serve as the visitor center. The museum is open daily from 10 a.m. to 4:15 p.m.

**GUENTHER HOUSE FREE**
**205 E. Guenther St.**
**(210) 227-1061**
**www.guentherhouse.com**

Built in 1860, this was the home of Carl Hilmar Guenther (the first syllable rhymes with "when"), founder of Pioneer Flour Mills. With its crystal chandelier, gold-leaf mirrors, and piano from Stuttgart, Germany, the parlor offers a lovely glimpse of the elegance once enjoyed by the Guenther family. The home's library is now a museum, displaying family and mill artifacts such as Dresden china anniversary plates, cookie cutters, and family photos. The San Antonio River Mill Store is housed in the former music room and bedroom, and visitors can purchase stoneware, baking accessories, and gift items here. Finally, the Guenther House Restaurant, decorated in the art nouveau style, serves breakfast and lunch 7 days a week (see the Restaurants chapter for details). The museum and River Mill Store are open Mon through Sat 8 a.m. to 4 p.m. and Sun 8 a.m. to 3 p.m. Neither the store nor the museum is wheelchair accessible, although a video tour can be shown downstairs on request.

**SAN ANTONIO ART LEAGUE MUSEUM FREE**
**130 King William St.**
**(210) 223-1140**
**www.saalm.org**

The headquarters for the San Antonio Art League is a historic structure built in 1896. Changing exhibits feature various types of art, from members' current works to pieces from previous decades. The museum is open Tues through Sat from 10 a.m. to 3 p.m.

## La Villita

La Villita (www.lavillita.com), the "little village," is nestled on the east bank of the River Walk. Although right off a bustling pedestrian area, La Villita has a much different atmosphere, with an emphasis on history and art. Dating back to the days when the Alamo served as a military outpost, La Villita developed as a temporary village of squatters, people without land title. These tradesmen, camp followers, and Spanish soldiers and their families lived in primitive huts.

For years, La Villita remained a temporary settlement until a disastrous flood in 1821. The San Antonio River rose and demolished much of the west bank, but La Villita, with its slightly higher elevation, was spared. Locals began to look at the "little village" as the place to be on the river, and soon the temporary huts were replaced with more permanent structures of adobe and stone.

La Villita came to historic prominence during the Texas Revolution, when Mexican troopers were defeated after the storming of Bexar. The surrender was signed at the Cos House in the neighborhood (see below). After Texas became a state, La Villita became a neighborhood of new immigrants. The look of the neighborhood changed from Spanish adobe to European-style limestone blocks.

Within 50 years, though, La Villita hit bottom, reduced to a collection of boardinghouses and bathhouses on the river's edge. Water was hauled from the river and sold for a quarter a barrel. The region became a virtual slum and remained one of the worst areas in the city until 1939. Then, as the city turned its attention to the river, planners realized that La Villita was long due for a renovation. The National Youth Administration and the city began an extensive program of renovation and re-creation. Today this is a National Historic District, filled with structures that recall Texas's early days.

The historic buildings now house artisans and craftspeople at work on everything from fine hand-blown glass to woven shawls. You'll find Latin American imports, from tin art to Indian rugs, sold alongside the creations of San Antonio artists. This artists' community lies between San Antonio's tallest structure and the age-old river. One square block in size, it has retained an air of separateness from the River Walk. Today it is one of the top shopping districts for fine souvenirs in a collection of buildings whose styles hark back to the days of Old San Antonio. La Villita is also the site of "A Night in Old San Antonio," a Fiesta week fixture that annually draws more than 3.5 million partygoers. See "Fiesta San Antonio" in the Annual Events and Festivals chapter.

Most shops are open from 10 a.m. to 6 p.m. daily.

**COS HOUSE** **FREE**
**418 Villita St.**

The Cos House is called by some the birthplace of Texas independence. Here the articles of capitulation were signed by General Martín Perfecto de Cos on December 9, 1835, relinquishing Mexico's claim to all lands north of the Rio Grande. When General Cos returned to Mexico City and told Santa Anna of the surrender, Santa Anna swore revenge and headed his troops for the Alamo. The home is not open to the public but you can observe and photograph the exterior. The house can also be rented for special events.

**LITTLE CHURCH AT LA VILLITA FREE**
**418 Villita St., Building #1300**
**(210) 226-3593**
**http://lavillita.com/church**

The cornerstone of this tiny historic chapel was laid March 2, 1879. First a German Methodist church, the chapel was built in Gothic Revival style, with lancet-shaped casement windows and handcarved pegs made by a Norwegian sailor.

Interdenominational services are held Sun and Thurs at 11 a.m., with music beginning at 10:30 a.m. both days. The church is open daily 10 a.m. to 5 p.m., although it's usually booked for weddings on Saturday.

i A tradition since 1963, the Little Church at La Villita sponsors the Starving Artist Show during the first full weekend of April.

### Monte Vista Historic District

One of San Antonio's oldest neighborhoods, this district was declared public land by King Philip of Spain in 1729. That makes the district's San Pedro Springs Park the second-oldest municipal park in the US. Settlers from the Canary Islands built an acequia (irrigation ditch) from San Pedro Springs to households and fields. The facility served the city for a century and a half.

In the 19th century, the site became a military camp on more than one occasion. In 1846 US soldiers camped here; they were later followed by camels assigned to the region as part of Jefferson Davis's Camel Corps (it didn't work). Today the neighborhood is a quiet residential district, best known as the home of San Pedro Springs Park (see the Parks & Recreation chapter).

## TOURS

The richest source of tour information is the Visitors Information Center operated by the San Antonio Convention and Visitors Bureau. It is located at 317 Alamo Plaza, directly across from the Alamo. The information center also has brochures, maps, and San Antonio gifts.

The San Antonio Convention and Visitors Bureau also operates a toll-free phone line: (800) 447-3372. Call to order a free visitors packet, get information on convention delegate housing, or obtain information on specific attractions.

### Guided Tours

**ALAMO HELICOPTER TOURS $$$$**
**Stinson Municipal Airport**
**8535 Mission Rd.**
**(210) 287-5797**
**www.alamohelicoptertours.com**

Get a bird's-eye view of San Antonio aboard a helicopter tour. Operating from Stinson Airport south of downtown, Alamo Helicopter Tours offers a variety of tours, from a quick 7-minute flight over the city all the way up to the Ultimate Tour, lasting 45 minutes with views of downtown, the Mission Trail, and the surrounding Hill Country. Tours are aboard Robinson R-44 helicopters and are limited to 3 passengers per flight. All passengers have a window seat and headsets for communication. Tours operate year-round; hours vary by season, so it's best to call ahead.

**✳RIO SAN ANTONIO CRUISES $$**
**205 N. Presa, Building B, Suite 201**
**(210) 244-5700, (800) 417-4139**
**www.riosanantonio.com**

These colorful barges have become icons of San Antonio. The company offers cruises on the river year-round on open-air barges that operate on environmentally friendly compressed gas. Tours are narrated and are a great way to get an overview of the River Walk. This is a "don't miss" among the many available opportunities here. You'll find ticket booths at Rivercenter Mall and across the river from the Hilton Palacio del Rio. The company also runs water taxis along the River Walk (see the Getting Here, Getting Around chapter). Charter cruises and dining cruises can also be arranged. Tours operate from 9 a.m. to 9 p.m. daily.

## Houston Street Walking Tour

Historic Houston Street runs through downtown San Antonio, offering visitors a peek into the city's history and culture with 19th-century architecture, boutique hotels, theaters, and River Walk views. Now it's easier than ever to explore this district, with the new Houston Street walking tour. Known for preserving its historic attributes, San Antonio has repurposed former telephone kiosks into components of a self-guided walking tour that shares Houston Street's history from the late 1800s to the early 20th century. Stops include Alamo Plaza, the Majestic Theatre, and the Hipolito F. Garcia Federal Building and US Courthouse.

**ALAMO SIGHTSEEING TOURS $$$$**
**Alamo Visitor Center**
**122 Loyosa**
**(210) 492-4199**
**www.alamosightseeingtours.com**

This company offers visitors several city tours. The full-day tour includes the Alamo, the IMAX Theatre, an optional riverboat ride, Market Square/El Mercado, Missions San José and Concepción, the Japanese Gardens, and the Texas Ranger Museum. A half-day tour is offered in the morning and afternoon with stops at the Alamo, Market Square, Mission Concepción, and Mission San José.

San Antonio City Tours also offers guided all-day tours to the Texas Hill Country for a look at Fredericksburg and the LBJ Ranch. Another all-day trip travels to the wine-growing region around Fredericksburg. Visitors can sample the local vintages and shop Fredericksburg's Main Street.

Tours depart from Loyosa Street near the Alamo; pickup service at downtown hotels is also available.

i The San Antonio Paranormal Investigations (SAPI) organization, which delves into the possibilities of spirits in the Alamo City, offers a video documentary featuring explorations of local haunts. The 80-minute DVD can be purchased online at http://paranormalinvestigations.org.

**GHOST HUNTS OF SAN ANTONIO TEXAS TOUR $$$**
**(210) 275-9957**
**http://satxghosttour.com**

For a look at the eerie side of San Antonio, this tour convenes nightly in Alamo Plaza near the Menger Hotel. The 90-minute walks seeking the city's haunted past are led by a former cast member of *Ghost Hunters International* who is well versed in the area's supernatural legends. Will you see a ghost? Well, they don't guarantee it, but bring your camera just in case. Tours begin at 9 p.m. and cover 10 downtown locations. Reservations are recommended and may be booked until 7:30 p.m. for that night's tour; drop-ins are accepted if space permits. See "Haunted San Antonio" Close-up in this chapter for the story on local ghosts.

# KIDSTUFF

There's no denying that San Antonio is a city with a youthful atmosphere. With its wide variety of activities, from a world-class zoo to top theme parks, the city attracts families looking for vacation fun.

That youthful atmosphere is also seen in the faces of San Antonio's residents. The median age in San Antonio is just 32.3 years, younger than the national average. Children are seen at attractions, restaurants, and establishments across town and make up a large part of the population.

An excellent guide to family-friendly San Antonio attractions is found on the San Antonio Convention and Visitors Bureau website,, offering information on attractions across town. See www.visitsanantonio.com/visitors/play/family-fun/index.aspx.

Another top source of information on children's activities and attractions is *Our Kids: San Antonio*. This free publication is distributed around town at grocery stores and Walmarts. The digital version is available on the magazine's website, http://sanantonio.parenthood.com.

Along with the numerous attractions, programs, and activities, both indoors and out, available in this kid-friendly city, we've included many attractions within a short drive of San Antonio. With all that's going on in the Alamo City, there's no reason for kids ever to complain "I'm bored" while they're here.

***Price Code***

The price ratings below are for an adult admission fee during the summer high season. Keep in mind that many attractions offer significant discounts for children, seniors, and military personnel.

| | |
|---|---|
| **$** | **Less than $5** |
| **$$** | **$5 to $10** |
| **$$$** | **$10 to $20** |
| **$$$$** | **More than $20** |

## AMUSEMENT PARKS

**KIDDIE PARK** **$–$$**
**3015 Broadway at Mulberry Avenue**
**(210) 824-4351**
**www.kiddiepark.com**

Since 1925, children have delighted in this old-fashioned amusement park filled with kid-size rides. The carousel, carved in 1918, is a longtime favorite and fills the park with festive calliope music. The Little Dipper roller coaster is also popular with small visitors, as is the Ferris wheel, kiddie cars, and the game room. Individual ride prices vary; unlimited-ride passes are available. Open daily 10 a.m. to 7 p.m.

**MORGAN'S WONDERLAND** **$$–$$$**
**5223 David Edwards Dr.**
**(210) 637-3434**
**www.morganswonderland.com**

This unique 25-acre attraction northeast of downtown is designed for individuals with special needs and is the "World's First Ultra Accessible Family Fun Park." A brand-new facility built on the site of a former stone quarry, Morgan's Wonderland is completely wheelchair-accessible. It features more than 25 elements and attractions including rides, playgrounds, gardens, an 8-acre fishing lake, an 18,000-square-foot special-events center, a 575-seat amphitheater, and picnic and rest areas throughout the park. All rides have been designed to safely accommodate riders with special needs. Founder Gordon Hartman was inspired to design and build the park by his special-needs daughter, Morgan Hartman. The philanthropist realized that, like Morgan, millions of children and adults with cognitive and physical challenges were effectively barred from enjoying typical recreation activities. Gordon Hartman dedicated the efforts of the Hartman Family Foundation to correct this imbalance and to create a special kind of amusement park where no one was excluded due to their special needs. Funding came from various charitable organizations, the City of San Antonio, the State of Texas, and contributions from private individuals. The park is open daily during Jul and Aug; hours are reduced the rest of the year, but it normally is open on weekends. Call ahead to check the schedule. Reservations are suggested. General admission is $15; individuals with special needs are admitted for free; persons accompanying those with special needs are admitted for $10.

***SEAWORLD OF SAN ANTONIO $$$$**
**10500 SeaWorld Dr.**
**(210) 523-3611, (800) 700-7786**
**www.seaworld.com**

With its multitude of marine animals, SeaWorld of San Antonio is a favorite with children. The park also offers many kid-friendly rides, most found at Shamu's Happy Harbor, a play area. This 3-acre playground in the center of the park pulsates with young energy and encourages children to climb and explore. The area includes a large sandbox as well as a swinging bridge, net climbing areas, and a square-rigger with water cannons. Stop by the Sea Star theater for a 4-D experience, R. L. Stine's *Haunted Lighthouse*.

Kids' rides range from the Jungle Jump to the Shamu Express. Pete's Pinwheel Ferris wheel is always a favorite. Summer visitors also love Li'l Gators Lagoon, a shallow area in Lost Lagoon that encourages plenty of splashing and watery fun. The park is open Mar through Nov; hours vary by season. For additional details, see the Attractions chapter.

**i** Allow at least a one-day visit for each amusement park. During the heat of the Texas summer, when temperatures topping 100 degrees are not unusual, consider arriving at the park early, returning to your motel in the afternoon for a swim and a chance to rest, and then venturing back in the evening. If you want to remain in the park all day, plan to move slowly, drink plenty of fluids, and rest often.

***SIX FLAGS FIESTA TEXAS $$$$**
**17000 I-10 West**
**(210) 697-5050**
**www.sixflags.com**

Six Flags Fiesta Texas is justly known for its thrill rides, but this popular park offers plenty of pint-size rides for younger visitors as well. The Amerigoround, a classic, old-fashioned carousel, amuses the younger set in Rockville, while Yosemite Sam's Wacky Wagons gives children the chance to ride a youngster-size Ferris wheel. Taz's Tornado features swinging seats, and the Little Castaways takes kids in circles in spinning teacups. Kids will enjoy driving mini sports cars and will thrill to the Scooby Doo Ghost Blasters Mystery of the Haunted Mansion ride.

The German-themed region of the park, Spassburg, is home to several child-size rides, including Bugs' White Water Rapids and Kinderstein (both for children at least 36 inches tall). Park hours vary by season. For additional details, see the Attractions chapter.

## ART CLASSES & WORKSHOPS

**ARTWORKS**
**1840 Nacogdoches Rd.**
**(210) 826-ARTS**
**www.artworkstx.com**

This art studio was especially designed for children. Starting with early childhood classes, the studio offers art instruction and creative field trips for children. Birthday parties for ages 3 to 12 are also available. The studios are open for general admission; hours vary by location. Two other locations are at 7715 Mainland, Suite 103 (210-256-2787), and 18771 FM 2252, Garden Ridge (210-655-2787).

**CARVER COMMUNITY CULTURAL CENTER**
**226 N. Hackberry St.**
**(210) 207-7211**
**www.thecarver.org**

Carver's School of Visual and Performing Arts offers a variety of classes for children and adults. Along with drama and movement, the center offers classes in,ceramics and visual arts.

**JEWISH COMMUNITY CENTER**
**12500 NW Military Hwy.**
**(210) 302-6820**
**www.jccsanantonio.org**

The courses for children ages 3 and older offered here are open to all residents of San Antonio. In addition to arts and crafts classes, there are sports programs and science classes. Fees vary.

**SAN ANTONIO MUSEUM OF ART $$**
**200 W. Jones Ave.**
**(210) 978-8100**
**www.samuseum.org**

Every month this museum features a "First Sundays for Families" art class for children ages 12 and under. The theme of the monthly event varies. The programs are free with paid admission to the museum.

**SOUTHWEST SCHOOL OF ART**
**300 Augusta St.**
**(210) 224-1848**
**www.swschool.org**

More than 1,600 children enroll in classes at this popular art and craft school every year. One of the favorite programs is the Saturday Morning Discovery, a free introductory art class scheduled every week during the school year. Aimed at children ages 5 to 17, this program has been in operation for more than 4 decades and has introduced thousands of children to the world of ceramics, drawing, photography, painting, origami, silk-screening, stained glass, and more.

Classes are offered in one-month sessions, and parents are required to remain with their children through the program;

often parents have the opportunity to work alongside their child. Advance reservations are required for the program; call (210) 224-1848, ext. 317.

The school also sponsors the Mobile Arts Program (MAP), which brings artists into hospitals, public schools, shelters, and community centers. The workshops in drawing, clay sculpture, weaving, architecture, design, and other activities complement classroom instruction; more than 25,000 San Antonio children participate each year. To schedule classes through MAP, teachers should call the Young Artist Programs director at (210) 224-1848, ext. 331.

## BOOKSTORES

### BARNES AND NOBLE BOOKSELLERS
**11711 Bandera Rd.**
**(210) 521-9784**
**www.barnesandnoble.com**

These extensive bookstores have a B&N Junior section and offer story hours with that include snacks and crafts. The free programs vary; check out the website for additional location information.

### THE TWIG BOOK SHOP
**200 E. Grayson, Suite 124**
**(210) 826-6411**
**http://thetwig.indiebound.com**

Recently relocated to the Pearl Brewery area, this bookstore offers a free story hour every Friday at 10:30 a.m. The children's bookstore also features a variety of special events every month. In the past the store has hosted Jan Brett, author of *The Mitten* and *On Noah's Ark,* and Paul Epner, author of *Herbert Hilligan and His Magical Lunchbox.* Special appearances by Curious George, Tacky Penguin, and other costumed characters also give young shoppers the chance to have a photo taken with their favorite storybook friends.

## CAMPS

### GREEN TREE TENNIS CLUB
**4721 Callaghan Rd.**
**(210) 681-5261**
**www.greentreetennis.com**

This tennis club sponsors a variety of summer programs for children. From late May through early August, the club offers a tennis camp, with new sessions beginning each week. The camp runs weekdays from 10 a.m. to 2 p.m.; fees range from $93 to $170 per week. Children learn tennis skills and also have the opportunity to go swimming. During the summer, the Sports Camp here runs weekdays from 8 a.m. to 5:30 p.m. and includes tennis, swimming, and more activities; the cost is $156 per week for members, $166 for nonmembers. This club also offers a spring-break camp in March.

### KIDS SPORTS NETWORK GOLF CAMPS
**8206 Roughrider Dr., Suite 104**
**(210) 654-4707**
**www.ksnusa.org/camps.htm**

Is your child an aspiring Tiger Woods? You just might want to check out this day camp, designed to teach golf to young players ages 7 to 14 of all levels of ability. Participants learn everything from rules and etiquette to keeping score. On the last day of camp, the kids play a partial round of golf to exhibit their new skills.

The weeklong camp is held at either San Pedro Golf Center or Alamo Golf Club, depending on the week. All sessions include 15 hours of instruction, a set of 5 golf clubs, a golf bag, a cap, a polo shirt, a golf rule book,

## Close-up

### San Antonio Area Wildlife Ranches

From the shade of the century-old tree, the wildebeest yawns and eyes a small herd of springbok on their way to the watering hole. Nearby, a lanky ostrich saunters across the field, a few wide paces away from a dusty zebra. It's a scene witnessed by a family from the comfort of their vehicle, enjoying a daylong safari—Texas style.

Within a short drive of San Antonio, you'll find several excellent wildlife parks that let families view exotic animals in a natural setting, away from the cages and confinement of a zoo. Here the animals exhibit natural behaviors, relating to fellow herd members, teaching their young, and in other ways acting as they would in the wild.

One of the largest drive-through animal parks in Texas is the **Natural Bridge Wildlife Ranch,** located next to the caverns of the same name. About half an hour north of San Antonio, the park is located west of I-35 near New Braunfels. This ranch features both native and exotic animals, ranging from some very pushy ostriches to some rather excited zebras. After the drive, enjoy a look around the petting area, which includes some cute critters such as pygmy goats, then shop for wildlife-related souvenirs in the gift shop. The park is open daily; for directions and price information, call (830) 438-7400 or visit www.wildlife ranchtexas.com.

North of San Antonio, the community of Johnson City is home to **The Exotic Resort,** a park that lives up to its name. On 137 acres, unusual species (including many endangered animals) roam across the wooded hill country. In this park you leave the driving to someone else and enjoy a guided ride aboard a safari truck. Professional guides conduct tours of the ranch and provide visitors with information about the animals as you feed the friendly park residents. After the tour, you can see some wildlife up close at the petting zoo. Kids enjoy petting child-size miniature donkeys, baby deer, llamas, baby elk, and even a kangaroo at this special area. For directions, call (830) 868-4357 or visit www.zooexotics.com

If your children enjoy petting zoos, then don't miss the largest one in Texas, located at San Marcos's **Wonder World.** Just north of San Antonio on I-35, this park is best known for its cave, created by an earthquake about 30 million years ago. There's plenty of action aboveground as well, though, at the 7.5-acre **Texas Wildlife Park.** Kids and parents can all hop aboard a miniature train for a ride through the animal enclosure. Along the way, the train stops to allow riders to pet and feed tame white-tailed deer, turkeys, and many exotic species. This park is open throughout the year; for information call (877) 492-4657 or look online at www.wonderworldpark.com.

Whichever park you visit, don't forget your camera. And for best viewing of the animals, try to arrive either early or late in the day. Especially during warm-weather months, most animals will retire to the cool shade at midday, so your best chance of seeing active animals is when the park first opens or just before sunset.

golf balls, and tees. Golf camps are held from 8:30 to 11:30 a.m.

**SAN ANTONIO CHILDREN'S MUSEUM**
**305 E. Houston St.**
**(210) 212-4453**
**www.sakids.org**

The museum sponsors several summer camps, each led by museum educators. The camps, are aimed at children ages 2 to 6. Themes for the summer camps vary but center on art and culture exploration; previous themes have been "Mask Mania," when participants had the opportunity to learn about cultures around the world as they made masks out of natural and man-made materials, and "Look at Culture through Food," where kids explored cultures from around the world by creating regional dishes. Costs for the camps run from $85 to $175 ($75 to $150 for museum members).

**SEAWORLD OF SAN ANTONIO**
**10500 SeaWorld Dr.**
**(210) 523-3611, (800) 700-7786**
**www.seaworld.com**

SeaWorld has long been a favorite destination for children, but the popular amusement park also offers many child-specific programs for children from pre-K through grade 8 and their families. Day camps include Shamu's Stroller Club (ages 1 to 2 with adult), introducing infants and toddlers to the sights and sounds of the sea; Shamu's SeaSchool (ages 3 to 4 with adult), exploring the sea with role play, songs, crafts, and hands-on exploration; Small Wonders (ages 3 to 4 with adult), where campers and their parents learn about the world of playful sea creatures including belugas and majestic killer whales; Ocean Quest (ages 5 to 12), for an up-close view of the lives of sea lions, whales, and penguins; and Let's Get Wet! (ages 5 to 12), in which campers cool off from the Texas heat in SeaWorld's wet and wild attractions.

SeaWorld also offers sleepover options for children of different ages. Sleepover activities include dinner, games, and other fun while spending the night at one of the park's animal habitats, and a continental breakfast the following morning. Like the day camps, sleepovers are divided into age-appropriate groups and some have special themes, such as those for Boy and Girl Scout groups, birthday groups, seasonal sleepovers, and some designed for whole families. All SeaWorld sleepovers conform to educational standards established by the National Science Education Standards and Texas Essential Knowledge and Skills.

Another option is the SeaWorld Resident Camps, which give older children a more in-depth look at the fascinating world of working with animals. Resident Camps include Expedition Camp (for grades 5 to 8), Career Camp (grades 9 to 12), Advanced Career Camp (grades 10 to 12), and Counselor in Training Camp (grades 11 to 12). All Resident Camps are multinight sleepaways that utilize hands-on learning about animals and their environment.

**SOUTHWEST SCHOOL OF ART**
**300 Augusta St.**
**(210) 224-1848**
**www.swschool.org**

This school offers weeklong art camps for children ages 5 to 18. Choose from all-day, morning, or afternoon sessions, which run from Jun until mid-Aug. Classes cover a range of topics such as photography, weaving, painting, drawing, architecture, and more. You'll even find specialized class topics such as anime cartoons, the art of the

Surrealists, 3-D animation, painting like an Egyptian, and clay crafting for teens.

Registration is required for these popular camps. You can register in person, by phone, online, or by mail or fax. Class size is limited, and registration is on a first-come, first-served basis. Scholarships based on merit and need are available. To be considered for a Young Artist Programs scholarship, students must submit written recommendations from a classroom teacher or qualified professional and parent or guardian.

The cost of the full-day camps (which include 5 full days, a supervised lunch hour, and 2 hours of supervised after-class activities) is $290 for nonmembers. Half-day programs are $140 for nonmembers.

**WITTE MUSEUM**
**3801 Broadway**
**(210) 357-1900**
**www.wittemuseum.org**

In the summer months and during holiday and spring-break weeks, the Witte Adventure Club provides plenty of interesting activities for children ages 6 to 11. Each of the camp sessions focuses on a particular topic such as "Amazon Adventure: Riches of the Rainforest" and "Expedition San Antonio River: Watercolors, Waterfalls, and Fountains."

Weeklong sessions run from 9 a.m. to 5 p.m. A limited number of need-based scholarships are available on a first-come, first-served basis. Reservations are required for all camp sessions; call (210) 357-1910.

**YMCA CAMP FLAMING ARROW**
**190 Flaming Arrow Rd., Hunt**
**(800) 765-YMCA, (830) 238-4631**
**www.ymcasatx.org**

The YMCA offers 1- and 2-week residential summer camp sessions for girls and boys ages 8 to 15 at a 213-acre camp. Located between the Hill Country and the Guadalupe River, the ranch is located in the town of Hunt, 90 minutes from San Antonio. Activities include horseback riding, canoeing, archery, swimming, folk arts and crafts, hiking, and more. Campers also learn about the natural world that surrounds them with sessions on the plant and animal life of Texas.

**Y.O. RANCH ADVENTURE CAMP**
**1736 Y.O. Ranch Rd. Northwest**
**Mountain Home**
**(830) 640-3220**
**www.yoadventurecamp.com**

The historic Y.O. Ranch, well known throughout Central and South Texas, hosts an adventure camp for children ages 7 to 16. Especially valuable for city children, the camp lets kids experience life on a 40,000-acre ranch. Campers learn ranch skills and more. One- and 2-week sessions are offered.

## GAMES & ARCADES

**GREEN ACRES GOLF & GAMES $$–$$$**
**9782 US 87 East**
**(210) 649-4653**
**www.greenacresminigolf.com**

One of San Antonio's newest attractions, Green Acres is a one-stop destination for youth-centric games and fun. The focus here is on outdoor action, from miniature golf to bumper boats to batting cages. You can also work out on the trampolines, have a water-balloon war, or pan for treasure in the Mining Sluice. Older kids can play paintball or have a go-kart race. A full-service snack bar serves burgers, hot dogs, pizza, and nachos, and the video arcade offers carnival-style prizes for the winners. Green Acres is also available for party rentals to celebrate birthdays and other special events. Open 10 a.m. to 10 p.m. Mon through Thurs, 10 a.m. to midnight Fri and Sat, and 1 to 9 p.m. Sun. After Labor Day the park is open 11 a.m. to 9 p.m. Mon through Thurs, 10 a.m. to 10 p.m. Fri and Sat, and 1 to 9 p.m. Sun.

**KIDDIE PARK** **$–$$**
**3015 Broadway at Mulberry Avenue**
**(210) 824-4351**
**www.kiddiepark.com**

This San Antonio institution, in operation since 1925, claims to be the oldest children's amusement park in the nation. It features an antique carousel, small roller coaster, and old-fashioned but still kid-pleasing rides such as helicopters and boats. More modern amusements are in the game room. Unlimited rides are $12.

**LASER QUEST** **$$**
**606 Embassy Oaks**
**(210) 499-4400**
**www.laserquest.com**

Laser tag is the name of the game at this high-tech gaming center that adds space-age lasers to the joy of hide-and-seek. The multilevel gaming area pits players against each other; the idea is to "shoot" other players and remove them from the game. Players can play alone or with friends; the center is also very popular for birthday parties and group gatherings. Reservations are accepted. A second location is at 6420 NW Loop 410 (210-520-8555).

**MALIBU GRAND PRIX** **$–$$**
**3330 Cherry Ridge Dr.**
**(210) 341-6663**
**www.malibugrandprix.com/site/sanantonio**

The grand-prix-style tracks are designed so all ages can experience the thrill of driving a mini race car. A video game room, miniature golf course, bumper boats, and batting cages add to the fun. There's a separate fee for each activity.

## HISTORIC SITES

**ALAMO** **FREE**
**300 Alamo Plaza**
**(210) 225-1391**
**www.thealamo.org**

Schoolchildren throughout Texas often see the Alamo on school-sponsored trips, but the historic site makes an excellent destination for family trips as well. The former mission church is a quiet, solemn place where children can learn more about the battle and the Texians and Mexicans who died here. Also part of the complex is the Long Barrack Museum, where a film about the event is shown. The film is of interest to children 10 and over; for younger children, the grounds are a nice place to walk on cool days.

The Alamo offers several educational programs, from teacher in-service to an orientation film produced by the History Channel to packets for 4th- and 7th-grade teachers. Teachers can find information online, and some of the information might also be of interest to parents: how to get the most out of your visit to the Alamo, how to build a model of the Alamo, and the Alamo History Hunt, a fill-in-the-blank form children can complete as they tour the facility.

The Daughters of the Republic of Texas, the caretakers of the Alamo, have constructed an amphitheater on the mission grounds. Located on the eastern end of the complex, the 78-seat amphitheater is used for lectures and seminars. For more information on the Alamo, see the Attractions chapter.

**QUADRANGLE AT FORT SAM HOUSTON** **FREE**
**Grayson Street and N. New Braunfels Avenue**
**(210) 221-1232**
Fort Sam Houston is best known for its extensive military history museum, but to its youngest visitors, the resident deer and peacocks are much more exciting. Many of the deer are so tame that they can be petted and hand-fed. Call for current information regarding visitors to the base.

**SAN ANTONIO MISSIONS National Historical Park** **DONATION**
**6701 San Jose Dr. (Visitor Center)**
**(210) 932-1001**
**www.nps.gov/saan**
This national park is spread along the Mission Trail, which encompasses 4 historic missions. Start your self-guided tour at the Mission San José Visitors Center, where you can pick up a Junior Ranger packet. Geared for children in the 2nd to 6th grades, the packet points out special attractions and activities of interest to children. A 23-minute film shown at Mission San José provides young visitors with a good overview of the purpose and history of the missions. See the Attractions chapter for detailed information on each mission. Be aware that fire ants are a problem in this area and can be very painful for young children. Good walking shoes are important for the irregular floors of the missions as well. The missions are open daily 9 a.m. to 5 p.m. but are closed Thanksgiving, Christmas, and New Year's Day.

## KID-FRIENDLY FESTIVALS

For schedules, admission fees, and other information about most of the following events, see the Annual Events & Festivals chapter.

### February

**SAN ANTONIO STOCK SHOW AND RODEO**
**1 AT&T Pkwy., AT&T Center at the Freeman Coliseum Grounds**
**(210) 225-5851**
**www.sarodeo.com**
The annual rodeo is definitely a family-friendly event. Along with a stock show, educational displays, and a carnival midway, families with children also enjoy the rodeo's Family Fair and World of Animals, which gives kids the chance to pet livestock. Check the website for tickets.

### March

**REMEMBERING THE ALAMO WEEKEND**
**Alamo Plaza**
**(210) 279-4973, (210) 723-1730**
**www.sanantoniolivinghistory.org**
When asked about the Alamo, many children only mention the fateful battle that took place within these walls. However, this former mission and the surrounding area once served as a home for the region's pioneers, both from Mexico and from the US. This special weekend, always scheduled the Saturday and Sunday nearest March 6 (the anniversary of the fall of the Alamo), takes a look at the life, not the death, of the people of that time period. Costumed actors bring the era to life with demonstrations of spinning, weaving, pioneer medicine, and more. Admission is free.

## April

### FORD CHILDREN'S FESTIVAL
**Rivercenter Mall Lagoon**
**(210) 227-4262**
**www.thesanantonioriverwalk.com**

Adults don't get to have all the fun at Fiesta; this officially sanctioned Fiesta event is especially designed for the youngest partygoers. Held along the River Walk at the Rivercenter Mall lagoon and sponsored by the Paseo del Rio Association, this 1-day event features live entertainment, face painting, and more. Admission is free.

## May

### TEXAS STATE ARTS AND CRAFTS FAIR
**4000 Riverside Dr., Kerrville**
**(830) 896-5711, (888) 335-1455**
**www.tacef.org**

Held on the grounds of the 7.5-acre River Star Arts & Event Park, this crafts fair is a favorite with adults for its excellent shopping, but it also offers good family fun. There's a special area where children can make and exhibit their own artwork, pet exotic species, and play on the rock-climbing wall. Other activities for children include train rides, cave painting, puppet-making, and fishing games.

## June

### FIESTA NOCHE DEL RIO
**Arneson River Theatre**
**(210) 226-4651**
**www.alamo-kiwanis.org/fiestanoche.html**

Children enjoy the colorful dances and catchy rhythms of this summer production, staged at the Arneson River Theatre. For 5 decades, this show has been sponsored by the Alamo Kiwanis Club as a fund-raiser for children's charities in San Antonio. It celebrates the many cultures of San Antonio through song and dance every Fri and Sat night mid-May through mid-Aug.

### TEXAS FOLKLIFE FESTIVAL
**Institute of Texan Cultures**
**801 E. Durango Blvd.**
**HemisFair Plaza**
**(210) 458-2224**
**www.texasfolklifefestival.org**

Kids love this June festival for its crafts exhibits, folk dances, and fun atmosphere. The festival is also an excellent way to introduce children to other cultures (not to mention other cuisines) and to enjoy a fun and educational family weekend.

## December

### FIESTA DE LAS LUMINARIAS
**Paseo del Rio**
**(210) 227-4262**
**www.thesanantonioriverwalk.com**

Thousands of luminarias, tiny candles in sand-weighted paper bags, guide visitors to the River Walk during this special Christmas celebration. The candles symbolize the lighting of the way for the Holy Family.

For children, a candlelit walk is a magical pre-bedtime treat. This event is sponsored by the Paseo del Rio Association and happens every Fri, Sat, and Sun in Dec; admission is free.

### SAN FERNANDO CATHEDRAL—LA GRAN POSADA
**115 Main Plaza**
**(210) 227-1297**
**www.sfcathedral.org**

La Gran Posada continues the centuries-old Spanish tradition of reenacting Mary and Joseph's search for shelter on the night of the birth of Jesus. The procession of costumed children, priests, and mariachi players starts at Milam Park and concludes at San Fernando Cathedral. La Gran Posada is held the Sunday before Christmas.

## LIBRARIES

In addition to the Central Library (listed here), San Antonio's library system includes 26 branch libraries throughout the city. The branch libraries all have children's sections and offer special programs for young readers throughout the year. The San Antonio Public Library System also operates an online program for students in 8th through 12th grade. Along with research assistance, the program's website (www.mysapl.org/teens.aspx) offers games, online magazines, and suggestions on teen fiction.

**SAN ANTONIO CENTRAL LIBRARY**
**600 Soledad Plaza**
**(210) 207-2500**
**www.mysapl.org**

Story time at the "Big Red Library" downtown takes place on the special Children's Floor. There are also puppet shows, arts and crafts classes, and musical activities for kids, all free.

## MUSEUMS

**BUCKHORN SALOON AND MUSEUM $$$**
**318 E. Houston St.**
**(210) 247-4000**
**www.buckhornmuseum.com**

This museum displays trophies and wax figures; of greatest interest to children, however, is the live entertainment. Although it varies by day, kids can visit the 120-year-old bar for a soda and watch trick roping, gunfighters, or a cowboy poet. The Buckhorn Arcade is also tops with young visitors. The museum is open daily. For additional details, see the Attractions chapter.

**INSTITUTE OF TEXAN CULTURES $$**
**801 E. Durango Blvd.**
**(210) 458-2300**
**www.texancultures.utsa.edu**

Texas was settled by more than 30 ethnic groups from around the world, all honored at this museum operated by the University of Texas. Families should start their visit at the Dome Theater; kids can lie back on the floor and watch the show—which highlights the many faces of Texas—overhead. Around the theater are exhibits on groups such as Native Americans, Swedes, and Canary Islanders. The Native American area is always of particular interest to young children; it houses a Sioux tepee tanned with buffalo brains. Docents are on hand to explain more about the life of the Sioux, and kids can even touch the tools these early residents used. The historic buildings behind the museum, including a one-room schoolhouse and a frontier fort, are also kid-pleasers. The museum is open 9 a.m. to 5 p.m. Mon through Sat and noon to 5 p.m. Sun, and closed on Christmas Eve, Christmas Day, and New Year's Day.

**✱SAN ANTONIO CHILDREN'S MUSEUM $$**
**305 E. Houston St.**
**(210) 212-4453**
**www.sakids.org**

Hands-on fun is the theme of this interactive museum. Targeted to children ages 0 to 10, it gives young visitors an opportunity to explore subjects from gardening to global communications. Kids learn to create all kinds of bubbles in the Hill Country

Bubble Ranch, while the Tot Spot features several play areas where babies can safely explore the physical world around them while developing their motor skills with interactive activities. This museum also offers many regularly scheduled children's events and classes. Weekly workshops help children develop a love of learning through classes such as Pint Sized Science, where kids explore such natural phenomena as weather, electricity, and animals, and Art Studio, where they develop self-expression through the creation of art projects. Admission to the workshops is free with museum admission. The museum is open from 9 a.m. to 5 p.m. Mon through Fri, from 9 a.m. to 6 p.m. Sat, and from noon to 5 p.m. Sun.

**WITTE MUSEUM** **$$**
**3801 Broadway**
**(210) 357–1900**
**www.wittemuseum.org**

This museum has long been a favorite with children because of its interactive exhibits. But for the past several years, families have had more reasons than ever to visit, thanks to the H-E-B ScienceTreehouse. Built like a genuine tree house, this 15,000-square-foot building spans 4 levels and is located on the museum grounds. Tucked in the trees and sheltered from the sounds of traffic, the Treehouse challenges young visitors with hands-on science exhibits. No matter how energetic the child, this center offers activities that entertain and teach at the same time. Kids can launch a tennis ball two stories in the air, use laser beams to produce music, or lift themselves with pulleys and ropes.

The first and second levels of the Treehouse contain most of the hands-on exhibits. The first floor contains "Move It," a vertical wave ladder made of undulating copper rods; "Flying Forces," a mechanized mobile controlled by joy sticks; and "Suddenly Superhuman," a multigear system that pits six people against one. Discovery Areas help visitors connect the concepts learned in these exhibits with their everyday lives. This floor also includes a museum store, an observation porch overlooking the San Antonio River, and "Small World Science," for kids up to 6 years old.

The second level of the Treehouse contains "Eye Spy and Magnify," a high-powered microscope that enables visitors to see inside their own ear; "Magnetic Tug-of-War," a variety of experiments using magnets; "Computer Animation Video," an opportunity for visitors to create unique three-dimensional animation; and the "Internet Surfing Station," with computer terminals offering access to the World Wide Web (special controls protect children from inappropriate material).

The underground level of the Treehouse includes an archaeological profile of the site of the Treehouse as well as exhibits on the region's past. One exhibit includes part of a hearth of a campsite dating back 4,000 years. Throughout the year, the museum plans overnight camps as well as live theater performances in this area.

At the top is the Treetop level, overlooking Brackenridge Park. Here children can use telescopes or view exhibits such as "Hang It and Clang It," musical science stations for creating sounds using natural and artificial materials; and "A-Maze Yourself," a large floor maze for visitors to navigate, patterned after a Navajo rug in the Witte's permanent collection.

The grounds are also home to a genuine tree house, which spans two levels. Created by San Antonio sculptor Carlos Cortes, the tree house is erected on two concrete "oak" trees; the upper level of the tree house offers binoculars for watching area wildlife.

The museum also hosts many special events throughout the year. During the summer months and holiday weeks, the facility sponsors the Witte Adventure Club (see Camps, earlier in this chapter).

The museum is open Mon through Sat 10 a.m. to 5 p.m. and Sun from noon to 5 p.m. On Tues the museum stays open until 8 p.m., and everyone gets in free between 3 and 8 p.m. Admission is $8 for adults, $7 for seniors 65 years and over, $6 for children ages 4 to 11, and free for children 3 and under. The admission fee includes both the Witte Museum and the H-E-B Science Treehouse. For more information about the Witte Museum, see the Attractions chapter.

## MUSIC

### JENSEN'S YAMAHA MUSIC SCHOOL

**2241 NW Military Hwy., Suite 202-B**
**(210) 366-5048**
**www.jensensyamahamusic.com**

Children ages 3 to 7 are taught according to the Yamaha method at this school, now in operation more than 30 years. Instruction is available in keyboard, singing, movement, solfège, and music appreciation. Call for a free preview class.

### SAN ANTONIO SYMPHONY

**130 E. Travis St., Suite 550**
**(210) 554-1010**
**www.sasymphony.org**

The San Antonio Symphony hosts 2 programs for young people. Its Family Series at Trinity University's Laurie Auditorium happens 5 times a year and includes a variety of hands-on activities such as the Instrument Petting Zoo, where kids get to handle and play instruments, and the Concert Close-ups that allow children to take conducting lessons on stage. The Young People's Concert Series is an excellent introduction to the world of classical music. The symphony also sponsors an annual Future Stars Concerto Competition for local students. (See more information in The Arts chapter.)

## OTHER INDOOR ATTRACTIONS

### IMAX THEATRE AT RIVERCENTER MALL $$

**849 E. Commerce St. at Rivercenter Mall**
**(210) 247-4629, (800) 354-4629**
**www.imax-sa.com**

*Alamo: The Price of Freedom,* the IMAX movie that is the main attraction here, is considered one of the best and most historically correct film versions of the famous event. And it is a pleasure to watch in this state-of-the-art big-screen theater. Other IMAX releases are also shown periodically. The IMAX also offers 3-D shows on a variety of subjects.

### LOUIS TUSSAUD'S WAXWORKS $$

**301 Alamo Plaza**
**(210) 224-9299**
**http://sanantonio.ripleys.com**

Located directly across the street from the Alamo, Louis Tussaud's Waxworks has more than 225 lifelike wax figures. For children, the most interesting sections are the Hollywood exhibits, which include replicas of present-day stars such as Brad Pitt and Britney Spears, and the Heroes of the Lone Star, featuring the historic figures who fought at the Alamo. A note to parents: The Theater of Horrors is especially scary for young (and even not-so-young) children. However, this attraction is accessible only by entering a well-marked door at the bottom of a staircase, so you can easily skip the stairs and bypass the creepy exhibits without even a peek. Of special interest to little ones is the Children's Land of Make Believe, filled with fantasy characters. The museum is open daily, though hours change by season. The ticket box office closes 1 hour prior to closing time. Combination tickets with the Believe It or Not! Odditorium (see listing) are available.

**RIPLEY'S BELIEVE IT OR NOT! ODDITORIUM** **$$**
**301 Alamo Plaza**
**(210) 224-9299**
**http://sanantonio.ripleys.com**
Located in the same facility as Louis Tussaud's Waxworks just across the street from the Alamo, Believe It or Not! Odditorium is filled with the unusual and odd. Some exhibits in the collection—the torture devices and shrunken heads, for example—may be a little too strange for very young children. Other children will enjoy such unusual exhibits as the Lord's Prayer on a grain of rice. In all, more than 500 oddities are housed in the museum. The collection is open daily; hours vary by season.

**SCOBEE PLANETARIUM AT SAN ANTONIO COLLEGE** **$**
**1300 San Pedro Ave.**
**(210) 486-0100**
**www.alamo.edu/sac/ce/scobee**
Would-be astronomers will enjoy the presentations projected on the planetarium dome on Friday nights; there are 3 different shows, at 6:30, 7:45, and 9 p.m. Children under 6 years of age are not admitted to the 2 later shows; tots under 4 are not admitted to any shows. The planetarium is named for NASA astronaut Commander Francis R. (Dick) Scobee, former student of San Antonio College, who was killed in the Space Shuttle *Challenger* disaster.

## OUTDOOR ATTRACTIONS

**LIGHTNING RANCH** **$$$$**
**Highway 16, Pipe Creek**
**(830) 535-4096**
**www.lightningranch.com**
Located 30 minutes from San Antonio, Lightning Ranch welcomes families for the day or overnight in bed-and-breakfast–style guest houses. Kids can help groom a horse, pet barnyard animals, or even ride a camel. The ranch offers daily guided horseback rides through the Hill Country. The shortest rides are an hour long; half-day rides are also offered. For the half-day ride, the wrangler packs you a saddlebag lunch to enjoy atop one of the area's hills overlooking Medina Lake. The cost for a 1-hour ride is $30 per person; 2-hour rides are $75 per person. Half-day rides (with lunch) are $155 per person. Parents who just want to lead while their small children ride are charged $10 per half-hour. Minimum riding age is 8 and there is a 225-pound weight limit for all riders.

**LOVE CREEK ORCHARDS**
**14024 Highway 16 North, Medina**
**(830) 589- 2202, (800) 449-0882**
**www.lovecreekorchards.com**
From April through mid-June, you can pick your own peaches and blackberries at this orchard in the small town of Medina. Later in the year, the focus changes to apples, figs, and persimmons. Call for ripe reports to find the best time for you and your children to

## Close-up

### San Antonio Area Caves

Caverns can be the perfect family activity, especially when the San Antonio summer is getting you down. Within a short drive of San Antonio are six commercial caves, each offering well-lighted, easy-to-follow trails that every member of the family can enjoy. Here you'll view a quiet world where progress takes place one drop of water at a time.The following is an overview of the intriguing worlds found under the region's surface, arranged according to their distance from San Antonio (closest to farthest).

Cave tours generally last from 45 minutes to 90 minutes. Good walking shoes are a must for the tours, although the caverns have broad, well-lit trails that even preschoolers can handle. Sweaters are a good idea, too—it's cool underground. Tours generally cost $10 to $12. All the caves are open year-round; call for specific hours.

**Cascade Caverns** (830-755-8080; www.cascadecaverns.com), outside of Boerne off I-10, is named for its 90-foot waterfall. Cascade Caverns has welcomed the public since 1932, but it's clear that both man and animals were here much earlier. One of the first visitors, more than 50,000 years ago, was a mastodon whose bones remain in the cave today. Later, ancient Indian tribes held ceremonies within the cave's first room, fearing to venture beyond the reassuring sunlight. The largest cave in the area is **Natural Bridge Caverns,** located north of San Antonio at exit 175 off I-35 (210-651-6101; www.naturalbridgecaverns.com). Tours take visitors through enormous rooms with names like "The Castle of the White Giants." The gargantuan halls of limestone were discovered in 1960 by four spelunkers from St. Mary's University. Cave developers later carved passages from room to room, resulting in a comfortable walk through this long cavern. Reminiscent of New Mexico's Carlsbad Caverns, Natural Bridge Caverns takes its name from a rock bridge between two sinkholes, the original entrance to the mouth of the cavern. The sinkholes have been known since the 19th century, but there is evidence of much earlier visitors. Bones of an American black bear at least 8,000 years old have been discovered, as well as human bones, stone weapons, and other Indian artifacts. North of San Antonio on I-35 is **Wonder World Cave** (512-392-3760), a cavern where you won't see sparkling cave formations, waterfalls, or auditorium-size rooms. But you will see one very unique attraction: a view of the Balcones Fault from inside the fault. The cave was produced during a 3.5-minute earthquake 30 million years ago. That same quake formed the Balcones Fault, an 1,800-mile line separating Texas's western Hill Country from the flat eastern farmland. Within the cave, you'll see boulders lodged in the fissure.

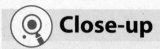

Farther north on I-35 is Georgetown, home of **Inner Space** (512-931-CAVE; www.myinnerspacecavern.com). The cave was discovered in 1963 when road crews building the highway drilled into one of the large rooms. Subsequent drilling and exploration revealed that a major cavern wound below the proposed highway. Remains of Ice Age mastodons, wolves, saber-toothed tigers, and glyptodons (a kind of prehistoric armadillo) have been discovered, and an 80-foot cavern wall has been decorated with a modern artist's renderings of these ancient creatures.

The granddaddy of all the Hill Country caves is **Longhorn Cavern** (877-441-CAVE; www.longhorncaverns.com), located near Burnet, 123 miles north of San Antonio. The cavern was used by prehistoric people, but its most dramatic events have occurred since the 1800s. Comanche once kidnapped a young woman named Mariel King and brought her back to the cavern. The Indians did not realize they had been followed by three Texas Rangers. When the Indians prepared a campfire, the Rangers fired on them, grabbed Mariel King, and raced for the entrance. Meanwhile, the surviving Comanche regrouped and began their counterattack, falling upon the Rangers before they reached the cavern entrance. A desperate hand-to-hand battle took place, with the Rangers finally escaping with Mariel King. Ending the story with a fairy-tale flourish, King later married one of her rescuers, Logan Van Deveer, and the couple made their home in Burnet.

Years later, Confederate soldiers used Longhorn Cavern's main room as a munitions factory. Bat guano from the cave was an ingredient in the manufacture of gunpowder. Additional small rooms in the back reaches of the cavern were used as storerooms for the gunpowder. The cave went unused for several decades until the Roaring Twenties. A local businessman opened a dance hall in the largest room of the cave, building a wooden dance floor several feet above the limestone. When it proved successful, he then opened a restaurant in the next room, lowering food through a hole in the cavern ceiling. Next, an area minister decided to take advantage of the cool temperature and built bleachers to accommodate crowds for Sunday services. When the Depression struck, the owners were forced to sell the cave. It was purchased by the state and opened as a state park in 1932.

**The Caverns of Sonora** (325-387-3105; www.cavernsofsonora.com) have been described by some cave experts as the most beautiful in the world. The one hour, 45-minute tour offers a look at spectacular stalactites, stalagmites, and unusual butterfly-shaped formations of the Crystal Palace. To reach the caverns, just follow I-10 through Junction and past the town of Sonora to RM 1989. They're about 180 miles northwest of San Antonio.

After a tour of some of the San Antonio–area caverns, you'll have to agree that this region's beauty reaches far below its surface.

go out and pick some fruit. Fruit pickers can bring their lunch and eat in a picnic area near the orchards. No admission fee; you pay for the fruit you pick.

**NATURAL BRIDGE CAVERNS $$$–$$$$**
**26495 Natural Bridge Caverns Rd., exit 175 off I-35**
**(210) 651-6101**
**www.naturalbridgecaverns.com**

The huge rooms and wide, well-lit walkways of this cavern make it especially popular with families. Most take part in the Discovery-Tour, which runs about 75 minutes. Children enjoy a look at rooms such as Sherwood Forest, named for its many stalagmite formations, and the Hall of the Mountain King, which is more than 350 feet in length. Even kids who don't want to visit the cave will enjoy the Natural Bridge Mining Company. A sluice (series of troughs) is seeded with small pieces of amethyst, sapphire, obsidian, topaz, and other stones. For a fee, kids can pan for jewels—and keep anything they find. Hours change seasonally. For additional details, see the Attractions chapter.

**NATURAL BRIDGE WILDLIFE RANCH $$$**
**26515 Natural Bridge Caverns Rd.**
**(830) 438-7400**
**www.wildliferanchtexas.com**

Want to take your children on an African safari? Here's a chance for an abbreviated version, Texas-style. More than 50 species of exotic animals reside at this, Texas's most-visited safari park. Children especially love Lemur Island and the petting zoo at the conclusion of the drive. The park is open daily, although hours change seasonally. For additional details, see the Attractions chapter.

**RIVER WALK (PASEO DEL RIO) FREE**
**Downtown**
**(210) 224-9951**
**www.thesanantonioriverwalk.com**

The River Walk is an excellent destination for children. Kids enjoy the colorful walk, the shops filled with piñatas and *cascarones* (confetti-filled eggs), and the festive atmosphere. You'll find a wheelchair-accessible route marked with signs along the River Walk; if you're pushing a stroller, this route will be the easiest to maneuver. For more information, see the Attractions chapter.

**SAN ANTONIO BOTANICAL GARDEN $**
**555 Funston Place**
**(210) 207-3250**
**www.sabot.org**

Kids with green thumbs will love the San Antonio Botanical Garden. These extensive gardens offer plenty of activities for the youngest visitors. One of the most popular programs is the annual Children's Garden. The program accepts children ages 8 to 13 on a first-come, first-served basis. Participants meet every Sat from 9 to 11 a.m. at the garden to learn more about planting, growing, and harvesting vegetables. All supplies are provided by the garden, and the children are assisted by volunteers from the San Antonio Men's Garden Club, Bexar County Master Gardeners, and the staff of the San Antonio Botanical Garden. Admission to the program is $25 per child, and kids should plan on attending all meetings. (If they have three absences, they may be dropped from the program.) To register, call the garden's office at (210) 207-3270.

Throughout the year, the garden also hosts many other child-focused programs. Little Sprout Mondays introduces kids ages

3 to 4 to the wonders of growing things through hands-on demonstrations, storytelling, and craft activities. Session themes include seeds, insects and butterflies, and garden animals. Sessions are held Mon from 10 to 11:30 a.m. and cost $3 plus garden admission.

The garden is open daily except Thanksgiving, Christmas, and New Year's Day. From Mar through Oct, the garden is open 9 a.m. to 6 p.m.; during the winter months, the hours are 9 a.m. to 5 p.m. For additional details about the Botanical Garden, see the Attractions chapter.

**i** The Texas Parks and Wildlife Department has a special Internet section dedicated to children's fun. Check out www.tpwd.state.tx.us/kids/fun_stuff for dinosaur information, a coloring book, games, and plenty of information designed for young outdoor lovers.

**SAN ANTONIO ZOO** **$$**
**3903 N. St. Mary's St.**
**(210) 734-7184**
**www.sa-zoo.org**

The San Antonio Zoo is one of the largest in the US and has operated on the same site (an old rock quarry) since 1914. Among its 3,800 different animals is an exhibit of endangered whooping cranes; kids will be amazed by their 7-foot wingspans. The zoo runs many educational programs for children. For instance, the S.A.fari Kids program for ages 7 to 10 meets one Sunday each month and includes animal encounters, projects, and games. Zoo School, for ages 3 to 5, introduces tiny naturalists to a variety of aspects of the zoo and up-close animal education. The zoo is open daily from 9 a.m. to 6 p.m. in summer, and until 5 p.m. the rest of the year. For additional information, see the Attractions chapter.

## PARKS & PLAYGROUNDS

**BRACKENRIDGE PARK**
**3910 N. St. Mary's St.**
**(210) 207-7275**

Brackenridge Park is a fine place for a picnic or a stroll, but for visitors it's also a major destination because of the many attractions found there. Families should budget at least half a day, for example, to visit the San Antonio Zoo (see listing). Garden lovers, too, will find a wealth of sites to explore. Brackenridge Park is home to the Japanese Tea Gardens (see listing), and nearby San Antonio Botanical Garden (see listing) displays plants from the Lone Star State and from around the globe. Other children's attractions are sprinkled throughout Brackenridge Park. A miniature railroad, the San Antonio Zoo Eagle (3810 N. St. Mary's St.; 210-735-7455), runs 2.5 miles through the park. Every train is a replica of an 1863 C. P. Huntington model. This ride has a small admission fee.

For additional information on Brackenridge Park, see the Parks & Recreation chapter.

**DWIGHT D. EISENHOWER PARK DONATION**
**19399 NW Military Hwy.**
**(210) 564-6400**
**www.sanaturalareas.org**

This park offers the Second Saturday program, which teaches parents and children more about the natural world. First Saturday Nature Walks offer guided hikes and talks focusing on the South Texas landscape, birdlife, wildlife, and plants. Reservations are recommended.

**FRIEDRICH WILDERNESS PARK**
**21395 Milsa Rd.**
**(210) 564-6400**
**www.sanaturalareas.org**

An unspoiled slice of the Texas Hill Country awaits the family just north of Loop 1604 at Friedrich Wilderness Park. Miles of well-marked hiking trails provide urbanites a rare chance to experience the peace and quiet of the country. If your family chooses, you can arrange for a guide by calling ahead. For more information, see the Parks & Recreation chapter.

**HEMISFAIR PARK** **FREE**
**Bowie Street at Durango Boulevard**
**(210) 207-7819**

HemisFair Park is best known as the home of the Tower of the Americas, a soaring symbol of San Antonio. Kids love to survey the scene from 579 feet up. The Tower's 1-minute elevator ride is also a hit with young visitors. (For more on the Tower, see the Attractions chapter.) Children also love the Downtown All Around Playground, with its extensive playscape and popcorn wagon, and the cooling water gardens.

**JAPANESE TEA GARDENS FREE**
**3853 N. St. Mary's St.**
**(210) 207-7275**

One of the city's most beautiful spots, these gardens are built in and around an old rock quarry. There are lots of fun places for kids to explore and for parents to relax and unwind.

**MILAM PARK**
**500 W. Commerce St.**
**(210) 207-7819**

Honoring one of the heroes of the Texas Revolution, this downtown park has several kid-friendly features. A playscape with tunnels and castles is the centerpiece, but children will also love the gazebo.

## RECREATION CENTERS & PROGRAMS

**SAN ANTONIO PARKS AND RECREATION DEPARTMENT**
**(210) 207-3000**
**www.sanantonio.gov/parksandrec**

The San Antonio Parks and Recreation Department offers a variety of programs for youths year-round. Each year, the department sponsors the Summer Youth Recreation Program from early June through early Aug. Approximately 65 sites participate in the program, which runs weekdays from 7:30 a.m. to 5:30 p.m. (with community centers open until 9 p.m.). The program offers a wide variety of recreational options for kids, including arts and crafts, cookouts, basketball and golf clinics, teen pool parties, and field trips.

Throughout the year, children ages 6 to 19 can enroll in the youth membership program. This public-private partnership was developed to encourage youths to participate in positive recreation and activities. Both local and national celebrities help promote the program and stress the importance of positive participation in school, youth programs, career planning, and other aspects of young lives.

Community centers throughout the city also offer year-round recreational options for local children and teens. Sports such as flag football, volleyball, basketball, and softball are offered along with activities such as arts and crafts, talent shows, and table games.

Community centers operated by the Parks and Recreation Department include:

**BODE**
901 Rigsby Ave.
(210) 532-1212

**COPERNICUS**
5003 Lord Rd.
(210) 648-1072

**CUELLAR**
5626 San Fernando St.
(210) 436-0908

**DAWSON**
2500 E. Commerce St.
(210) 227-1627

**DENVER HEIGHTS**
300 Porter St.
(210) 533-5242

**DORIE MILLER CENTER**
2802 Martin Luther King Dr.
(210) 333-4650

**FATHER ROMAN CENTER**
11030 Ruidosa
(210) 627-2138

**GARZA**
1450 Mira Vista
(210) 435-6806

**GILL**
7902 Westshire Dr.
(210) 675-2123

**HAMILTON**
10700 Nacogdoches Rd.
(210) 654-7749

**HARLANDALE**
7227 Briar Place
(210) 924-8021

**MEADOWCLIFF**
1240 Pinn Rd.
(210) 674-0820

**MILLER'S POND**
6175 Old Pearsall Rd.
(210) 623-2900

**NORMOYLE**
700 Culberson Ave.
(210) 924-0770

**PALM HEIGHTS CENTER**
1201 W. Malone Ave.
(210) 207-3099

**RAMIREZ CENTER**
1011 Gillette Blvd.
(210) 921-0681

**SAN JUAN BRADY GARDENS CENTER**
2307 S. Calaveras
(210) 225-5410

**SOUTH SAN CENTER**
2031 Quintana Rd.
(210) 927-1640

**SOUTHSIDE LIONS CENTER**
3100 Hiawatha St.
(210) 532-1502

**TOBIN**
1900 W. Martin St.
(210) 225-0941

**WARD CENTER**
435 E. Sunshine Dr.
(210) 732-2481

**WOODARD CENTER**
1011 Locke St.
(210) 225-5445

**YATES COMMUNITY CENTER**
528 Rasa Dr.
(210) 673-1152

## SPORTS & FITNESS

For details on youth sport leagues in San Antonio, see the Parks & Recreation chapter.

**KIDS SPORTS NETWORK**
**8206 Roughrider Dr.**
**(210) 654-4707**
**www.ksnusa.org**

The best resource for information on San Antonio–area children's sports is the Kids Sports Network. This nonprofit organization acts as a clearinghouse for children's sports information, provides coach training, and conducts special events. The network's website includes extensive listings of sports organizations, ranging from flag and tackle football to baseball, volleyball, and soccer.

## THEATERS

**CHILDREN'S FINE ART SERIES $$**
**3201 West Ave.**
**(210) 340-4060**
**www.childrensfineartseries.org**

Aimed at children ages 5 and older, this series features a variety of productions that take place in theaters around the city. Past shows have included the Kennedy Center on tour, the Paul Mesner Puppets, and the Austin Ballet.

**MAGIK THEATRE $$–$$$**
**420 S. Alamo St.**
**(210) 227-2751**
**www.magiktheatre.org**

San Antonio is the home of a professional repertory theater that produces shows especially for children and families. Since 1994 its Theatre for Young Audiences Series has presented favorites such as *When Dinosaurs Rocked the World* and *The Grinch*. One of the troupe's most popular performances was *The Best Christmas Pageant Ever*, which attracted 25,000 people in a 5-week run.

The theater produces 7 to 9 shows for young audiences per year and has a cast of 14 full-time actors. More than half the productions are original plays, such as *Phantom of the Alamo*, for both elementary-school-age children and teens. Children with an interest in drama can participate in the Acting and Creativity Academy, which offers semester-long acting classes, as well as an intensive summer workshop, Camp Showbiz. Each season free and discounted tickets are distributed through the theater's Tickets to Literacy program to help disadvantaged children learn about the joy of theater.

**STEVEN STOLI'S BACKYARD THEATRE $$**
**11838 Wurzbach Rd.**
**(210) 605-2575**

Award-winning director Steven Stoli produces a variety of shows for children such as *The Little Mermaid* and *Jack and the Beanstalk* at this 120-seat theater. Shows are held Wed, Thurs, and Sat at 11 a.m. For San Antonio–area residents, the theater also offers a discounted Backyard Pass for 11 shows.

Children with an interest in acting can also take part in Steven Stoli's weeklong acting camp for kids. Open to kids ages 3 to 17, the camp covers techniques for both TV and stage acting. Sessions cover improvisation, theater games, memorization, and more. The final day includes a performance.

## TOY STORES & CHILDREN'S SHOPS

**THE DISNEY STORE**
**849 E. Commerce St.**
**Rivercenter Mall**
**(210) 227-3202**
**www.disneystore.com**

The Disney Store has 3 convenient locations in San Antonio for all things related to the mouse. From stuffed Poohs and Donald Duck T-shirts to Sleeping Beauty ball gowns and Disney animation cels, this place has something for the kid in all of us. Additional locations are at 7400 San Pedro Ave., North Star Mall (210-366-3331), and 6301 NW Loop 410, Ingram Park Mall (210-509-6256).

**GYMBOREE PLAY AND MUSIC**
**16632 San Pedro Ave., at Park Oaks Center**
**(210) 490-3710**
**www.gymboreeclasses.com**

Gymboree's 2 locations—an additional location is at 11703 Huebner Rd., #205 (210-490-3710)—introduce young visitors to the world of music and movement. Parents and children from newborn to 5 years old can learn together through singing, motion, and sharing time.

**TOYS "R" US**
**321 NW Loop 410, Suite 108**
**(210) 524-0117**

**8270 Agora Pkwy.**
**(210) 658-2183**

**BABIES "R" US**
**6955 NW Loop 410**
**(210) 681-2229**

**BABIES "R" US**
**17610 La Cantera**
**(210) 694-2087**
**www.toysrus.com**

The large toy giant, Toys "R" Us, has 2 locations, 2 in town and another in nearby Selma, with everything from toys to baby wipes. There are also 2 Babies "R" Us locations in San Antonio.

## WATER PARKS

***SCHLITTERBAHN WATERPARK RESORT** **$$$$**
**305 W. Austin St., New Braunfels**
**(830) 608-8532**
**www.schlitterbahn.com**

Just up I-35 from San Antonio lies a leader in the world of water parks: Schlitterbahn. This family-oriented park offers water activities for kids of every age, from toddlers to teens.

Schlitterbahn is the sister company of New Braunfels General Store International, a leader in the water feature industry. NBGS was founded in 1984 to manufacture and distribute coated-foam water park products that had been developed and used by Schlitterbahn Waterpark. Today NBGS has expanded to include themed play elements in use by water parks, amusement parks, municipal pools, indoor recreation centers, and even cruise lines.

The trial-and-error process that honed the high-tech features for which NBGS is known today were worked out at Schlitterbahn, a park founded in a way that sounds like a scene straight out of the movies. In the 1970s during a vacation to Walt Disney World, Jeff Henry and his two siblings fell in love with water slides. The youngsters came home and worked with their parents to build four water slides at their riverfront resort in New Braunfels.

Those four slides have grown into the most popular seasonal water park in the US. Today Schlitterbahn spans 65 acres and features rides and family activities across 5 themed areas. With 2 uphill water coasters, 9 tube chutes, 5 giant hot tubs, 17 water slides, a surfing ride, a family wave pool, 5 swimming pools, 7 children's playgrounds, water and sand volleyball courts, 4 gift shops, 2 restaurants, and 20 refreshment centers all operated by nearly 1,600 seasonal employees, the park truly boasts Texas-size proportions and profits. Schlitterbahn plays upon local features, both cultural and topographical. Meaning "slippery road" in German, the name Schlitterbahn is a first hint at the German heritage that plays an important role in the community of New Braunfels and indeed in the park itself. The symbol of Schlitterbahn is a 60-foot-tall castle, a replica of the guard tower of Solms Castle in Braunfels, Germany. The park's many sections carry on the theme, with names like Kinderlund, Slidenplatz, Das Lagune, and Surfenburg, home of the world's first uphill water coaster. The park also utilizes its natural surroundings, including the Comal River, which serves as the starting and stopping points of a 45-minute tube ride and also supplies 72-degree spring water to the tube chutes.

Schlitterbahn has held the record for many "firsts" in the water park world. The park is considered the home of the world's first swim-up refreshment bar, first family wave pool with maximum 4-foot depth, first continuous wave surfing ride, and first professional competition on a man-made wave. It's also the world's largest tubing park, with more than 10,000 inner tubes from which to choose.

The park introduces new and innovative attractions every year. In past years the venue added such thrill rides as the Torrent, a high-tech ride in the new Blastenhoff section of the park. The Torrent features a 20-foot-wide river in which waves surge at 10-second intervals, taking guests on a wild white-water ride. The waves break onto a 25,000-square-foot sloping beach.

Schlitterbahn is open on weekends in the spring and daily in summer. High-season hours are 10 a.m. to 8 p.m.

**SEAWORLD OF SAN ANTONIO $$$$**
**10500 SeaWorld Dr.**
**(210) 523-3611, (800) 700-7786**
**www.seaworld.com**

SeaWorld may be best known for its marine life, but the park also offers visitors plenty of chances to get wet. The park's water park, Lost Lagoon, features numerous water rides guaranteed to cool visitors even on the hottest San Antonio days. The Texas Splashdown, the longest and tallest flume ride in the state, takes riders along a 0.5-mile route with plunges from as high as 5 stories. The Rio Loco (Crazy River) transports 6 riders on circular rafts down a raging stream under a waterfall. And there's also a beach, a 3-story funhouse (don't miss the 500-gallon bucket!), and a 5-story tube ride that plunges riders from the top of a slide tower to a splashdown pool. Younger children will find plenty of water features, wave pools, and water slides. In all there are more than a dozen attractions on 5 acres. SeaWorld of San Antonio is open daily during the summer months and weekends only during the spring and fall. Call for the current schedule.

**SIX FLAGS FIESTA TEXAS $$$$**
**17000 I-10 West**
**(210) 697-5050**
**www.sixflags.com**

The water park at Six Flags Fiesta Texas is a good place to escape the summer heat, with several water rides and attractions. Some top offerings include Splash Water Springs, a water pool with a slide, the million-gallon Lone Star Lagoon (the largest wave pool in Texas), and the Texas Treehouse, a 5-story tree house complete with a 1,000-gallon cowboy hat that fills with water. Some of the water park rides have height restrictions. Park hours vary by season.

**SPLASHTOWN $$$$**
**3600 I-35 North**
**(210) 227-1400**
**www.splashtownsa.com**

This water park, located along I-35, offers 20 acres of water rides, ranging in speed from lazy river rides to white-knuckle tube rides. In all, the park offers more than 50 rides and attractions. The Lone Star Luge sends riders sliding the length of more than 2 football fields, while Siesta Del Rio provides a relaxing river ride. Starflight sends riders soaring through total darkness in 1 of 2 tubes (and there's a Junior Starflight for young visitors). The park includes a large kiddie area with child-size rides and slides as well as sand volleyball courts and full-court basketball on-site. Tubes and lockers are available for rent; the park also has concession stands. The park is open weekends only from mid-Apr through the end of May then daily until Aug, returning to a weekend-only schedule until mid-Sept. The park opens at 11 a.m. and closes at 7, 8, or 9 p.m. depending on the day and time of year.

# ANNUAL EVENTS & FESTIVALS

**They don't call San Antonio the Fiesta City for nothing. This is one city that parties in style, whatever the reason, whatever the time of year. From bacchanalian gatherings to solemn remembrances, San Antonio knows how to mark an occasion.**

**Many events here are scheduled for the fall through spring months. Winter days can be a bit nippy sometimes, but that doesn't slow down the holiday festivities. December is one of the busiest months on the calendar, thanks to the many festivals with religious significance. The River Walk/Paseo del Rio really comes to life at this time of the year, lit by thousands of miniature lights as well as luminarias, candles in sand-filled sacks. The river reflects the thousands of lights, transforming the area into a truly magical spot.**

**The peak of the festival season is April, time of Fiesta. This is the granddaddy of San Antonio's festivals, a true Texas-size blowout. Festivities take place all over the city during this period, and traffic can be trying, especially in the downtown area. Hotel space can get tight during this period as well, so make plans early if you plan to attend Fiesta.**

**Numerous other celebrations here mark special days in Mexican history, such as Cinco de Mayo and Diez y Seis de Septiembre. These cultural festivals, to be enjoyed by everyone, are an excellent window into the Latino heritage of the region and a good way to sample the food, dance, and song that the Hispanic culture has given San Antonio.**

## OVERVIEW

Although the following list is extensive, it doesn't include every event hosted in San Antonio; that would be a book in itself. We've listed our favorites and longtime events, ones that consistently take place year after year. The exact dates on which many of these events take place varies from year to year, so the entries listed under each month may not be in chronological order. For a month-by-month listing that's updated frequently, check out the San Antonio Convention and Visitors Bureau website at www.visitsanantonio.com. This site includes details and contact information for both one-time and annual events, including festivals, concerts, fund-raisers, and more.

Admission prices are included in many of these listings, but please realize that these can and do change frequently. You'll want to contact the event organizers directly to verify the scheduled date and time of the festival as well as the current admission price.

## JANUARY

### MARTIN LUTHER KING JR. MARCH AND RALLY

**Citywide**
**(210) 207-7224**
**www.sanantonio.gov/mlk**

This annual march is considered the nation's largest honoring Dr. Martin Luther King Jr., the civil rights leader. The march begins at the MLK Freedom Bridge and ends at Pittman-Sullivan Park. Admission is free.

### RIVER WALK MUD FESTIVAL

**River Walk**
**(210) 227-4262**
**www.thesanantonioriverwalk.com**

It takes a mighty festive city to turn the draining and cleaning of a river into a party, but, hey, San Antonio's just that kind of place. Since 1987 this 3-day event has elevated mudslinging to an art. The fun begins with the Mud Pie Ball. The peak of the celebration is the election of the Mud King and Mud Queen to preside over the festivities. The King and Queen rise to their positions by collecting the most nickels, money to be used by the Paseo del Rio Association to hold free events along the River Walk throughout the year. The prospective Kings and Queens (usually celebrities, politicians, or business leaders) can obtain nickels any way they choose, and don't think that mud wrestling is out of the question for these campaigners. When the nickels are tallied, the winners enter the "Brown House on Pig Pen-sylvania Avenue" and wear a sand-colored royal robe. Admission to all the festivities is free.

### GO WESTERN GALA

**AT&T Center, 1 AT&T Center Parkway**
**(210) 225-5851**
**www.sarodeo.com/annual/go_western_gala.html**

For more than 3 decades, this annual event has brought the spirit of the West to San Antonio through dance, song, and food. The gala draws many big-name performers; among those who have appeared in the past are Lorrie Morgan and Neal McCoy. Tickets include dinner, drinks, dancing, and more. For an additional fee, attendees can sit in the Golden Corral, a special area directly in front of the stage that is staffed by private waiters; Golden Corral tickets also include valet parking and other extras. Proceeds from this annual event go to the San Antonio Livestock Exposition's Scholarship Fund.

### COWBOY BREAKFAST

**Cowboys Dance Hall**
**3030 NE Loop 410**
**(210) 646-9378**
**www.cowboysdancehall.com/San-Antonio**

This may very well be the world's largest breakfast. Sponsored by the Cowboy Breakfast Foundation, the event benefits scholarship funds raised through the rental of entertainment stages and vendor tables. And just what is a cowboy breakfast, you ask? In this case, it means a real Texas favorite: breakfast tacos along with tender biscuits beneath plenty of country gravy.

### ASIAN NEW YEAR FESTIVAL

**Institute of Texan Cultures**
**801 E. Durango Blvd.**
**(210) 458-2224**
**www.texancultures.utsa.edu**

The Asian communities of Texas are in the spotlight during this annual celebration of the Asian New Year. Sponsored by the Institute of Texan Cultures, the festival includes dance, music, food, and crafts. The ethnic cuisine served at the festival is a favorite part of the festivities; look for Chinese fried rice, Indian *samosas* (a fried filled snack), Japanese *yakisoba* (a noodle dish), Korean *bulgogi* (marinated beef) and *kimchi* (fermented vegetables), Malaysian/Singaporean beef and chicken satay, Filipino *pancit* rice noodles, Hawaiian/Polynesian almond cookies, and traditional Pakistani foods. The event also includes hands-on activities featuring Asian crafts and traditions such as Chinese calligraphy, brush-painting, paper-cutting, and mah-jong; Indian sari-wrapping, *rangoli* (traditional Indian art), and palm-reading; Japanese calligraphy and origami; Hawaiian/Polynesian hula-dancing, tapa cloth–painting, and lei-making; and Vietnamese fortune-telling. Throughout the festival, local groups give demonstrations of yoga, martial arts, tai chi, and more. Admission is $8 for adults, $4 for children ages 3 to 12, and $4 for seniors and military personnel; free for children 2 and under.

## FEBRUARY

### MARDI GRAS ARTS & CRAFTS SHOW

**River Walk**
**(210) 227-4262**
**www.thesanantonioriverwalk.com**

This 3-day event is sponsored by the Paseo del Rio Association and showcases the artists of the region. The shady walkways of the River Walk are lined with easels and shelving for the popular event, where jewelry, watercolors, oils, sculpture, and crafts compete with the beauty of the Paseo del Rio itself during this twice-annual show. Admission is free.

### *SAN ANTONIO STOCK SHOW AND RODEO

**1 AT&T Pkwy., AT&T Center**
**(210) 225-5851**
**www.sarodeo.com**

Ready, set, rodeo! If you're looking for a taste of a traditional Texas get-together, attend this 16-day show and rodeo. One of San Antonio's largest events, the annual Western festival attracts more than 1 million attendees every year. Activities include a rodeo, stock show, educational displays, a concert series, a carnival midway, and plenty of Western fun.

The event is very family friendly. The Family Fair is a top stop for parents and kids, with educational displays, entertainment of special interest to younger visitors, plenty of food, and more. The Hall of Heritage takes visitors back to the days of the Old West. At the World of Agriculture, some of the state's top cooks offer up a taste of their creations. Craftspeople are also on hand to display their wares. A favorite with children is the World of Animals, where kids and critters can get up close and cuddly. Kids also love the carnival midway, with rides, games of skill, and old-fashioned fun. More than 1,000 cowboys and cowgirls provide much of the entertainment at the rodeo, which includes competition in the fields of bull riding, calf roping, barrel racing, and other sports sanctioned by the Professional Rodeo Cowboy Association (PRCA).

The event also features America's largest junior livestock show; teens from across Texas exhibit and sell award-winning cattle, swine, sheep, poultry, and horses. The competition for the title of Grand Champion is fierce.

Entertainment also comes in the form of live music, and that includes all types of Texas sounds, from Tejano to country to rock. Performers change every year, but top-name performers at previous rodeos have included George Jones, Martina McBride, Brooks and Dunn, Alan Jackson, Toby Keith, Alabama, and other recognized names. There's a live performance every night.

Parking is at a premium in the AT&T Center area during the rodeo, but there's a 15-acre paved, lighted, and secured parking lot nearby on Gembler Road. To reach the parking facility, exit at AT&T Center Parkway (formerly Coliseum Road), turn left on Gembler, and proceed to the parking area. The free Rodeo Shuttle runs continuously from the parking lot. Cost of parking for the rodeo is $10.

Tickets to rodeo competitions are priced at $10 and $25, with tickets also covering ground admission. Ground admission only is $7 for adults, $5 for seniors, and $3 for children under 12.

### RIVER WALK MARDI GRAS

**River Walk**
**(210) 227-4262**
**www.thesanantonioriverwalk.com**

This pre-Lenten event celebrates Mardi Gras with music, a parade, and more. The fun begins on the Sunday before Lent with a fleet of barges gliding down the river in a floating Mardi Gras Parade. Costumed krewes cruise down the river while throngs of onlookers gather along the riverbanks. Performers keep the parade lively; in previous years, the San Antonio Street Dance and Drum Company, and the San Antonio Iguanas Cheerleaders and Iggy have participated. Later in the week, the festivities continue with an arts and crafts fair scheduled for Fri through Sun. In previous years, free concerts have also been scheduled at the Rivercenter Mall lagoon, featuring local and regional bands performing mariachi, conjunto, and contemporary tunes. Admission to the festival is free.

### CINEFESTIVAL

**Guadalupe Cultural Arts Theater**
**1300 Guadalupe St.**
**(210) 271-3151**
**www.guadalupeculturalarts.org**

CineFestival holds the title as the country's largest and oldest Latino film festival. Now in its third decade, the event showcases shorts, features, experimental, and documentary works either by Latinos or about the Latino experience.

**i** The Alamo City celebrates Black History Month with a variety of events ranging from poetry readings to screenings of black cinema masterpieces. For a comprehensive listing of events, visit the Carver Community Cultural Center's website, www.thecarver.org.

## MARCH

### REMEMBERING THE ALAMO WEEKEND

**Alamo Plaza**
**(210) 273-1730**
**www.sanantoniolivinghistory.org**

Sponsored by San Antonio's Office of Cultural Affairs, the San Antonio Convention and Visitors Bureau and the Downtown Operations Department, this 2-day annual event is scheduled for the Saturday and Sunday nearest March 6, the anniversary of the fall of the Alamo in 1836. The weekend includes education programs and demonstrations about life during the period. Costumed actors help visitors learn more about music of the time as well as food preparation, spinning, weaving, herbal medicine and early medical practices, and warfare. Attendees can visit and pose for photos with them. The programs help visitors learn more about the men, women, and children who lived on both sides of the famous conflict between the Texians and the Mexicans. The event also includes an exhibition of Alamo archaeological displays. Admission is free.

**✳DAWN AT THE ALAMO**

**Alamo Plaza**

**(210) 273-1730**

**www.sanantoniolivinghistory.org**

Members of the San Antonio Living History Association are joined by reenactors from across the country in portraying the armies of the Texian defenders and the Mexican soldiers led by General Santa Anna. The event occurs on March 6, the anniversary of the fall of the Alamo in 1836. The battle is also remembered with quiet solemnity. Thirteen candles are lit to symbolize the 13-day siege of the Alamo; other solemn remembrances include the reading of a reconciliation peace prayer in English and Spanish and the laying of commemorative wreaths. Sponsored by the San Antonio Living History Association, Dawn at the Alamo also includes a flintlock musket volley, with the sounds of the gunfire echoing against the historic walls of the shrine, as well as the reading of eyewitness accounts of the bloody battle. Visitors must get up early for this special event—the 1-hour ceremony takes place the hour before dawn. Admission is free.

**WREATH LAYING CEREMONY AT THE ALAMO SHRINE**

**Alamo**

**(210) 344-4317**

**www.harpandshamrock.org**

For more than 3 decades, the Harp and Shamrock Society of Texas has presented a wreath at the Alamo to honor the fallen heroes of the battle. Admission is free.

**ALAMO IRISH FESTIVAL**

**La Villita and Arneson River Theatre**

**(210) 207-8612**

**www.harpandshamrock.org**

Grab your green and head to the river. This 3-day festival, held the weekend closest to March 17, celebrates St. Patrick's Day in true Irish-American tradition with music, food, arts and crafts, cultural displays, and dancing. The festival is sponsored by the Harp and Shamrock Society of Texas. The event also includes the city's St. Patrick's Day St. Parade, one of the largest in the Southwest and now in its fourth decade. Admission to the parade is free.

**i** **Rooms can be at a premium during San Antonio's top festival seasons: April's Fiesta San Antonio and the December holiday celebrations along the River Walk. Book early to reserve a downtown room during either of these months.**

**CONTEMPORARY ART MONTH**

**Blue Star Contemporary Art Center**

**116 Blue Star and citywide**

**(210) 227-6960**

**http://contemporaryartmonth.com**

For nearly 2 decades, the work of San Antonio's artists has been recognized with exhibits and performances. More than 70 events celebrate the city's performing and visual arts—everything from Latino photography exhibitions to a show featuring one-of-a-kind lamps made by local artists. Events are held at galleries around town, museums, studios, and the Blue Star Contemporary Art Center.

### GUINNESS ST. PATRICK'S DAY RIVER PARADE AND PUB CRAWL

**River Walk**
**(210) 227-4262**
**www.thesanantonioriverwalk.com**

It's not your imagination—on St. Patrick's Day, the San Antonio River is a little greener than its usual tint, thanks to the Paseo del Rio Association. The river is actually dyed green for the day and renamed "The River Shannon." In early March mariachi music gives way to Irish song and dance in San Antonio, and the River Walk turns into a huge Pub Crawl. The next day, the river hosts a floating parade with Irish dignitaries, pipers and drummers, and the pervasive spirit of the Old Country. Tickets are sold for the Pub Crawl, but the river parade is free.

### LUMINARIA

**Hemisfair Park**
**(210) 271-2842**
**www.luminariasa.org**

Luminaria is a 1-day event when the city glows with colorful and free celebrations, exhibitions, and performances in honor of the arts in San Antonio. Visitors are surrounded by simultaneous and innovative programming: storefront exhibitions; art lighting; alley galleries and numerous stages with theater, dance, and music performances. Citywide celebrations go until early morning and include studio tours, art demonstrations, museums, and galleries that stay open for the festive night.

## APRIL

### TEJANO MUSIC AWARDS

**La Villita Assembly Hall**
**(210) 558-3400**
**www.tejanomusicawards.com**

This internationally recognized event is considered the Grammy Awards of Tejano music. Sponsored by the Texas Talent Musicians Association, the awards show is designed to honor the top performers in the field of Tejano music, a Latino music that utilizes accordions and 12-string guitars. The event began in 1980 and today draws more than 40,000 onlookers. Online reservations can be made at the Tejano Music Awards website. The show is also broadcast on radio and television.

### VIVA BOTANICA FESTIVAL

**San Antonio Botanical Garden**
**555 Funston Place**
**(210) 207-3255**
**www.sabot.org**

Celebrate spring blossoms at the San Antonio Botanical Garden during this colorful festival. Sponsored by the San Antonio Botanical Society, the 2-day annual event showcases the blooms of San Antonio. You'll have the chance to buy blooming plants if the surrounding greenery inspires you. Along with 33 acres of spring flowers, the festival includes a children's parade, art displays, live entertainment, and food booths. Admission is $8 for adults, $5 for children.

**i** **During Fiesta, there's no escape from *cascarones,* dyed eggshells filled with paper confetti and covered with tissue paper. Everyone—strangers and friends alike—is a target for these little bombs, sold in many stores.**

### *FIESTA SAN ANTONIO

**Citywide**

**(210) 227-5191, (877) 723-4378**

**www.fiesta-sa.org**

Though all of San Antonio's annual events and festivals draw a crowd, Fiesta San Antonio is in a league of its own when it comes to popularity. One of Texas's most-attended celebrations, this April blowout draws 3.5 million partygoers every year for more than 150 events, lots of food, and barrels of margaritas. Add to that mix a good dose of Texas pride and the spirit of Old Mexico and you've got a party that draws revelers from across the US and Mexico.

The 10-day Fiesta dates back to 1891. First a celebration of Texas independence, it later grew to recognize the many diverse cultures that made San Antonio the city it is today. The exact dates of the festival change from year to year, but the focal point of the event is always April 21, the anniversary of the Battle of San Jacinto, when Texas won its independence from Mexico.

Fiesta's origins may have been serious and solemn, but today this event is pure entertainment. Standard Fiesta fare includes music festivals, colorful parades, and serious grazing through food booths that offer everything from Cajun to Tex-Mex to German specialties. The official partying winds down about midnight each night, but unofficially it continues in the River Walk bars until about 2 a.m. In fact, the River Walk is one of the busiest Fiesta locations, especially from La Mansión del Rio hotel at Navarro Street all the way around the horseshoe-shaped stretch of the river to La Villita historic area. A river parade is among the more unusual aspects of this rollicking celebration. If you're lucky, you can snag a riverside table at one of the crowded restaurants. (But don't just rely on luck; you'll need to arrive plenty early to nab these prime seats as thousands of revelers pack the parade route.) Reservations are encouraged. The Texas Cavalier's River Parade is the first of 3 popular Fiesta parades, cruising the river past some 250,000 spectators. The event features more than 40 floats, each bursting with musicians, singers, and celebrities. Later in the week, the Battle of Flowers Parade, with brightly colored floats and the Queen of the Order of the Alamo, draws as many as 500,000 onlookers. Finally, the nighttime Fiesta Flambeau Parade fills the streets with lighted floats, marching bands, and 400,000 onlookers. For tickets to the parades, call the River Parade Ticket Line at (210) 22-RIVER anytime after December 1, or obtain them online at www.texascavaliers.org.

The parades feature the "royalty" of Fiesta. At the Battle of the Flowers, keep an eye out for the Queen and Princesses of the Order of the Alamo. Bedecked in expensive and ornately jeweled gowns, the Queen and her court are crowned at Municipal Auditorium earlier during Fiesta.The biggest Fiesta event is A Night in Old San Antonio, better known by its nickname, NIOSA ("n-eye-O-sa"). The party, featuring music and food in 15 cultural areas, takes place in La Villita, a restored 18th-century village on the River Walk. Dance to live Western, conjunto, oompah, or mariachi music, and when you've worked up an appetite, work your way over to the food booths selling everything from escargots to German sausages to *antichuchos,* a spicy marinated meat on a stick. This event draws enormous crowds, so come early in the evening if you can. Tickets for A Night in Old San Antonio are available at the gate or through NIOSA at (210) 226-5188 or at www.niosa.org.

The Mariachi Festival, one of the oldest in the country, features amateurs and pros battling for the spotlight. The event is filled with all the color and spirit of San Antonio. Admission for some Fiesta events is free.

**i** The Fiesta Flambeau Parade is the largest illuminated night parade in the nation.

**FORD CHILDREN'S FESTIVAL**
**Rivercenter Mall Lagoon**
**(210) 227-4262**
**www.thesanantonioriverwalk.com**
Adults don't get to have all the fun at Fiesta; this officially sanctioned Fiesta event is especially designed for the youngest revelers. Held along the River Walk and sponsored by the Paseo del Rio Association, the 1-day event offers plenty of pint-size fun and games. Admission is free.

**FIESTA RIVER ART SHOW**
**Alamo Plaza**
**(210) 226-8752**
**www.riverartgroup.com**
This annual event is sponsored by the River Art Group Inc., a group that has been operating for more than half a century. If you've visited the Alamo City at other times of the year, you may be familiar with the group's River Art Group Gallery in historic La Villita (see the Shopping chapter for more details). During the 3-day art show each April, the group expands its coverage to display works not only in La Villita but also in Alamo Plaza. Admission is free.

**A TASTE OF NEW ORLEANS**
**Sunken Garden Theater**
**Brackenridge Park**
**(210) 637-8328**
**www.fiesta-sa.org or www.saza.org**
If you're staying downtown, grab a bus for a ride out to the Sunken Gardens in Brackenridge Park for A Taste of New Orleans. Gumbo, jambalaya, Cajun catfish, boudin, and beignets top the list of offerings, while everything from jazz to salsa to Big Band sounds keeps things hopping. This event is sponsored by the San Antonio Zulu Association Commission. Admission is $12 for adults, free for children 10 and under.

**KING WILLIAM FAIR**
**King William Historic District**
**(210) 271-3247**
**http://kwfair.org**
This 1-day festival, an official part of Fiesta San Antonio, showcases the historic neighborhood of King William. Since 1968, the event has featured the usual fair attractions: arts and crafts, food, and entertainment. Proceeds fund the charity work of the King William Association.

**LOWRIDER FESTIVAL**
**Mateo Camargo Park**
**Highway 90 West at Callaghan Road**
**(210) 432-1896**
**www.centroculturalaztlan.50megs.com**
Presented by Centro Cultural Aztlan, a promoter of lowrider shows and competitions in Texas, the 1-day Lowrider Festival attracts hundreds of local and regional competitors who have transformed their factory-built cars into one-of-a-kind machines. There are more than 40 categories of competition, including cars that hop, cars with upholstery, cars with murals, and more. The family-oriented event includes food and drink booths, games for children, and live music of the 1950s and '60s. The event is held at Camargo Park; to reach the park, travel west on Highway 90 and take the

## Close-up

### A Bloomin' Good Time

Grab the car keys in one hand, your camera in the other, and get ready for a bloomin' good time! When the wildflowers are in bloom throughout Central and South Texas, there's no better excuse to hit the roads for a day trip. Here's a bouquet of the best getaways during this spring season:

**Texas Hill Country Wild Flowers and Wine Trail.** The Hill Country blooms not just with wildflowers but also with vineyards. This trail traces its way through numerous wineries in the region. Wine aficionados should pick up a copy of the "Texas Hill Country Wine Trail" brochure from the Fredericksburg Chamber of Commerce and Convention and Visitors Bureau (830-997-6523) or online at www.texaswinetrail.com.

**Wildseed Farms, Fredericksburg.** The largest family-owned wildflower seed farm in the US is the site of the annual Wildseed Farms Wildflower Celebration, scheduled for early to mid-April, when the fields are filled with bluebonnets and other Texas wildflowers. You can stroll along a walking trail and even cut your own wildflower bouquet; weekend visitors can also enjoy a taste of local wines and the sound of Texas music. Each spring, the Butterfly Haus opens for visitors to walk through its free-flying butterfly habitat. The farm is located 7 miles east of Fredericksburg on US 290. It's open daily from 9:30 a.m. to 5 p.m. Admission to the farm is free; the Butterfly Haus is extra. For information, call (800) 848-0078 or visit www.wildseedfarms.com.

**Lady Bird Johnson Wildflower Center, Austin.** Don't know a primrose from a paintbrush? Or would you like to learn more about how you could incorporate wildflowers into your landscaping? Whatever you know or don't know about wildflowers, if you love beautiful blooms, the Lady Bird Johnson Wildflower Center is the place for you. Located about 85 miles from San Antonio, the only facility in the nation devoted to native plants and flowers offers educational programs as well as plenty of flower-filled walks among its blooming acres. After planting in excess of 2,000 pounds of wildflower seed every fall, the center is a showcase in the spring. The centerpieces here are the Wildflower Meadows, which explode with color. And flowers are combined with festivities at the Spring Plant Sale and Gardening Festival, scheduled for early April. It's your chance to learn more about native plants and wildflowers and how they can be included in your own garden. Along with demonstrations and lectures, this event includes the sale of native plants from the center's greenhouses. Call (512) 232-0100 or visit www.wildflower.org. Admission rates vary by season.

Callaghan Road exit. The park is across the street from the Nelson Wolf Baseball Stadium. Admission is $10; children 12 and under are free.

## MAY

### CINCO DE MAYO

**Market Square**
**(210) 207-8600**
**www.sanantonio.gov/marketsquare**

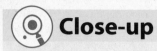

**Kerrville.** This Hill Country community, about 60 miles from San Antonio on I-10, is home to the Riverside Nature Center (830-257-4837; www.riversidenaturecenter .org). Located at 150 Francisco Lemos St., the center is filled with more than 200 varieties of native Texas plants, including wildflowers. Drop by the visitor center, then take a self-guided walk along the tree trail. While you're in Kerrville, don't miss the Willow City Loop between Fredericksburg and Llano off Highway 16. (North of Fredericksburg on Highway 16, take the second Willow City Loop turn to the right; there are three Willow City exits.) This 16-mile loop through unfenced ranch land includes canyon views, bluffs, spectacular wildflowers, and wildlife. Another popular wildflower drive is HIghway 16 South out of Kerrville toward Medina. For more on Kerrville, call (800) 221-7958.

**Boerne.** Check out the wildflowers growing around Boerne, 22 miles northwest of San Antonio on I-10; if you're inspired by all the greenery, don't miss the Cibolo Nature Center Plant Sale, scheduled yearly for early April. Held at the Kendall County Fairgrounds on Highway 46, the event features native trees, plants, and seeds as well as a kids' activity area. While you're in Boerne, be sure to visit the Nature Center and the Cibolo Wilderness Trail (830-249-4616; www.cibolo.org), where you'll see some of the area's natural habitats, including a reclaimed prairie and marsh. You'll find several walking trails, including a historic farm trail, a prairie trail, a creekside trail, and a marsh loop. The trails wind past native plants and wildflowers as well as birds and animals indigenous to the Hill Country. For more details, call the Greater Boerne Chamber of Commerce at (830) 249-8000.

**Corpus Christi.** Don't forget the beautiful coastal blooms as you plan your wildflower drives. One of the best places to enjoy the wildflowers is the South Texas Botanical Garden and Nature Center at 8545 S. Staples. This 180-acre park traces the banks of Oso Creek; you can enjoy a walk along the Bird and Butterfly Trail or see the blooms of the plumeria collection or the orchid greenhouse. As you look around the gardens, you will notice that they're a favorite with winged visitors as well. Spring means bird migration, and the gardens are part of the Greater Texas Coastal Birding Trail. For more information, call (361) 852-2100 or visit www.stxbot.org.

**Hot Lines.** Before you reach for the car keys, spend a few minutes listening to the various hot lines that pinpoint the best sites for flower power. Call the Texas Department of Transportation at (800) 452-9292; along with road information, this number offers reports on wildflower sightings throughout the state. Reports are updated weekly with news of spectacular roadside wildflower displays. Or you can visit www.dot.state.tx.us.

This event celebrates the Battle of Pueblo, which won Mexico's independence from France. The battle was waged on May 5, Cinco de Mayo in Spanish. The city celebrates with a Cinco de Mayo festival with music, food, arts and crafts exhibits, and other fun. It's sponsored by the Farmer's Market Plaza Tenants Association. Admission is free.

### CLASSIC CRUISE ALONG THE CORRIDOR

**Tripoint Family YMCA**
**3233 N. Saint Mary's St.**
**(210) 213-1984**
**www.aacog.com**

Sponsored by the Alamo Area Council of Governments, this event is a favorite with classic-car buffs. More than 12 classic-car clubs participate in this annual drive from San Antonio down the Alamo–La Bahia corridor. Cars depart from the Tripoint Family YMCA. The drive passes through towns including Seguin, Floresville, Goliad, Poth, Sutherland Springs, Helena, Karnes City, Panna Maria, and others, and features special events in each community. Now in its second decade, the Classic Cruise showcases both vintage cars and motorcycles. Admission is free.

### RETURN OF THE CHILI QUEENS

**514 Market St., Market Square**
**(210) 207-8600**
**www.sanantonio.gov/marketsquare**

This is the time to indulge your taste for chili, the spicy concoction created by local women known as "chili queens." To celebrate the state dish, booths are set up every Memorial Day for a 3-day tasting sponsored by the El Mercado Merchants Association. The festivities include a chili cook-off sanctioned by the Chili Appreciation Society. The public can sample the tasty dishes starting at 2 p.m.; live music adds to the fun. Admission is free.

### TEJANO CONJUNTO FESTIVAL EN SAN ANTONIO

**Guadalupe Theater, 1301 Guadalupe St.**
**Rosedale Park at 303 Dartmouth**
**(210) 271-3151**
**www.guadalupeculturalarts.org**

Take the liveliness of Mexican music, mix in German accordion, and you have conjunto, a unique sound born in South Texas. Tejano music adds a newer beat to this old favorite. This festival celebrates conjunto, Tejano, and *norteño* (Mexican-Latin) music, and it is considered the largest one of its kind in the world. The 6-day event features more than 35 hours of live music performed by some 25 artists. Previous performers have included 5-time Grammy Award–winner Flaco Jimenez, Esteban Jordan, the Hometown Boys, Los Dos Gilbertos, Mingo Saldivar, Grup Vida, Los Desperados, Jay Perez, Dee, the Garcia Brothers, and Michael Salgado. Special events include inductions into the Conjunto Music Hall of Fame. Admission Fri is $14; Sat and Sun is $18. An all-events pass, including the Hall of Fame dinner, is available for $100.

### ✷KERRVILLE FOLK FESTIVAL

**Quiet Valley Ranch, Highway 16**
**9 miles south of Kerrville**
**(830) 257-3600, (800) 435-8429**
**www.kerrville-music.com**

Starting in late May and continuing into early June, this annual festival is not only one of the largest in the San Antonio area but also one of the largest in the Lone Star State. The Kerrville Folk Festival features more than 100 songwriters and their bands from Texas, other states, and other countries, too. The festival includes daily 6-hour evening concerts as well as 2-hour sundown concerts, plus dozens of arts and crafts booths, and multiple daytime events. One of Texas's best-loved music gatherings, this extravaganza of song is held 9 miles south of town at the Quiet Valley Ranch. In previous years, headliners have included Tish Hinojosa, Peter Rowan, David Wilcox, actor Ronny Cox, Guy

Clark, Butch Hancock, Riders in the Sky, Jimmy LaFave, Sara Hickman, and Ray Wylie Hubbard. New songwriters are featured at the New Folk Concerts held early in the festival. Previous winners of this prestigious contest include Nanci Griffith, Lyle Lovett, James McMurtry, and Tish Hinojosa. The concert is a casual event, and guests are invited to bring lawn chairs. Ice chests, bottles, cans, or glass containers are not permitted on the fairgrounds, however. If you want to extend your day trip for a weekend of good music, consider camping at the ranch. There are 20-plus acres, complete with picnic tables, restrooms, solar-heated showers, and a country store.

### TEXAS ARTS AND CRAFTS FAIR
**River Star Arts and Event Park**
**(830) 896–5711**
**www.tacef.org**

Every Memorial Day weekend, this festival opens its gates on the grounds of the River Star Arts and Event Park. Founded by the State of Texas, this enormous show features the paintings, sculptures, jewelry, and other artwork of more than 200 Texas artists, all available to answer questions about their work. A special children's area includes crafts instruction and a petting zoo. Musical entertainment rounds out the day. Cost is $7 for Mon only or $10 for a 3-day pass.

## JUNE

### FIESTA NOCHE DEL RIO
**Arneson River Theatre, River Walk**
**(210) 226-4651**
**www.alamo-kiwanis.org/fiestanoche.html**

You know it's summer when Fiesta Noche Del Rio begins. The Arneson River Theatre has hosted this summer production since 1956. Sponsored by the Alamo Kiwanis Club as a fund-raiser for children's charities in San Antonio, the show celebrates the many cultures of San Antonio through song and dance every Friday and Saturday night in June through August. The event includes acts showcasing the music of Spain, Argentina, Mexico, and Texas; there's romantic Latin music, too. Tickets are $15 for adults, $5 for children ages 6 to 14, and $12 for seniors.

### JUNETEENTH FAMILY PICNIC
**Comanche Park #2**
**2600 Rigsby Ave.**
**(210) 527-1830**
**www.juneteenthsanantonio.com**

Juneteenth (June 19), also known as Emancipation Day, is an official Texas holiday honoring the day in 1865 when Union General Gordon Grainger publicly read Executive Order #3, proclaiming that "all slaves are free." The San Antonio celebration is held in Comanche Park and offers a free, family-friendly event with a freedom parade, picnic, golf tournament, and various other fun activities over 2 days. A slate of live entertainment rounds out the festivities.

### SAN ANTONIO SUMMER ART & JAZZ FESTIVAL
**Crockett Park at 1300 N. Main Ave.**
**(210) 772-2900**
**http://sanantoniosummerartjazzfestival.com**

From bebop to blues, a bevy of musicians have gathered at Crockett Park each year since 2003 for this free 3-day, 10-concert celebration of a purely American sound. Attendees can spread a blanket over a patch of grass, sit back and listen while the mellow tones of trumpets and saxophones paint musical portraits, or stroll among canvases splashed with a symphony of vivid colors at the arts and crafts fair. Aspiring musicians in junior high or high school can attend free jazz workshops.

**✱TEXAS FOLKLIFE FESTIVAL**
**Institute of Texan Cultures**
**801 E. Durango Blvd.**
**HemisFair Plaza**
**(210) 458-2224**
**www.texasfolklifefestival.org**
This 3-day celebration is one of San Antonio's top events. Dating back to 1972, it has grown from 2,000 to 70,000 attendees. Held at the Institute of Texan Cultures, the festival carries out the museum's mission—to recognize the contributions of the many cultures that settled Texas—through song, folk dance, game demonstrations, crafts exhibits and demonstrations, and lots of ethnic food. Eleven stages throughout the grounds showcase ethnic song and dance ranging from flamenco dancers to Celtic Airs to hula. Advance tickets can be purchased at retail locations and through the Texas Folklife Festival website. The festival also sells a special wristband that allows unlimited admission to all events. The wristband is nontransferable and must be purchased by late May.

## JULY

**FIESTA NOCHE DEL RIO**
**Arneson River Theatre**
**(210) 226-4651**
**www.alamo-kiwanis.org/fiestanoche.html**
This nightly summer festival continues through July; see the June listings for details.

## AUGUST

**FIESTA NOCHE DEL RIO**
**Arneson River Theatre**
**(210) 226-4651**
**www.alamo-kiwanis.org/fiestanoche.html**
This nightly summer festival continues through August; see the June listings for details.

## SEPTEMBER

**EL GRITO CEREMONY**
**Municipal Auditorium**
**100 Auditorium Circle**
**(210) 207-8511**
**http://portal.sre.gob.mx/sanantonio**
On September 15, 1810, Father Hidalgo y Costilla gave his "El Grito" (Cry for Freedom) speech, which launched Mexico's rebellion against Spain. The reenactment of El Grito takes place at the Plaza Mexico in HemisFair Park each September 15 and is followed by plenty of music and dance. Admission is free.

**DIEZ Y SEIS DE SEPTIEMBRE**
**Citywide**
**(210) 207-8600**
**www.visitsanantonio.com**
Diez y Seis de Septiembre (September 16), the anniversary of Mexican independence, is celebrated with festivals and special events at La Villita, the Arneson River Theatre, Market Square, and Guadalupe Plaza. Highlights include a parade and performances by folkloric dance groups.

## OCTOBER

### GO RODEO ROUNDUP

**Expo Hall at the AT&T Center**
**3201 E. Houston St.**
**(210) 225-5851**
**www.sarodeo.com**

A fund-raiser for the San Antonio Livestock Exposition Scholarship Fund and Junior Livestock Auction, this elegant event is a favorite with country music lovers. The evening function features live music and gourmet dining. Tickets are $75 per person; tables for 10 people can be reserved for $750.

### GREEK FUNSTIVAL

**St. Sophia Greek Orthodox Church**
**2504 N. St. Mary's St.**
**(210) 735-5051**

Enjoy Greek food, dances, and music at the St. Sophia Greek Orthodox Church during this 3-day fall festival, now in its fourth decade. The event offers guests a taste of such traditional Greek goodies as baklava, dolmades, and souvlaki. You can also purchase Greek jewelry or imported Greek wines to accompany the homemade food prepared by the women of the church. Admission is $3 for adults; children under 12 are admitted free.

### INTERNATIONAL ACCORDION FESTIVAL

**La Villita Historic Arts Village**
**South Alamo at Nueva**
**(210) 865-8578**
**www.internationalaccordionfestival.org**

For 3 days, the toe-tapping sounds of squeeze-boxes reverberate on the grounds of La Villita as music lovers kick up their heels and dance to tunes ranging from Celtic to Klezmer. Performers on 3 stages keep the tunes flowing as folks search for souvenirs among the rows of vendor stalls or sample south-of-the-border fare from one of the food booths.

**i** Get into the Halloween spirit with the Coffins on Parade as All Hallow's Eve–themed boats, each bearing a casket, float down the River Walk. This free event, courtesy of the Paseo del Rio Association, takes place every year on October 31.

## NOVEMBER

### EL DÍA DE LOS MUERTOS

**Various locations**
**(210) 432-1896**
**www.sacalaveras.com**

El Día de los Muertos, literally "the Day of the Dead," is an important and ancient celebration in the Mexican cultural tradition. Families welcome back departed loved ones to share their lives with them as their memories live on in their hearts. Altars are set up with *ofrendas* around town in homes, art galleries, cultural centers, restaurants, and elsewhere to commemorate deceased loved ones. Cemeteries are popular with families picnicking and decorating the graves, particularly with marigolds, *pan de muerto* ("dead bread"), sugar skulls, and other traditional items. The day may also include *calavera* processions, with participants dressed as skeletons.

### DIWALI: FESTIVAL OF LIGHTS

**Hemisfair Park**
**Bowie Street at Durango Boulevard**
**(210) 207-8083**

Diwali (also known as Deepavali) is a significant festival celebrated in India recognizing the victory of good over evil. The Diwali:

Festival of Lights event is the only citywide celebration showcasing Indian culture. The celebration comes complete with Indian dance, food, an Indian craft market, and a special lighting ceremony where 1,000 candles are released into the fountains at HemisFair Park. The evening also includes a spectacular fireworks display after dark. Admission is free; Indian cuisine and crafts are available for purchase.

### *WURSTFEST
**178 Landa Park Dr.**
**Landa Park, New Braunfels**
**(830) 625-9167, (800) 221-4369**
**www.wurstfest.com**

The month of November starts with a bang—and a bratwurst—at Wurstfest, a celebration of sausage, suds, and song held north of San Antonio in the city of New Braunfels on I-35. Since 1961 Wurstfest has been drawing the attention of merrymakers looking to enjoy the German heritage of this community. Held on the banks of the Comal River in Landa Park, Wurstfest is consistently rated as one of the best fests in the US. An estimated 100,000 visitors from across the nation participate in this special festival each year. Get ready to polka to the sounds of accordion tunes and to sample the sausage for which this event is known.

The Wurstfest fun is scattered throughout the community thanks to related special events. The local art league offers a Wurstfest Art Show, or "Artoberfest" (830-629-8022), highlighting area talent. History buffs can browse the Heritage Exhibit at the New Braunfels Civic Center to see how the first settlers founded this town. And bicyclists can ride in the Tour de Gruene (www.tourdegruene.com), a scenic 26- and 36-mile recreational bicycle tour that follows River Rd. through the Gruene Historic District. Tickets for Wurstfest can be obtained online at www.wurstfest.com; by writing Wurstfest Association, P.O. Box 310309, New Braunfels, TX 78131; or by calling the telephone number above.

## LATE NOVEMBER & DECEMBER

### *HOLIDAY RIVER PARADE AND LIGHTING CEREMONY
**Alamo Plaza**
**(210) 227-4262**
**www.thesanantonioriverwalk.com**

What better place than the Alamo to make official holiday declarations? Every year on the day after Thanksgiving, Alamo Plaza is the site of music and entertainment, culminating with the arrival of Santa, who throws the switch to light up the 45-foot Christmas tree on the plaza. Within about 30 minutes, the mayor and grand marshal of the San Antonio Christmas River Parade throw a switch from the Arneson River Theatre to illuminate 122,000 tiny Christmas lights on the majestic trees arching over—and reflected in—the San Antonio River. The grand light-up signals the beginning of the river parade, which glows with illuminated floats populated by local celebrities, politicians, bands, and lavishly costumed participants. Reserved seating is available for $20 to $25 from the Paseo del Rio Association, (210) 227-4262. On weekend evenings through Christmas, thousands of luminarias (traditional Mexican holiday lights) add candlelight to the already spectacular panorama. It's a sight you won't forget. Add to that the caroling on the river barges, and you've got a Technicolor picture of a San Antonio Christmas.

### Pancho Claus

If you think Santa's the only fellow who delivers presents to children, then you've never met Pancho Claus, who identifies himself as Santa's cousin living south—really, really south!—of the border. Wearing a traditional Mexican poncho and a red mariachi-style sombrero, this black-bearded deliverer of cheer lives at the South Pole, where his faithful companion isn't Rodolfo of red-nosed fame but Chuy the donkey. Spanish-speaking Pancho isn't crazy about cookies and milk—he'd much rather that children leave him a plate of tamales.

**FIESTAS NAVIDEÑAS**
**Market Square**
**(210) 207-8600**
**www.visitsanantonio.com**

The first three weekends in December, Market Square spreads the holiday spirit with special events such as piñata parties, a blessing of the animals ranging from llamas to parrots, and, of course, a visit from Pancho Claus.

**HECHO A MANO**
**Guadalupe Cultural Arts Theater**
**1300 Guadalupe St.**
**(210) 271-3151**
**www.guadalupeculturalarts.org**

This arts and crafts festival, held for 3 days in late November or early December, showcases the work of local artisans. Only handmade items are allowed at this event, which has been held annually since 1986. Jewelry, woodwork, furniture, clothing, folk art, toys, ceramics, and more are displayed and sold during the event, which attracts in excess of 10,000 shoppers. No admission is charged.

**CELEBRATE SAN ANTONIO**
**Downtown, La Villita**
**(210) 212-8423**
**www.saparksfoundation.org**

Celebrate San Antonio, the Alamo City's countdown to a new year, generally begins around sunset in the heart of Downtown and La Villita, and ends at midnight with a spectacular fireworks display. Live music performed at multiple stages, a children's area featuring carnival games, family entertainment at the Arneson River Theatre, strolling street performers, and dozens of food and beverage booths are all part of this huge celebration. The event is free and open to the public.

**LOS PASTORES**
**Mission San José, 6701 San Jose Dr.**
**(210) 932-1001**
**www.nps.gov/saan**

The National Park Service hosts this Christmas play at Mission San José every season. Usually scheduled for the Saturday following Christmas, Los Pastores (The Shepherds) is considered one of San Antonio's oldest Spanish traditions, dating back more than 250 years. At that time, the play was presented by Franciscan priests at the mission to explain the story of the birth of Christ to the local Indian population. The Franciscans had brought the play with them from Spain, where it originated in the 1500s. It is a story of good versus evil, with masked devils trying to prevent the shepherds from arriving in Bethlehem. Although the story is Spanish, the presentation has some local touches such as the handmade costumes that hark

## Close-up

### Holidays in the Hill Country

The 12 Days of Christmas is fine, but the Hill Country does the holiday up in South Texas fashion with a whole month of activities. One of the largest Christmas events in the area is the **Texas Hill Country Regional Christmas Lighting Trail,** stretching north from San Antonio to encompass many of the communities of this region. Shops, historic sites, courthouses, and churches welcome travelers with a show of spectacular lights and Christmas cheer.

The Christmas Lighting Trail runs from late November through New Year's Day, spreading the holiday spirit with free activities that recall Christmases gone by in historic Hill Country towns. Some activities take place on weekends only; others, especially lighting displays, occur nightly. Grab a coat, the camera, and the kids and jump aboard the sleigh—or at least the minivan—for a look at the dazzling show that awaits just beyond San Antonio's city limits.

**Blanco.** One of the largest Hill Country light displays is found at the Old Blanco County Courthouse, a historic building aglow with some 100,000 tiny white lights. Blanco, 35 miles north of San Antonio, hosts a month of activities to celebrate the season, including the Christmas Market, which offers plenty of opportunities for holiday shopping. Later in the month, visitors can take a tour of homes, enjoy a holiday meal, and then witness the reenactment of Las Posadas at St. Ferdinand's Catholic Church. For more information, call (830) 833-5101.

**Boerne.** This German community starts the holiday season on Thanksgiving weekend with Dickens on Main, which features scenes from Dickens's classic *A Christmas Carol,* art galleries, specialty shops, visitors and residents in period clothing, and food galore. Early December brings the Weihnachts Fest Parade in the historic district and Oma's (Grandmother's) Christmas Fair at the Kendall County Fairgrounds. Additional information is available at (888) 842-8080 or www.visitboerne.org.

**Bulverde.** Start your Hill Country lighting tour in Bulverde, located 9 miles north of Loop 1604 and 1 mile west of US 281. This small town has a lot of Christmas spirit and shows it starting in early December with the Christmas tree lighting in Spring Branch and the Bulverde Senior Holiday Craft Show. The following weekend, the town enjoys a living Nativity scene at St. Paul Lutheran Church and an open house at the Krause House Theater. For more details, call (830) 438-4285 or visit www.bulverdechamber.com.

**Fredericksburg.** The holiday fun starts at the end of November or beginning of December with a lighted Christmas parade on historic Main Street and continues right through the end of the month in this charming community 66 miles northwest of San Antonio. The parade marks the opening of Weihnachten in Fredericksburg, a Christmas market and festival. Designed in the style of an open-air German Christmas market, Weihnachten offers everything from crafts to Christmas beers.

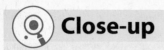

There's plenty of holiday fun for the children, too, thanks to the Kinderfest. A real highlight of the season is the Christmas Candlelight Tour, with self-guided tours of historic homes and buildings. The fun continues after Christmas as well. On December 26, the Pioneer Museum Complex hosts Zweite Weihnachten, or Second Christmas. According to this German tradition, the day after the holiday was meant to be shared with friends. For more information, call (888) 997-3600 or visit www.fredericksburg-texas.com.

**Johnson City.** They named it right—Lights Spectacular is downright spectacular, thanks to more than 750,000 lights. At the center of the festivities stands the Blanco County Courthouse, adorned with some 100,000 lights; it's open weekend evenings so visitors can view the Christmas tree and antique toy display. The community, 63 miles north of San Antonio, also has "light art displays," illuminated panels with up to 1,200 lights that portray the 12 days of Christmas. And don't miss the Pedernales Electric Co-op, with more than 275,000 shining lights. The free lighting displays take place nightly through New Year's Day, but December is also filled with special events, including Christmas in the County Carriage Rides, lamplight tours of the LBJ Boyhood Home and the Johnson settlement, and the living Nativity scene at the United Methodist Church. Shoppers in the family will want to check out the Blanco County Artists International Art Show, held on the courthouse square. For more information, call (830) 868-7684 or visit www.johnsoncitytexaschamber.com.

**New Braunfels.** In late November, New Braunfels (800-572-2626; www.nbcham.org) kicks off the Yule season with a parade and Weihnachtsmarkt, a German Christmas shopping market featuring unique gift items and antiques from distinctive merchants and artisans, which is held in the New Braunfels Civic Center. Wassailfest comes in early December, when the downtown area offers samples of different types of wassail and diverse entertainment. The Gospel Brunch with a Texas Twist occurs mid-month in Gruene Hall. It's a New Orleans–style buffet brunch with seasonal music and Christmas decor. Tickets are $19.50, available by visiting www.gruenehall.com or by calling (830) 629-5077 or (830) 606-1281.

**San Marcos.** The home of Texas State University is also the home of an event called the Sights and Sounds of Christmas (512-393-5900 or 512-393-8400; www.sights-n-sounds.org). Held on the banks of the San Marcos River (ride a free shuttle from Strahan Coliseum on the university campus), this annual festival includes activities ranging from butter churning and Indian dancing to train rides and sock skating (complete with falling snowflakes!). With lights shimmering over the river, the event creates a festive Yuletide scene with music, food, and fun. In nearby Wimberley (512-847-2201; www.wimberley.org) the big event is called a "Creekside Christmas" in honor of Cypress Creek there. Special events include a gourmet dinner and a Christmas Trail of Lights. Lighting of the Menorah is one of the featured activities.

back to Texas traditions. The play itself is a Texas tradition and was sponsored by the San Antonio Conservation Society from 1947 to 2002. It remains very much a homegrown effort; the cast consists of members of Our Lady of Guadalupe Catholic Church. Local foods are sold at the performance. Admission is free.

## Holiday Sparks

Fireworks are a big part of South Texas celebrations. Although the rest of the US enjoys most of its fireworks around July 4, the most popular time to break out the sparklers and Roman candles here is between Christmas and New Year's Eve. Fireworks within city limits are prohibited, and weather conditions affect the legality of using fireworks in the county, so be sure to check before you light the sky. Also, be sure to avoid illegal fireworks (they often carry no labels or instructions) and buy from a reputable dealer such as Mr. W. Fireworks or Wald and Co.

**LA GRAN POSADA**
**San Fernando Cathedral**
**115 Main Plaza**
**(210) 227-1297**

Las Posadas, the reenacted Christmas journey of Mary and Joseph in search of shelter, is a cherished event that brings together visitors of many faiths. At one time, the celebration was sponsored by the San Antonio Conservation Society but today is sponsored by the San Fernando Cathedral. This cherished event finds parishioners, visitors, and even government officials taking part as costumed marchers wind through downtown San Antonio from Milam Park. A musical procession accompanies children portraying Mary and Joseph, whose way is lit by luminarias. Their first stop is City Hall, where the mayor refuses them lodging, followed by a stop at the Bexar County Courthouse, where the reception is the same. The procession ends at San Fernando Cathedral, where the group finally finds refuge. A fiesta featuring the traditional tamales, *buñuelos,* and cinnamon chocolate awaits the marchers and guests.

**TAMALES AT PEARL**
**200 E. Grayson**
**(210) 212-7260**
**www.atpearl.com**

The Hispanic tradition of making tamales during the holiday season is celebrated during Tamales at Pearl, a festival for the entire family held in mid-December at the historic Pearl Brewery. Enjoy traditional San Antonio fare, tamale-making and cooking demonstrations, family activities, musical entertainment, dancing, and a fireworks display. You will discover numerous genres of tamales: traditional pork, bean and cheese, chicken, pumpkin, chocolate, and more. Also on the menu are San Antonio favorites like empanadas, beef *antichuchos,* rib eye fajita tacos, chicken-stuffed poblano rellenos, and pulled-meat tacos from the outdoor roasting pits at the neighboring Culinary Institute of America San Antonio campus. But save room for dessert—*buñeulos, tres leches* cupcakes, and *capirotada* (bread pudding), all washed down with Mexican coffee and hot chocolate.

# THE ARTS

**The San Antonio arts scene is vibrant and varied. The cultural diversity that makes this city special is reflected in its creative community, which includes Latino artists, Southwestern artists, and representatives from many other genres, who work in both the performing and visual arts in a variety of media.**

**San Antonio is a patchwork of artistic areas, from the commercial district to the King William Historic District. One aspect that has attracted many artists to the city is its attitude toward art. "It offers a 'big sky' attitude where anything is possible," says Alexander Gray, a native New York art administrator and former member of the staff of ArtPace, a San Antonio gallery. "Artists support each other and welcome new people to the community. They turn their homes into galleries and invite the public inside to enjoy and learn from their work."**

**Blue Star Arts Complex, San Antonio's art space, also brings international talent to a South Texas venue. According to Executive Director Bill Fitzgibbons, "Since 1985, artists and advocates for contemporary art have used the Blue Star Art Space to spearhead trends in San Antonio." For those who seek to learn more about art and its creation, the Southwest School of Art provides instruction in a variety of media. Every year, 2,400 adults and 1,600 children take part in classes taught by local and international artists. An additional 10,000 children are taught in special programs in schools, shelters, and community centers. Paula Owen, director of the school, notes that "San Antonio is a fantastic place for artists. There is a new interest in regionalism, and San Antonio is a city that catches the imagination. It is different and spirited and it feels as if something is about to happen. Artists feel that energy and welcome the opportunity to learn, exhibit, and interact."**

## OVERVIEW

The city's appreciation for art is reflected in many of San Antonio's public buildings. For example, the renovation of the Henry B. Gonzales Convention Center included the installation of 16 pieces of public art. Mexican artist Juan O'Gorman created the mosaic mural at the Lila Cockrell Theater for the Performing Arts at the convention center; it tells the story of the region from the days before the conquest to the present day.

At other points in the city, public art also makes an appearance. At the trolley transit center, tile medallions have been designed by quilt artist Ann Adams. The artist also created the mosaic mandala in the sidewalk along the River Walk. At the airport, local artist Bill Fitzgibbons has crafted a gateway of airplane wings and tail sections that links the parking garage and Terminal Two. San Antonio also has many nonprofit organizations that educate the citizens of the city about the joys of the performing and visual arts. Guadalupe Cultural Arts Center (210-271-3151; www.guadalupeculturalarts.org), located at 1300 Guadalupe St., was founded in 1980. The largest organization of its kind in the US, it aims to promote the arts and culture of the Native American, Latino, and Chicano peoples. Arts San Antonio! (210-226-2891; www.artssanantonio.com) sponsors performances for the children of the city in an effort to help them develop an appreciation of art. Incorporated as a nonprofit organization in 1992, Arts San Antonio! tries to make the performing arts an accessible avenue of entertainment for everyone in the community.

**i** **To find out what's going on in San Antonio's art realm, pick up a copy of the *San Antonio Current*. The free weekly paper is known for its good coverage of the art scene and its comprehensive art and entertainment listings.**

## CHOIRS

### ALAMO CITY MEN'S CHORALE

**106 Auditorium Circle**
**(210) 495-SING**
**www.acmc-texas.org**

Since it was founded in 1987, the Alamo City Men's Chorale has sought "to provide quality choral music, performed by gay and gay-friendly voices, that enriches the lives of its audience." For 20 years, it has apparently fulfilled that goal. ACMC performs a range of music, including pop songs, spiritual works, and classics. One critic praised them as "one of the finest men's choruses in the country." At any given time the choir is made up of around 40 individuals. Members must pass an audition process.

Alamo City Men's Chorale has performed across the state and around the country in venues including the Center for the Performing Arts in Tampa, San Jose's Center for the Performing Arts, and the Wortham Center in Houston. It also has appeared with the San Antonio Symphony several times. Over the years Alamo City Men's Chorale has lost 10 members to AIDS. To join the fight against HIV and AIDS, the chorale performs regularly at the annual Procession of Hope, sponsored by the Hope Action Care Agency.

### TEXAS BACH CHOIR

**11 St. Luke's Lane**
**(210) 828-6425, ext. 201**
**www.texasbachchoir.org**

The Texas Bach Choir has been performing for San Antonio audiences since 1976. TBC sings a variety of choral arrangements from a range of years and styles but specializes in the works of composer Johann Sebastian Bach. Each season there is at least one concert devoted solely to his work. The choir, which has performed all of Bach's major works for choral choir, is made up of the finest voices in the San Antonio area, who must try out in a competitive audition process.

The Texas Bach Choir has performed in many churches and concert halls throughout the San Antonio area. It has also taken two European concert tours, performing in Central and Eastern Europe. In an effort to educate the community about the beauty of choral music, TBC runs educational programs at San Antonio schools.

## DANCE TROUPES

### SAN ANTONIO METROPOLITAN BALLET

**2800 NE Loop 410, Suite 307**
**(210) 650-8810**
**www.sametballet.org**

This professional company is aimed at providing entertainment to San Antonio citizens while supplying young dancers with the opportunity to gain experience and broaden their artistic scope. The San Antonio Metropolitan Ballet has been in operation since 1983, first as the San Antonio Dance Theatre before its name change in 1995. Two major productions are presented every year, one in spring and one in winter. The company performs modern dance and jazz as well as ballet. Classes are held from August through April each year.

### BALLET CONSERVATORY OF SOUTH TEXAS

**5200 Broadway**
**(210) 820-3400**
**http://balletsouthtexas.org**

This preprofessional dance company offers classes in contemporary American ballet for dance students ages 3 to 21, allowing serious young dancers to develop their craft in a nurturing environment. The performing company is made up of dancers ages 11 through 21, who conduct public performances several times a year. The organization raises funds for scholarships to allow deserving students from all economic backgrounds to participate. The conservatory also encourages students from underserved communities, offering free tickets to performances and conducting workshops in schools and social service centers in San Antonio. Classes run from late August through mid-June.

## EDUCATION

### SOUTHWEST SCHOOL OF ART

**300 Augusta St.**
**(210) 224-1848**
**www.swschool.org**

The building that now houses the Southwest School of Art has a history that is almost as interesting as that of the city of San Antonio itself. In the 1840s Bishop Jean-Marie Odin bought 10 acres of land for $1,000 with the intent of starting a girls' school in San Antonio. The first group of teachers, Ursuline nuns, was brought to San Antonio from Galveston in 1851, and the school was opened. By 1900 there were 300 students enrolled in the Old Ursuline Academy. In 1965 the school moved to northwest San Antonio; later that year the San Antonio Conservation Society bought the building from the Ursuline Order.

Southwest School of Art was organized by a group of citizens who felt there was a void in San Antonio that could be filled by the teaching of handicrafts and art. The 1968 World's Fair in San Antonio provided the opportunity for the school to sponsor a gallery, and enrollment grew quickly. The San Antonio Conservation Society offered the use of the Old Ursuline Academy to the school, and in 1971 the Southwest School of Art moved into its new quarters. Massive renovation was needed, and the school and the Conservation Society both worked hard to raise money for the restoration, which lasted for 12 years.

Today the school has 2 campuses: the original Ursuline Campus and the adjacent Navarro Campus, which was opened in 1998. It offers programs for all age groups, with classes taught by local, regional, and national artists. More than 100 classes and workshops are offered each term, and the annual enrollment is about 4,000 adults, children, and teenagers.

There are 2 galleries at the school, which are open to the public from 9 a.m. to 5 p.m. Mon through Sat; the Navarro Campus gallery is also open 11 a.m to 4 p.m. Sun. The Ursuline Hallway Gallery shows works by up-and-coming artists, while the Russell Hill Rogers Gallery on the Navarro Campus displays pieces by more well-known regional, national, and international artists.

## FILM

**CINEFESTIVAL**
**Guadalupe Cultural Arts Theater**
**1300 Guadalupe St.**
**(210) 271-3151**
**www.guadalupeculturalarts.org**

This February event is the country's largest and oldest Latino film festival. Since 1978, CineFestival has showcased shorts, features, and experimental and documentary works either by Latinos or about the Latino experience. Tickets range from $8 to $30.

i Faith is at the forefront of the San Antonio Independent Christian Film Festival (www.independentchristianfilms.com) and the Jewish Film Festival (http://jccsanantonio.org), while cutting-edge cinema is explored during the San Antonio Underground Film Festival (www.safilm.com).

**SAN ANTONIO FILM COMMISSION**
**203 S. St. Mary's St., Suite 200**
**(210) 207-6730**
**www.visitsanantonio.com/film**

The San Antonio Film Commission's purpose is to bring film and video productions to San Antonio. It has lured a number of movie, television, and commercial shoots to the Alamo City. San Antonio has a lot to offer film studios. Within an hour's drive of the city, there are rolling hills, farmland, and arid plains. There are well-preserved historic buildings as well as new buildings downtown that can present a modern look.

For these reasons, San Antonio is becoming a popular movie location. Among the films that have been shot here are *Syriana* (2005), *Spy Kids* (2000), *All the Pretty Horses* (1999), and *The Newton Boys* (1997).

## ART GALLERIES

**ARTPACE**
**445 N. Main Ave.**
**(210) 212-4900**
**www.artpace.org**

This contemporary arts gallery was founded by the late Linda Pace, daughter of David Earl Pace of Pace Foods fame (if you've been in San Antonio for long, you've sampled their picante sauce). The gallery opened its doors in January 1995 and quickly attracted attention with its artists-in-residence programs. The 18,000-square-foot facility houses three artists at a time: one international, one national, and one from the San Antonio region. The artists live and work at ArtPace for two months; at the end of that period there is an exhibition of their work. The gallery is open Wed through Sun from noon to 5 p.m. and by appointment.

**BLUE STAR CONTEMPORARY ART CENTER**
**116 Blue Star**
**(210) 227-6960**
**www.bluestarart.org**

Located directly across from the Pioneer Flour Mills, this collection of former warehouses spans 137,000 square feet and is home to San Antonio's most expansive arts complex, a collection of art galleries, student exhibition space, alternative theater venues, and restaurants. Blue Star was founded by several local artists, including Jeffrey Moore, Richard Thompson, Kent Rush, Richard Mogas, Adair Sutherland, and Lewis Tarver; the complex first opened in 1986 with an exhibit featuring the work of local artists. The following years brought more successful shows as well as funding by the City of San Antonio, the National Endowment for the Arts, and the Texas Commission on the Arts.

Within two years of that first exhibit, the complex expanded to include studios and both work and living space for artists. Today Blue Star hosts over 20 exhibitions each year. Shops and galleries here feature a variety of art forms, from folk art to glass objects to jewelry. Open Tues through Sat, noon to 6 p.m., till 8 p.m. Thurs.

### GALERIA ORTIZ

**102 Concho St.**
**(210) 225-0731**
**http://samarketplace.com**

This distinctive gallery showcases mainly contemporary Southwestern art. Lisa Ortiz moved to San Antonio from New York in 1978. She took over the DagenBela Galeria in 1995 and changed the name to Galeria Ortiz. Up-and-coming artists' work is featured alongside that of internationally recognized artists. Painting, jewelry, and sculpture are displayed and sold.

### GREENHOUSE GALLERY OF FINE ART

**6496 N. New Braunfels Ave.**
**(210) 828-6491, (800) 453-8991**
**www.greenhousegallery.com**

This gallery is one of the most respected in the US. Its 12,000 square feet are filled with works by many nationally and internationally known artists, including oil paintings and bronze sculptures by some of the 21st-century art world's biggest stars. The Greenhouse Gallery is closed Sun and Mon.

## MUSEUMS

### MARION KOOGLER MCNAY ART MUSEUM

**6000 N. New Braunfels Ave.**
**(210) 824-5368**
**www.mcnayart.org**

Works by famous artists such as Picasso, Matisse, O'Keeffe, and Cézanne are featured in this art museum, which is housed in the home of the late Marion Koogler McNay, heiress to an oil fortune and an artist herself. Built in the 1920s, the Spanish Colonial Revival–style 24-room house was converted to a museum after Mrs. McNay's death in 1950. She left her art collection, home, and endowment "for the advancement and enjoyment of modern art." The collection numbers more than 20,000 prints, drawings, and sculptures and is considered among the finest in the Southwest US. The museum also features a 30,000-volume research library, an auditorium, and a museum store.

The museum's education department provides educational programs for 42,000 local schoolchildren, teachers, and other adults each year. Tours of the expansive museum are offered each week. Art historians and museum curators give presentations about the exhibits as part of the Gallery Talks on Exhibitions program. Lectures by visiting curators, artists, and scholars are presented on select Sundays. Also on some Sundays, local musicians and actors perform at McNay's Leeper Auditorium.

Free Family Days allow parents and children to enjoy art in a fun atmosphere; check the McNay calendar for specific dates. On the last Sunday of each month, special family activities are held at 2 p.m.

The museum's library is open to visitors who wish to use its collection for research and reference. The library is open Tues, Wed, and Fri from 10 a.m. to 3:45 p.m., and from 10 a.m. to 7:45 p.m. Thurs. The library is closed on most holidays and the entire month of December.

The museum store is located on the first floor of the museum. It sells art books, posters, and souvenirs.

Marion Koogler McNay Art Museum is closed Mon as well as New Year's Day, July 4th, Thanksgiving, and Christmas. Admission is $8, with children under 12 free.

## Jane & Arthur Stieren Center for Exhibitions

In 2008, the McNay Art Museum doubled in size with the opening of the **Jane & Arthur Stieren Center for Exhibitions,** adding 14,000 square feet of exhibition space to the museum. The Stieren Center was designed by Jean-Paul Viguier, a Paris-based architect known worldwide for his public-space projects. One of his best-known projects is the Parc André Citroën, the largest urban park built in Paris since the mid-1800s. The Stieren Center, Viguier's first museum design in the US, enhances the viewing of the collections by maximizing natural light with soaring glass walls and ceilings. The center's galleries and sculpture gardens host changing exhibitions.

**✱SAN ANTONIO MUSEUM OF ART**
**200 W. Jones Ave.**
**(210) 978-8100**
**www.samuseum.org**

The San Antonio Museum of Art is one of the largest museums in the Southwest, and the building that houses it is as unique as the museum itself. It's the former Lone Star Brewery, and even today the building maintains a factory-like atmosphere with bright, airy spaces, skywalks, and even glass elevators.

The museum has a permanent collection of ancient glass and pottery as well as artifacts from around the world. It is especially noted for its ancient Egyptian, Greek, and Roman antiquities; Asian art; and American works.

But the pride of the museum is the Nelson A. Rockefeller Center for Latin American Art, considered the finest collection of Latin American art in the Americas. Opened in late 1998, this 3-story, 30,000-square-foot center, designed by San Antonio's Overland Partners, is a repository of all types of Latin American art. Located on the east side of the museum, it features an introductory gallery with computer stations that help visitors learn more about the region's art history and culture. Exhibits portray the long history of Latin American art starting with the Pre-Columbian Period. and continuing through the 20th century with works by Diego Rivera, Miguel Covarrubias, Chilean artist Roberto Matta, and many others.

Indeed, education is an important aspect of the center's mission. The center plans special events and educational programs throughout the year. The museum is open Tues from 10 a.m. to 9 p.m.; Wed through Sat from 10 a.m. to 5 p.m.; and Sun from noon to 6 p.m. Admission is $8 for adults, $7 for seniors, $5 for college students and active military with ID, and $3 for children ages 4 to 11.

## MUSIC

### SAN ANTONIO OPERA

**909 NE Loop 410, Suite 636**
**(210) 225-5972**
**www.saopera.com**

Local businessman Mark A. Richter founded the San Antonio Opera in 1997 with the stated mission "to produce fully staged opera in an evolving fashion, starting with modest budgets, increasing its production and musical values with each opera until the level of grand opera is achieved." The company grew at such a rate that only three years later the opera's production of *Madame Butterfly* was budgeted at $70,000. It produces full operas with a full symphony orchestra and professional costumes. A night at the opera is a popular outing for San Antonio locals and visitors alike.

For those hoping to perform professionally, the San Antonio Opera hosts chorus auditions several times a year. Most Opera events are currently performed at the Lila Cockerell Theatre, but the company plans to move into the San Antonio Performing Arts Center in 2012.

### SAN ANTONIO SYMPHONY

**224 E. Houston St.**
**(210) 554-1010**
**www.sasymphony.org**

The San Antonio Symphony performs in the beautiful Majestic Theatre in downtown San Antonio. Composed of 76 professional musicians, the symphony performs several times a year. The San Antonio Mastersingers is the symphony's chorus, made up of 120 volunteers from the San Antonio area. The symphony is a highly competitive organization; as many as 600 candidates from around the globe compete for every opening through an anonymous audition process.

The symphony's Young People's Concert Series, started in 1945, has taught generations of San Antonio youngsters about the joys of music. The series of 4 concerts is very affordable and is aimed at children in grades 4 and 5.

**i** Formerly a movie house, the ornate Aztec Theatre (201 E. Commerce St.; 877-43-AZTEC; www.azteconthe river.com) debuted its new role as a 700-seat concert venue in the spring of 2008. Having undergone a $4 million transformation, the 1920s-era venue features a 3,000-square-foot stage now graced by country music's top performers during the "San Antonio Rose Live" music series.

## THEATER TROUPES

### JUMP-START PERFORMANCE COMPANY

**108 Blue Star**
**(210) 227-5867**
**http://jump-start.org**

Found in the Blue Star Arts complex (see listing), Jump-Start Performance Company presents enjoyable shows of contemporary theater. Jump Start is committed to bringing artists together, despite ethnicity or other differences. The nonprofit company produces works by its members and features local and international artists in a guest series. It also offers classes and workshops.

Jump-Start presents some of San Antonio's most innovative theater work.

**MAGIK THEATRE**
**420 S. Alamo St.**
**(210) 227-2751**
**www.magiktheatre.org**

This troupe aims to provide an enjoyable theatergoing experience for audience members of all ages. More than 150,000 people attend a performance by the group every year. Magik Theatre is committed to bringing affordable yet quality productions to the stage; a quarter of the tickets each season are distributed to disadvantaged children. Many of the plays performed are chosen from local school reading lists, but in the evenings, classical and cutting-edge productions are staged for adults.

## VENUES

**ARNESON RIVER THEATRE**
**River Walk**
**(210) 227-4262**
**(Paseo del Rio Association)**
**http://lavillita.com/arneson**

This unique theater was erected in 1939, designed by River Walk architect Robert Hugman, and built by the WPA. When you are on the River Walk, have a seat on the grass-covered steps and enjoy a look. In this open-air format, the river, not a curtain, separates performers from the audience. Some of San Antonio's top events take place here, including Fiesta Noche Del Rio, a summer show that has been in operation nearly 5 decades (see the Annual Events and Festivals chapter for more information).

**CARVER COMMUNITY CULTURAL CENTER**
**226 N. Hackberry St.**
**(210) 207-7211**
**www.thecarver.org**

In the past, when it was known as the Library Auditorium, this historic structure hosted Ella Fitzgerald, Duke Ellington, Nat King Cole, Paul Robeson, and many other nationally known performers. Later rescued from demolition and reopened in 1977 as the Carver Community Cultural Center, it continues to stage a wide range of shows. Over the years the auditorium has featured the Dance Theatre of Harlem, a performance of Gershwin's *Porgy and Bess*, and a concert by the Muddy Waters Tribute Band.

### Tobin Center for the Performing Arts

In the fall of 2013, San Antonio's venerable Municipal Auditorium will be reborn as the **Tobin Center for the Performing Arts** (www.tobincenter.org), becoming the finest performance facility in San Antonio. Though the unique character of Municipal Auditorium will be preserved in the new design, the reborn center will feature state-of-the-art sound and lighting as well as greatly expanded audience facilities. It is expected to become the new home of the San Antonio Symphony, San Antonio Opera, and the Metropolitan Ballet of San Antonio.

**MUNICIPAL AUDITORIUM**
**200 E. Market St.**
**(210) 207-8500**
**www.sahbgcc.com**

Located adjacent to the San Antonio Convention Center, Municipal Auditorium has been one of the city's premier venues since its construction in 1926. Built in Mission style, the auditorium's twin domes have been a familiar landmark to thousands of conventioners and event attendees. With its decorative arches and extensive curtain and lighting accoutrements, the lavishly designed stage area has been the scene for countless special events. It boasts a Mediterranean-themed lobby and a main auditorium that can accommodate up to 5,000 guests.

**MAJESTIC PERFORMING ARTS CENTER**
**224 E. Houston St.**
**(210) 226-3333**
**www.majesticempire.com**

One of San Antonio's most famous theaters, the Majestic was built in 1928 by John Eberson as a vaudeville and movie palace. This proud building holds the title as the nation's oldest city-built playhouse. At the time it was built, it was the second-largest cinema venue in the US. Built in 1929 in baroque Mediterranean Villa style, the building is ornamented with unique architectural touches everywhere you look. Walls and columns are adorned with stylized trees and vines, and the vaulted ceiling twinkles with "stars," suggesting a mystical European village scene. The Majestic is now home to the San Antonio Symphony as well as national touring Broadway shows and traveling concerts. Comedian Jerry Seinfeld and other top acts perform at the Majestic. Parking for the theater is on Houston Street and costs about $5.

**SAN PEDRO PLAYHOUSE**
**800 W. Ashby Place**
**(210) 733-7258**
**www.sanpedroplayhouse.com**

The exterior of the San Pedro Playhouse is a reproduction of an old market house, making the building truly one of a kind. The structure was built in 1929 and has 2 stages, the main stage and the cellar theater. Usually musicals are shown on the main stage, while the downstairs theater usually offers experimental productions. This is a great place to see an informal show staged by local actors.

# PARKS & RECREATION

Whether your interests lie in golf, biking, swimming, or just plain enjoying the outdoors, you're in luck in the Alamo City. San Antonio is filled with parks and recreation facilities of all types, sprinkled from downtown to the city's outer reaches. Within the city's boundaries, you'll find parkland maintained by the city, county, state, and even national government. And still more parks are just a short distance away. Many of the local parks and recreation facilities are free; others have a small admission fee.

In all, the San Antonio Parks and Recreation Department operates 236 city-owned parks and recreational facilities, which include swimming pools, gyms, many municipal golf courses, and more. The list also includes some of the city's top attractions such as the Japanese Tea Garden and the San Antonio Botanical Garden. In all, the Parks and Recreation Department oversees and maintains more than 14,300 acres of parkland and 118 miles of hike and bike trails. For more on city parks, call (210) 207-PARK or visit www.sanantonio.gov/parksandrec.

You can reserve facilities at city- and county-owned parks by calling (210) 207-PARK, (210) 207-6545, or (210) 207-6150. Reservation specialists at these numbers can assist you with reserving facilities for a group picnic, birthday party, reunion, or other group function. (Fees vary by facility.)

Along with city parks, this region is rich with state parks, facilities that offer visitors the chance to enjoy ecological or historic attractions. Several are located right around the city; others are found within a short drive that's well worth the time.

## OVERVIEW

San Antonio is also home to a national park, the **San Antonio Missions National Historical Park.** Although the Alamo is often thought of as the prime mission in the city, San Antonio boasts a Mission Trail with several historic facilities that give visitors a better feeling of mission life. San Antonio Missions National Historical Park is covered in the Attractions chapter.

Whether you plan to visit a city, state, or national park, be sure to keep San Antonio's environment in mind. Temperatures during the summer months can be very high. Morning visits are best from June through September. Parks in the surrounding area that feature water recreation are very popular during the summer months, so they may be crowded, especially on weekends and holidays.

Also, please remember that the parks are natural settings, filled with nature's creatures, some of which bite and sting. Central and South Texas are home to several poisonous snakes, including rattlesnakes, copperheads, water moccasins, and coral snakes. Though these are typically shy creatures and would prefer to flee rather than bite, be wary when hiking. Bites are fairly rare, but if you are bitten, seek medical attention immediately. The region is also home to several nasty crawly creatures, such as scorpions and fire ants. Their bites are painful but not poisonous. Mosquitoes can be the most annoying insect during warm-weather months; pack repellent to enjoy your trip.

This chapter is divided into two sections: parks and recreation. The parks section focuses on all types of parks in and around San Antonio. The recreation section is divided into recreation activities you can enjoy in the region, from bicycling and bowling to swimming and tennis.

## PARKS

Admission to parks is free unless otherwise noted. The website for all city parks and recreational programs is www.sanantonio.gov/parksandrec unless otherwise noted.

### City Parks

**✳BRACKENRIDGE PARK**
**3910 N. St. Mary's St.**
**(210) 207-7275,**
**(210) 207-8590 (park police)**

Located 2 miles north of downtown, this is the granddaddy of San Antonio's parks; if you have time for only one park visit, this is the one. The sprawling 343-acre facility is home to the San Antonio Zoo (3903 N. St. Mary's St.; 210-734-7184), widely considered one of the best zoos in the nation. Housed in a former rock quarry, the zoo spans 35 acres and holds the distinction of being the only zoo in the country to exhibit the endangered whooping crane. For more on the zoo, see the Attractions chapter.

The park also has many other special features, including a miniature railroad (3810 N. St. Mary's St.; 210-735-7455) that runs 2.5 miles through the park. The train is a replica of an 1863 C. P. Huntington steam locomotive.

Brackenridge Park also has plenty of shady picnic areas, swings and slides, and green space for play. One of the park's most beautiful areas is the Japanese Tea Garden (3853 N. St. Mary's St.; 210-207-PARK). San Antonio's semitropical climate encourages the lush flowers, climbing vines, and tall palms found inside this quiet, serene place. The ponds, with beautiful rock bridges and walkways, are home to numerous koi (large goldfish). For more information on the gardens, see the Attractions chapter.

The history of this swath of land dates back far earlier than its days as a park. Archaeologists have unearthed proof that this region has been visited by human beings for more than 11,000 years. A few centuries ago, the Spanish settlers in the region used the river here to feed their acequias (irrigation ditches). One of these ditches, the Upper Labor acequia, can still be seen at the zoo.

This region remained largely uninhabited, however, until the mid-19th century. After the Civil War, the local rock quarry enjoyed a booming business, thanks to the discovery that its limestone could be used to manufacture cement.

In 1866 George W. Brackenridge came to San Antonio from Austin; he and his mother later began to purchase riverfront property. A few decades later, Brackenridge developed a waterworks system to supply the city with artesian spring water. Eventually he donated nearly 200 acres to the city for use as a public park. Brackenridge Park was born.

Development of the park began almost immediately. A zoo was built, incorporating old quarry walls and an old tannery site. Later came a public golf course, designed by A. W. Tillinghast of Philadelphia. This was the state's first public golf course. In 1917 work began on the Japanese Tea Garden, also in the abandoned quarry. Prison laborers created the lush gardens, and local residents donated the plants. The Witte Museum was built on the northeast edge of the park in 1926, and during the Great Depression several public works projects were completed in the park. Today Brackenridge Park remains much as it was 50 years ago.

**COMANCHE LOOKOUT PARK**
**15551 Nacogdoches Rd.**
**(210) 207-PARK**

This 96-acre park is indeed a lookout—it is home to the fourth-highest point in Bexar County. Perched at an elevation of 1,340 feet (that's nosebleed territory for South Texas), the lookout was first used by Apache and Comanche Indians searching for game. It was later acquired by Mirabeau B. Lamar, the second president of the Republic of Texas. Lamar's land was passed down through his family, who eventually sold it to German immigrants for farming. It was finally purchased by the city in 1994. The view includes miles of native trees such as Mexican buckeye, chinaberry, mesquite, huisache, and ash juniper.

**i** The medieval-inspired tower located within Comanche Lookout Park was constructed in the 1920s by Army Colonel Edward H. Coppock, who had dreamed of building a castle residence on the site.

**DAWSON PARK**
**2500 E. Commerce St.**
**(210) 207-PARK**

This neighborhood park, first named East End Park, was later named in honor of aviator Charles A. Lindbergh. In 1986, at the urging of local citizens, the park was renamed for still another aviator, Robert A. Dawson. The first licensed African-American pilot was a graduate of the local Phillis Wheatley High School. The aviation pioneer trained as an Army Air Corps flying cadet during World War II and was later killed in an air crash. Today the park is a favorite getaway for neighborhood residents.

**DWIGHT D. EISENHOWER PARK**
**19399 NW Military Hwy.**
**(210) 564-6400**
**www.sanaturalareas.org**

Once part of Camp Bullis, this park opened to the public in 1988 and is now a favorite with birders. Dotted with juniper and oak, the rocky park is home to many native birds, including the black-crested titmouse and the ladder-backed woodpecker. Many deer, raccoon, rabbits, and armadillos also live here. It boasts 5 miles of hiking trails, with the Cedar Flats Trail leading to the park's highest point. A lookout tower offers good views of the surrounding countryside. Special programs sponsored by San Antonio Natural Areas and the Bexar County Audubon Society are offered on the second Saturday of the month. Dwight D. Eisenhower Park is open from dawn to dusk; no admission fee is charged.

**i** The San Antonio Parks and Recreation Department maintains an online calendar of events, including special activities at area facilities. See www.sanantonio.gov/parksandrec.

**FRIEDRICH WILDERNESS PARK**
**21395 Milsa Rd.**
**(210) 564-6400**
**www.fofriedrichpark.org**

Nature lovers flock to Friedrich Wilderness Park for its birding opportunities and its hiking trails. Located near Six Flags Fiesta Texas, across I-10 from the Dominion Golf Course, it is the city's only nature preserve. The 633-acre park offers more than 5 miles of hiking trails, including the Forest Range Trail, which is both scenic and wheelchair accessible. The park is known not only in Texas but also internationally for its birding opportunities. It is shaded by thick juniper trees that provide nesting sites to the golden-cheeked warbler and the black-capped vireo, both endangered species. The park is also home to many other forms of wildlife, including white-tailed deer, raccoons, rabbits, squirrels, and more. Guided hikes are scheduled for the first Saturday of each month. A donation of $3 for individuals or $5 for a family is requested, and reservations are required.

Pets are not allowed in this nature reserve; also prohibited are fires, camping, hunting, and smoking on the trails. Hikers must stick to marked trails.

Nature lovers can take part in the park's 40-hour Master Naturalists Program to learn more about local ecology, native plants, site maintenance, and more. After completing the course, participants give 40 hours or more in volunteer work. For more on the program, call the park number or see the website. The park is open from 7:30 a.m. to sunset.

**MONTERREY PARK**
**5909 W. Commerce St.**
**(210) 207-PARK**

Established in 1962, this park is named for San Antonio's sister city in Mexico. Especially popular for its recreational facilities, the park offers a community center, a swimming pool, picnic sites, a football field, a soccer field, basketball and tennis courts, and more.

## Dog Parks

Two Alamo City parks are designed with man's best friend in mind. Fire hydrants, play features, and canine-level water fountains dot the 1.5-acre **McAllister Park** dog park (13102 Jones-Maltsberger Rd.) and the 1.5-acre **Pearsall Park** dog park (4700 Old Pearsall Rd.). The two fenced areas are open seven days a week from 5 a.m. until 11 p.m. For more dog parks in San Antonio, see www.sanantonio.gov/parksandrec/dog_parks.aspx.

**RIVERSIDE PARK**
**100 McDonald**
**(210) 207-PARK**

This was once a privately owned park and a popular picnic grounds. Formerly located at the end of a streetcar line, it was a favorite getaway for San Antonians. In the late 19th century, the park was used as a training ground for the Rough Riders, Teddy Roosevelt's troops gathered for the Spanish-American War.

For years the park was overshadowed by Brackenridge Park. In 1927 the city purchased additional land and added a 9-hole golf course; today the course boasts 27 holes, and the park has reclaimed its place as a good getaway on a weekend afternoon.

**✳SAN ANTONIO BOTANICAL GARDEN**
**555 Funston Place**
**(210) 207-3250**
**www.sabot.org**

Roses, herbs, a garden for the blind, and native plants are all found within these lovely 38-acre gardens. The centerpiece here is the Lucile Halsell Conservatory, a 90,000-square-foot architectural masterpiece designed by Emilio Ambasz, formerly curator of design at New York's Museum of Modern Art. Opened in 1988, the Halsell Conservatory departs from the house-shape of typical conservatories, relying instead on conical and triangular roof shapes. To take advantage of the cooling effect of the earth during hot Texas summers, the greenhouse is built 16 feet underground. Separate structures showcase palm trees from around the world, desert plants, and tropical foliage. For more on the conservatory, see "A Texas Oasis" in this chapter. The garden is open year-round from 9 a.m. to 5 p.m. except for Thanksgiving, Christmas and New Year's Day. Cost is $8 for adults, $6 for seniors and military, and $5 for children.

**SAN PEDRO SPRINGS PARK**
**1415 San Pedro Ave.**
**(210) 207-PARK**

This is the city's oldest designated park and in fact is one of the oldest in the country. (Only Boston Common predates it.) This land was first reserved for public use by the Spanish government in the 18th century, although history shows that the site has been used by humans for more than 12,000 years. The natural springs on the site were first named San Pedro Springs in 1709, and soon thereafter the first permanent settlement in the area was founded nearby. The Spanish later constructed an acequia to carry water from the springs into town.

The cool springs and shady surrounding trees drew many visitors, and in 1852 the city established a reserve around the site. Soon pavilions were constructed to sell food and drink. In 1856 the US Army decided to stable camels here as part of an experimental camel corps. A few years later, Sam Houston spoke at a rally here; later the park was used as a site for holding prisoners during the Civil War.

Sadly, the springs began to dwindle when artesian wells were drilled for city use. The park was renovated in 1899, however, and again began to attract visitors. It was again renovated a century later, and in 1979 it was added to the National Register of Historic Places. The latest renovation, completed in 2000, retained the historical uses while restoring the landscape and structural features. The pool remains the centerpiece.

**TRAVIS PARK**
**301 E. Travis St.**
**(210) 207-PARK**

This small downtown greenspace across from the St. Anthony Hotel was originally part of a farm supporting Mission San Antonio de Valero (the Alamo) and later sold to Samuel Maverick, who deeded it to the city in 1870. It was named for Col. William Barrett Travis, who commanded the Alamo defenders. It frequently hosts outdoor concerts, and it's a popular place with downtown employees, who like to take a picnic lunch and enjoy a little quiet time here.

**WALKER RANCH HISTORIC LANDMARK PARK**
**12603 West Ave.**
**(210) 207-PARK**

Opened in May 1999, the Walker Ranch Historic Landmark Park is located on the city's northwest side. This park may be new, but the site was used by hunter-gatherers 8,000 years ago. Later the park site was part of the Monte Galvan, a ranch that supplied the Mission San Antonio de Valero, better known as the Alamo.

The long-standing popularity of the site is due to its location near the confluence of Panther Springs Creek and Salado Creek. Today it offers hiking, an exercise trail, a pavilion, and information stations. The park is open daily from 5 a.m. to 11 p.m.

**i** Frequent visitors can purchase a $60 Texas State Parks Pass at a Texas state park. You can also order one at (512) 389-8900. The pass gives you free admission to more than 120 state parks as well as a discounted subscription to *Texas Parks & Wildlife* magazine. Members also get special access to restricted wildlife-management and state natural areas.

## State Parks near San Antonio

The year was 1923. Texans were enamored with the automobile, eagerly looking to weekends for a chance to cruise along paved roads and enjoy the state's scenic byways.

Governor Pat Neff recognized the need to set aside parcels of land along those roads to be enjoyed by all the citizens of the state and by visitors and worked to ensure the passage of the state parks bill. And so the Texas state parks system was born.

Today Texas boasts an extensive state park system. When it comes to state parks, San Antonio residents and visitors have only one problem: selecting from a long list of excellent facilities. Here's a look at parks you can enjoy as a day trip or a weekend getaway.

**BASTROP STATE PARK, BASTROP**
**97 miles northeast of San Antonio via I-35 and Route 21**
**(512) 321-2101**

**BLANCO STATE PARK, BLANCO**
**35 miles north of San Antonio via US 281**
**(830) 833-4333**

Located along the Blanco (locally pronounced "BLANK-oh") River, this park once drew early explorers and settlers who used it as a campsite. Modern-day developments arrived when the Civilian Conservation Corps made the first improvements. Blanco State Park today includes a variety of amenities and is located near several other attractions, including the Lyndon B. Johnson State Historical Park. Admission is $4.

**ENCHANTED ROCK STATE NATURAL AREA**
**84 miles north of San Antonio via I-10 and US 87**
**(830) 685-3636**

This park features a huge, pink granite dome that rises 425 feet above the ground and 1,825 feet above sea level, covering 640 acres. It is one of the largest batholiths (underground rock formation uncovered by erosion) in the US, second only to Georgia's Stone Mountain. Humans have visited

## Close-up

### A Texas Oasis

It was a Texas-size problem: How do you keep delicate greenhouse plants from roasting in the heat of the summer? The typical greenhouse, with its glass walls and ceiling, would only intensify the extreme temperatures typical of this sunny state. But the San Antonio Botanical Society came up with a Texas-size answer: the **Lucile Halsell Conservatory.**

This unique conservatory, which opened in 1988, is an important feature of the **San Antonio Botanical Garden.** Located 16 feet underground, the building uses the cooling effects of the earth to help maintain a stable temperature even on the hottest of days.

This 90,000-square-foot structure is an architectural masterpiece, designed by Emilio Ambasz, former curator of design at New York's Museum of Modern Art. Ambasz created a new type of conservatory, choosing a form that's as functional as it is eye-catching.

Instead of a typical box-shaped conservatory, the Halsell Conservatory consists of seven tall glass spires that surround a center courtyard. The glass and steel cones, which give the conservatory a futuristic look, rise to the height of a five-story building. Visitors enter the conservatory via a ramp that feeds into the first exhibit area. The **Exhibit Room** is your first look at one of the glass structures that provide controlled light to the delicate plants. Here, as in the other conservatory rooms, temperature and humidity are read automatically, and the data are fed into a central computer that controls the very different environments of the conservatory's five areas.

As you leave the Exhibit Room, a stunning view of the main section of the conservatory lies before you. Unlike the Exhibit Room, this large area is not protected by glass, only by the coolness of the surrounding earth. The courtyard's focal point is a lagoon-shaped pool crisscrossed with walkways and stepping stones. Take any route you want through the conservatory at this point: You're in for a treat no matter which direction you choose.

To the right lies the **Desert Room,** one of the most extreme environments found in the conservatory. Feel the blast of warm air as you enter through the glass doors of the Desert Pavilion. At 94 degrees, the temperature's hot enough for the cacti, which come in shapes from pencil to barrel, with names as colorful as chocolate drop, strawberry, and rainbow.

Be ready for a complete change of climate as you continue through the conservatory into the **Gretchen Northrup Tropical Conservatory.** Suddenly you drop into the world of the jungle, missing only the slither of a snake or the raucous call of an

here for more than 11,000 years, notably the Tonkawa Indians, who believed ghost fires flickered at the top. The Tonkawas heard weird creaking and groaning, which geologists now say resulted from the rock's heating by day and contracting in the cool night. Enchanted Rock was designated a National Natural Landmark in 1970 and was placed on the National Register of Historic Places in 1984.

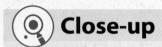

exotic bird. You'll find plants from as far away as India and Cambodia in the humid tropical room as well.

After the dense tropical room, head for the airy **Palm House**—a 5-story structure that dominates the conservatory. The wide, 110-foot base of the Palm House is planted with palms and cycads from the New World, including Florida's royal palm, the saw palmetto from the southeast US, the peaberry palm from the Florida Keys, and Cuba's queen palm.

The Palm House is built in a spiral design, so you'll ascend to the higher levels by means of a winding sidewalk, passing more New World palms on your way to the Old World palms of the upper area. These include Africa's queen sage, South Africa's whitebird of paradise, and exotic palms from New Guinea, Thailand, and Madagascar.

When you reach the top of the Palm House, step outside for a bird's-eye view of the conservatory. From this vantage point, it's easy to see what's hidden at the front entrance: the conservatory, the whole half-acre of it, is truly underground. Off in the distance you can see the skyscrapers of downtown San Antonio and the towers of Trinity University.

You'll take a staircase back down to the **Orangerie,** where exotic fruit trees produce a bounty of guavas, cherries, limes, and oranges. Look for unusual trees such as coffee, breadfruit, chocolate, allspice, and miracle fruit along the narrow walkway.

The Orangerie ends in perhaps the most popular room of the conservatory—the greenery-filled **Fern Grotto.** Open the doors and step into the humidity-laden air where the ferns thrive, climbing the simulated rock walls to reach to the sky. Many visitors believe the walls are limestone, but simulated rock was used to provide a germ-free, clean environment.

The focal point of this room is a double-tier waterfall that fills the air with the sound of falling water. A large pond planted with lilies lies at the foot of the waterfall. Enjoy a cool (but damp!) walk behind the waterfall as you circle the crowded room. Exotic plants such as bear's foot fern from Malaysia, climbing fern from China, and tailflower from tropical America grow alongside giant elephant ears and Hawaiian fern trees in this, the lushest of the conservatory's environments.

Given its inexpensive admission fees ($8 for adults, $6 for seniors and military, $5 for children), the Botanical Garden is one of Central Texas's best bargains. After all, where else could you travel from the starkness of the Mojave Desert to the humid Amazon jungle in just one afternoon?

The website for all Texas state parks is www.tpwd.state.tx.us/spdest, and the phone number for all park information is (800) 792-1112.

People of all ages in reasonably good physical condition can enjoy a climb up Enchanted Rock. The walk takes about an hour, and hikers are rewarded with a magnificent view of the Hill Country. Those interested in technical rock climbing can practice their skills here as well; rock climbers must check in at park headquarters.

Consider planning your visit to Enchanted Rock on nonpeak weekends because there is a limit on the number of cars allowed in the park. Admission is $6.

**GUADALUPE RIVER STATE PARK**
**47 miles northwest of San Antonio via I-10 and Route 46**
**(830) 438-2656**

The star of this park is the clear, cold Guadalupe River. This park stretches along 4 miles of riverbanks and offers visitors the chance to enjoy the scenic beauty of the Texas Hill Country. On Saturday mornings, take an interpretive tour of the Honey Creek State Natural Area to learn more about the plants and animals of the region. Call ahead to confirm tour schedules. Admission is $7.

**LANDMARK INN STATE HISTORIC SITE**
**20 miles west of San Antonio via US 90**
**(830) 931-2133**
**www.visitlandmarkinn.com**

The historic Landmark Inn and museum was first a home and general store before becoming the Vance Hotel. Robert E. Lee and Bigfoot Wallace, a famous Texas Ranger, were said to have stayed here on the banks of the Medina River. Located in Castroville, this site today offers overnight accommodations at the inn as well as activities for the day visitor. A museum contains displays illustrating Henri Castro's early efforts to recruit settlers to this region as well as exhibits covering early Castroville life. On the river, visitors can swim, fish, or canoe.

Guest rooms contain antique furnishings but no televisions or telephones. All rooms are nonsmoking and include air-conditioning; some rooms offer private baths.

**LOST MAPLES STATE NATURAL AREA**
**90 miles northeast of San Antonio via Highway 90 and FM 336**
**(830) 966-3413**
**www.tpwd.state.tx.us**

This lovely natural area got its name from a large, isolated stand of uncommon Uvalde Bigtooth Maple, whose fall foliage can be spectacular. Generally, the foliage changes the last two weeks of October through the first two weeks of November but doesn't do much of anything in years when the onset of cool weather is sudden. Fortunately, there's plenty more to enjoy here since Lost Maples is considered an outstanding example of Edwards Plateau flora and fauna. Located 5 miles north of Vanderpool on Ranch Road 187 on the clear Sabinal River, the area features combinations of steep, rugged limestone canyons, springs, plateau grasslands, wooded slopes, and clear streams. Try to plan any trip taken in the fall for a weekday, as the park is generally crowded on the weekend and parking is limited. Visit the website or call (800) 792-1112 for fall foliage updates.

**✳LYNDON B. JOHNSON STATE PARK & HISTORIC SITE**
**77 miles northwest of San Antonio via US 281 and US 290**
**(830) 644-2252**

During Johnson's life, the ranch was closed to all but official visitors. In hopes of catching a glimpse of the president, travelers often stopped along RR 1, located across the river from the "Texas White House," the nickname for the Johnsons' home. Today the park draws visitors from around the world who come for a look at the history behind the Hill Country, the presidency of LBJ, and a working Texas ranch.

A visitor center presents displays on LBJ's life; nearby, historic cabins offer a look back at early Texas living. Guided tours (a fee is charged for these) of the LBJ Ranch, operated by the National Park Service, stop at the 1-room Junction School where Johnson began his education, slow down for a photo of the Texas White House, then continue past the president's airstrip and cattle barns. Other stops include a look at the reconstructed birthplace home as well as the family cemetery where the former president is buried. The Sauer-Beckmann Living Historical Farm, two 1918 farm homes, are furnished in period style and staffed by costumed interpreters who garden, tend livestock, and perform chores. Children enjoy petting the farm animals. Although the park does not have overnight facilities, there are two picnic areas and hiking trails for day use. Admission is free.

**✳THE NATIONAL MUSEUM OF THE PACIFIC WAR**
**340 E. Main St., Fredericksburg**
**66 miles north of San Antonio via I-10 and US 87**
**(830) 997-8600**
**www.pacificwarmuseum.org**

Formerly known as the Admiral Nimitz Center, this expansive museum attracts visitors from around the globe. The 7-acre site consists of the historic Nimitz Steamboat Hotel, which is now the Admiral Nimitz Museum; the Japanese Garden of Peace; the Pacific Combat Zone; Plaza of the Presidents; Memorial Courtyard; Nimitz Education and Research Center; and the George H. W. Bush Gallery. The renovated Steamboat Hotel, the nucleus of the site, once was operated by the grandfather of Fredericksburg's most famous son. Admiral Chester Nimitz served as World War II commander in chief of the Pacific (CinCPac). He commanded 2.5 million troops from the time he assumed command 18 days after the attack on Pearl Harbor until the Japanese surrendered.

The museum now offers far more than it did during its earlier years. Special features include a living history presentation at a re-created Pacific War battlefield complete with foxholes, trenches, bunkers, and pillboxes (for more information, contact 830-997-8600) and a larger collection of memorabilia ranging from beer passes on Mog Mog Island to aircraft and tanks; a Japanese two-man submarine, captured the day after the 1941 Pearl Harbor attack; and more. Behind the museum lies the Japanese Garden of Peace, a gift from the military leaders of Japan. Follow the signs from the Garden of Peace for 1 block to the Pacific Combat Zone. Guided tours show visitors the hangar deck of an aircraft carrier, a South Pacific PT boat base with the world's only combat-proven, restored PT boat, and an island battlefield, modeled on the Japanese defenses at Tarawa. Tours of this outdoor exhibit take place on the hour between 10 a.m. and 4 p.m. The newly expanded George H. W. Bush Gallery features the story of the Pacific War. One of the major exhibits is HA-19, one of 5 Japanese two-man submarines. Interactive computer installations take visitors to the fall of Bataan, one of many displays the museum says makes a visit here a "high-impact experience." Finally, the outdoor Plaza of the Presidents features monuments to 10 presidents, from FDR to the first President Bush, each of whom had a role in World War II. The museum is open from 9 a.m. to 5 p.m. daily, except for Thanksgiving and Christmas, and admission is $12 for adults, $10 for senior citizens and retired military with ID, and $6 for students with ID; children under age 6 are admitted for free. Plan to spend half a day here—there's a lot to see.

**PALMETTO STATE PARK**
**63 miles northeast of San Antonio via I-10 and US 183**
**(830) 672-3266**

Along the banks of the San Marcos River, Palmetto State Park is a topographical anomaly amid gently rolling farm- and ranchland. According to scientists, the river shifted course thousands of years ago, leaving a huge deposit of silt. This sediment absorbed rain and groundwater, nurturing a marshy swamp estimated to be more than 18,000 years old. Now the swamp is filled with tropical dwarf palmettos as well as moss-draped trees, 4-foot-tall irises, and many bird species. Nature trails wind throughout the area. Located near Gonzales, the park has full hookups and tent sites. There's also picnicking, but during the warmer months bring along mosquito repellent. Admission is $3.

# RECREATION

## Baseball

**LITTLE LEAGUE DISTRICT 19**
**P.O. Box 6114, San Antonio, TX 78209**
**(no phone)**
**www.salittleleague.org**

District 19 encompasses northern San Antonio as well as the northern portions of Bexar County. Operated by a volunteer crew, the organization is composed of 11 programs covering various portions of the region. Player registration is held in mid-Jan.

## Basketball

**SAN ANTONIO PARKS AND RECREATION DEPARTMENT**
**(210) 207-3000 or (210) 207-3109**
**www.sanantonio.gov/parksandrec**
**http://eteamz.active.com/sapar**

You may not be San Antonio Spurs material, but if you enjoy a little hoops, consider participating in the adult men's or women's basketball leagues. Games are played weekdays at Jesse James Leja Gym, 319 W. Travis St., and at Woodlawn Gym, 1103 Cincinnati Ave.

## Bowling

Bowling is booming in San Antonio, with more than 15,000 league bowlers in the city spread among 500-plus leagues. The city is home to 20 bowling centers, both commercial and military.

i Voted the city's best bowling center by the *San Antonio Current* magazine, University Bowl (12332 I-10 West at De Zavala Road; 210-699-6235; www.ubbowl.com) has 32 Quabica AMF high-performance lanes and bumpers for beginners.

**GREATER SAN ANTONIO USBC**
**13307 San Pedro Ave.**
**(210) 490-6010**
**www.sanantoniobowling.org**

As the local affiliate of the US Bowling Congress, the national organization that promotes bowling nationwide, the GSAUSBC takes an active role in the sport by sponsoring tournaments and encouraging adult and youth bowling programs around town. The GSAUSBC website includes a comprehensive list of bowling centers in the San Antonio area.

## Choose Your Own Adventure

San Antonio is making it easier for adventurers to conquer the city with new hike and bike maps, and a dedicated website (http://sanantonio.gov/oep/sabikes) packed full of trail information. In just minutes, journeys can be plotted with directions, photos, bike rack locations, and can't-miss attractions along the way.

With miles of on- and off-road amenities, San Antonio has a diverse selection of routes to choose from. Bikers can explore Mission Trail, which runs alongside San Antonio Missions National Historical Park, the largest concentration of Spanish colonial missions in North America. Joggers can conquer the Museum Reach, the River Walk's new extension. This scenic trek is brimming with public art and leads to the Pearl Brewery, a 127-year-old brewery that has been redeveloped into an eco-friendly hot spot to eat, live, and work. There are many more trails to choose from: through historic districts, cultural corridors, and urban segments.

## Cycling & Mountain Biking

**BRITTON'S BICYCLE SHOP**
**16636 N. US 281**
**(210) 656-1655**
**www.brittonbikes.com**

This shop rents bicycles by the day, week, or weekend. To rent, you must have a credit card and/or valid identification. Rentals for high-end road bikes or mountain bikes are usually $35 per day or $55 per weekend, with helmets supplied if necessary.

**SAN ANTONIO WHEELMEN**
**(210) 241-3479**
**www.sawheelmen.com**

San Antonio's local bicycling club, the Wheelmen, has been in existence more than 3 decades and has a membership list of around 600 men and women. The club plans evening rides as well as weekend rides through the Hill Country and along the Mission Trail. Throughout the year, at least 2 organized weekend rides are planned, along with other events. Helmets are required.

**VIA METROPOLITAN TRANSIT**
**(210) 362-2020**
**www.viainfo.net**

Take your bike for a ride, literally, aboard one of the VIA buses. VIA now has 460 bike racks on all its vehicles except the downtown streetcars, making it easier than ever for bicyclists to take their wheels out to the less-traveled reaches of the city. Bike lockers are available at select VIA locations (see website for the latest listing).

## Dance, Music & Arts

**SAN ANTONIO PARKS AND RECREATION DEPARTMENT**
**Youth dance and music classes**
**(210) 207-3132, (210) 207-3134, (210) 207-3133**
**www.sanantonio.gov/parksandrec**

Boys and girls of all ages can learn ballet, tap, jazz, hip-hop, Mexican folkloric, flamenco, and other types of dance through the city's special programs division. Youngsters also can sign up for basic tumbling skills and flexibility training. Music programs include guitar, keyboard, and percussion.

All classes provide possibilities for exhibition and performance. Classes are offered during the school year and in the summer at a cost of $30, with discounts for enrolling in 2 or more courses concurrently. Call for schedule information.

## Fitness Centers

**D. R. SEMMES FAMILY YMCA AT TRIPOINT**
**3233 N. St. Mary's St.**
**(210) 384-2232**
**www.ymcasatx.org**

One of 7 YMCA locations in San Antonio, the TriPoint YMCA opened downtown in 2009. It features state-of-the-art exercise equipment and personal and group training programs, plus programs for seniors, teens, and youth. The YMCA also operates a summer day camp as well as preschool day care during the school year.

## Golf

San Antonio is a golfer's paradise, with numerous courses in and around the Alamo City. All but a handful are open to the public; some are municipal courses owned and operated by the city, and some are privately owned courses that are open to anyone. All share the same golf-friendly weather, which allows year-round play, and most offer views of San Antonio's scenic beauty. Green fees, including cart rentals, range from $30 to around $100, with $45 being about average. Average green fees for municipal courses are $34; private courses, $80.

**MUNICIPAL GOLF COURSES**
**Brackenridge Park Golf Course**
**2315 Avenue B**
**(210) 226-5612**

This course, designed by Philadelphia's A. W. Tillinghast (who also designed Inverness, Baltusrol, and Winged Foot), holds the distinction as the oldest 18-hole public course in the state. Opened in 1916, the course was designed to utilize the river and the many tall oak and pecan trees of the park, especially on the front 9. The par 71 course first hosted the Texas Open in 1922 and today is listed in the Texas Registry of Historic Sites, the Texas Golf Hall of Fame, and the Texas Open Hall of Honor. Renovations in 2008 added 30 new bunkers to the course.

***CEDAR CREEK GOLF COURSE**
**8250 Vista Colina**
**(210) 695-5050**

This course is often named the best municipal golf course in South Texas. Nestled in the scenic Hill Country, the demanding 18-hole, par 72 layout incorporates limestone hillsides, creeks, and several waterfalls.

**MISSION DEL LAGO GOLF COURSE**
**1250 Mission Grande**
**(210) 627-2522**

This 18-hole, par 72 course spans 7,285 yards, much of it in links-style design. The course has 124 bunkers as well as water features on 10 of its holes.

**OLMOS BASIN GOLF COURSE**
**7022 N. McCullough Ave.**
**(210) 826-4041**

This course, designed by George Hoffman, has hosted the Men's City Championship 27 times and remains one of the city's most popular municipal courses. The 18-hole, par

72 course has many long par 3 holes and narrow, demanding fairways.

**RIVERSIDE GOLF COURSE**
**203 McDonald**
**(210) 533-8371**

Located in historic Riverside Park along the San Antonio River, this course got its start in 1918 as a 9-hole course; today it offers 27 holes: a par 3 course and a full-size, 18-hole championship course. The course's biggest challenge is on the 7th hole, where trees block the right side of the fairway.

**WILLOW SPRINGS GOLF COURSE**
**202 AT&T Pkwy.**
**(210) 226-6721**

This course dates back to 1923, and through the years many famous players have competed here, including Ben Hogan, Sam Snead, and Byron Nelson. The 18-hole, par 72 long course has many tough par 4 holes as well as the city's longest hole: The second hole is a par 5 and spans 663 yards.

***Private Golf Courses***

These privately owned courses are all open to the public.

**CANYON SPRINGS GOLF CLUB**
**24405 Wilderness Oaks**
**(210) 497-1770**
**www.canyonspringsgc.com**

This 18-hole, par 72 course, located north of San Antonio in the Hill Country, is known for its wide fairways as well as its bunkers and natural hazards. On the 10th hole, golfers tee off on the cliff top. The club also has a driving range, adult and youth golf instruction programs, practice greens, and a pro shop.

**HYATT HILL COUNTRY RESORT**
**9800 Hyatt Resort Dr.**
**(210) 647-1234**
**www.hillcountry.hyatt.com**

Designed by Arthur Hills, this championship club utilizes native cacti, oaks, and a beautiful setting. Three par 36 courses feature 8 holes facing water challenges. Other facilities include a restaurant and bar housed in a ranch-style clubhouse, a driving range, a practice green, and a pro shop.

**JW MARRIOTT SAN ANTONIO HILL COUNTRY RESORT & SPA**
**23808 Resort Pkwy.**
**(210) 276-2500**
**www.jwsanantonio.com**

San Antonio's newest luxury resort offers golfers an upscale golfing experience amid Hill Country scenery. Guests of the resort have privileges at the adjacent TPC San Antonio private golfing facility featuring 2 courses, both tournament venues. The 18-hole, par 72 AT&T Canyons course, designed by Pete Dye, is a rugged, challenging course dominated by dramatic elevation changes and overlooks a 750-acre nature preserve. The course measures 7,545 yards. The companion course, AT&T Oaks, was designed by Greg Norman and is the new home of the PGA Valero Texas Open. The 7,435 yards, par 72 course displays traditional design balancing narrow, tree-lined fairways with wider fairways offering multiple routes and strategic options to the greens. The Oaks course is an intimate design with narrow corridors carved through oak trees with only 100 feet of fall from the highest point of the course to the lowest, making it walker-friendly. The TPC clubhouse offers private locker rooms, a full-service golf shop, and the upscale Members" Grill. Fees for JW Marriott guests are $70 for 18 holes and $30 for 9 holes.

**✳LA CANTERA GOLF CLUB**
**Westin La Cantera Resort**
**16641 La Cantera Pkwy.**
**(210) 558-GOLF, (800) 4-GOLFUS**
**www.westinlacantera.com**
**www.lacanteragolfclub.com**

Westin La Cantera boasts 2 golf courses, including the Palmer Course, designed by golf legend Arnold Palmer. With its own clubhouse and restaurant facilities at 17865 Babcock Rd. (210-558-2365; 800-4-GOLFUS), it plays out over 225 acres of ruggedly beautiful terrain. The Resort Course at La Cantera, the original course at the resort, was designed by Jay Morrish and Tom Weiskopf. It utilizes the walls of a former limestone quarry as well as acres of live oak trees to challenge golfers. The 18-hole, par 72 course was the site of the Valero Texas Open for 14 years. (The Open is now held at TPC San Antonio.) Among the unusual features here is the tee shot from an 80-foot quarry wall looking right out at Fiesta Texas's Rattler roller coaster. The club includes a driving range, practice green, restaurant, and golf academy.

**PECAN VALLEY GOLF CLUB**
**4700 Pecan Valley Dr.**
**(210) 333-9018, (800) 336-3418**
**www.pecanvalleygc.com**

This 18-hole, par 71 course has been rated one of the top 25 public courses in America by *Golf Digest* magazine. Its assets include oak-lined fairways and beautiful greens. This was the site of the 50th PGA Championship in 1968; the course was also selected by the USGA as the site of the 2001 US Amateur Public Links Championship. Pecan Valley's original architect was J. Press Maxwell, although the course underwent a $5.5 million renovation under the direction of architect Bob Cupp in 1998. The club includes a restaurant, pro shop, driving range, and practice green.

**THE QUARRY GOLF CLUB**
**444 E. Basse Rd.**
**(210) 824-4500, (800) 347-7759**
**www.quarrygolf.com**

Designed by Keith Foster, this links-style 18-hole, par 71 course is yet another example of San Antonio's creative reuse of limestone quarries. The back 9 of this beautiful course are set in a century-old quarry pit; the front 9 are tucked in rolling grasslands. Tee times are accepted up to 30 days in advance. The Quarry also has a clubhouse and a pro shop.

**SILVERHORN GOLF CLUB**
**1100 W. Bitters Rd.**
**(210) 545-5300**
**www.silverhorngolfclub.com**

This course, which opened in 1997, is located about 20 minutes from downtown. Designed by Randy Heckenkemper with input from PGA pros Scott Verplank and Willie Wood, the course utilizes 262 acres of wooded land. Patterned after the highly successful Silverhorn layout in Oklahoma City, the 18-hole, par 72 course features narrow fairways and soft, undulating greens. The club also includes a pro shop and a driving range.

**TAPATIO SPRINGS RESORT AND CONFERENCE CENTER**
**314 Blue Heron Blvd., Boerne**
**(800) 999-3299**
**www.tapatio.com**

This course boasts 27 holes, the first 18 designed by Bill Johnston. The additional 9 holes give golfers 3 options: The Lakes, The Valley, and The Ridge; the latter is the most challenging of the three. Tapatio (pronounced "tap-a-TEE-oh") Springs is consistently named one of the top 10 resort courses in Texas by the *Dallas Morning News.*

***Area Golf Courses***

These courses are all within a 50-mile drive of San Antonio.

**THE BANDIT**
**6019 FM 725, New Braunfels**
**(830) 609-4665, (888) 923-7846**
**www.banditgolfclub.com**

This Keith Foster Signature Course, located just north of San Antonio in the community of New Braunfels, is a lot of fun. The 18-hole, 6,928-yard, par 71 layout features elevation changes as well as beautiful greens.

**CANYON LAKE GOLF CLUB**
**405 Watts Lane, Canyon Lake**
**(830) 899-3372**
**www.canyonlakegolfclub.com**

This 18-hole course features Canyon Lake as a backdrop; you might also spot white-tailed deer while you play. The 6,500-yard, par 72 course is known for its tight fairways.

**FLYING L GOLF COURSE**
**Highway 173 South and Wharton Dock Road, Bandera**
**(800) 292-5134**
**www.flyingl.com**

Located northwest of San Antonio, this 18-hole, par 72 course is located at the Flying L Resort. The layout has a slope rating of 123 and can be enjoyed by players of all abilities.

**THE GOLF CLUB OF SEQUIN**
**300 Chaparral Dr., Seguin**
**(830) 303-0669**
**www.thegolfclubofseguin.com**

This 7,058-yard, 18-hole course is par 72. Former University of Texas football coach Darrell Royal once was a club member here.

i San Antonio Parks and Recreation has designated 10 skate parks in the city. The most developed is Lady Bird Johnson Park at 10700 Nacogdoches Rd., which features a 7,000-square-foot skate bowl.

***Driving Ranges***

**ALAMO GOLF CLUB**
**9700 Rochelle St.**
**(210) 696-4000**
**www.alamogolfclub.net**

This range is both covered and lighted. On-site extras include a pro shop, concessions, and professional instruction. The range is open from 7 a.m. to 10 p.m. daily.

**BLOSSOM GOLF CENTER**
**13800 Jones Maltsberger Rd.**
**(210) 494-0002**
**www.blossomgolfcenter.com**

This driving range offers private instruction as well as clinics. Greens are dedicated to putting, pitching, and chipping. The range is open from 7 a.m. to 10 p.m. daily.

**CARUSO GOLF CENTER**
**16900 Blanco Rd.**
**(210) 492-7888**

Weekly putting contests are sponsored by this range, which also offers a pro shop, club rental, club repair, professional lessons, and clinics. In addition to the driving range, this lighted complex includes a putting and a chipping green, as well as a sand trap. Open daily.

**ROLLING OAKS GOLF CENTER**
**5550 Mountain Vista Dr.**
**(210) 656-4653**
This range includes target greens, putting and chipping greens, and sand traps along with professional lessons, a pro shop, and club repair. The facility is open daily.

**SAN PEDRO DRIVING RANGE AND PAR 3**
**6102 San Pedro Ave.**
**(210) 349-5113**
This large range can accommodate up to 50 players. It has a driving range that spans 350 yards and is illuminated at night. The facility includes 2 practice greens for putting and chipping and a 9-hole, par 3 course. Lessons are available. The facility opens daily at dawn.

## Hockey

**ICE AND GOLF CENTER AT NORTHWOODS**
**(210) 490-9550**
**http://northwoodsice.net**
The Ice and Golf Center offers hockey lessons for youth and adults. The facility is located at the southeast corner of Loop 1604 and US 281 next to Regal Cinema. The ice rink features a National Hockey League (NHL) regulation-size ice sheet. The facility also offers related amenities, including skate rental, a pro shop for hockey and figure skating, dressing rooms, meeting space, party rooms, a restaurant, and a video arcade that appeals to enthusiasts of all ages. Admission is $7 and skate rental is $3.

## Running & Walking

San Antonio has many great trails to run or walk on. Some of the most popular are found at McAllister Park, Alamo Heights, and Mission Park.

## Scuba Diving

**DIVE WORLD SCUBA CENTER**
**2250 Thousand Oaks, Suite 212**
**(210) 403-3721**

**DIVE WORLD WEST**
**2110 West Ave.**
**(210) 734-5526**
**www.diveworldscuba.com**
Dive World is a family-owned business that's been teaching San Antonio families to scuba dive the PADI way for more than 30 years. Features include an on-premises heated pool that makes it convenient to train regardless of the weather. Rental equipment, airfills, and rinse tanks are located poolside. Additionally, Dive World sponsors trips to various tropical sites throughout the world.

## Skating

***THE ROLLERCADE**
**223 Recoleta Rd.**
**(210) 826-6361**
**www.therollercade.com**
This family-owned roller-skating rink has been keeping San Antonians rolling for more than 40 years. It features a wooden skating surface and state-of-the-art music and lighting systems. Lessons are available from professional instructors for all ages. The rink is especially popular for birthday parties; call about public skating hours. Admission is $5 to $6, depending on the day and time.

i Sundays are Family Days at The Rollercade on Recoleta Road. For the regular price of a child's admission, one parent can skate for free.

## Soccer

Soccer is available through a number of groups within San Antonio, including the YMCA, Catholic Youth Organization, youth centers, Boys and Girls Clubs, and more.

### *Soccer Clubs*

Club soccer is a popular activity in San Antonio. Various clubs offer different levels of competition for boys and girls, with some including opportunities for men and women.

**ALAMO AREA YOUTH SOCCER ASSOCIATION**
**(210) 568-0491**
**www.aaysa.org**

**ALAMO CITY YOUTH SOCCER ORGANIZATION**
**(210) 647-1019**
**www.acyso.org**

**ALAMO INDOOR SOCCER**
**(210) 744-1143**
**www.sanantonioindoorsoccer.com**

**GREATER RANDOLPH AREA YOUTH SOCCER ORGANIZATION**
**(210) 497-1100**
**http://eteamz.active.com/graysa**

**NORTH EAST YOUTH SOCCER ORGANIZATION**
**(210) 495-3477**
**www.neyso.org**

**SOCCER ASSOCIATION FOR YOUTH OF SAN ANTONIO**
**(210) 860-4648**
**www.saysat.org**

### *Soccer League*

**SAN ANTONIO PARKS AND RECREATION DEPARTMENT**
**(210) 207-3030**
**www.sanantonio.gov/parksandrec**
The Parks and Recreation Department offers a spring soccer league for boys and girls ages 6 to 19. Some 2,000 players participate.

## Softball

**TIME WARNER PARK**
**12001 Wetmore Rd.**
**(210) 545-2700**
**www.theparkonline.com**
This well-maintained park has 6 manicured softball fields for league play and tournaments of men's and coed teams. The teams play one night a week, and players are assigned according to skill level.

**SAN ANTONIO PARKS AND RECREATION DEPARTMENT**
**(210) 207-3153, (210) 207-3127**
**www.sanantonio.gov/parksandrec**
The Parks and Recreation Department sponsors several softball leagues: adult slow pitch (men's, women's, and coed), and youth fast pitch (ages 10 and under, 12 and under, 14 and under, 16 and under, and 18 and under). Games are played on weekdays, and fall, spring, and summer leagues are offered. To register, check the Parks and Recreation website. Games are held at the following locations:

**ALVA JO FISCHER SOFTBALL COMPLEX**
**10700 Nacogdoches Rd.**

**KENNEDY SOFTBALL COMPLEX**
**3101 Roselawn Rd.**

**KOGER STOKES COMPLEX**
**611 W. Myrtle**

**LAMBERT BEACH SOFTBALL FIELD**
**4000 N. St. Mary's St.**

**RUSTY LYONS COMPLEX**
**6300 McCollough Ave.**

**TONY "SKIPPER" MARTINEZ COMPLEX**
**3610 N. St. Mary's St.**

## Swimming

### *Indoor Pools*

**PALO ALTO COLLEGE NATATORIUM**
**1400 W. Villaret Blvd.**
**(210) 486-3800**
**www.alamo.edu/pac**

Located in the southwest section of San Antonio at Palo Alto College, this pool is frequently used for competitive events. The pool is a 50-meter, 8-lane facility with a movable bulkhead. The City of San Antonio co-owns this excellent facility, which is open to the public for open swim and lap swim. The schedule varies due to classes and swim meets, so call for a current schedule.

**SAN ANTONIO NATATORIUM**
**1430 W. Durango Blvd.**
**(210) 207-3299**
**www.sanantonio.gov/parksandrec**

This indoor pool is open Mon through Sat and offers lap swimming, learn-to-swim programs, senior swims, and more. Call for a schedule of classes and fees. The general public can swim from noon to 6:45 p.m. (5 to 6:45 p.m. in winter) for $3; children ages 16 and under are admitted for $1.

### *Outdoor Pools*

The San Antonio Parks and Recreation Department (210-207-PARK; www.sanantonio.gov/parksandrec) oversees 24 outdoor pools, most of which are open only from mid-June until mid-Aug. Pool hours are typically 1 to 7 p.m. daily, and no admission fee is charged. Regional pools remain open on weekends throughout August and continuing through Labor Day weekend. The outdoor pools operated by the Parks and Recreation Department are:

**CASSIANO**
**1140 S. Zarzamora St. and Cassiano Park**
**(210) 434-7482**

**CONCEPCION**
**600 E. Theo Ave. and Concepcion Park**
**(210) 532-3473**

**CUELLAR**
**503 SW 36th St. and Cuellar Park**
**(210) 434-8028**

**DELLVIEW**
**500 Basswood Dr. and Dellview Park**
**(210) 349-0570**

**ELMENDORF**
**4400 W. Commerce St. and Elmendorf Park**
**(210) 434-7380**

**FAIRCHILD**
**1214 E. Crockett St.**
**(210) 226-6722**

**GARZA**
**5800 Hemphill Dr.**
**(210) 434-8122**

**HERITAGE**
1423 S. Ellison Dr.
(210) 645-9465

**JOE WARD**
435 E. Sunshine Dr.
(210) 732-7350

**KENNEDY**
3299 SW 28th St. and Emerson
(210) 436-7009

**KINGSBOROUGH**
350 Felps St.
(210) 924-6761

**LADY BIRD JOHNSON**
10700 Nacogdoches Rd.
(210) 599-0122

**LINCOLN**
2803 E. Commerce St. and Lincoln Park
(210) 224-7590

**MONTERREY**
5919 W. Commerce St. and Monterrey Park
(210) 432-2727

**NEW TERRITORIES**
9023 Bowen Dr.
(210) 681-2929

**NORMOYLE**
700 Culberson Ave. and Normoyle Park
(210) 923-2442

**ROOSEVELT**
500 Lonestar Blvd. and Roosevelt
(210) 532-6091

**SAN PEDRO**
2200 N. Flores and San Pedro Park
(210) 732-5992

**SOUTHCROSS**
819 W. Southcross Blvd. and Flores Park
(210) 927-2001

**SOUTHSIDE LIONS**
3100 Hiawatha St. and Springfellow Park
(210) 532-2027

**SPRING TIME**
6571 Spring Time St.
(210) 558-0491

**SUNSET HILLS**
103 Chesswood Dr.
(210) 435-4011

**WESTWOOD**
7601 W. Military Dr.
(210) 673-3382

**WOODLAWN**
1100 Cincinnati Ave. and Woodlawn Park
(210) 732-5789

***Swimming Lessons***

**SAN ANTONIO PARKS AND RECREATION DEPARTMENT**
(210) 207-3113
www.sanantonio.gov/parksandrec

Several of the outdoor pools offer 3 sessions of swimming classes during the summer. Sessions run for 2 weeks, Wed through Fri. Morning sessions are held at Dellview, 500 Basswood Dr.; Garza, 5800 Hemphill Dr.; Joe Ward, 435 E. Sunshine Dr.; Heritage, 1423 S. Ellison Dr.; Lady Bird Johnson, 10700 Nacogdoches Rd.; Kingsborough, 350 Felps St.; New Territories, 9023 Bowen Dr.; San Pedro, 2200 N. Flores St.; Spring Time, 6571 Spring Time St.; South Side Lions, 3100 Hiawatha St.; and Woodlawn, 1103 Cincinnati Ave.

**SAN ANTONIO SWIM ACADEMY**
4857 Fredericksburg Rd. (Administrative Office)

**ROGERS RANCH (SPECTRUM CLUB)**
**2711 Treble Creek**

**ALAMO HEIGHTS (SPECTRUM CLUB)**
**1246 Austin Hwy.**

**TEZEL (SPECTRUM CLUB)**
**9240 Guilbeau Rd.**

**UNIVERSAL CITY (SPECTRUM CLUB)**
**2925 Pat Booker Rd.**
**(210) 404-2782**
**www.sanantonioswimacademy.com**
San Antonio Swim Academy provides year-round swim instruction at this facility for all ages, from 6 months to adult. All lessons are offered in small groups in indoor heated pools at 4 Spectrum Club locations in San Antonio. Classes are geared to all levels of swimmers. Children are divided by age; private lessons are also available.

**i** Five pools also offer evening lessons: Dellview, 500 Basswood Dr.; Heritage, 1423 S. Ellison Dr.; Lady Bird Johnson, 10700 Nacogdoches Rd.; New Territories, 9023 Bowen Dr.; and Spring Time, 6571 Spring Time St. Registration is held at all city pools; the cost is $30 per session.

**TIME WARNER PARK**
**12001 Wetmore Rd.**
**(210) 545-2700**
**www.theparkonline.com**
This sports complex has a 25-meter swimming pool where instructors use the state-of-the-art Swim America method for school-age lessons, stroke school, and swim team classes for infants, children, and adults. Safety classes are also available.

## Tennis

More than 140 tennis courts throughout the city are managed by the Parks and Recreation Department. The largest facility in town is the McFarlin Tennis Center at San Pedro Park, where reservations are required for court use. Other tennis courts are available on a first-come, first-served basis without charge. For more on San Antonio tennis, call (210) 732-1223.

**✳MCFARLIN TENNIS CENTER**
**1503 San Pedro Ave.**
**(210) 732-1223**
San Antonio's premier tennis facility is McFarlin Tennis Center. The US Tennis Association has recognized this site as one of the best public facilities in the country. The center was designed in 1974 and includes 22 lighted hard tennis courts as well as a pro shop. The facility offers lessons and clinics as well as leagues for adult play. The San Antonio Tennis Association sponsors tournaments at the center throughout the year.

**SAN ANTONIO PARKS AND RECREATION DEPARTMENT**
**(210) 207-PARK**
**www.sanantonio.gov/parksandrec**
The San Antonio Parks and Recreation Department operates tennis courts throughout the city at the following parks:

**ARNOLD**
**1011 Gillette Rd.**

**BENAVIDES**
**1500 Saltillo St.**

**CAMARGO**
**5500 Castroville Rd.**

**COLLINS GARDENS**
601 S. Park Blvd.

**COPERNICUS**
5003 Lord Rd.

**CUELLAR**
5626 San Fernando St.

**DAFOSTE**
210 Dafoste Ave.

**DAWSON**
2500 E. Commerce St.

**ESCOBAR FIELD**
1400 S. Zarzamora St.

**FLORES**
743 Flores St.

**FORGE**
1900 W. Pyron Ave.

**GARZA**
5627 Seacroft St.

**HIGHLAND**
900 Rigsby Ave.

**J STREET**
800 J St.

**KENNEDY**
3101 Roselawn Rd.

**LAS PALMAS**
503 Castroville Rd.

**MARTINEZ**
200 Merida St.

**MARTIN LUTHER KING**
3503 M. L. King Dr.

**MONTERREY**
5900 W. Commerce St.

**NEW TERRITORIES**
9023 Bowen Dr.

**NORMOYLE**
800 Culberson Ave.

**OAKHAVEN**
16400 Parkstone Blvd.

**PALM HEIGHTS**
1201 W. Malone Ave.

**PALO ALTO**
1500 Palo Alto Rd.

**PITTMAN SULLIVAN**
1101 Iowa St.

**ROSEDALE**
303 Dartmouth St.

**ROYALGATE**
5900 Windy Hill Dr.

**SAN JUAN BRADY**
2307 S. Calaveras St.

**SOUTHSIDE LIONS**
900 Hiawatha St.

**TEJEDA**
500 Division Ave.

**VILLA CORONADO**
10420 Renova St.

**WINDSOR**
2300 Ingleside Dr.

## Volleyball

**TIME WARNER PARK**
12001 Wetmore Rd.
(210) 545-2700
www.theparkonline.com
This sports club offers San Antonio's largest number of volleyball courts, both sand and clay varieties. Call ahead—these courts are frequently used for league play.

## FATSO'S SPORTS GARDEN

**1704 Bandera Rd.**
**(210) 432-0121**
**www.fatsossportsgarden.com**

This popular sports bar is best known as a place to kick back and enjoy happy hour while watching spots on the big-screen TVs. However, for those looking for more active diversions, Fatso's has 6 sand volleyball courts. The bar hosts leagues nightly and offers the courts for rental.

## SIDELINERS GRILL

**15630 Henderson Pass**
**(210) 404-0121**
**www.fsgnorth.com**

This eatery on the north side of San Antonio has all the ingredients for sports-minded families. It's the scene for year-round beach volleyball and soccer league play for all skill levels. Sideliners also boasts a host of large-screen TVs tuned to whatever sports are in season. Pool tables and a climbing wall complete the sports menu.

# SPECTATOR SPORTS

**Spectator sports in San Antonio can be divided into two eras—before 1973 and after 1973. Before 1973 it was a toss-up as to whether the biggest game in town was college football or minor-league baseball. In 1973 the San Antonio Spurs moved to town, bringing the unmistakable aura of big-time sports to the Alamo City. That year began a series of developments, each of which solidified the city's infatuation with the professional basketball team: In 1976 the Spurs became part of the National Basketball Association; and in 1993 the Alamodome opened as the Spurs' home court. The peak of Spurs worship occurred in 1999 when the team won its first NBA Championship. Spurs worship continued with 2003, 2005, and 2007 World Championship wins. Other team sports have benefited from the Spurs' popularity, too, as shown by the 2003 arrival of the Silver Stars WNBA team and the Rampage AHL hockey team.**

**Let's face it: San Antonians just love their sports.**

## BASKETBALL

***SAN ANTONIO SPURS**
**AT&T Center**
**1 AT&T Center**
**(210) 444-5000**
**www.nba.com/spurs**

It's hard to overestimate the impact the Spurs have had in San Antonio. Now four-time winners of the NBA Championship, the Spurs have a 35-year history in San Antonio. In the beginning, the focus was on George Gervin, the sweet-shooting guard who led the team for nine seasons, beginning in 1973 when he won a spot on the All-Rookie team of the American Basketball Association. When the Spurs hit the big time in 1976, the "Iceman," as Gervin was affectionately known, continued his winning ways, earning NBA All-Star honors for nine consecutive seasons. He was the NBA's scoring leader in 1978, 1979, 1980, and 1982 and still holds the NBA record for the most points scored in a single quarter—33 points. His No. 44 jersey was retired by the Spurs after he left the NBA in 1986.

Despite the Iceman's heroics, which led the Spurs to five division titles, the thrill of winning it all eluded the team and its loyal fans until the 1999 season. Inspired by long-time center David Robinson and Tim Duncan, the Spurs put together a sterling season, which they topped off by winning the World Championship series. It was San Antonio's first major sport championship, and the city was jubilant. The San Antonio Spurs would go on to win NBA Championships in 2003, 2005, and 2007. They remain among the NBA's elite teams and are still the hottest ticket in town. The Spurs played in the Alamodome from 1993 to 2002, when they moved to the AT&T Center (known at the time as the SBC Center). The Alamodome, a $186 million multipurpose dome built with flexibility in mind, also hosts conventions, business conferences and trade shows, concerts and performances, and other sporting events such as NCAA football's Alamo Bowl and several National Football League preseason games. The Spurs' home today, the AT&T Center, located near Freeman Coliseum a few miles north of downtown, offers a more intimate viewing environment—all the seats are much closer to the action on the court. A facility built with fans, particularly NBA fans, in mind, it includes the Fan Fiesta area featuring video games; a Tex-Mex–styled courtyard with food kiosks, picnic tables, and plenty of shade; a variety of restaurants; and even a $1 million art collection. With the new venue and the team's high-profile players, the future looks like smooth ridin' for the Spurs.

Spurs' tickets are easy to get—but buy early. You can charge by phone at (800) 745-3000 or buy online at www.ticketmaster.com. Tickets cost from $12 to $60.

Season tickets for Spurs games range from $1,000 to a whopping $11,000 for floor seats. To buy season tickets, call (210) 444-5050 on weekdays or visit www.nba.com/spurs.

**i** Known for their good looks and high-energy dance routines, the San Antonio Spurs cheerleaders/dancers are called, appropriately enough, the Spurs Silver Dancers. The 15-member team often makes school and community appearances around San Antonio.

**SAN ANTONIO SILVER STARS**
**AT&T Center**
**1 AT&T Center**
**(210) 444-5000**
**www.wnba.com/silverstars**

After three years of working to bring a WNBA team to San Antonio, the dream finally came true in November 2002 when the WNBA announced that they had granted a WNBA franchise to Spurs Sports and Entertainment. Soon after, SS&E assumed ownership of the Utah Starzz, one of the WNBA's original 8 franchises that began play in 1997. The name changed to the Silver Stars, and the Fox (a silver fox wearing a Stars uniform) became the team's mascot.

San Antonio's new team began its inaugural season with a training camp delayed by discord between players and league officials over the collective-bargaining agreement. After the dust settled, however, the Silver Stars kicked off the regular season with a win over the Los Angeles Sparks in front of a crowd of almost 15,600 fans. Ticket prices range from $10 to $125, and youngsters under 24 months old sitting in laps can get in free of charge. Tickets are available through the same sources as the San Antonio Spurs.

## BASEBALL

**SAN ANTONIO MISSIONS**
**Wolff Stadium**
**5757 US 90 West**
**(210) 675-7275**
**http://web.minorleaguebaseball.com**

As members of the Texas League, the Missions have been around in one form or another for more than 100 years. Currently the team is part of the San Diego Padres organization. The team has a proud past, winning championships in 1897, 1908, 1933, 1950, 1961, 1964, and 1997. A host of Missions players also went on to become major league stars, among them Brooks Robinson, Joe Morgan, Pedro Martinez, Mike Piazza, Orel Hershiser, and Fernando Valenzuela.

Before Municipal Stadium (since renamed for longtime Missions patron and former city mayor, Nelson W. Wolff) opened in 1994, the Missions played for 26 seasons at V. J. Keefe Stadium on the campus of St. Mary's University. Wolff Stadium is located west of the downtown area, on US 90 at Callaghan Road; it seats 6,200 (with an additional 3,000 more on the grass beyond the outfield walls) and also boasts 14 skyboxes. One unique aspect of the park is the presence of 2 bell towers, which mirror a feature of long-gone Mission Field, where the team played between 1947 and 1968. Games at Wolff Stadium usually begin at 7:05 p.m. Mon through Sat, and at 4:05 p.m. Sun, but call for confirmation. A postgame fireworks show follows every Saturday home game. Advance or same-day tickets can be purchased at the ticket window on the first-base side of the stadium. Tickets can be purchased for any future home game through the 5th inning. For additional information call (210) 675-PARK. Advance tickets may also be purchased by visiting the website. Tickets cost $7.50 to $10.50. Smoking is not allowed inside the stadium but is permitted on the concourse area and on the left field berm. A spacious parking lot can accommodate up to 2,600 vehicles; additional parking is located at Mateo Camargo Park. Wheelchair-accessible seating is available in sections 100, 101, 102, 113, 114, 115, 116, 209, and 210 and on the concourse.

## COLLEGIATE SPORTS

A variety of sports ranging from football to tennis to baseball offered by universities here should be enough to appease any fan of college sports. All are part of the National Collegiate Athletic Association and the Heartland Conference. In addition to football, Trinity has a rich tradition in its tennis program, which saw both the men's and women's teams win national championships in 2000. Other popular sports include men's and women's basketball (the women have won an NCAA Division III national championship), baseball, and softball. The men's soccer team also won an NCAA Division III national championship in 2003. Look for more information at www.trinitytigers.com. At the University of the Incarnate Word, a Division II school, 17 sports are offered, including football, men's and women's basketball, softball, baseball, and men's and women's soccer. Both the men's basketball and men's soccer teams are nationally ranked. Additional information is available www.cardinalathletics.com

**i** **Billed as "San Antonio's sports station," Sports Radio 760 AM The Ticket provides up-to-the-minute coverage of the city's college, minor, and major league teams as well as a live sports chat. The broadcast can also be heard online at www.ticket760.com.**

Also competing in Division II is St. Mary's University. The Rattlers baseball team, which plays in the old V. J. Keefe Stadium where the Missions once played, won a national NCAA championship in 2002; the softball team earned a national NCAA title a year later. Both the men's and women's basketball teams are highly competitive as well. Other sports include men's and women's soccer, tennis, and volleyball. Schedules are listed at www.stmarytx.edu/athletics.

At the University of Texas at San Antonio, athletes compete in Division I. UTSA recently added football to its sports program; the team will play home games in the Alamodome. Men's and women's basketball remain a big draw here, with the women's team taking the conference championship in 2003. Although the baseball and softball programs just began in 1992, the Roadrunner softball team led the nation in 2001–2002. Additional information on these sports, plus tennis and volleyball, is available at www.goutsa.com.

i The San Antonio Sports Hall of Fame, located in the Alamodome, honors sports legends such as George Gervin, Johnny Moore, James Silas, Clarissa Davis-Wrightsil, Rita Crockett, Pat Knight, Red McCombs, Joe Williams, and others. It's open to the public 9 a.m. to 5 p.m. Mon through Fri. Enter from the south side of the Dome at the security desk.

## GOLF TOURNAMENTS

**VALERO TEXAS OPEN AT TPC SAN ANTONIO**
**23808 Resort Pkwy.**
**(210) 491-5800**
**http://valerotexasopen.org**

The third-oldest pro golf competition in the US, the Valero Texas Open annually raises millions of dollars for charity while offering great golf for spectators and players as well. This official PGA Tour event is played over 72 holes and 4 days in April on the AT&T Oaks Course, designed by Greg Norman and PGA consultant Sergio Garcia. The 7,252-yard, par 70 course incorporates the natural beauty of the Texas Hill Country. Tickets are available online at http://valerotexasopen.front gatetickets.com.

**AT&T CHAMPIONSHIP**
**TPC San Antonio**
**23808 Resort Pkwy.**
**(210) 491-5800**

Since 1985, the Champions Tour has drawn big names in the golfing world, including Tom Watson, Lee Trevino, Larry Nelson, Tom Weiskopf, and others. The tournament is played on the 7,406-yard AT&T Canyons Course at TPC San Antonio. Pete Dye, with help from PGA consultant Bruce Lietzke, designed the course with distinctive wide fairways and scenic views of Cibolo Canyon.

## ICE HOCKEY

**SAN ANTONIO RAMPAGE**
**AT&T Center**
**1 AT&T Center**
**(210) 444-5554**
**www.sarampage.com**

Come on now, ice hockey in San Antonio? Well, they laughed at the Wright Brothers and probably at Bill Gates, too! As it happens, a lot of San Antonians like the sport and celebrated when in May 2002 the American Hockey League approved selling the inactive AHL franchise owned by the Detroit Red Wings to San Antonio Hockey LLC. The latter was a joint venture of the San Antonio Spurs and the Florida Panthers.

The San Antonio team, called the Rampage, follows other hockey teams—representing other hockey leagues—who "broke the ice" in the Alamo City. Serving as the AHL affiliate for the Panthers, the Rampage enjoyed a successful inaugural season during the 2002–2003 campaign, ultimately qualifying for the AHL playoffs. The Rampage's mascot is a blue and gray bull named T-Bone. The team plays in the AT&T

Center and game tickets range in price from $40 to $62 and can be purchased at the AT&T Center Box Office or by calling (210) 444-5554.

## RODEO

### SAN ANTONIO STOCK SHOW AND RODEO

**AT&T Center**
**1 AT&T Center**
**(210) 225-5851**
**www.sarodeo.com**

If you are in town around mid-February, you can take in some real down-and-dirty sports action, Texas-style. No, it's not championship wrestling; it's the San Antonio Stock Show and Rodeo. This annual event is one of San Antonio's biggest happenings, drawing more than 1 million attendees every year. Activities include a rodeo, a stock show, educational displays, a concert series, a carnival midway, and plenty of Western fun. Some 1,000 cowboys and cowgirls provide much of the entertainment at the rodeo, which includes competition in the fields of bull riding, calf roping, barrel racing, and other Western sports sanctioned by the Professional Rodeo Cowboy Association (PRCA). Top country-and-western and Tejano entertainers are also featured. For the livestock show, cattle, sheep, swine, and horses are exhibited, judged, and sold. Competition for the Grand Champion animal in each division is intense, and the stakes are high. The rodeo is also home to the largest junior livestock show in the country. Cattle, sheep, poultry, swine, and horses are exhibited by hardworking teenagers from across the state, all hoping that their animals will be awarded the title of Grand Champion. The rodeo also boasts exhibits such as the Hall of Heritage, a look at the days of the Old West, and the World of Agriculture, showcasing the creations of some of the state's best cooks. Children instinctively head for the World of Animals, with its petting zoo, and the carnival midway, filled with old-fashioned games and rides. Parking is at a premium in the AT&T Center area during the rodeo, but the event offers a 15-acre paved, lighted, and secured parking lot a block away on Gembler Road. To reach the parking facility, exit at AT&T Center Parkway (formerly Coliseum Road), turn left on Gembler, and proceed to the parking area. From the parking lot, you may take the free AT&T Rodeo Shuttle; the shuttle runs continuously. Cost of parking for the rodeo is $10.

Tickets to rodeo competitions are $10, and $25, and include admission to the grounds. Ground admission only is $7 for adults, $5 for seniors, and $3 for children under 12.

**i** **Every performance night at the San Antonio Rodeo includes all seven rodeo events: bareback bronc riding, steer wrestling, calf roping, team roping, saddle bronc riding, barrel racing, and bull riding.**

## RUNNING & MARATHONS

### ROCK 'N' ROLL SAN ANTONIO MARATHON

**http://runrocknroll.competitor.com/san-antonio**

This event, held each November, blends music and running competitions in a celebration that enlivens the whole city. Two dozen stages along the course blast out rock and roll to urge the runners on as they race through downtown and the King William Historic District to the finish line at the Alamodome, where the race concludes with the Finish Line Fiesta. In addition to the full marathon, the event also features a half-marathon and a 2-person half-marathon relay. The Rock 'n' Roll San Antonio Marathon is a qualifier for the Boston Marathon. Non-runners can attend the event and enjoy the music for free. The day before the official marathon events begin, the YMCA sponsors Kids Rock San Antonio, in which children grades K–5 run an untimed 1-mile course through Brackenridge Park.

## THOROUGHBRED RACING

### RETAMA PARK

**1 Retama Pkwy., Selma**
**(210) 651-7000**
**www.retamapark.com**

During the summer and fall, the thoroughbred racing season at Retama Park offers the thrill of live horse racing and the chance to win big at the betting window. Opened in 1995, Retama is located a few miles northeast of downtown, just off I-35. It's a handsome, impressive structure with comfortable seating for up to 20,000 spectators among several levels, including outside and enclosed-seating areas. The lower level includes good views of the action on the track as well as a food court. The grandstand level also has a food court as well as a large off-track simulcasting area where fans may watch and wager on races being run elsewhere in the US. The clubhouse level is fully enclosed and air-conditioned and offers several dining options, including the Terrace Dining Room, the Sports Bar, and the members-only Player's Club. Up one floor, the Press Box level is the site of the luxurious Turf and Field Club as well as suites for race announcers and judges and, as the name indicates, the racing press. Races are generally held Thurs through Sun. Although the live racing season is limited, the park is open every day for simulcast viewing and wagering. Call for specific dates and times.

Retama tries hard to be a family-friendly facility where parents will feel good about taking their kids for an evening's entertainment. Several special-event nights are scheduled during each racing season, often offering discounted prices on food and drink and activities such as pony rides and face painting for the children. The park does manage to project a more or less wholesome atmosphere, at least when there's live racing. It is quite a spectacle to see several thousand pounds of muscular animal churning around the turns and to sense the excitement of the horses and their riders. Even without the wagering, Retama can be a good bet for a fun outing.

# MILITARY

**From its earliest days as an isolated outpost of Spain, San Antonio has enjoyed a long and distinguished history as a military base. Small garrisons of Spanish troops were dispatched to Bexar to guard the first colonists and the early missions. In 1721 the Marques de San Miguel de Aguayo, governor of the "New Philippines," commanded the construction of a permanent barracks of adobe, a fort, and the Plaza de Armas, a parade ground that later became Military Plaza.**

**These early Spanish regiments never attained sufficient size to end the raids by the Apache and Comanche. In 1730 Apache attacked the garrison, killing 15 soldiers. A desultory war of raid and counterattack continued for the next 150 years before San Antonio's survival was assured.**

## EARLY YEARS

The colonization of San Antonio by Americans under the leadership of Moses and Stephen F. Austin began a parade of different military forces to the area: Spanish, insurrectionary Mexican Republicans, Mexican Royalists, Texian volunteer militia, and Mexican Army. Each controlled the city for a time, San Antonio's strategic value being obvious, as the only fort within hundreds of miles in any direction. By the time of the Texians' famous defense against Santa Anna in 1836, the Alamo fortress consisted of an area of some 4 acres, enclosed by a series of stone walls and fences. Although General Sam Houston had ordered the fort destroyed and its defenders to fall back to Goliad, Santa Anna's forced march across the Rio Grande prevented them from doing so. Although the Texians died in battle, their spirited defense from the walls of the Alamo bought precious time for Sam Houston's main army, which defeated the Mexicans at San Jacinto a few weeks later.

Yet even the founding of an independent Republic of Texas did not allow the frontier town much peace. Range war with the Comanche intensified as more settlers moved into the area. And there was a continued threat of Mexican troops foraging into what some still believed was their territory. In 1842 a Mexican army under General Woll attacked and captured San Antonio. Many prominent citizens and town officials were taken prisoner, transported to Mexico, and jailed. The early Texas Rangers stationed in San Antonio were better equipped to deal with the Comanche than with Woll's army of 1,200 Mexicans. Only a reorganized Texas militia checked his advance at the Battle of Salado Creek, 7 miles from San Antonio.

**i** **When the young Robert E. Lee was assigned to the army post in San Antonio, he was responsible for making maps later used in the Mexican-American War.**

## STATEHOOD & THE CIVIL WAR

With the annexation of Texas by the US in 1845, a new chapter of military history was written in San Antonio. As Americans chased their Manifest Destiny west, San Antonio became important as a garrison and supply depot for troops and settlers headed toward the Rio Grande and distant California. Army troops were stationed in Military Plaza, in the barracks first built by the Spanish. The army also leased the Alamo from Catholic Church authorities, reroofed it in 1849–1850, and used it as a supply warehouse. The city became the principal headquarters for forts extending south and west. The army became the first big business to locate in San Antonio, and its presence, in turn, attracted other businesses to town.

San Antonio's military importance made it a prime target for secessionists at the beginning of the Civil War. On February 6, 1861, more than a month before Texas formally joined the Confederacy, General David E. Twiggs of the US Army's Second Cavalry Regiment surrendered munitions and supplies totaling around $3 million to a secessionist force headed by Army Major Ben McCullough. Robert E. Lee of Virginia, the base's inspector-general, was likewise beset by a mob of secessionists who demanded that he join them or leave town immediately. Lee refused to obey "any revolutionary government of Texas," returned to Washington without bothering to pack, and then went on to serve his native Virginia. Thus San Antonio passed the Civil War years as a Confederate city; legions of Confederate troops were mustered and trained in Military Plaza. Involuntary conscription into the Confederate army began in 1862 and proved very unpopular, especially with the immigrant German population. These farmers tried to remain neutral to the conflict but reacted with rebellion against the military draft, some even forming their own militia. A number of serious confrontations erupted between these militia and Confederate forces. One of the most tragic of these conflicts occurred in 1862, when several dozen German Union sympathizers were chased and shot down by Confederate troops near the Nueces River. Yet, on the whole, the city was spared many of the horrors of the war, even prospering in a fashion by serving as a shipping point for Mexican goods bound for the Confederate states in defiance of Union blockades.

## POSTWAR GROWTH

When the US Army reoccupied San Antonio in 1865 at the conclusion of the Civil War, the town resumed its role as headquarters for the great westward expansion. The poet Sidney Lanier, who lived in San Antonio at the time, observed in a historical sketch published in 1873: "The United States Government selected San Antonio as the base for the frontier army below El Paso, and the large quantities of money expended in connection with the supply and transportation of all material for so a long a line of forts have contributed very materially to the prosperity of the town."

San Antonio's growing military population led to the town's development as an American city. Businesses catering to the military began to establish a presence in the city. During the war between Mexico and the US, volunteer troops serving under General Zachary Taylor drilled and trained in San Antonio. In 1875 the city donated 93 acres of land, a parcel known as Government Hill, for a permanent military base called

Post San Antonio. Work on the primary walls, forming the original quadrangle, began in 1876. Other facilities were added in the next few years: officers' quarters, post commander's quarters, and a base hospital. The defeated Apache chief Geronimo was held at the post in 1886. In 1890 Post San Antonio was renamed Fort Sam Houston, in honor of the hero of the Texas Revolution. Over the next few years, the fort was enlarged several times as US presence in the West increased.

## THE ROUGH RIDERS

One of the most memorable episodes in San Antonio's long military history occurred with the beginning of the Spanish-American War of 1898. The US sought to increase its ranks by enlisting volunteer cavalry. The only such unit to actually see combat was the First US Volunteer Cavalry, informally known as the "Rough Riders." The regiment was mustered in San Antonio, where it met its famous leader, Theodore Roosevelt. The group needed strong leadership, as it was composed of many types of individuals from all walks of life: cowboys, Indian fighters, and bandits as well as Ivy Leaguers and society swells. Many arrived from the Wild West, bearing names as colorful as their dispositions—Rocky Mountain Bill, Bronco George, Dead Shot Jim, and Rattlesnake Pete. Others, such as William Tiffany, were Easterners who became known as the "millionaire recruits" for their refined tastes in food and clothing. However, a newspaper of the time saw them all as "one homogeneous mass of patriotism and pluck, representing and illustrating our fierce democracy where every man is equally a sovereign. . . . The rough frontiersman, daring but uncouth, and the cultured collegiate, genteel but full of spirit, stand upon a common level and mingle in a common purpose."

The unit was bivouacked in Riverside Park (now Roosevelt Park), where they drilled and trained to fight using Krag-Jorgensen repeating carbines. Although the nominal commander of the regiment was Col. Leonard Wood, its actual leader was Lt. Col. Roosevelt, who had resigned his post as US assistant secretary of the Navy to serve under Wood's command. Roosevelt proved to be a popular leader and was lionized by the press while he was in town. Roosevelt, in turn, was effusive in his praise of his men, especially the recruits from Texas. "We drew a great many recruits from Texas," wrote Roosevelt, "and from nowhere did we get a higher average, for many of them had served in that famous body of frontier fighters, the Texas Rangers. Of course, these rangers needed no teaching. They were trained to obey and to take responsibility. They were splendid shots, horsemen, and trailers. They were accustomed to living in the open, to enduring great fatigue and hardship, and to encountering all kinds of danger."

On May 30, a scant month after the Rough Riders arrived in San Antonio, they were ordered into action in Cuba, the first US troops to land there. After a bloody battle with Spanish forces at Las Guisimas, the Spanish retreated to the well-fortified San Juan Hill. There, on July 1, 1898, the regiment joined other US divisions to successfully storm San Juan Hill in one of the most famous battles in US history. The Rough Riders and their ebullient leader Teddy Roosevelt are memorialized in San Antonio by Roosevelt Park, where the regiment camped; Roosevelt Street; and the Roosevelt Bar of the Menger Hotel, where the Riders frequently stopped to wet their whistles.

## FLIGHT & FORTS

On February 15, 1910, the US Army's first airplane arrived at Fort Sam Houston, thanks to Lt. Benjamin Foulois, who is credited with performing the first flight in US military history. By the time of World War I, Fort Sam Houston was home base for nine airplanes, in addition to its regular contingent of infantry, cavalry, artillery, and military engineers. In all, more than 200,000 army troops bound for the trenches of Europe in World War I trained at the fort.

**The picturesque clock tower on Fort Sam Houston's historic Quadrangle was originally designed as a water cistern.**

Several other military bases were established in San Antonio in the first decades of the 20th century. Kelly Field, named for Lt. George Kelly, the first US military pilot killed in a crash of a military aircraft, opened in 1917. The base had two initial missions: training of airmen and aircraft maintenance and supply. Nearly all US aviators in World War I trained here, including some famous pilots such as Charles Lindbergh, Flying Tigers organizer Claire Lee Chennault, and Curtis Lemay, former Air Force chief of staff. The demands of World War I also led to the opening of Brooks Field. Known as Gosport Field when it opened in 1917, it was renamed a year later in honor of Cadet Sidney Johnson Brooks, who died in a training accident at Fort Sam Houston in 1911. In addition to its flight instructor school, Brooks also trained B-25 bomber pilots, airship personnel, and paratroopers. In 1929 it was the scene of the first large paratroop deployment in US military history. The School of Aviation Medicine, first relocated to the base from New York in 1926, was charged with research in the area of aircraft-related health issues such as crew airsickness, injury hazard reduction, and cold-related health problems.

The Aviation Medicine School later moved to nearby Randolph Field, founded in 1930 as a facility dedicated to pilot training. Randolph Field began as an Army Air Corps base, and so many future military pilots trained there that it was once known as "The West Point of the Air." Its exact mission varied over the years from basic training to advanced programs for bomber and fighter pilots and flight engineers. The base is located about 15 miles northeast of San Antonio, near the city of Schertz. At the time of the base's construction, 1928–1933, it represented the largest project undertaken by the US Army Corps of Engineers since the Panama Canal. It was designed by Lt. Harold Clark and features Spanish Renaissance–style architecture and more than 30 miles of roads, ramps, runways, and streets radiating from the central administrative area like spokes of a wheel.

## WORLD WAR II

A large army hospital, Brooke Army Medical Center, was built on Fort Sam Houston in 1938, and by 1940, as the country again prepared for war, "Fort Sam" was the largest of all US Army bases. Several important tactical strategies in US military history were devised here, and a number of officers who served at the fort went on to important posts in World War II, among them Lt. General Walter Krueger and Lt. General Courtney Hodges, who served with the US Third Army, and General Dwight D. Eisenhower. In 1942 Lackland Army Air Field, originally part of Kelly Field, was detached to become a high-volume training facility for aviation personnel, including not only pilots but also navigators, bombardiers, fiscal officers, nurses, medical technicians, even chaplains bound for World War II. As the US war effort accelerated, Lackland's population swelled to 31,000 military personnel. After the war, the name was changed to Lackland Air Force Base when the Air Force became a separate military entity, but Lackland's nickname, "The Gateway to the Air Force," still rang true, as all new Air Force personnel processed through Lackland during their basic training. In addition to its training mission, the base has expanded its operations to include marksmanship, cryptography, and other programs. Wilford Hall Air Force Medical Center (www.whmc.af.mil), the Air Force's largest hospital, is also located here.

Also in 1947, Randolph Field became Randolph Air Force Base, and the name of Kelly Field officially changed to Kelly Air Force Base. At that time Kelly assumed responsibility for strategically important aircraft such as the B-29, B-47, and B-58 bombers and fighters such as the F-102 and F-106. The world's largest clear-span hangar, covering more than 1 million square feet, was built to accommodate planes such as the C-5 transport, one of the largest aircraft in the world, with its 223-foot wingspan and 270,000-pound payload capacity.

## FURTHER DEVELOPMENTS

After the war, Fort Sam Houston, then home of the US Fourth Army, continued to expand. The Institute of Surgical Research was added in 1946, and the Burn Center opened in 1949. At that time the fort's 1,500 buildings covered more than 3,000 acres. Fort Sam Houston's large concentration of military medical facilities was further augmented in 1973 with the addition of the Health Services Command. The fort now calls itself "The Home of Army Medicine" and hosts various commands, including the US Army Medical Command, the US Army Medical Department Center and School, Brooke Army Medical Center, and the Fifth US Army and Fifth Recruiting Brigade. The post's National Landmark and Historic Conservation District designations include more than 900 historic structures, including the US Army Medical Department Museum and the Fort Sam Houston Museum. The Fort Sam Houston National Cemetery is also located on the post.

In 1959 the School of Aviation Medicine at Randolph AFB was again moved, this time to Brooks Air Force Base as the US Air Force School of Aerospace Medicine. The primary mission of the school, dedicated in 1961 by newly elected President John F. Kennedy, was support of the national space exploration program, all regular flight-training operations having been curtailed the previous year. Researchers here developed many of the discoveries that enabled both unmanned and manned space missions, such as an early space capsule used in a 1959 flight.

In the early 1980s other organizations relocated to Brooks AFB. Among them were the Air Force Human Resources Laboratory and the USAF Occupational and Environmental Health Laboratory. Brooks also became home to the Air Force Drug Testing Laboratory and the Air Force Systems Command's Systems Acquisition School. Brooks celebrated its 70th anniversary in November 1987. In 1991 four of its laboratories—the Harry G. Armstrong Aerospace Medical Research Laboratory, the

Air Force Drug Testing Laboratory, the Air Force Human Resources Laboratory, and the Air Force Occupational and Environmental Health Laboratory—merged to create the Armstrong Laboratory, one of the Air Force's "super labs." In 1992 the Air Force Systems Command and the Air Force Logistics Command merged into a new organization called the Air Force Materiel Command. Brooks's Human Systems Division changed its name to the Human Systems Center. Brooks Air Force Base, now called Brooks City Base, continues to pursue as its mission "the development of combat power and efficiency through the many facets of aerospace medicine."

The demand for additional troops during the Korean and Vietnam Wars forced Lackland Air Force Base to rapidly expand, including construction of the 1,000-person steel and brick Recruit Housing and Training (RH&T) facility. Flight training was conducted in shifts around the clock to supply pilots bound for Vietnam and later for Desert Storm. At Randolph Air Force Base in the early 1970s, the 12th Tactical Fighter Wing became the 12th Flying Training Wing. Many Air Force pilots in Vietnam trained here. At the end of the Vietnamese conflict, Randolph became the site of Operation Homecoming, in which US military pilots who had been prisoners of war in Vietnam retrained and requalified to fly. About the same time, another era of training at Randolph began with the formation of the Undergraduate Navigator Training squadrons.

As part of the Base Realignment and Closure process, Kelly Air Force Base was closed in July 2001. Now Port San Antonio, the former Kelly AFB serves as a Foreign Trade Zone and an inland port to service the vast international trade industry.

With the privatized Port San Antonio, San Antonio has five bases with approximately 36,000 military and an additional 34,000 civilian personnel. San Antonio's military bases also were involved in the Afghanistan conflict, followed by the war with Iraq and the subsequent rebuilding mission.

### Visiting a Military Base

To visit one of San Antonio's military bases, you will need to obtain a free visitor pass at the base. After entering, you'll find a visitor center that will supply the required pass.

Personal identification is required of all visitors age 16 and older. You'll need to show a state or federal photo ID—your valid driver's license, passport, or state-issued identification card will work.

## MILITARY BASE ATTRACTIONS

You don't have to be a military buff to appreciate San Antonio's long military tradition. All of the city's bases have public attractions, although the bases can be closed to visitors during wartime for security reasons. Call for current schedules and restrictions.

**FORT SAM HOUSTON**
**1212 Stanley Rd.**
**(210) 221-1151**
**www.samhouston.army.mil**

Now designated a National Historic Landmark, Fort Sam Houston welcomes visitors with several attractions that are fully open to the public. The original Quadrangle features a famous clock tower and resident wildlife such as deer and peacocks. It's the fort's oldest structure. The Fort Sam Houston Museum (210-221-1886, http://ameddcs.army.mil) features exhibits that tell the story of the fort's past as well as the more general history of the military in San Antonio. Admission to the museum is free, as is admission to the Gift Chapel, dedicated by President William Howard Taft in 1909. The US Army Medical Department Museum (210-221-6358) traces the development of military medicine in US history. It includes displays of uniforms, medical instruments, army ambulances, even a railroad hospital car. There is also a gift shop and bookshop in the museum. Admission is free. In addition to its public areas, Fort Sam Houston boasts a number of other notable places that are at least worth a drive-by. However, these remain part of the working base, so call before visiting sites such as the Pershing House, named for General of the Army John J. "Blackjack" Pershing; the Infantry Post, built in 1885; and the First Flight Memorial, marking the spot where, in 1910, Lt. Benjamin Foulois made the first US military flight. Also notable are 2 residences where General Dwight D. Eisenhower lived during two tours of duty at the fort.

**BROOKS CITY-BASE**
**8081 Inner Circle Rd., Brooks AFB**
**(210) 536-1110**
**www.brooks.af.mil**

Brooks offerings include Hangar 9, a World War I wooden hangar that is now a National Historic Landmark. It holds exhibits on the history of Brooks, manned flight, and aerospace medicine. The museum includes a gift shop. There is no admission charge. The museum operates from 8 a.m. to 4 p.m., but the annex and gift shop stay open until 5 p.m.

**LACKLAND AIR FORCE BASE**
**37th Training Wing**
**1701 Kenly Ave., Lackland AFB**
**(210) 671-3055**
**www.lackland.af.mil**

Lackland is the home of the US Air Force History and Traditions Museum at 2051 George Ave., Building 5206. The museum is dedicated to the history of military aviation, with 30 aircraft on display covering the period from World War I to the present. There is also a museum gift shop. Admission is free, but groups of more than 15 require an appointment.

**RANDOLPH AIR FORCE BASE**
**12 FTW Public Affairs**
**1 Washington Circle, Suite 4, Randolph AFB**
**(210) 652-4407**
**www.randolph.af.mil**

Tours of the "Showplace of the Air Force" must be scheduled at least 3 weeks ahead of time by writing or calling the above address. Tours normally last approximately 2 hours.

# DAY TRIPS

**Mention "Texas" and some travelers might picture the Texas of the movies: miles of rugged, uncivilized land where outlines of cattle and lonely windmills stretch above the horizon. For others, the land near the Louisiana border might come to mind, a region of tall pine forests and bountiful lakes. Some might see the high-tech cities bustling with world-class attractions, shop-'til-you-drop opportunities, and a pulsating nightlife.**

**And they'd all be right. For years Texas has promoted itself as the "land of contrasts." Rolling hills, rugged deserts, verdant forests, and sandy beaches are all found within its borders. For city slickers everything from the culture of Dallas to the cowboy fun of Fort Worth, from the south-of-the-border style of El Paso to the youthful exuberance of Austin, awaits within a few hours of San Antonio. Nature lovers find plenty of fun as well, thanks to the rolling hills and fish-filled lakes of Central Texas's Hill Country, and the beautiful beaches of the Texas coast. All of the following destinations are within a two-hour drive of the Alamo City.**

## NORTH OF SAN ANTONIO

### Austin

Maybe it's the college-student population that tops 50,000. Maybe it's the music industry that has made this city a haven for fans and performers alike. Or maybe it's just geography—the city has a downtown lake and is perched at the edge of a second lake, a rambling Hill Country one that offers everything from sunbathing to windsurfing.

Whatever the reason, there's one thing for certain: **Austin** is a town that doesn't want to grow up. Like a perpetual teenager, the capital city of Texas—83 miles north of San Antonio via I-35—is brash, sassy, and sometimes just downright silly. The city is home to both high-tech industry and countless state officials, but residents use any excuse to toss off the ties and three-piece suits. They don elaborate costumes for an annual party in Pease Park to celebrate (believe it or not) the birthday of Eeyore, the pal of Winnie the Pooh. But those costumes are just a dress rehearsal for the Halloween party that's considered one of the nation's largest, complete with 20,000 to 70,000 merrymakers.

This carefree attitude is just one of the reasons that Austin is a great day trip destination from the Alamo City. Less than a two-hour drive from San Antonio, the Texas capital offers visitors plenty of ways to spend their time: historic sites, museums, water sports on the lake, other outdoor activities, good restaurants, and a lively nightlife. There's even a spa and, in summer, the chance to see thousands of bats fill the sky at sunset.

As the state capital, Austin is steeped in history. When Mirabeau B. Lamar, the president-elect of the Texas Republic, set out to hunt buffalo in the fall of 1838, he returned home with a much greater catch than a prize buffalo: a home for the new state capital. Lamar fell in love with a tiny settlement surrounded by rolling hills and fed by cool springs. Within the ensuing year, the government arrived, and construction of the Capitol building began. Austin was on its way to becoming a city.

Today Austin is a city of 800,000 and it continues to prosper and grow. High-tech industries have migrated to the area, making this Texas's answer to Silicon Valley. But this big city still has a small-town atmosphere that makes it attractive to residents and visitors alike. Even Hollywood has taken notice of Austin—it's not uncommon these days to see film crews blocking off an oak-lined street.

**i** As much a tribute to childhood as a celebration of spring, Eeyore's Birthday Party (www.eeyores.com) has been a beloved Austin tradition since the 1960s. The fun-for-all-ages event is held each April at 1100 Kingsbury St. in Pease Park.

Downtown, the **Colorado River** slices through the heart of the city. Once an unpredictable waterway, the Colorado has been tamed into a series of lakes, including two within the Austin city limits. The 22-mile-long **Lake Austin** begins at the foot of the Hill Country and flows through the western part of the city into **Lady Bird Lake** (formerly Town Lake), a narrow stretch of water that meanders for 5 miles through the center of downtown Austin. Several hotels overlook the beautifully planted greenbelts that line the lake shores.

**i** In honor of her role as former First Lady of the United States and her determination to beautify the roadways of her home state, Town Lake was renamed Lady Bird Lake in July 2007 in a unanimous decision by the Austin City Council.

Visitors who enjoy natural beauty and outdoor activities join locals along the shores of Lady Bird Lake, in the clear waters of **Barton Springs** swimming hole, or at **Zilker Park,** a favorite with joggers, picnickers, swimmers, soccer teams, and kite flyers. The park also features Japanese gardens, a rose garden, and a nature center. **Chuy's** (1728 Barton Springs Rd.; 512-474-4452; www.chuys.com), a restaurant at the entrance to Zilker Park, is a good place to stop for lunch. With its funky Elvis paintings on velvet and decor that includes everything from hubcaps to plastic dinosaurs, it's a fun example of Austin style and offers a menu of Tex-Mex delights. Beyond the borders of Austin lies nearby **Lake Travis;** in summer it's a great place to boat, swim, or just enjoy a sunny day.

A sightseeing excursion through Austin should start at the **State Capitol** (11th Street and Congress Avenue; 512-463-0063; www.capitol.state.tx.us), truly a building of Texas-size proportions. Taller than its national counterpart, the pink granite structure is filled with history and legend; there are exhibits on the building and the state, and guided tours are available. A block south of the Capitol, the **Governor's Mansion** (1010

Colorado St.; 512-463-5516; www.txfgm.org) was home to Texas governors for more than 150 years. The mansion suffered a catastrophic fire in June 2008 and underwent renovations; at press time renovations are ongoing. The most famous resident of the Texas Hill Country did not live in Austin, but he is remembered at the city's **LBJ Presidential Library** (2313 Red River St.; 512-721-0200; www.lbjlibrary.org). This grand facility houses more than 35 million historic documents, films, and exhibits on Johnson's life and career. There's even a reproduction of the White House Oval Office.

LBJ's first lady was the powerhouse behind the **Lady Bird Johnson Wildflower Center** (4801 LaCrosse Ave.; 512-292-4100; www.wildflower.org), located on the south side of town. This unique institution is the only one in the nation devoted to the conservation and promotion of native plants and flowers. Bring your camera for self-guided tours of the blooming grounds.

Visitors from San Antonio will have seen the Alamo and heard the story of the pre-dawn battle that fueled the fire for Texas independence. But while San Antonio is the site of that famous shrine, Austin now boasts a world-class museum that takes a closer look at the Alamo and the history of Texas. The **Bob Bullock Texas State History Museum** (Congress Avenue and Martin Luther King Boulevard; 512-936-8746, 888-369-7108; www.thestoryoftexas.com), opened in 2001, is a showcase for the history of the Lone Star State from early European exploration to recent times. There are three floors of exhibits, including the multimedia **Texas Spirit Theater,** the only one of its kind in Texas, and an IMAX Theatre that can show both 2-D and 3-D movies.

**i** **Twice the size of the former facility, the new Austin Music Hall was unveiled in November 2007. Styled with giant glass windows that frame a view of the Warehouse District, the 43,000-square-foot building, located on the same grounds as the original (208 Nueces St.), offers exclusive box and club seating and a full bar for its patrons.**

The second floor of the museum focuses on the Alamo. In the Revolution Theater, built to resemble the Alamo the day after the battle, a video told from the point of view of military leader Juan Seguin takes visitors back to the fateful day. Just outside the theater, a display showcases a letter written from within the Alamo's walls by William B. Travis urging the independence fighters to send more troops.

Another popular area attraction, located on the outskirts of Austin, is a historic steam railroad. Operated by the **Austin Steam Train Association** (512-477-8468; www.austinsteamtrain.org), this historic train, built in 1916, offers several routes. From fall through spring, the Hill Country Flyer travels from Cedar Park to Burnet every weekend. During the summer months, there are two routes from which to choose: the Bertram Flyer, winding from Cedar Park to Bertram every Sunday, and the Hill Country Flyer, a Saturday trip that travels from Cedar Park to Burnet.

When the sun sets on summer days in Austin, attention turns to the Congress Avenue bridge, location of the country's largest urban colony of Mexican free-tailed bats. The bats make their nightly exodus after sunset to feed on insects in the Hill Country.

Austin has plenty to keep visitors amused after the sun goes down. If it's nightlife you seek, you may want to stay in town overnight. Many of the city's clubs are found along downtown's 6th Street, an entertainment district that's sometimes compared to New Orleans's Bourbon Street. But here blues, rather than jazz, is king along with rock, alternative, and eclectic. The area offers several lunch and dinner options as well, such as the inexpensive hamburgers and onion rings at **Hut's Hamburgers** (807 W. 6th St.; 512-472-0693; www.hutsfrankand angies.com).

**Hotel rooms can be very difficult to book in Austin during University of Texas football weekends. Plan to return to San Antonio for the night or book early.**

An increasingly popular nighttime destination is Austin's **Warehouse District.** This area, extending from 2nd to 6th Streets and east–west from Congress Avenue to Shoal Creek, was once lined with dilapidated warehouses. More than a decade ago, however, things started to change. Quiet evening venues moved into the area, soon joined by highbrow restaurants. But a 1993 change in Texas law that paved the way for brewpubs really changed the face of this district. Today several brewpubs are joined by nearby coffeehouses, fine restaurants, and plenty of places such as the **Austin Music Hall** (208 Nueces; 512-263-4146; www.austinmusichall .com) that showcase homegrown musical talent.

Another reason to consider an overnight in Austin is **Lake Austin Spa Resort** (1705 S. Quinlan Park Rd.; 512-372-7300, 800-847-5637; www.lakeaustin.com). A venue ranked one of the "Top 10 Destination Spas in North America" by the readers of *Condé Nast Traveler,* this resort rejuvenates guests with its spa treatments, healthy cuisine, and tranquil setting, providing a vacation for mind, body, and spirit. For more information, contact the Austin Convention and Visitors Bureau at (800) 926-ACVB, see www.austintexas.org, or stop by the downtown Visitor Information Center at 209 E. 6th St.

## Georgetown

Located 113 miles north of San Antonio on I-35, **Georgetown** has all the ingredients of small-town Texas in one neat package. Start with a small Texas county seat. Add a sprinkling of cultural attractions, a pinch of recreational sites, a dash of locally owned businesses, and a heaping helping of restored historic buildings. What do you have? The perfect day trip destination from San Antonio.

Although it is the seat of the second-fastest-growing county in the nation, Georgetown continues to hang on to its cozy charm. It's still the kind of place where folks can walk around the square and be welcomed by a smile and a friendly nod. Now celebrating more than a century and a half of small-town life, Georgetown has found the secret to its survival in one important ingredient: preservation.

**For old-fashioned, hometown fun, the Red Poppy Festival (http://poppy.georgetown.org) held each April in downtown Georgetown offers more than 125 booths selling arts and crafts, a variety of musical performers, a kids' village, and a Red Poppy Parade.**

The community's small-town foundations date back to July 4, 1848, when Georgetown was founded on a 10-acre site donated by George Washington Glasscock Sr. and his partner, Thomas B. Huling. For years the sleepy town stirred to life only when the cotton or grain harvest came in from the fields. After the Civil War, however, the railroad sliced through those fertile fields. About the same time, the cattle industry rode in and the oldest university in the state relocated to this Central Texas town. Georgetown was on the map, and before long the streets were busy with the sound of construction. Local limestone was quarried to create elegant downtown buildings. In 1911 a Classic Revival–style courthouse took its place in the square.

Eventually Georgetown stepped out of the limelight, overshadowed by its big-city neighbor to the south, Austin. Stores closed, shopping habits changed, and downtown Georgetown became just a place to pick up necessities between trips to Austin.

No more. Today shoppers stroll **Georgetown's square,** just as their predecessors did more than a century ago, looking for local bounty picked fresh from the fields. Fruits and vegetables glisten in the afternoon sunshine at the farmers' market, held on the square on a weekly basis during harvest season. The square is also a place to stroll cobbled sidewalks and visit the many small boutiques. From 1982 to 1986 Georgetown participated in the Main Street project, renovating and rejuvenating historic structures to bring back the look of the 1890s. With the help of the National Trust for Historic Preservation, more than $8 million was invested in this project. The investment paid off in both appearance of the downtown and its appreciation not only by the residents of Georgetown but also by the nation. In 1997 Georgetown was selected as one of five national winners of the Great American Main Street Award. Cosponsored by the National Trust for Historic Preservation's National Main Street Center, the award recognizes communities that have grasped the reins of preservation and guided their towns to stronger economic positions. Today that future is looking bright for residents who own and operate downtown businesses. For travelers the square holds special appeal because of its many specialty shops. The square really comes alive during seasonal special events, when visitors and residents saunter these streets for a little shopping and a lot of socializing. Beyond the square, the small-town spirit continues, even as big-city recognitions have turned the spotlight on this community and its longtime institutions. East of downtown stands **Southwestern University,** the oldest college in Texas, and now also one of the most recognized.

Opportunities for visitors lie in every direction. North of the courthouse square, **San Gabriel Park** has served for centuries as a gathering site. Native Americans camped on the verdant grounds, pioneers met here, and early Georgetown residents congregated on the riverbanks for parades and meetings, including one event that featured speaker Sam Houston. Today park lovers enjoy shady picnics on the oak- and pecan-dotted grounds. Children romp on the playscape while anglers try their luck from the grassy riverbanks. Crystal-clear springs bubble up at three sites on the park grounds, and often you can watch these little "salt and pepper" springs spewing up chilly spring waters.

West of the park at **Blue Hole,** where river waters reflect limestone cliffs, a revitalization project has made this beautiful spot again a place to be appreciated by residents and visitors. At Blue Hole, walkers and joggers hurry along the wide paths that wind beside waters as green as fresh spring leaves. At this deep-water swimming hole on the South San Gabriel, teens take daredevil plunges off the sheer cliffs into the watery depths, and on quiet mornings anglers try their luck with just the sound of an occasional cardinal singing its friendly song in the distance.

Upstream, the North San Gabriel River has been controlled to create **Lake Georgetown,** a 1,310-acre lake popular with anglers, boaters, water-skiers, and swimmers. A favorite getaway with nature lovers is the 17-mile **Good Water Trail,** named in honor of the Tonkawa, a people who made the region near the San Gabriel River their home. Known for their flint arrowheads and tools, these Native Americans called this region "takatchue pouetsu," or "land of good water."

## From the Cinema to the Stage

Formerly the oldest continuously operated movie house in Williamson County, the **Palace Theatre** (810 S. Austin Ave.; 512-869-SHOW; www.thegeorgetownpalace.org) has a new life today as the home for performing arts in Georgetown. Iconic plays, including *Jesus Christ Superstar, Cats,* and *A Funny Thing Happened on the Way to the Forum,* are acted out on stage by the region's top thespians, and children's theater workshops are offered to budding Broadway stars.

The trail is marked by mileposts as it snakes its way along the lake, passing through several historical points of interest. One such spot is Russell Crossing, which was later known as the **Second Bootys Crossing,** located near milepost 1. In the late 1860s Frank Russell resided at this crossing, and his rock house served as a postal substation. From saddlebags, mail was distributed to the local residents. Between mileposts 2 and 3, hikers can see **Crockett Gardens,** a natural spring. A flour mill was operated here in 1855, and a few decades later the first strawberries in Williamson County were grown in truck gardens at this site. Today the remains of the springhouse and corrals can still be seen.

Besides man-made attractions, hikers are also surrounded by natural beauty. White-tailed deer, coyote, skunk, raccoon, ringtail cat, armadillo, and opossum thrive in this area. From February to August the region is home to the endangered golden-cheeked warbler, a small bird that nests in older juniper trees.

Visitors can drive south on I-35 to reach Georgetown's subterranean attraction: **Inner Space Cavern** (west of I-35 at exit 259; 512-931-CAVE, 877-931-2283; www.myinnerspacecavern.com), discovered during road construction. The highway was built as planned, and soon afterward the cavern was developed for commercial use. It remains one of the most accessible caverns in the state due to its roadside location. Guests enter the cavern on a cog-railroad car, descending from the visitor center to a well-lit, easy-to-follow trail.

More than 80,000 years of dripping water carved Inner Space Cavern from the limestone. Today visitors view discoveries such as the remains of Ice Age mastodons,

## Close-up

### Lower Colorado River Authority Parks

When it comes to parks, San Antonians have only one problem: selecting from a long list of excellent facilities located a short drive from the Alamo City. Many of these parks are part of a conservation and reclamation district that generates and transmits electricity produced by the powerful Colorado River. As such, they are overseen by the **Lower Colorado River Authority (LCRA).** The LCRA also manages the waters of the river and assists riverside and lakeside communities with their economic development. But most people think of the parks when they hear of the LCRA. Scattered from the shores of Lake Buchanan, down through the rest of the Highland Lakes, and along the riverbanks of the Colorado River all the way to Matagorda County on the Gulf coast, these reservoirs offer vacationers a great place to relax.

The LCRA's parks begin along the shores of **Lake Buchanan,** in the upper reaches of the **Highland Lakes.** Contained by one of the largest multiple-arch dams in the world, Buchanan covers 23,000 acres—more than 30 miles in length and 8 miles in width. Here travelers can select from numerous recreation areas to enjoy summer fun—from boating and swimming to quieter pursuits such as bird-watching and hiking.

Small fishing and resort communities are found along Buchanan's shoreline, but miles of land are untouched by development. The land bordering this lake is the wildest of any on the Highland Lakes chain. Lucky boaters often see wild goats and javelina venturing down for a drink, as well as white-tailed deer, especially in the early-morning and late-evening hours. From November through March, many American bald eagles live in the tallest trees along the banks. Surprisingly, the eagles are very tolerant of boats, and one chartered boat tour takes visitors right up to the spectacular birds. At other times of the year, expect to see great blue herons wading in the shallows or perched atop stumps, eyeing passersby. The lake is also an angler's paradise, filled with striped bass, white bass, black bass, perch, yellow catfish, and crappie.

Many of those anglers are familiar with one of the most popular sites along Lake Buchanan: **Black Rock Park** (northwest of Burnet, 123 miles north of San Antonio). This location underwent a major renovation, with improvements that include new campsites and restrooms. Anglers can try their luck with either bank or boat fishing. Boats can launch without charge from the ramp at neighboring Llano County Park.

This park is also a favorite destination among birders. The northeast side of the lake offers one of the best opportunities to spot the American bald eagle from

wolves, saber-toothed tigers, and glyptodons (a kind of prehistoric armadillo) as well as delicate cave formations on their walk through the cool cave.

Doing things the old-fashioned way is just part of everyday life in Georgetown. More than a century and a half after the city's founders settled these banks of the San Gabriel River, Georgetown wouldn't have it any other way.

Contact the Georgetown Convention and Visitors Bureau (800-GEO-TOWN or 800-436-8696; http://visit.georgetown.org) for brochures on attractions, lodging,

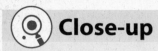

November through March. Other species often sighted include great blue herons, kingfishers, double-crested cormorants, roadrunners, osprey, red-breasted mergansers, common loons, horned grebes, and Bonaparte's gulls.

If you'd like to extend your stay at Black Rock, the park has 21 tent sites, 15 RV sites, and 12 AC/heat cabins. Campsites can fill up on busy weekends, and they are offered on a first-come, first-served basis.

Birders also flock to another nearby park: **Canyon of the Eagles Nature Park** (north side of Lake Buchanan, 137 miles north of San Antonio). Named for the American bald eagles that nest in this wilderness area, this park offers back-to-nature activities such as bird-watching from an observation platform to canoeing along quiet waters.

Another top LCRA park is **Shaffer Bend Recreation Area** (north side of Lake Travis, 95 miles north of San Antonio). This free park is one of the largest on Lake Travis, covering 523 acres. Shaffer is a favorite with day-trippers and campers looking for an undeveloped site that offers good lake views, plenty of wildlife, and various kinds of vegetation. The recreation area, located between Marble Falls and Lago Vista on the lake's north shore, is dotted with hills lined with dense cedar. From these peaks, you can enjoy good lake views at several points along the park road. The hills gradually give way to savanna shaded by oaks and pecan trees. Here you can also see the guayacan, a plant not usually seen east of Del Rio. A milelong swimming area offers a chance to cool off after hiking.

While Shaffer offers undeveloped fun, downstream on Lake Bastrop two LCRA parks offer visitors more facilities. **North Shore** (north side of Lake Bastrop, 100 miles northeast of San Antonio) has campsites, RV sites, group pavilions, a two-lane boat ramp, a fishing pier, playgrounds, trails, and more. Extensive renovations on the **South Shore Park** (south side of Lake Bastrop, 99 miles from San Antonio) have also been completed. The park was totally renovated by the Texas Parks and Wildlife Department at the cost of $1.6 million. The LCRA leases both shoreline parks to Texas Parks and Wildlife, and to meet the increased visitor numbers at these parks, the agency revitalized the visitor facilities. Today the South Shore Park includes 38 recreational vehicle sites with water and electricity, 18 mini-cabins, paved parking and roads, more than 3 miles of hiking trails, a bathhouse, a pavilion, and improvements to the pier, boat dock, and boat ramp. A day-use facility offers picnic tables, grills, a playground, a swim area, and volleyball nets.

For more information on LCRA parks, call (800) 776-5272 or check out the website at www.lcra.org.

shopping, and special events. In town, stop by the Georgetown History and Visitor Information Center on the square at 101 W. 7th St. (512-863-5598) for information and assistance.

## San Marcos

Ready to shop 'til you drop? Then set your compass north toward the community of **San Marcos.** Located 50 miles north of San Antonio on I-35, this city offers the largest outlet malls in Texas as well as plenty of hometown relaxation, outdoor recreation, and fun-loving festivals.

San Marcos's most popular shopping stops are located alongside I-35 at exit 200. This is the location of the **San Marcos Premium Outlet,** an open-air mall that features more than 140 factory-direct shops. Luggage, shoes, leather goods, outdoor gear, china, kitchen goods, and other specialty items are sold. Along with stores, shoppers find plenty of special features: a food court, children's playground, free stroller use, wheelchair loans, and tourist information. On Tuesday the mall offers 50 Plus Shopper Perks, with special discounts for senior citizens.

## Get an Inside Look

Flashlights in hand, guides at **Inner Space Cavern** take tourists of any age on a 95-minute excursion into areas previously closed to the public during the **Explorer's Tour,** one of two recently added tours at the Georgetown attraction. For a behind-the-scenes gander at the cave, take the **Wild Cave** tour. Advance reservations are required for this off-the-beaten-path trip, which is offered Saturday and is limited to ages 13 and up.

Next door to Prime Outlets lies the expansive **Tanger Factory Outlet Center** (512-396-7446; www.tangeroutlet.com). Here you can shop for name-brand goods ranging from housewares and footwear to home furnishings and fine perfumes. And shoppers, don't miss downtown San Marcos, where you'll find many specialty shops selling everything from cigars to collectibles along the square.

Literature lovers should make time for a visit to the **Wittliff Collections at the Alkek Library** at Texas State University (512-245-2313; www.thewittliffcollections.txstate.edu). The extensive holdings showcase the writers of the region, including J. Frank Dobie, Cormac McCarthy, John Graves, and others. If you're a history buff, don't miss the **Calaboose Museum of African American History** (Martin Luther King Drive and Fredericksburg Street; 512-393-8421; www.toursanmarcos.com/CalabooseAfricanAmerican; open Sat and weekdays by appointment). Housed in the first jail in Hays County, the building became known as the Calaboose. Later it served as a USO Center for African-American servicemen during World War II. Today the historic structure preserves the history of African Americans in San Marcos from the 19th century to the present.

Another not-to-be-missed stop is the **historic downtown.** Take time to stroll through this scenic district, which has been transformed into a shopping and dining area. Here visitors can see the work of Texas artists, dine on Texas cuisine, and/or drink Texas beer or wines. San Marcos has been recognized by the Texas Historical Commission and the National Trust for Historic Preservation as one of 39 National Main Street cities in Texas. San Marcos has been participating in the Main Street program since 1984, and during that time the program has helped garner the public and private reinvestment of more than $29 million in the city. Save time for a look at the natural attractions that have given this town the nickname "San Marcos, A Texas

Natural." Many of these attractions lie on the banks of the **San Marcos River,** an area that is considered by many to be the oldest continually inhabited area in North America. The river is a popular swimming and snorkeling destination in the summer months, but year-round it is home to the **Aquarena Center** (921 Aquarena Springs Dr.; take I-35 to the Aquarena Springs exit; 512-245-7575, 800-999-9767; www.aquarena.txstate.edu), a family park that features glass-bottom boat rides, an endangered species exhibit, the San Xavier Spanish Mission, historic homes from San Marcos's earliest days, and plenty of educational fun. Admission to the park, which is operated by Texas State University, is free; there are fees for glass-bottom boat rides and group tours.

Nearby, **Wonder World** (I-35 at Wonder World Drive; 512-392-3760, 877-492-4657; www.wonderworldpark.com) offers a look at San Marcos's natural attractions both above and below the ground. Guided tours last nearly two hours and cover the entire park, including the 7.5-acre **Texas Wildlife Park,** Texas's largest petting zoo. But the highlight of the tour is **Wonder Cave,** created during a three-and-a-half-minute earthquake 30 million years ago. It was the same earthquake that produced the Balcones Fault, an 1,800-mile line separating the Texas western Hill Country from the flat eastern farmland. At the end of the cave tour, visitors take the elevator ride to the top of the 110-foot **Tejas Tower,** which offers a spectacular view of the Balcones Fault and the contrasting terrain it produced.

For more information, call the San Marcos Convention and Visitors Bureau at (888) 200-5620 or (512) 393-5930, or visit www.toursanmarcos.com.

## Gruene

The pronunciation of **Gruene** is one of those things that set a real Texan apart from visitors and newcomers. To sound like a local, just say "Green."

This former ghost town now booms with live music, outdoor recreation, and shopping. Gruene is a neighborhood of New Braunfels, located north of San Antonio along I-35. To get there, take I-35 to exit 191 (Canyon Lake/FM 306 exit), go west 1.5 miles, and turn left at the first traffic light (Hunter Road), continuing for 0.5 mile into Gruene.

Tucked under tall live oaks near the banks of the Guadalupe River, the Gruene of today is a "shop-'til-you-drop" kind of town, filled with antiques stores and boutiques, alfresco restaurants, and historic buildings. The hamlet is quiet on weekdays, but on Friday afternoons the streets fill with shoppers, river rafters and tubers, and city folks looking for a small-town weekend escape.

**i** **For more than 30 years, costumed guides from the Heritage Association have opened doors into yesteryear with tours of some of the most refined homes in San Marcos. Heritage Home Tours/Tours of Distinction are offered in late April.**

Gruene's days have not always been so prosperous. The town was founded in the 1870s by H. D. Gruene at a time when cotton was king. With its swinging dance hall and busy cotton gin, prosperity reigned until the boll weevil arrived in Texas, with the Great Depression right on its heels. H. D.'s plans for the town withered like the cotton in the fields. Gruene became a ghost town.

A century after its founding, investors began restoring Gruene's historic buildings, and little by little, businesses began moving into the once-deserted structures. Gruene eventually was placed on the National Register of Historic Places. Today all the downtown structures are filled with thriving establishments that range from restaurants to a potter to a general store. The commercial area of Gruene is a T-shape formed by Gruene and Hunter Roads.

**i** **China Grove, a tiny town that lies 87 miles from the Alamo City but also within Bexar County, became a part of rock 'n' roll history when the Doobie Brothers sang its praises in the 1970s hit, aptly titled "China Grove."**

The heart of the community remains **Gruene Hall** (1281 Gruene Rd., New Braunfels; 830-606-1281; www.gruenehall.com), the oldest dance hall in the Lone Star State. Since 1878 this joint has reverberated to the sounds of Texas music; crowds still line up to listen to all types of music, from gospel to country.

Nearby, the **Gruene General Store** (1610 Hunter Rd.; 830-629-6021, 800-974-8353; www.gruenegeneralstore.com) brings back memories of Gruene's heyday as a cotton center. This was the town's first mercantile store, built in 1878 to serve the families that worked on the cotton farms. It also served as a stagecoach stop and a post office. Instead of farm implements and dry goods, however, this modern general store now sells cookbooks, fudge, Texas-themed clothing, and sodas from an old-fashioned fountain.

As the population of Gruene rose, so did the need for merchandise, and in 1904 the original general store moved to a new brick building. This was once the biggest store in Comal County, selling everything from lamp oil to caskets. Today the **Gruene Antique Company** (1607 Hunter Rd.; 830-629-7781; http://grueneantiqueco.com) fills this huge building with the wares of numerous vendors.

Located on the banks of the Guadalupe River, the **Gristmill River Restaurant and Bar** (1287 Gruene Rd.; 830-625-0684; www.gristmillrestaurant.com) is housed in the ruins of a 100-year-old cotton gin. In the early days, an explosion blew a hole in the side of the building that today serves fried chicken, chicken-fried steak, and other Texas favorites.

The Guadalupe River also fuels Gruene's most popular summer activities: river rafting and tubing. Several operators take visitors of all abilities—from families to daredevils—to one of the drop-off points on the Guadalupe. From there you can drift beneath the tall cypress trees for hours. Although there's always plenty going on in town, Gruene really springs to life during Market Days, the third weekend of every month. These arts and crafts festivals attract more than 100 vendors from across the state along with shoppers from Central and South Texas who come to look for everything from handmade furniture to hot sauces.

For more information on Gruene Hall's scheduled performers, see www.gruenehall.com or call (830) 606-1281. For information on Gruene, call (830) 629-5077 or visit www.gruenetexas.com.

## New Braunfels

Located 33 miles north of San Antonio on I-35, **New Braunfels** combines a full menu of day trip attractions with a rich history. More than a century and a half ago, the German Prince Carl of Solms, Braunfels, and a group of German settlers founded the city of New Braunfels, naming it for their homeland. Afraid of attack, the prince donned an iron vest, wearing it everywhere, even in the sweltering summer heat.

**i** **While visitors may not develop a Texas twang during their stay in the Lone Star State, mastering the proper pronunciation of its towns will bring travelers one step closer to sounding like a native. From Boerne (BUR-nee) to Uvalde (you-Val-dee), the audio files at www.texastripper.com/pronounce will help tourists say it like a Texan.**

After 11 months in Texas, Prince Solms returned to Germany to marry Sophie, a woman he had hoped would return to Texas with him. Sophie had no interest in coming to this frontier land, however, so the prince remained in Germany, leaving New Braunfels in the hands of its German settlers.

Today you'll find that this community has never forgotten those German roots. It says *Wilkommen* throughout the fall and winter months, with plenty of festivals and fun for the whole family. While the city is a popular summer attraction thanks to its Texas-size Schlitterbahn water park, the cooler months also mean plenty of outdoor fun—both above and below the ground.

Drive out to Texas's largest cave, **Natural Bridge Caverns** (RR 3009, southwest of New Braunfels; 830-651-6101; www.naturalbridgecaverns.com), for a look at what lies beneath the Hill Country. Natural Bridge is a limestone cave, formed by underground waters. It's a showcase of glittery stalactites and stalagmites, with huge flowstones and rooms larger than football fields.

Just next door, animals are the star attractions at **Natural Bridge Wildlife Ranch** (26515 Natural Bridge Caverns Rd.; 830-438-7400; www.wildliferanchtexas.com). Texas's most visited safari park (and the state's oldest) was established on the family's century-old ranch and now boasts species from around the globe. More than 50 species of animals roam these fields. You'll receive a bucket of food when you arrive, and the animals come right up to the car to greet their guests. Don't miss the expanded rhinoceros facility, a specially designed building to help rhinos endure the chilly winter days.

No trip to New Braunfels should overlook the historical side of this Hill Country town. Stop by the **Sophienburg Museum** (401 W. Coll St.; 830-629-1572; www.sophienburg.com) for a look at the early days of this German settlement. You'll see exhibits on founder Prince Solms at the Sophienburg, named for his bride. The museum is open Tues through Sat from 10 a.m. to 4 p.m. Admission is $5 for adults, $2 for students, and $1 for children under 13.

The history of **downtown New Braunfels** is drawing the attention of many visitors, thanks to the Main Street Project and the Downtown Association of New Braunfels. Colorful plantings, a renovated fountain, old-fashioned lampposts, benches, and the rehabilitation of many of the downtown buildings has brought renewed focus on this section of town. You'll even find walking-tour brochures available, highlighting stops in the downtown region.

Decorative and folk arts hold a special place in New Braunfels, which is nicknamed the **"Antique Capital of Texas."** With dozens of shops, this community is a shopper's dream. In addition to the downtown area, there are shops along

I-35 and in neighboring Gruene. Art lovers find plenty of temptation at the local small galleries, and bargain hunters flock to **New Braunfels Marketplace** (I-35 at exits 187 and 189; 830-620-6806; www.nbmarketplace.com), with outlet shops that draw busloads of shoppers from as far as Dallas and Houston.

So that visitors don't literally shop 'til they drop, the city is home to many varied restaurants. **Oma's Haus** (541 Route 46 South; 830-625-3280; www.omashaus.com) serves moderately priced German dishes as well as Texas favorites, and **New Braunfels Smokehouse** (Route 46 and US 81; 830-625-2416; www.nbsmokehouse.com) specializes in barbecued sausage.

All these attractions and more make New Braunfels a special place to visit any time of year, but in November this town really starts to oompah. The biggest blowout is **Wurstfest** (www.wurstfest.com), a 10-day "Salute to Sausage" in early November. One of the top German celebrations in the nation, Wurstfest celebrates with sausage, strudel, suds, and plenty of song.

But the fun doesn't end with Wurstfest. **Festtage** (Holidays) in New Braunfels includes myriad special events including **Weihnachtsmarkt,** a German Christmas shopping market, and **Art for the Holidays,** scheduled for late November.

New Braunfels is a good destination year-round, whether your interests are shopping or spelunking. And unlike Prince Solms, you can leave your iron vest at home. You'll find the locals are very friendly.

For more information on New Braunfels attractions, call the New Braunfels Chamber of Commerce at (800) 572-2626 or visit the town's website at www.nbjumpin.com.

## Wimberley

Looking for more shopping and outdoor fun? Just north of San Antonio, the community of **Wimberley** offers something for everyone. This day trip begins with a 35-mile drive north on US 281 to just south of the town of Blanco. Turn east on Route 32 and continue to Route 12, your turnoff for Wimberley. Bring along your camera for the drive that's often cited as one of the most scenic in the Lone Star State: the **Devil's Backbone.** It stretches along Route 32 from the little community of Fischer to the intersection with Route 12. There aren't any steep climbs or stomach-churning lookouts; a high ridge of hills provides a gentle drive with excellent views along the way. At the end of the Devil's Backbone, Route 32 intersects with Route 12, and the road drops from the steep ridge to a fertile valley where the Blanco River and the town of Wimberley are nestled. The small town of Wimberley boasts dozens of specialty stores, art galleries and studios, and accommodations ranging from river resorts to historic bed-and-breakfasts. The busiest time to visit is the first Saturday of the month, from March through December. This is **Market Day,** when hundreds of vendors set up to sell antiques, collectibles, and arts and crafts. Even if you can't visit on Market Day, you'll find plenty of potential purchases at the shops on the square and surrounding area.

Many springtime visitors come to enjoy the town's two water sources: the **Blanco River** and clear, chilly **Cypress Creek.** Both are filled with inner-tubers and swimmers during hot summer months. During the spring, the waterways provide a temporary home for campers and vacationers who stay in resorts and cabins along the shady water's edge. Family travelers especially appreciate

Wimberley's popular **Pioneer Town** (7A Ranch Resort; 512-847-2517; www.7aresort.com), located 1 mile west of Route 12 on County Road 178. Visitors can watch a blacksmith at work, tour a general store museum, or spend some time at the town jail in this Wild West village. Stop by the Pioneer Museum of Western Art or the Jack Glover's Cowboy Museum to see Western memorabilia. You might feel like a time traveler as you leave the highway for roads lined with hitching posts and return to the early days of this region.

## Corral Outdoor Theatre

Bringing a bit of Hollywood to the Hill Country, the **Corral Outdoor Theatre** (http://corraltheatre.com; 512-847-5994) has been a summertime staple in Wimberley since 1948. Each Friday, Saturday, and Sunday evening from mid-May through late September, movie fans can watch first-run flicks in a no-frills atmosphere at the Rocky River Ranch. Admission is $5 for adults, with children under the age of 4 and seniors 85 and over getting in for free.

For more information, call the Wimberley Chamber of Commerce at (512) 847-2201 or visit www.wimberley.org.

## NORTHWEST OF SAN ANTONIO

### *Enchanted Rock State Natural Area

**Enchanted Rock** looms over the Texas hillside like a massive bald mountain, an enormous dome of pink granite that rises 425 feet above the small stream flowing at its base. Covering more than a square mile, the formation is second in size only to Georgia's Stone Mountain. Located northwest of San Antonio near Fredericksburg, in the heart of the Hill Country, Enchanted Rock can be reached via US 281 (to Johnson City) and US 290 (west to Fredericksburg). In Fredericksburg follow Route 965 for 18 miles to this unique geological formation.

Over the years, rumors about the rock have been plentiful: It glows in the dark, human sacrifices were held on its smooth granite surface, it moans at night, it hides veins of gold and diamonds, and it is haunted. Everything about the rock, from its name to its legends, is enchanted.

The land here is covered with live oaks, sharp rock formations, and steep hills that jut from the land. No hills in the area compare to this granite monolith, though, which catches the attention of travelers even miles away. Today the park is a favorite playground for rock climbers, backpackers, and even sedentary tourists who don't mind a lung-expanding walk up the dome for a look at mile after mile of rural Texas.

The story of Enchanted Rock dates back more than a billion years, when underground upheavals created the rock. When it was first formed, the giant dome was covered by dirt. The actual face of the rock appeared on the scene about 600 million years ago, when erosion removed all the sediment and left the bald mountain exposed. Over the years, the rock has been heated and cooled so many times that giant cracks have been left in the surface, giving the appearance of giant sheets of rock that look like they're ready to flake off and slide down the mountain. This heating and cooling process continues every day, and it's said to be accountable for the noises that come from the rock in the dark, cool hours of the night.

Native Americans believed that those creaking sounds came from a less worldly source. A legend told of a young Indian woman who was brought to the apex of the stone by her father, an ambitious chieftain. Eager to win the favor of his gods, he sacrificed his daughter. Too late he learned that the offering was condemned. As punishment the gods commanded his unhappy spirit to wander forever the surface of Enchanted Rock.

Not all the tales of Enchanted Rock are fiction, however. Near the summit, a bronze plaque recounts the escape of Texas Ranger Captain Jack Hays from the Comanche in 1841. Surprised and cut off from his companions, Hays fled up the rock and hid in one of the cracks that cover its surface, pursued by the angry Comanche, who were convinced that Hays had violated the sanctity of their sacred mountain. The ranger managed to avoid capture and, thanks to his superior weapons, killed so many Comanche that the rest quickly abandoned the chase when Hays's companions arrived on the scene.

Today the face of Enchanted Rock is little changed from those pioneer days. Although at first glance the granite appears to be barren of any plant life, scattered shallow pools of rainwater grow wild onion and lichen, and several small trees grow near the summit.

**i The best times to visit Enchanted Rock are spring and fall, when temperatures are moderate and visibility is high.**

Wildlife is also found here. The collared lizard, a green, yellow, and red iguana cousin with a black-and-white collar, calls Enchanted Rock home. Many species of birds circle the rock, and most days you'll be able to see buzzards, miles away, circling a potential meal. Keep an eye out for mockingbirds, as well as hawks, doves, and bobwhites.

The entire park is of interest to biologists, botanists, and geologists, who now know that Enchanted Rock is composed of granite. Years ago, however, speculators had different ideas about the rock. The promise of precious metals and gems lured the earliest Europeans to the vicinity of Enchanted Rock. The Spanish began organizing explorations of the area in 1753 after hearing reports of "a red mountain." Small samples of silver-bearing ore were sent back to San Antonio for analysis, but the silver was found to be of inferior quality. Rumors of vast gold and silver treasures hoarded by the Indians continued to attract the Spaniards' attention. By the time settlers from the US arrived in Texas, the folklore concerning Enchanted Rock dictated that the entire rock was a giant gold nugget. Later, Texas pioneer Stephen F. Austin said that experiments had proven that the hill was made of pure iron.

See the granite for yourself with a walk up the dome. Bring your best walking shoes for the trek. Except when wet or icy, it is a fairly easy climb, though, and the view is worth the effort. Experienced climbers can also scale the smaller formations located adjacent to the main dome. These bare rocks are steep and dotted with boulders and crevices, and their ascent requires special equipment.

If you'd like to extend your stay at the park, tent camping and primitive backpack camping are available. For more information on Enchanted Rock, call (830) 685-3636.

## Comfort

Located 39 miles northwest of San Antonio on I-10, **Comfort** is a community with strong German roots and ties to earlier generations. Settlers were first planning to name the town "gemütlichkeit," meaning peace, serenity, comfort, and happiness. Fortunately, they settled on the easier-to-pronounce name of Comfort.

That name still perfectly describes the atmosphere of this Hill Country community. The streets here are as busy today as they were a century ago, when customers would come in to the local establishments for kerosene, oil, and washboards. The only difference is that many of these historic structures now house antiques shops, restaurants, and bed-and-breakfast inns instead of the feed, dry goods, and grocery stores of a century past. The downtown historic district boasts numerous buildings.

Today the former Ingenhuett-Faust Hotel is the **Comfort Common** (717 High St.; 830-995-3030), a combination bed-and-breakfast inn and antiques cooperative. Travelers watch small-town life from rocking chairs on the wide porches of the 2-story inn. Day-trippers can shop for antiques in the hotel and in several outbuildings located in the shady backyard.

At one time, however, things were far from comfortable here. This town suffered a massacre of many of its citizens, an event called "the blackest day in the history of the Civil War." Comfort was first settled in 1854 by German immigrants who were followers of the "Freethinker" philosophy. These settlers felt an intense loyalty to their new country and its commitment to democracy and freedom of religion. When the Civil War broke out and Texas began to talk of seceding from the Union, the German immigrants strongly opposed secession because of their feeling of allegiance to their adopted country and because they were against the institution of slavery. Some of the German farmers openly backed the Union government, an act that the Confederates considered treasonous. To make matters worse, the local residents of Comfort formed the Union Loyal League to protect themselves from Indian and outlaw attacks. A nervous Confederacy felt that the group might be a serious threat to their government.

Finally, martial law was declared, and the Texas Rangers were sent to order all males over 16 years old to take an oath of allegiance to the Confederacy. When many refused, farms and homes were burned, and some dissidents were lynched. Some accounts say as many as 150 citizens were killed. With these mounting troubles and threats to their families, a group of Comfort men decided to leave Texas and head to Mexico to wait out the war. A band of 60 left on August 1, 1862. They did not know that the Confederates had been told of their move by an informant. The Unionists were followed to the banks of the Nueces River before the attack began. When it was over, 19 Comfort citizens had been killed in battle. Nine others were captured, but they were later executed by the leader of the Confederates.

On October 18, eight other Unionists were killed while crossing the Rio Grande near the Devil's River. The bodies of these farmers and those killed on the Nueces River were left unburied until the end of the war. It was three years later when the remains were returned and buried in a mass grave in Comfort. The next year, on August 10, 1866, the first monument in Texas was erected at the gravesite to remember this grim battle.

## US Passport Card for Border Crossings

***Note:*** Due to continuing violence in Mexico, especially near the border, **travel to these areas cannot be recommended.** If you do decide to visit these areas, check the US Embassy in Mexico (http://mexico.usembassy.gov) and the US Department of State (http://travel.state.gov/travel/cis_pa_tw/cis/cis_970.html) for up-to-date information on the safety of visiting the border cities. For those of you still wishing to travel to Mexico, here's what you need.

In the old days, you could head off to Laredo for a day trip and stroll back across the border with just your word and a driver's license showing that you were a US citizen. Times have changed. You now need proof of identity and proof of citizenship, such as a birth certificate or, even better, a passport. The US State Department has an alternative to the passport: a US passport card, designed especially for people who cross the border frequently. Since 2009 a passport or passport card has been mandatory for land crossings from Mexico.

The card is good only for land and sea crossing, so you won't be able to fly home from Mexico or any other country using it, but it is cheaper than a passport. The cards are $55 for adults and are good for 10 years. If you already have a passport and just don't want to carry it back and forth (and fill up all your pages), you can get a passport card as well; the cost for passport holders is just $30. Children under 16 will pay $40 for their card, which is good for five years.

For more information on US passport cards, visit the US State Department website, http://travel.state.gov.

The Treue der Union, or True to the Union, Monument was a simple obelisk, inscribed with the names of the men who were killed. Outside of National Cemeteries, this remains the only monument to the Union erected in a state south of the Mason-Dixon Line. The **Treue der Union Monument** is located on High Street, between 3rd and 4th Streets. For more information on Comfort's many historic attractions, contact the Comfort Chamber of Commerce at (830) 995-3131 or visit www.comfortchamberofcommerce.com.

### Fredericksburg

What's your idea of a vacation? An international trip to explore new cultures, music, and cuisines? A shopping excursion to seek out one-of-a-kind items? A romantic getaway, tucked in historic lodging, just you and yours? Or a fiesta, a chance to kick up your heels and enjoy a few carefree days?

In **Fredericksburg** you'll have the chance to fulfill any of those vacation fantasies. This Hill Country community, located 66 miles northwest of San Antonio on US 290, has something for everyone. To reach Fredericksburg, travel north on US 281 through Blanco to Johnson City; turn west in Johnson City on US 290 and continue to Fredericksburg. There are several outstanding wineries in the Fredericksburg area, including **Grape Creek Vineyard** (US 290, 4 miles west of

Stonewall or 10 miles east of Fredericksburg; 830-644-2710; www.grapecreek.com), **Fredericksburg Winery** (247 W. Main St.; 830-990-8747; www.fbgwinery.com), **Chisholm Trail Winery** (2367 Usener Rd., 9 miles west of Fredericksburg on US 290; 830-990-CORK; www.chisholmtrailwinery.com), and **Becker Vineyards** (10 miles east of Fredericksburg, off US 290 on Jenschke Lane; 830-644-2681; www.beckervineyards.com). Wine aficionados should pick up a copy of the "Texas Hill Country Wine Trail" brochure, available from the Fredericksburg Chamber of Commerce and Convention and Visitors Bureau or online at www.texaswinetrail.com. The trail showcases 22 wineries throughout the region.

Or are fine art and sculpture more your style? You're in luck: Fredericksburg is home to many excellent galleries that represent nationally and internationally known talents. **Whistle Pik Galleries** (425 E. Main St.; 830-990-8151; www.whistlepik.com), **Fredericksburg Art Gallery** (251 E. Main St.; 830-992-3188; www.fbgartgallery.com), **Beckendorf Gallery** (105 N. Adams; 800-369-9004; www.beckendorf.com), and many others offer shoppers unique opportunities to purchase original works of art.

This community is also a prime destination for day-trippers looking for antiques, gifts, books, and crafts. The shops along Fredericksburg's Main Street and nearby side streets offer travelers myriad shopping opportunities, no matter their tastes. One-of-a-kind gifts can be found at shops like the **Fredericksburg Herb Farm** (407 Whitney St.; 830-997-8615; www.fredericksburgherb farm.com) and the **Wildseed Farms Market Center** (100 Legacy Dr., east of town on US 281; 800-848-0078; www.wildseed farms.com).

History buffs also find plenty of attractions in the town and its environs. For a look at early Fredericksburg, visit the **Pioneer Museum Complex** at 325 W. Main St. (830-990-8441; www.pioneermuseum.net). This collection of historic houses includes an 1849 pioneer log home and store, the old First Methodist Church, and a smokehouse and log cabin. Also on the premises you'll see a typical 19th-century "Sunday house." These houses catered to farmers and their families who would travel long distances to do business in town, often staying the weekend.

Have another look at Fredericksburg's rich history at the **Vereins Kirche Museum** (325 W. Main St.; 830-990-8441; www.pioneer museum.net). You can't miss this attraction: It's housed in an exact replica of an octagonal structure erected in 1847. The museum is sometimes called the Coffee Mill (or Die Kaffe-Muehle) Church because of its unusual shape. Exhibits here explore Fredericksburg's German heritage; there are also Indian artifacts from archaeological digs. More about the town's early history can be learned at **Fort Martin Scott Historic Site,** located 2 miles east of town on US 290 (830-997-9895). Established in 1848, this was the first frontier military fort in Texas. Today the original stockade, a guardhouse, and a visitor center with displays on local Indians are open to visitors; historic reenactments keep the history lesson lively. More recent military history is explored at the **National Museum of the Pacific War** (formerly the Admiral Nimitz State Historical Park) at 340 E. Main St. (830-997-8600). Admiral Chester Nimitz, World War II commander in chief of the Pacific (CinCPac), was Fredericksburg's most famous resident. He commanded 2.5 million troops from the time he assumed command

18 days after the attack on Pearl Harbor until the Japanese surrendered.

The Nimitz name was well known here even years earlier. Having spent time in the merchant marines, Captain Charles H. Nimitz, the admiral's grandfather, decided to build a hotel here, adding a structure resembling a ship's bridge to the front of his establishment. Built in 1852, the Nimitz Steamboat Hotel today houses a three-story museum honoring Admiral Nimitz and Fredericksburg's early residents. Discover more about one of our nation's leaders with a tour of the George H. W. Bush Gallery, showcasing the wartime service of the former president.

For a look at the life and times of another former president, drive west on US 290 from Fredericksburg to Stonewall, site of the **Lyndon B. Johnson National and State Historical Parks** (830-644-2252; www.nps.gov/lyjo). These combined parks span approximately 700 acres. The visitor center offers displays on LBJ's life, which include mementos of President Johnson's boyhood years. While you're in the visitor center, obtain a driving permit for a self-guided auto tour of the LBJ Ranch with an optional stop at the **Sauer-Beckmann Living Historical Farm,** operated like a 1918 farm, furnished in period style, and staffed by costumed interpreters.

Just a short drive farther west on US 290 is **Johnson City,** home to the **LBJ National Historical Park** (9th Street between Avenues F and G; 830-868-7128). The visitor center showcases the life and history of Lyndon Johnson and his ancestors and the role the family played in the Hill Country. Adjacent to the center lies the Johnson Settlement, with 1860s cabins that once belonged to LBJ's cattle-driving grandfather. Nearby, the LBJ Boyhood Home is still furnished with the Johnsons' belongings and can be seen on guided tours. Admission is free.

If you want to extend your day trip into a weekend visit, Fredericksburg is the capital city of Texas bed-and-breakfast inns. More than 300 B&B accommodations are located in Gillespie County, in everything from Sunday houses to local farmhouses to residences just off Main Street. For more information on Fredericksburg, call the Convention and Visitors Bureau at (888) 997-3600 or (830) 997-6523.

## Boerne

**Boerne** is located 22 miles northwest of San Antonio on I-10. Boerne (pronounced "Bernie") was founded in 1847 by German immigrants, members of the same group who settled nearby New Braunfels. They named the town for author Ludwig Börne, whose writings inspired many settlers to leave Germany for the New World.

During the 1880s, Boerne became known as a health spot, and vacationers came by railroad to soak in mineral water spas and enjoy the clean country air. Although no mineral spas remain today, Boerne still offers a quiet country atmosphere and plenty of attractions to fill a day trip.

For many of those day-trippers, Boerne means shopping, especially for antiques. Many of the antiques you'll see reflect the German heritage that is so strong in this region. Most of the antiques shops are found along **Main Plaza,** the site of many of the town's historic structures. The perfect spot for a weekend getaway is **Ye Kendall Inn** (128 W. Blanco St.; 800-364-2138; www.yekendallinn.com). Located on the Main Plaza, this historic inn dates back to 1859; today's guests find all the modern comforts in historic rooms filled with period antiques. If you can't make this a weekend getaway, budget some time to stop by the inn's village of shops and its **Limestone Grille** (128 W. Blanco St., Main Plaza), an eclectic restaurant featuring Southwestern, Cajun, Northern Italian, and classic French influences. Next door, the Coffee Cafe serves coffees from around the globe as well as breakfast and lunch.

In summer the Main Plaza hosts **Abendkonzerte,** concerts performed by the Boerne Village Band. For more than 140 years, this German band (the oldest continuously active German band in the country and the oldest in the world outside of Munich) has entertained residents and visitors with its Old World sound.

Outdoor lovers will be thrilled with Boerne's many natural attractions. **Cibolo Nature Center** (Boerne City Park, Route 46 at Cibolo Creek; 830-249-4616; www.cibolo.org) preserves some of the natural habitat of this area with a reclaimed prairie and reclaimed marsh. You'll find several walking trails, including a 1-mile historic farm trail, a 0.25-mile prairie trail, and a 0.5-mile marsh loop. These areas are filled with native plants as well as birds and animals native to the Hill Country. Look for great horned owls, opossum, white-tailed deer, and cottontail rabbits. Outdoor lovers will also find plenty of fun at the **Guadalupe River State Park** (Park Road 31; 830-438-2656; www.tpwd.state.tx.us), located 13 miles east of Boerne on Route 46. Swim in the cool waters of the Guadalupe River or try to spot wildlife, which ranges from coyotes to the endangered golden-checked warbler. You can turn your day trip into a weekend excursion by camping here (both tent and RV camping sites are available).

If golf's your game, head over to **Tapatio Springs Golf Resort and Conference Center** (800-999-3299; www.tapatio.com), located 22 miles northwest of San Antonio. This hotel is home to one of the nation's best resort courses, with 27 holes of championship golf.

History buffs will also find plenty of activity in Boerne. On Saturday and Sunday afternoons, tour the **Kuhlmann-King Historical House and the Graham Building** (Main Street and Blanco Road; 830-249-2030). The home was built by a local businessman in 1885 for his German bride, and today it is staffed by volunteer docents who provide weekend tours. Next door, the Graham Building, an 1880s office building, is today a museum and store with exhibits on local history.

Farming was important to the history of this community, and its contribution is remembered at the **Agricultural Heritage Center** (Route 46, 1 mile from Main Street; 830-249-6007; www.agmuseum.org). This museum features farm and ranch tools used by pioneers in the late 19th and early 20th centuries, including a working steam-operated blacksmith shop. Six acres surrounding the museum are dotted with hand-drawn plows, wagons, early tractors, and woodworking tools. For more information on Boerne attractions, give the Chamber of Commerce a call at (830) 249-8000 or (888) 842-8080 or visit http://boerne.org.

## Kerrville

From Boerne, continue north on I-10, then turn south on Route 16 for another 19 miles. With its surrounding hills and the clear waters of the Guadalupe River, **Kerrville** is an outdoor lover's paradise, especially during the spring months. Make time for a visit to the Kerrville-Schreiner State Park, which offers 8 miles of hiking trails, as well as fishing and swimming in the Guadalupe River. If you'd like to extend your day trip, screened shelters and campsites are also available. You can learn more about the flora and fauna of the Hill Country with a stop at the **Riverside Nature Center** (150 Francisco Lemos St.; 830-257-4837; www.riversidenaturecenter.org). This informative center includes walking paths, a wildflower meadow, butterfly gardens, and gardens featuring native grasses, trees, and flowers.

Those rolling hills have also been the inspiration for many artists, so it's not surprising that Kerrville is home to many internationally recognized artists. For a look at world-class Western art, make a visit to the **Museum of Western Art** (1550 Bandera Hwy./Route 173; 830-896-2553; www.museumofwesternart.org). This hilltop museum features Western-themed paintings and sculpture by members of the Cowboy Artists of America.

**i** The early summer Kerrville Folk Festival is a favorite with campers who stake out their space on the ranch to enjoy a few days of live music. The festival has a following of diehard fans who call themselves "Kerrverts."

Kerrville's appreciation for the arts continues in its revitalized downtown, where antiques shops and art galleries offer excellent shopping. The high quality of the artwork available in Kerrville attests to the community's status as a magnet for artists from across the Southwest. Whatever type of art you're looking for, you'll find it at one of the festivals for which Kerrville is known throughout the state. The **Texas State Arts and Crafts Fair** (830-896-5711; www.tacef.org), scheduled for late May, draws more than 200 artists from across the state. No manufactured, mass-produced, or molded items are permitted, and artisans must reside in Texas to participate. Mark your calendar for the annual **Kerrville Folk Festival** (830-257-3600; www.kerrville-music.com), held from late May through early June. This Texas-size festival features songwriters and their bands from Texas as well as numerous other states. One of Texas's best-loved music gatherings, this extravaganza of song is held 9 miles south of town at the **Quiet Valley Ranch.** The ranches that surround Kerrville are as much an attraction as the city itself. One of the best known is the **Y.O. Ranch** (800-YO-RANCH; www.yoranch.com). This famous ranch once spanned more than 600,000 acres, covering a distance of 80 miles. Today the Schreiner family still owns the ranch, located in nearby Mountain Home. You can visit and tour the ranch for a look at its Texas longhorns and many exotic species.

For more about Kerrville's many attractions, call the Kerrville Convention and Visitors Bureau at (800) 221-7958 or see www.kerrvilletexascvb.com.

## EAST OF SAN ANTONIO

### Seguin

Many Texas towns boast nicknames, but **Seguin,** located 36 miles east of San Antonio on either US 90 or I-10, must hold the title for most unusual monikers: "The Mother of Concrete Cities" and, later, the "Athens of Texas." In the 19th century a chemist in this town held several concrete production patents, and his invention was used to construct more than 90 area buildings.

Today many of those early buildings still greet visitors to this community on the banks of the Guadalupe River. Seguin (pronounced "se-GEEN") was named for Lieutenant Colonel Juan Seguin, a hero of the Texas Revolution. Seguin is a shady place that combines historic attractions with the natural beauty of its surroundings. Don't miss **Starcke Park,** the perfect spot for a picnic beneath towering pecan, oak, and cypress trees. Those pecan trees cover not just the park but also the yards of most downtown residences, and several local pecan houses sell the nut by the pound. The town even calls itself the home of the **"World's Largest Pecan,"** a statue located on the courthouse lawn at Court Street.

There are plenty of special reasons to make a day trip to this city of over 24,000 residents. History and architecture buffs should plan a visit to **Sebastopol House State Historical Park** (704 Zorn St.; 830-379-4833; www.tpwd.state.tx.us), one of the best examples of the early use of concrete in the Southwest. Sebastopol, once a private home, was constructed of concrete with a plaster overlay. Today it is open for tours and contains exhibits illustrating the construction of this historic building and its restoration in 1988.

Other historic sites in Seguin are familiar to readers of the best-selling novel ***True Women,*** an epic tale that combines frontier heroism with love, murder, and war. Readers can pick up a free brochure at the Seguin Convention and Visitors Bureau visitor center at 116 N. Camp St. (830-379-6382; www.visitseguin.com) to trace the path of this novel and visit the locations where the book's exciting events, from the Wild West Show to the saving of the horses from the flood, took place. Sites such as **Courthouse Square,** the **King Cemetery,** the **Juan Seguin Gravesite,** and the former **Magnolia Hotel,** one of the first structures that used concrete, are marked along the trail.

A popular spot for families is the **Wave Pool** (Starcke Park East; 830-401-2482; www.ci.seguin.tx.us/parks/wave.htm). In this 15,000-square-foot pool, youngsters can cool off under the Mushroom Shower or splash in the simulated waves. Nearby, the $100,000 **Kids Kingdom Playscape** (Starcke Park East; 830-401-2480; www.ci.seguin.tx.us/parks/parks.htm) makes an excellent stop for energetic young travelers as well.

For more information on Seguin, call (800) 580-PECAN.

## SOUTH OF SAN ANTONIO

### Laredo

Silver and serapes. Pottery and piñatas. For a getaway that combines shopping with historical and cultural fun, it's time to make a run for the border. **Laredo** and its sister city, **Nuevo Laredo,** have enough shops, street vendors, and markets to satisfy any souvenir hunter. And when it's time to take a break from the buying, you'll find plenty of attractions to turn your shopping excursion into a day or weekend of fun.

You might start your shopping in downtown Laredo, with its dozens of shops in the **San Agustin and Mercado Historic Districts.** This area has often been called America's largest urban outlet mall. Near the International Bridge, wholesalers along **Zaragoza Street** entice shoppers with goods ranging from electronics to clothing and shoes to jewelry. Linger in perfume shops where you can purchase the world's famous fragrances at prices far lower than you might expect.

Nearby, the **Republic of the Rio Grande Museum** (1005 Zaragoza St.; 956-727-3480) traces the history of the city. This unique museum, a must for history buffs, utilizes a historic structure. Constructed in the 1830s as a home, the building later served as the Capitol of the Republic of the Rio Grande, a country formed when Northern Mexico seceded from Mexico in 1839. The new state existed until 1841. Today the museum contains guns, saddles, and household belongings from the short-lived Republic.

Beyond the city streets lies a whole other side to Laredo—a place filled with desert wildlife, walking trails, fish-filled lakes, and more. The **Brush Country** offers plenty of winter activities for travelers, regardless of their interest. Birders find more than 300 species on record in the Brush Country, including several rare species such as the white-collared seed eater, the red-billed pigeon, and the gray-crowned yellow-throat. Some popular sightings include the long-billed dowitcher, the purple martin, and the green kingfisher. More interested in marine life? Anglers find plenty of challenge at **Lake Casa Blanca,** located 5 miles east of the city off US 59 on Loop 20. This human-made lake is filled with black bass as well as blue and yellow catfish. The lake is also popular for boating, sailing, and picnicking. Not far from the lake lies the **Casa Blanca Golf Course** (956-721-2621), an 18-hole challenge that you can play year-round. Whether you're in search of historic sites, exuberant festivals, or nonstop shopping, one thing's for certain: Laredo is the place to make a little history of your own.

Contact the Laredo Convention and Visitors Bureau at (800) 361-3360, or see the official website, www.visitlaredo.com, for information on hotels, shopping, and dining.

***NOTE:* At press time, Nuevo Laredo was experiencing increased violence and kidnappings; check with the US State Department (http://travel.state.gov/travel/cis_pa_tw/cis/cis_970.html) for any current advisories on the situation in Nuevo Laredo and other border cities before traveling.**

## WEST OF SAN ANTONIO

### Castroville

Imagine a place where the 19th and 20th centuries join together, treating visitors to modern conveniences and comforts in an Old World atmosphere. Add to this a gazpacho of cultures, a blend of French, German, English, and Spanish with a heavy dose of Alsatian heritage.

What you have is **Castroville,** located only 20 miles west of San Antonio on US 90 West. This town, nicknamed "The Little Alsace of Texas," may be near the Alamo City, but in terms of mood and atmosphere it is in another world. The community was founded by Frenchman Henri Castro, who contracted with the Republic of Texas to bring settlers from Europe. These pioneers came from the French province of Alsace in 1844, bringing with them the Alsatian language, a Germanic dialect. Today only the oldest residents of Castroville carry on the mother tongue.

Traditional Alsatian houses sport European-style, nonsymmetrical, steeply sloping roofs. To have a look at this distinctive architecture, take a self-guided tour of **Old Castroville.** Pick up a free map from the Castroville Chamber of Commerce (802 London St.). This town boasts 97 historic homes and buildings, including Henri Castro's homestead, a 1910 meat market, an 1854 gristmill, and homes dating back to the earliest pioneers. The entire section known as Old Castroville is now a National Historic District.

But perhaps the best way to absorb the atmosphere of Castroville is with a stay in one of its bed-and-breakfast inns. The most famous is the inexpensive **Landmark Inn** (402 E. Florence St.; 830-931-2133; www.visitlandmarkinn.com), operated by the Texas Historical Commission. This inn was first a home and general store before becoming the Vance Hotel. Robert E. Lee and Bigfoot Wallace, the famous Texas Ranger, were said to have stayed at the hotel that was renamed the Landmark Inn during World War II. Today's guests select from historic rooms decorated with antique furnishings. The absence of telephones and televisions helps transport visitors back to the time when travelers to the hotel enjoyed a welcome rest from the stagecoaches traveling the Old San Antonio El Paso Road. Even if you don't have the pleasure of staying overnight in one of the historic rooms, stop by the inn for a look at the museum, with displays illustrating Henri Castro's early efforts to recruit settlers, as well as exhibits covering early Castroville life. You can also enjoy a self-guided tour of the beautifully manicured inn grounds and have a look at the 1850s gristmill and dam and the old bathhouse.

With Castroville's rich history, it's not surprising that the community is a magnet for antiques dealers. Fifteen antiques shops dot the downtown area. Park and walk historic streets with names such as Paris, London, Madrid, and Petersburg, where you'll find shops offering furniture, glassware, china, pottery, and collectibles of all kinds. Castroville's cuisine also reflects its varied history. The **Old Alsatian Steakhouse** (1403 Angelo St.; 830-931-3260), housed in a historic 19th-century cottage typical of the provincial homes of Castroville, specializes in Alsatian and German food; **Haby's Alsatian Bakery** (207 US 290 East; 830-931-2118) offers inexpensive Alsatian and German baked goods.

Castroville hosts many special events throughout the year. Each August, the town celebrates the feast day of St. Louis. Local residents pitch in to prepare barbecue, Alsatian sausage, cabbage slaw, and potato salad, all served picnic-style in Koenig Park. The afternoon is filled with a country auction, arts and crafts, singers, and performances by Alsatian dance groups. On the second Saturday of the month from March through December, Castroville hosts **Market Trail Days,** a shopping extravaganza with everything from arts and crafts to antiques to food. Whether you come to shop, tour, or dine, the local residents have one bit of Alsatian advice: "Kum Sah Castroville," or "Come See Castroville!"

For more information on Castroville, call the Castroville Chamber of Commerce at (800) 778-6775 or visit www.castroville.com.

# WEEKEND GETAWAYS

**In addition to the many day trip options from San Antonio, there are several destinations within range of the city that make for perfect weekend getaways. Many of these getaways lie to the south and west of San Antonio. When you head in those directions, you quickly move from the busy metropolis to the sparsely populated brushland and coastal plains. A trip to the Coastal Bend can combine the fun of a beach weekend with other back-to-nature activities like camping, birding, fishing, or hiking.**

**To turn your excursion into a "two-nation vacation," don't forget the border towns. Along the US–Mexico border, numerous weekend getaways allow travelers to enjoy an easy trip into Mexico. From the cities of the Rio Grande Valley to the sister cities of Laredo and Nuevo Laredo to ecotourism attractions of Del Rio and Ciudad Acuña, you'll find plenty of south-of-the-border charm with north-of-the-border conveniences.**

## SOUTH OF SAN ANTONIO

### Corpus Christi

One of America's 10 busiest ports, there's always something happening in this lively bayside town. To reach **Corpus Christi** from San Antonio, follow I-37 south for 145 miles. The heart of Corpus Christi is **Shoreline Drive,** which boasts proud palms and spectacular views of the bay. Shoreline Drive's northern stretch is its most active, especially near the piers. Each of these piers bustles with life—whether in the predawn hours when the shrimp boats head out for their day's work or at midnight when night cruises offer anglers a chance at that trophy catch.

Attractions throughout Corpus Christi are offering travelers more reasons than ever before to plan a visit. Just over the Harbor Bridge, the **USS *Lexington* Museum on the Bay** (2914 N. Shoreline Blvd.; 361-888-4873, 800-LADY-LEX; www.usslexington.com) is now home to the **Mega Theater.** This state-of-the-art theater has a three-story giant screen and is capable of showing IMAX productions. While you're at the ship, known as the most decorated aircraft carrier in US naval history, save time to take part in one of five self-guided tour routes. Wear good walking shoes for your tour of the Lexington, as you will climb the stairs that sailors once raced up and down during wartime more than half a century ago. Visitors can follow routes to the flight deck and bridge, the captain's quarters, the sick bay and engine room, and the hangar deck as well as other areas. Step into the flight simulator if you'd like to feel what it's like to be on a bomber plane making an attack and then coming in for a landing on the carrier. If you feel like you recognize the USS *Lexington,* you very well might—the gray ship is somewhat of a star. If you saw the film *Pearl Harbor,* you saw the *Lexington;* the carrier has also appeared in the movie *Midway* as well as on the TV series *JAG*.

Next door to the *Lexington* lies the **Texas State Aquarium** (2710 N. Shoreline Blvd.; 800-477-GULF; www.texasstateaquarium.org), which showcases the aquatic animals and habitats indigenous to the Gulf of Mexico. Considered Corpus Christi's most popular tourist attraction, the aquarium has welcomed more than seven million visitors since it opened in 1990. Its tanks are filled with nurse sharks, amberjack, beautiful coral gardens, moray eels, tarpon, rays, and more. The aquarium hosts several daily programs to help visitors gain a deeper understanding of these marine creatures. Three times a day, visitors can touch a small shark or a stingray, while several times daily guests can watch scuba divers to learn more about coral reefs and their inhabitants. Outdoors, young visitors enjoy touch tanks filled with small sharks and rays; Otter Creek, where playful river otters amuse visitors with their antics; and Floating Phantoms, where visitors can watch the balletic beauty of jellyfish from around the globe.

Another top family attraction is the **Corpus Christi Museum of Science and History and the Ships of Columbus** (1900 N. Chaparral; 361-826-4667; www.ccmuseum.com). Ships of Columbus allows visitors to step aboard a life-size replica of the *Pinta*. The adjacent museum offers displays to fascinate all ages, covering everything from dinosaurs to Spanish shipwrecks. Don't miss the "Seeds of Change" exhibit, designed by the Smithsonian's National Museum of Natural History for the 500th anniversary of the European discovery of America. And no visit to the coast would be complete without a look at America's longest national seashore: Padre Island (www.nps.gov/pais). The drive to the island takes you past several excellent seafood restaurants and seaside accommodations. Several parks offer fun for all members of the family. Padre Island National Seashore is open year-round for beachcombing, fishing, and swimming and also has a visitor center with exhibits on the region. Campers can enjoy covered picnic areas and overnight hookups at Padre Balli Park on Park Road 22.

Weekend visitors to Corpus Christi find a full range of dining and accommodations options. Seafood, often caught that morning, is the specialty of many restaurants such as the moderately priced **Water Street Oyster Bar** (309 N. Water St.; 361-881-9448; www.waterstreetrestaurants.com) and **Landry's Seafood House** (600 N. Shoreline Blvd.; 361-882-6666; www.landrysseafoodhouse.com). Accommodations in Corpus Christi include the **Omni Bayfront** (900 N. Shoreline Blvd.; 361-887-1600, 800-THE-OMNI), **Omni Marina** (707 N. Shoreline Blvd.; 361-887-1600; www.omnihotels.com/FindAHotel/CorpusChristiMarina.aspx), and the **Holiday Inn Emerald Beach** (1102 S. Shoreline Blvd.; 361-883-5731), the only hotel in downtown Corpus Christi with its own beach.

For more information, call the Corpus Christi Convention and Visitors Department at (800) 678-6232 or visit www.visitcorpuschristitx.org.

## Rockport

**Rockport** is considered a bird-watching paradise, with more than 500 species on record. For a weekend of communing with nature, take I-37 south from San Antonio for 145 miles to Corpus Christi. Continue across the Harbor Bridge and follow US 181 north to Route 35 to Aransas Pass. In Aransas

Pass, continue on Route 35 for 11 miles to Rockport.

Rockport's annual **Hummer/Bird Celebration,** scheduled for mid-September, features both fun and educational activities, from boat trips to butterfly feeding, although the real star of the show is the hummingbird, which stops here in a final feeding frenzy before the nonstop migration across the Gulf of Mexico.

If you visit Rockport during the winter months, the attention turns to the rare **whooping crane,** the 5-foot-tall bird that makes its home at the nearby **Aransas National Wildlife Refuge** (45 minutes northeast of Rockport; 361-286-3559). These statuesque birds, with a 7-foot wingspan, once numbered below 20 and were placed on the endangered species list. Today their numbers have increased considerably, and naturalists excitedly make a head count every year, always on the lookout for a new chick.

After a day of bird-watching, Rockport offers many activities to give you a break from the binoculars. **Rockport Beach Park** boasts more than a mile of sandy beach, with swimming, boating, fishing, and water sports. History buffs will also find plenty of activities in Rockport and nearby Fulton. The **Fulton Mansion State Historic Site** (3 miles south of Rockport off Route 35 at the corner of Henderson Street and Fulton Beach; 361-729-0386), preserved today by the Texas Historical Commission, was somewhat of a futuristic home when first built in 1876. The house included central forced-air heating, and a central cast-iron furnace in the basement provided heat through a series of flues to false, decorative fireplaces in the main rooms. Hot and cold running water was achieved with a tank located in the tower attic. A gas plant located at the back of the house provided fuel for gas chandeliers. For a look at even earlier coastal history, stop by the **Texas Maritime Museum** (1202 Navigation Circle; 866-729-2469; www.texasmaritimemuseum.org), which traces maritime history from the Spanish shipwrecks off the Gulf Coast to the offshore oil industry. Nearby, the **Rockport Center for the Arts** (902 Navigation Circle; 361-729-5519; www.rockportartcenter.com) serves as a showcase for regional artists. Many of Rockport's accommodations are fishing cottages and furnished condominiums such as **Key Allegro Rentals** (1798 Bayshore Dr.; 361-729-3691) and **Kontiki Beach Motel and Condominiums** (2290 N. Fulton Beach Rd.; 800-338-0649). Although many people use the kitchen facilities to cook meals, Rockport is also home to a wide selection of restaurants, among them the casual **Boiling Pot** (201 S. Fulton Beach Rd.; 361-729-6972), which serves spicy seafood on paper-covered tables.

For more information, call the Rockport-Fulton Area Chamber of Commerce at (800) 242-0071 or check out their website at www.rockport-fulton.org.

## Port Aransas

Not far from Rockport lies **Port Aransas**—just "Port A" to most Texans—perched on the northern tip of **Mustang Island.** To reach Port Aransas, take I-37 south from San Antonio for 145 miles to Corpus Christi. Continue across the Harbor Bridge and follow US 181 north to Route 35 to Aransas Pass. Follow Route 361 from Aransas Pass across the Redfish Bay Causeway to Harbor Island and Port Aransas.

One of the area's top attractions is **Mustang Island State Park,** the perfect place for a beach campout. The park offers 1.5 miles of beach camping, and many visitors like to go horseback riding along the island's beaches.

Another popular activity is spending an afternoon out on the Gulf on a deep-sea fishing cruise. Large tour boats, taking as many as 100 passengers, provide bait and tackle. Serious anglers looking for big game fish such as marlin and shark should book charter excursions for personalized service. For a chance to see dolphins, stop by the Roberts Point Park on Highway 361. Dolphins often chase the ferries as they make their way across the ship channel. If you'd like to learn more about marine life, stop by the small aquarium at the **University of Texas Marine Science Institute** (Ship Channel; 361-749-6729; www.utmsi.utexas.edu); admission is free.

Another good way to see the local wildlife is a nature cruise aboard ***The Mustang II*** (Woody's Sports Center; 361-749-5252; www.woodysonline.com). Travelers can take a two-hour nature tour to watch dolphins and birds. Families enjoy the dolphin watch, a tour scheduled throughout the day. Other cruises departing from Woody's include a sunset cruise and a sightseeing tour with a look at the **US Naval Station** (home of the largest US mine-sweeping fleet), the **Lydia Ann Lighthouse,** and the **intracoastal waterway.**

This city is also home to the **Leonabelle Turnbull Birding Center** (Ross Avenue, off Cut Off Road; 800-45-COAST), part of the **Great Texas Coastal Birding Trail.** The center is landscaped with plants to attract migrating hummingbirds and also harbors two alligators and a family of nutria, members of the rodent family who nest in fallen reeds. Port Aransas offers numerous lodging places—everything from resorts to condominium complexes to mom-and-pop motels that cater to visiting anglers. A longtime favorite has been the **Tarpon Inn** (200 E. Cotter Ave.; 800-365-6784; www.thetarponinn.com), which dates back to 1923. Many families enjoy the conveniences of condominium complexes such as the **Dunes Condominiums** (1000 Lantana; 877-296-3863; www.thedunescondos.com), which offers kitchenettes as well as resort amenities such as a pool and tennis.

For more information, call the Port Aransas Tourist and Convention Bureau at (800) 45-COAST.

**i** **Feeling lucky? The only legal casino in the Lone Star State, the Kickapoo Lucky Eagle Casino (www.kickapooluckyeaglecasino.com), is located 6.5 miles southeast of Eagle Pass on the Kickapoo Indian Reservation.**

## Kingsville

King Ranch is almost synonymous with the Texas ranching industry, and today it welcomes visitors from around the world to the community of **Kingsville,** 39 miles south of Corpus Christi on US 77. Larger than the state of Rhode Island, the King Ranch sprawls across 825,000 acres. The ranch has long been known for its role in the American ranching industry and is still a worldwide leader. Here the Santa Gertrudis and King Ranch Santa Cruz breeds of cattle were developed, as was the first registered American quarter horse. For vacationers the **King Ranch** (Highway 141 West; 361-592-8055; www.king-ranch.com) is an important ecotourism destination, thanks to its population of migratory birds. The green jay has been named the bird of Kingsville, and more than 350 bird species such as pygmy owls and common paurauque are spotted on different areas of the ranch. In addition to excellent birding, the King Ranch has nature trails that offer glimpses of white-tailed deer, javelinas, coyotes, and other animals native to this region, which was first known as the Wild Horse Desert.

Vacationers can enjoy a one-and-a-half-hour tour of the ranch aboard air-conditioned buses. The drive around the ranch includes a look at longhorns, horses, and the many breeds of cattle that made this ranch famous.

One of the most popular annual events at the ranch is the **Ranch Hand Breakfast,** scheduled for the Saturday before Thanksgiving. More than 7,000 visitors show up for a real ranch breakfast.

Beyond the ranch in the town of Kingsville, the King legacy is also apparent. The **King Ranch Museum** (405 N. 6th St.; 361-595-1881) provides visitors with a look at the history of the ranch, including a stunning photographic essay of life on King Ranch in the 1940s. There's also a collection of saddles, antique carriages, and antique cars.

Kingsville is home to the **Conner Museum** (905 W. Santa Gertrudis St.; 512-593-2810; www.tamuk.edu) on the campus of Texas A & M University. Highlighting the natural and social history of South Texas, the museum includes exhibits on ranching, South Texas ecosystems, and area fossils and minerals.

Many Kingsville visitors make the journey a day trip from their home base in Corpus Christi or on Padre Island; others opt to stay at one of the city's motels, such as the **Rodeway Inn Kingsville** (3430 US 77 South; 361-595-5753; www.rodewayinn.com).

For more information on area activities, contact the Kingsville Convention and Visitors Bureau at (361) 592-8516 or (800) 333-5032 or visit www.kingsvilletexas.com.

## WEST OF SAN ANTONIO

### Del Rio

Whether you define a nature getaway as a weekend of camping, birding, houseboating, fishing, waterskiing, or exploring, there's one Texas destination that has it all: **Del Rio,** located 152 miles west of San Antonio via US 90.

The city that's known as "the best of the border" certainly lives up to that title when it comes to outdoor fun. Perched at the edge of the **Chihuahuan Desert,** Del Rio is an oasis lush with vegetation thanks to the **San Felipe Springs**, artesian wells that gush more than 90 million gallons of water each day.

While the town offers a full getaway's worth of activities—everything from the **Val Verde Winery** (100 Qualia Dr.; 830-775-9714; www.valverdewinery.com) to the **Whitehead Memorial Museum** (1308 S. Main St.; 830-774-7568; www.whitehead-museum.com)—many of Del Rio's natural attractions are located beyond the city's borders. Three rivers, including the Rio Grande, form **Lake Amistad.** Amistad, derived from the Spanish word for friendship, was a joint project between Mexico and the US. Today it's a vacationer's delight, offering water sports of all varieties and plenty of great fishing. Anglers try for black bass, crappie, catfish, and striper, and professional guides are available to help lead the way to a great fishing spot.

The best way to see the lake is aboard a boat, and the most luxurious ride is aboard a houseboat. With innumerable coves tucked inside sheer canyon walls, houseboaters can find seclusion as well as some beautiful, spring-fed swimming holes. Several operators rent houseboats that include all the comforts of home, from separate bedrooms to fully equipped kitchens—some boats even include a hot tub on deck! You'll also find fishing boats, powerboats, and personal watercraft for rent if you'd like to explore the lake on something smaller.

If you'd rather let someone else take the wheel, guided boat tours journey into the far reaches of the Pecos and Devil's Rivers for a look at prehistoric Indian pictographs painted on the canyon walls. Call the Chamber of Commerce for more information on guided tours to these picturesque areas.

About 45 miles northwest of Del Rio lies **Seminole Canyon State Historical Park** (US 90, 9 miles past the town of Comstock; 432-292-4464). This is a stop archaeology buffs shouldn't miss and a perfect getaway for bird enthusiasts as well. More than 300 bird species have been recorded in the Del Rio area, so bring your binoculars and birding guide for this getaway.

Seminole Canyon is home to a mystery that has never been solved. Delicate pictographs were drawn on canyon walls by ancient Indians about 8,500 years ago. The paintings in the caves and on canyon walls represent animals, Native Americans, and supernatural shamans, but their meaning is still unknown.

Archaeologists believe the early residents of Seminole Canyon were hunter-gatherers. Hunting was limited to deer and rabbits, and instead the residents survived as foragers, living on sotol, prickly pear, and lechugilla. The culture that made its home in this canyon produced the artwork now seen on guided tours. At 10 a.m. and 3 p.m., Wed through Sun, take a ranger-led walk to the Fate Bell Shelter. This rock overhang boasts ochre, black, and white paintings that are the oldest rock art in North America. One painting, known as "The Three Shamans," portrays three figures, one with antlers atop his head.

**i** Operated by three successive generations of the Qualia family, the Val Verde Winery (www.valverdewinery.com) is the oldest continuously run winery in Texas. Tours are given Monday through Saturday for those over the age of 21.

This park has some quiet campsites located high above the canyon. They offer a spectacular view of the Chihuahuan Desert, dotted with cactus. If you'd rather have a roof over your head than a tent canvas, you'll find a variety of accommodations in Del Rio, ranging from bed-and-breakfast inns like **Villa del Rio** (123 Hudson Dr.; 800-995-1887; www.villadelrio.com) to full-service motels such as the **Ramada Inn** (2101 Veterans Blvd.; 800-775-1511; www.ramadainndelrio.com).

For more information on Del Rio area attractions, call the Del Rio Chamber of Commerce at (800) 889-8149 or see www.drchamber.com.

## South Padre Island

The livin' is definitely easy on **South Padre Island**—whether it's summer or not. Whether a good weekend getaway to you means gulls or gambling, shops or surf, this island destination has got it all.

South Padre is an easy drive from the Alamo City. Travel I-37 south toward Corpus Christi. Just 15 miles before reaching Corpus Christi, turn south on US 77 and continue to Kingsville. In Kingsville head south on US 77 for 75 miles to Harlingen. From Harlingen, continue south on US 77 for 12 miles to the intersection with Route 100; turn east on Route 100 and continue to Port Isabel and across the causeway to South Padre Island. Air service to South Padre Island is also available from San Antonio through several communities in South Texas. Harlingen's Valley International Airport, a 45-minute drive from the island, and the Brownsville–South Padre Island International Airport, a 30-minute drive, offer numerous flights.

South Padre stretches for 34 miles, hugging the Texas coastline and serving as a protective barrier against Gulf storms. At its widest point, the island is just a half-mile across, providing all its hotel rooms with an unbeatable view.

Your visit to Texas's southernmost island begins with a drive over the **Queen Isabella Causeway,** the longest bridge in the state. It spans 2.5 miles, starting at the base of the **Port Isabel Lighthouse.** In **Port Isabel** you'll find plenty of opportunities to fish or just enjoy the catch of the day at one of the excellent seafood restaurants.

For some visitors the chance to enjoy miles of pristine beach is reason enough to journey to South Padre. Miles of toasted sand invite travelers to enjoy horseback riding, sailboarding, surfing, building sandcastles, or just wave-hopping in the surf.

But there are plenty of activities to keep travelers busy in and out of the water. Try your luck at fishing, one of the most popular activities both in bay and Gulf waters. For little more than the price of a movie ticket, you can go out on a cruise and have a chance at any one of the species that populate these waters: whiting, drum, flounder, trout, wahoo, and even sailfish.

Everyone thinks of South Padre as a magnet for college students looking for a spring-break party, but few know that the island is a classroom for students at the **University of Texas–Pan American Coastal Studies Laboratory** (956-761-2644; http://portal.utpa.edu/utpa_main/daa_home/cose_home/csl_home). Research here focuses on coastal ecosystems, including a study of the sea turtles and dolphins that live in the area. You can stop by the lab Mon through Fri afternoons for a look at aquariums filled with marine life.

Regardless of your interests, you'll spend part of your visit along Padre Boulevard, the main street in town. This road is lined with restaurants, shell shops, and tourist facilities that can make your trip easier and more fun. Park your car and catch a ride on "The Wave," a motorized trolley that stops at attractions along the way. For more information, call the South Padre Convention and Visitors Bureau at (800) SOPADRE or stop by the visitor center at 600 Padre Blvd. They also have a website, www.sopadre.com.

## Rio Grande Valley

While you are at South Padre Island, don't miss the treasures of the **Rio Grande Valley.** Here, among miles of citrus groves and coastal flats filled with birds from throughout North America, you'll find many attractions. Have a look at the website of the Rio Grande Valley Partnership Chamber of Commerce, www.valleychamber.com, for a look at the region's many activities and events.

Most South Padre visitors spend at least part of their trip enjoying an excursion to Brownsville, Matamoros, and other communities of the Rio Grande Valley. The southernmost city in Texas, **Brownsville** features one of the top 10 small zoos in the country, a must-see for families. The **Gladys Porter Zoo** (500 Ringgold St.; 956-546-7187; www.gpz.org) is home to about 2,000 animals, most contained by waterways rather than fences. From Brownsville, it's a quick 5-minute walk across the International Bridge to **Matamoros,** Mexico. Follow Route 48 downtown to the convention center and park at the free municipal lot. After crossing the bridge, it's a short taxi ride to the mercado. Here you can bargain for silver jewelry, leather goods, glassware, blankets, serapes, Baja jackets, and onyx creations.

**Harlingen** is a top destination in the Valley and makes a good central point from which to enjoy a look at all of the southern tip of Texas. The rich history of this region is traced at the **Rio Grande Valley Museum in Harlingen** (956-430-8500). This attraction includes a traditional museum as well as historic buildings: the Harlingen Hospital, the restored home of Harlingen's founder, and a stagecoach inn. For more history in this area, be sure to pick up a copy of Harlingen's Heritage Trail brochure. It details historic churches, theaters, and homes throughout the city.

West of Harlingen, **McAllen** also offers activities both in the city and in Mexico. Home to nearly 130,000 residents, McAllen is located just 8 miles from the Mexican city of Reynosa, a favorite with families looking for a chance to shop at a traditional mercado. Several hotels offer van service to the International Bridge, or you can drive to Hidalgo and park for the day on the Texas side for just a couple of dollars.

McAllen is also a favorite with weekend travelers looking to spend some time enjoying nature and the great outdoors. Birding is especially popular. About 16 miles southeast of the city, the **Santa Ana National Wildlife Refuge** (956-784-7500) challenges birders with many rare species. Interpretive tram rides are available during winter months. Twice a year (in April and October) McAllen holds the **McAllen International Birding Tour** celebrating the bountiful bird and wildlife of South Texas, Central Texas, and Mexico. For more information on Brownsville, call (800) 626-2639 or visit www.brownsville.org; on Harlingen, call (800) 531-7346 or go to www.visitharlingentexas.com, and on McAllen, call (877) MCALLEN or (956) 682-2871, or go to www.mcallencvb.com.

## EAST OF SAN ANTONIO

### Houston

Sometimes a getaway means big-city fun, and in Texas that means **Houston,** the nation's fourth-largest city. Houston is a sprawling mix of cultures, and it offers plenty of sightseeing, family attractions, shopping, and nightlife. To reach Houston, follow I-10 east of San Antonio, a drive of 200 miles.

The arts play a major role in Houston. One of the most noteworthy sights is the **Museum of Fine Arts** (1001 Bissonnet; 713-639-7300; www.mfah.org). Founded in 1900, this was the first municipal art museum in Texas. Among its permanent collections are the Strauss Collection of Renaissance and Eighteenth-Century Art, the Glassell Collection of African Gold, and the Beck Collection of Impressionist and Post-Impressionist Art. On the museum grounds is the Bayou Bend Collection and Gardens.

Art buffs also won't want to miss **The Menil Collection** (1515 Sul Ross; 713-525-9400; www.menil.org). More than 15,000 pieces of art are displayed here. Check out the collection of African tribal art, as well as the modern art. The Menil Collection also has one of the largest Surrealist collections in the world.

Located in walking distance of other attractions in the Houston Museum District, the **Contemporary Arts Museum** (5216 Montrose; 713-284-8250; www.camh.org) is set in a striking metal building that's a local landmark. A tight focus on art of the past 40 years allows the CAM to explore its specialty in great detail. Changing exhibits ensure that the galleries remain fresh and provocative.

The beauty displayed in the city's many art museums is a stark contrast to one of its most solemn sights: the **Holocaust Museum Houston** (5401 Caroline St.; 713-942-8000; www.hmh.org). Houston residents who suffered through the Holocaust are remembered here, along with the victims throughout the world. At the Ethel and Al Herzstein Theater, the film *Voices* is a sobering account of the Holocaust told by Houston residents who witnessed it. The museum's Josef and Edith Mincberg Gallery features artwork inspired by the Holocaust, and the Eric Alexander Garden of Hope remembers the children who died in the Holocaust. Some parts of this museum might be too intense for young children.

One museum that's appropriate for children of all ages is the **Houston Museum of Natural Science** (5555 Hermann Circle Dr.; 713-639-4629; www.hmns.org). In addition to the expected hands-on, kid-friendly exhibitions, this extremely popular museum has a number of specialty collections that shouldn't be missed. The Cullen Hall of Gems and Minerals is a vast and unique attraction, more impressive because of its skillful lighting. The Strake Hall display of seashells is similarly stunning. Favorites with children are the Discovery Works and the Challenger Learning Center. And all visitors are delighted by the Cockrell Butterfly Center, where free-flying butterflies are spotted along the walkways.

Wildlife of all sizes and shapes is found at the **Houston Zoological Gardens** (6200 Hermann Park Dr.; 713-533-6500; www.houstonzoo.org). Houston's 55-acre zoo is home to more than 5,000 animals. The sea lion training exhibit is very popular with visitors, as is the vampire bat feeding. The zoo is one of the most visited in the entire Southwest.

**Space Center Houston** (1601 NASA Pkwy.; 281-244-2100; www.spacecenter.org), located near the community of Clear Lake about 20 minutes south of Houston, is another popular local attraction. Starting with a mock-up of the space shuttle, the center is filled with interactive displays. The $70 million facility is usually filled to bursting with children engaging in hands-on learning. Video exhibits let kids try their hands at piloting a shuttle or driving a lunar rover. NASA's real technology can be seen via the four- to five-hour Level 9 Tour. Tour guides lead visitors behind the scenes to see the nuts-and-bolts world of astronaut training and Mission Control. The Level 9 Tour includes lunch in the astronauts' cafeteria. This tour is by far the most popular; wait times can exceed one hour. It's sea, not space, travel that's the focus of the **Battleship *Texas* State Historic Site** (3523 Highway 134; 281-479-2431; www.tpwd.state.tx.us), located 21 miles from downtown Houston on Route 225. One of the state's top historic attractions, the USS *Texas* fought in both World War I and II and was renovated by money raised by the schoolchildren of Texas. The largest part of the park is aboard the massive battleship, which has been restored and is open for self-guided tours.

Directly across from the Battleship *Texas* stands the **San Jacinto Battleground State Historical Site.** Here the Battle of San Jacinto was fought, winning Texas its freedom from Mexico. The museum has an extensive collection on the Texas Revolution, the Republic of Texas, and the early days of statehood. For more on Houston, visit the website of the Greater Houston Convention and Visitors Bureau, www.visithoustontexas.com, or call (800) 4-HOUSTON.

## Galveston

When you're ready for a weekend at the beach, drive 50 miles southeast of Houston to the resort community of **Galveston,** a place known for fun in the sun. Any time of year there's always something to do in this coastal community.

Shoppers find numerous antiques shops along **Post Office Street,** a shopping district that runs from 20th to 25th Streets. Along with restaurants and specialty shops, Post Office Street is also home to **The Grand 1894 Opera House** (2020 Post Office St.; 800-821-1894; www.thegrand.com), which once hosted performers such as Sarah Bernhardt, John Philip Sousa, and Anna Pavlova. It has been restored to its turn-of-the-20th-century grandeur.

After a morning at Post Office Street, stroll over to **The Strand,** just 3 blocks away. In the late 19th century, The Strand was the city's business district. It's a block away from the busy seaport, where shippers unloaded merchandise from around the world and took on a cargo of Texas cotton. Bankers and traders filled the buildings of The Strand, so it was known as the "Wall Street of the Southwest." Stroll the historic streets, which transport visitors through a district filled with specialty shops and restaurants housed in one of the nation's largest collections of Victorian commercial architecture. The district is also home to the ***Elissa,*** a restored 1877 tall ship that's open for self-guided tours. The ship is housed at the **Texas Seaport Museum** (Pier 21; 409-763-1877; www.galvestonhistory.org/Texas_Seaport_Museum.asp), which has displays on Galveston's shipping history as well as a database with information about more than 133,000 immigrants who entered the US through Galveston. Thousands of immigrants made their way through the port, earning it the name "little Ellis Island." Eventually Galveston went on to become the richest city in the state and home of many Texas firsts: post office, naval base, grocery store, insurance company, jewelry store, private bank, gaslights, hospital, cotton exchange, electric lights, telephone, golf course, real estate firm, and more.

**i** **Moody Gardens offers a variety of field trip programs depicting both ocean and rain forest exploration for grades K–12. Call (800) 582-4673, ext. 4203 or ext. 4362, for more information and reservations.**

Galveston's thriving economy took a downswing on September 8, 1900, with the arrival of one of the worst storms in US history. Known as the Great Storm, the hurricane killed more than 6,000 residents and destroyed one-third of the city. To prevent future damage by storm surges, the city constructed a 7-mile seawall and raised the level of the island. Near the Texas Seaport Museum, you can watch a documentary film on the Great Storm and its aftermath.

While the storm took many of the island's oldest buildings, others were spared and still welcome guests. One of the most famous is **The Bishop's Palace,** located at 1402 Broadway. Built as a private home by a local railroad founder, the home is built of Texas granite and is open for guided tours. Among its unique features are fireplaces and mantels from around the world.

Galveston also has plenty of modern-day attractions, and one of the best is **Moody Gardens** (1 Hope Blvd.; 800-582-4673; www.moodygardens.com). Save an entire day for this Texas-size attraction, now even larger with the Aquarium Pyramid, a 130,000-square-foot structure that houses 1.5 million gallons of water and more than 10,000 marine animals. The aquarium features North Pacific, Caribbean, South Pacific, and South Atlantic displays with true-to-life habitats. Moody Gardens' first major attraction was the Rainforest Pyramid, where more than 1,700 exotic plants, fish, birds, and insects from the world's rain forests live. The complex is also home to the nation's first 3-D IMAX theater. The Discovery Pyramid showcases the world of science with educational interactive displays. The Discovery Pyramid also features the IMAX Ridefilm Theater with a 180-degree wraparound screen. Other attractions at Moody Gardens include Palm Beach, constructed using sand shipped in from Florida, and *The Colonel*, a re-created paddlewheeler. Moody Gardens is just steps from the Moody Gardens Hotel, one of many reasons to turn a day trip into a weekend excursion. Throughout the island, January brings lower room rates and the chance to enjoy a relaxed atmosphere. Along Seawall Boulevard, one of the top properties is the **San Luis Resort Spa and Conference Center** (5222 Seawall Blvd.; 800-445-0090; www.sanluisresort.com), a 30-acre complex consisting of the San Luis Hotel, the Hilton Galveston Island Resort, the San Luis Condominiums, the Sealy Mansion, and eight restaurants. The resort offers a spa and fitness center, the perfect way to warm up and relax on a winter day. If you're in the mood for a more historic hotel, look to one of Galveston's grande dames. **The Hotel Galvez** (2024 Seawall Blvd.; 409-765-7721, 877-999-3223), known as the "Queen of the Gulf," opened a 9,000-square-foot spa and workout facility in the spring of 2008. On The Strand, the **Tremont House** (2300 Ship's Mechanic Row; 409-763-0300, 877-999-3223) is a favorite for guests looking for European-style luxury just steps from the shopping and entertainment district.

Many of Galveston's hotels and resorts are located in walking distance of its excellent restaurants. Fresh Gulf seafood is the specialty at many restaurants—shrimp, oysters, and fresh fish prepared in a variety of ways fill the menus.

For more information on Galveston, call the Convention and Visitors Bureau at (866) 505-4456 or go online to www.galveston.com.

Appendix

# LIVING HERE

In this section we feature specific information for residents or those planning to relocate here. Topics include real estate, education, health care, and much more.

# RELOCATION

**If you're moving to San Antonio, most people would assure you that it's a fine place to live, and its uniqueness only adds spice to the experience. These million-plus people are descendants of Canary Islanders, Scots, Germans, and tough-as-an-old-boot Texians who came to the frontier to make a new life in the American West. A great many of them are Hispanic, ranging from the "Green Card" ranch worker to the third-generation CEO, or Slavic and Asian refugees who fled political strife. Some are international scholars and medical students here for top-flight training or an opportunity for research. A surprising number of sons and daughters return to San Antonio after college or another sojourn, rejoining multiple generations who decided for themselves to stay in their earlier years. Many are members of the military and military retirees who have come back "home." San Antonio's mild winters also lure a lot of "snowbirds."**

**People continue coming to San Antonio because of the educational opportunities, an appetite for authentic tortilla soup, a love of bluebonnets in the spring, and the migrating monarch butterflies in October. They enjoy the easy fellowship of strangers here, the happy abandon of countless festivities, and the grandeur of centuries past integrated into the present.**

## OVERVIEW

San Antonio isn't for everyone, of course. Some people just don't acclimate to the more relaxed lifestyle. Others pine for a city with more sophistication, greater wealth, and a more liberal mind-set. (San Antonio is undeniably conservative, less moneyed than, say, Chicago or Boston, and generally casual in attitude.)

Additionally, the weather in this colorful community is just plain hot in the summer. Some people don't want to deal with the high mercury readings. Residents don't like it much, either, but the public buildings, our homes, buses, cars, and taxis are air-conditioned, often for months on end. In truth, it's occasionally hot as late as November. In December it's not uncommon to see people wearing shorts and washing their cars near Christmastime (many people find this one of the city's more attractive features). Nor is it uncommon to see residents battle sleet on the freeway in December. San Antonio weather is simply fickle.

Beyond the weather, people—whether they love the city or not—will tell you that San Antonio does have affordable housing and utilities (even in the summer), superior medical care, multiple educational opportunities, and an impressive array of leisure opportunities. Additionally, geography finds San Antonio within a few hours of surf, sand, and sport fishing on the coast to the southeast and about the same distance from the lure of an international border at Laredo to the southwest.

If you're considering retirement here, you'll find the city more accommodating than most, possibly because the large number of military retirees have already paved the way for abundant services and housing options (three of the largest independent-living facilities are military-related). Quality medical care is a given, whether the source is military or civilian.

One final attribute appeals to both retirees and new residents for another reason: Family and friends will enjoy visiting you here. Between the Alamo, SeaWorld, day trips to Mexico or the Hill Country, Fiesta Week, and Christmas lights on the River Walk, how can they resist?

Then it will be your turn to extol the virtues and idiosyncrasies of this fascinating city.

## NEIGHBORHOODS & DISTRICTS

### King William District

One of the earliest neighborhoods in San Antonio grew up on the land surrounding the San Antonio de Valero, the Alamo. Settled by Spanish missionaries, this territory soon gave rise to the King William District, built on mission land that was sold at a public auction. Settled in the 1840s by German immigrants, many of them merchants, this region became known as "Sauerkraut Bend" to San Antonio residents outside the neighborhood. For years this was considered the most cosmopolitan neighborhood in the city, with tree-lined streets, beautiful mansions, and homes built as investments by the wealthy merchants.

King William eventually fell into disrepair and remained run-down until downtown living was again in vogue. In 1967 King William was designated the first Historic Neighborhood District in Texas, thanks to the many 19th-century mansions and structures here that had been restored to their original grandeur. Today the district is again one of San Antonio's most desirable addresses, either for a permanent home or for a temporary residence in one of the neighborhood's elegant bed-and-breakfast inns.

### Government Hill

Beyond King William's boundaries, northeast of downtown, lies another historic section of town known as Government Hill. This area is adjacent to Fort Sam Houston, home to military personnel from around the world who train for military combat medicine. Around the fort stand numerous historic buildings.

### Tobin Hill

Just west of Government Hill stands the neighborhood of Tobin Hill, a favorite with college students and faculty from the University of the Incarnate Word, Trinity University, and San Antonio College. Located at St. Mary's and Josephine Streets, this district is lively with restaurants, theaters, and a diversity of cultures. The neighborhood is home to St. Sophia Greek Orthodox Church, Our Lady of Sorrows, and numerous other houses of worship that have served neighborhood residents for generations. The district is also the site of Brackenridge Park. Many homes in this area are newly renovated. Another revitalized neighborhood is Monticello, once considered San Antonio's rural cousin, with its numerous dairy and goat farms. Development came in the 1920s with a crop of architecturally diverse homes in styles including Colonial,

Monterey, French Revival, Tudor, Art Deco, and Mediterranean. Also architecturally noteworthy are the public buildings in this neighborhood; the centerpiece of the district is Thomas Jefferson High School, built in 1929 at a cost of $1.2 million. The building is a miniature version of Spain's Alhambra and once appeared on the covers of *Life* and *National Geographic* magazines.

## Prospect Hill

West of downtown lies Prospect Hill. Originally populated primarily by German immigrants, it later became primarily Hispanic. Comedienne Carol Burnett, actress Carol Channing, and former San Antonio mayor and HUD secretary Henry Cisneros grew up here. Prospect Hill remained a middle-class neighborhood until nearby Kelly Air Force Base declined; today it is home to only a few of the young families who once resided there to be close to the base. However, the neighborhood is now experiencing a revitalization of sorts.

## Ellis Alley

East of downtown is Ellis Alley, one of the first San Antonio neighborhoods to be settled by African-American residents following the Civil War. The area was long home to many African-American–owned newspapers, nightclubs, restaurants, and other businesses. Located east of the Alamodome, the neighborhood's centerpiece is the 1902 Sunset Depot; the train station now is a collection of nightclubs and restaurants. One historic structure that retains its original use is St. Paul United Methodist Church, established in 1866. This is the oldest African-American church in San Antonio.

## Alamo Heights

Within San Antonio's boundaries also lie several neighborhoods that are officially separate municipalities. One of these neighborhood/cities is Alamo Heights, which occupies most of the residential areas off Broadway. This beautiful, wealthy community was originally a project of the Alamo Heights Land and Improvement Company of Texas. Starting in 1890 with a private waterworks, a few streets, and some parks, the developers waited for growth that never came due to the neighborhood's distance from downtown. The company failed, and the development was later taken over by more successful companies, which by 1922 had the benefit of the automobile to bring residents to this neighborhood. Today Alamo Heights has its own independent school district and is home to the University of the Incarnate Word.

## Olmos Park

Another historic neighborhood/city is Olmos Park, located southeast of Alamo Heights. The city was incorporated in the 1940s, when it had a population of 1,822 residents, a number that nearly doubled by the 1950s. Today the number of Olmos Park residents is lower than it was during that peak period. The residential neighborhood's property values remain high, however; the average price for a single-family dwelling is $626,000.

## Universal City

On the east side of San Antonio near Randolph Air Force Base stands Universal City, a community that primarily serves the base. Property values remain modest here, with single-family houses averaging under $143,000.

## Bexar County

In all, 21 incorporated cities including San Antonio lie within Bexar County, which covers 1,247 square miles. Bexar County residents pay property tax at approximately 57 cents per $100 valuation at 100 percent market value. The school districts all have their own rates, as do the incorporated cities. For the City of San Antonio, the rate is approximately 58 cents per $100.

**i** If you spot Michael Nesmith Street in a Leon Valley neighborhood, you might be interested to know the street name is a tribute to the former Monkees rocker. His uncle helped develop Leon Valley.

## REAL ESTATE

The San Antonio real estate picture has been excellent in recent years, thanks to corporate relocations, including Toyota. Some of that growth can be attributed to the city's relatively low cost of living. According to the latest *Kiplinger's Personal Finance* magazine's research, San Antonio's cost of living score of 93 is well below the national average (100). Home prices in San Antonio also compare very favorably with other cities across the nation. A $110,400 home in San Antonio would sell for $143,300 in Phoenix, $156,000 in Austin/San Marcos, and $379,320 in San Diego, according to the Association of Applied Community Researchers (ACCRA). The median price of a new home in San Antonio is $110,400. In short, home prices here run 29 percent below the national median and are available at less than half the cost of comparable housing in New England and some California cities. An additional bonus is that the homes are large and solidly constructed because the city offers an abundance of building materials, labor, and land plus an extended building season.

The northern sector of the city, particularly the northwest side, is enjoying the fastest growth. Also growing rapidly is the north-central area, including the I-10 and I-35 corridors. Now, with Toyota locating a plant on the south side, growth is picking up there, as well.

San Antonio is also home to many subdivisions. In the north-central portion of town, these include Canyon Rim, Champions Ridge, Champion Springs, Mesa Verde, Mesa Vista, and Mountain Lodge. Additional up-and-coming subdivisions include Lookout Canyon, Stonewall Ranch, and the Heights at Palisades. Many of these areas south of Loop 1604 are gated communities.

In the northwest portion of town near the South Texas Medical Center, subdivisions include Chase Oaks and the Retreat at Oak Hills inside Loop 1604. Outside Loop 1604, areas include Shadow Canyon, Canyon Park Estates, Fossil Springs Ranch, Helotes Park Terrace, and Retablo Ranch. Some of these communities are gated.

**i** Within the city, much of I-10 West actually runs north or northwest.

In the north-central section of the city, several subdivisions have been constructed outside Loop 1604 in recent years, including Encino Mesa, Encino Ranch, Encino Rio, Evans Ranch, Fossil Creek, Redland Heights, Remington Heights, The Terraces of Encino, and Verde Mountain Estates. The north-central area also has subdivisions at Olympia, Olympia Oaks, Woodland Oaks, Jonas Woods, Woodridge, Deer Creek (in Cibolo), Greenshire, and Forrest Ridge. Inside the Loop, real estate buyers find houses at subdivisions such as Redland Estates and Stafford Heights South.

On the west side of the city, subdivisions have been constructed near the theme parks and the Air Force bases; these include Westover Hills, Legacy Trails, Westcreek, El Sendero of Westlakes, Retreat at Oak Hills, Sunset, and the Heights of Westover Hills. East of the city, subdivisions near Randolph Air Force Base include Arroyo Verde, Trails of Deer Creek, and Oak Trail Estates. Real estate also is strong in the multifamily market. On average, the city has a 93.9 percent occupancy level for apartments and multifamily dwellings. Although rent is on the rise in San Antonio, at 83 cents per square foot, it remains lower than that of many other metropolitan cities in the state, such as Dallas, which rents at 89 cents per square foot, and Austin, at 95 cents per square foot. A two-bedroom apartment rents for an average of $938 per month.

## REAL ESTATE AGENCIES

**BEST HOMES REALTY**
**11845 I-10 West, Suite 406**
**(210) 691-4622**
**www.reallivingsa.com**

Best Homes Realty, part of the national Real Living network, provides a full line of real estate services ranging from marketing new and pre-owned homes to worldwide relocation. This firm includes a Luxury Homes Division that showcases luxury properties to provide broad exposure to a global audience.

**BRADFIELD PROPERTIES**
**18830 Stone Oak Pkwy.**
**(210) 340-6500, (210) 496-4949**
**www.bradfieldproperties.com**

A San Antonio business since 1982, Bradfield Properties is active in the San Antonio, Boerne, Bulverde, and New Braunfels real estate markets. The firm has 8 regional real estate offices with approximately 250 agents. Included in its services are property management, corporate listings, business brokerage, and more.

**CENTURY 21 REAL ESTATE**
**14235 Blanco Rd.**
**(210) 408-1177**
**www.century21.com**

With 9 offices in San Antonio, Century 21 offers a full range of real estate services, including proprietary marketing tools to provide maximum services for purchasing a home, and relocation services to help sell homes across the US and abroad. This office also offers Century 21 Connections, which can provide discounted storage facilities, free installation of security systems, and more.

**COLDWELL BANKER D'ANN HARPER, REALTORS**
**7523 NW Loop 1604**
**(210) 483-6400**

Recognized by Coldwell Banker Real Estate Corporation in 2002 for outstanding achievement, this company represents buyers in San Antonio, Boerne, and New Braunfels and participates in transactions on both a national and international level. Properties it handles range from the middle of the market to the premier upper-tier market.

**KELLER WILLIAMS/LEGACY GROUP**
**1102 E. Sonterra Blvd., #106**
**(210) 482-3200**
**www.sanantoniorealestatevalues.com**

Specializing in residential properties, the agents at the Legacy Group are experts in helping first-time buyers and families relocating to San Antonio. The firm has over 30 years of experience in the San Antonio area.

**KUPER REALTY CORPORATION**
**6606 N. New Braunfels Ave.**
**(210) 822-8602**
**http://kuperrealty.com**
Founded in 1972, Kuper Realty Corporation is affiliated with Sotheby's. Locally, Kuper operates 3 offices with more than 100 professional sales associates. It offers a farm and ranch brokerage, residential brokerage, and relocation divisions. Kuper is a leader in upscale realty and provides virtual tours on its website.

**PHYLLIS BROWNING COMPANY**
**6101 Broadway**
**(210) 824-7878, (800) 266-0676**
**www.phyllisbrowning.com**
Phyllis Browning Company started out in 1989 with 5 people and 31 property listings between them. Today the company is among San Antonio's 10 largest residential real estate companies, with 3 office locations and over 150 agents, showing San Antonio residences, Hill Country homes, and South Texas ranch properties.

**RE/MAX ASSOCIATES INC.**
**300 E. Sonterra Blvd., Suite 1180**
**(210) 340-3000, (888) 209-2001**
**www.remaxa2734.remaxtexas.com**

**RE/MAX NORTHEAST REALTORS**
**4655 Walzem Rd.**
**(210) 590-5000**
**http://greatersanantoniohomes.com**
Focusing on the city's northeastern sector, this firm does business in all the surrounding communities as well. Among the areas represented are Helotes, Schertz, Medina, Devine, Canyon Lake, Kirby, Somerset, and other communities. The company offers both commercial and residential properties, including condos and garden homes, plus new and pre-owned homes.

## INFORMATION FOR NEWCOMERS

If you're new to the San Antonio area, here are some things you should know:

### Pet Licenses

Vaccinations and licenses for dogs and cats are required by the City of San Antonio. If your pet has a current vaccination certificate, bring it to the Animal Control Services at 4710 Highway 151 (210-207-4PET) or fax to ACS at (210) 207-6673. You can also obtain a pet license from a local veterinarian when the pet is vaccinated. Animal Control Services periodically sponsors vaccination clinics, where pets can receive shots at a reduced rate. Also note that San Antonio has a leash law, so your pet must be either on a leash or in a fenced yard.

### Animal Defense League of Texas

Looking for a loyal canine companion or a faithful feline friend? Check out the Animal Defense League of Texas (210-655-1481; www.adltexas.org), the Southwest's largest no-kill, nonprofit animal shelter. In operation since 1934, the shelter is located on over 12 acres of land at 11300 Nacogdoches Rd. Adoption costs $90 for pets under the age of four months, $65–$70 for those over the age of four months.

**i** The San Antonio Chamber of Commerce maintains an online directory of real estate agencies at www.sachamber.org.

## Auto & Driver's Licenses

Permanent residents of Texas must obtain a Texas driver's license and Texas license plates within 30 days of arrival. For more information, call the Motor Vehicle Registration Department at (210) 335-2251. Thereafter, registration must be renewed annually, which can be handled by mail, allowing two weeks for delivery. License tags also can be purchased at Bexar County Tax Offices, located on the north side at 3370 Nacogdoches Rd., on the south side at 660 SW Military Dr., on the northwest side at 8407 Bandera Rd., and downtown at 233 N. Pecos La Trinidad. Renewals may also be made at any H-E-B market in Bexar County. If you already have a current driver's license from another state, you need take written, driving, and vision tests to obtain a Texas driver's license. For test locations, look in the telephone book "blue" pages under Texas Department of Public Safety. Driver's licenses cost $25 and are issued for six years.

## Auto Insurance

In Texas, automobiles must be covered by minimum limits of liability insurance in accordance with the Texas Motor Safety Responsibility Act of 1981. Minimum limits are $25,000–$50,000 bodily injury liability and $25,000 property damage liability. These are required for any licensed motor vehicle. Current proof of financial responsibility is required (usually auto insurance) to obtain or renew a driver's license, to register a car, and upon issuance of a vehicle inspection sticker.

## Auto Inspection

Auto inspections are required and must be completed before registering the auto in Texas or obtaining a Texas license plate. Vehicle inspections are conducted at some local gas stations and cost $14.50 for one year or $23.75 for two years.

**i** To connect city utilities, just dial 311. This 24-7 service also allows existing city-service customers to report anything from potholes to graffiti and to ask questions about recycling regulations and removal of dead animals.

## Religious Organizations

For information on churches, contact the San Antonio Community of Congregations (210-733-9159; www.sacoc.info) or refer to the telephone numbers of denominational executive offices below.

- **Christian (Disciples of Christ)**—(210) 822-4345
- **Church of God (Spanish)**—(210) 310-2194
- **Episcopal**—(210) 824-5387
- **Jewish Federation**—(210) 302-6960
- **Latter-Day Saints**—(210) 538-0034
- **Lutheran**—(210) 951-3478
- **Nazarene**—(210) 342-7406
- **Presbyterian (USA)**—(210) 826-3296
- **Roman Catholic**—(210) 734-2620
- **Southern Baptist**—(210) 525-9954
- **United Church of Christ**—(210) 403-9084
- **United Methodist**—(210) 408-4500

## Registering to Vote

You may register to vote as soon as you arrive in San Antonio either by going to the Bexar

County Elections Department, 203 W. Nueva, or the Bexar County Voter Registration Office at 233 N. Pecos La Trinidad, Suite 350 or by calling (210) 335-VOTE to ask that a registration form be mailed to you. You may vote in any election 30 days after your register.

**i** Trash pickup begins one week after your new electrical service is turned on.

### Low Water Crossings

Low water crossings are marked by a larger rulerlike device sticking out of the ground. Drivers are urged, especially in sudden and violent thunderstorms during spring and fall, to heed these warnings. Because of the intensity of these storms, many areas and roads flood quickly. Cars often stall in these low water crossings, and people have been swept to their deaths by swift currents. Also, drivers not heeding low water crossing barricades can be ticketed and fined, and a driver needing rescue after driving past a low water crossing barricade will be billed for the cost of the emergency rescue.

## ECONOMIC & DEMOGRAPHIC INFORMATION

**ECONOMIC RESEARCH DEPARTMENT GREATER SAN ANTONIO CHAMBER OF COMMERCE**
602 E. Commerce St.
(210) 229-2100
www.sachamber.org

**NORTH SAN ANTONIO CHAMBER OF COMMERCE**
12930 Country Pkwy.
(210) 344-4848
www.northsachamber.com

**ALAMO CITY BLACK CHAMBER OF COMMERCE**
600 HemisFair Plaza Way, Building 406-10
(210) 226-9055
www.alamocitychamber.org

**AFRICAN AMERICAN CHAMBER OF COMMERCE**
1717 N. Loop 1604 East, Suite 220
(210) 490-1624
www.aaccsa.com

**RANDOLPH METROCOM CHAMBER OF COMMERCE**
9374 Valhalla, Selma
(210) 658-8322
www.randolphmetrocomchamber.org

**SAN ANTONIO HISPANIC CHAMBER OF COMMERCE**
200 E. Grayson, Suite 203
(210) 225-0462
www.sahcc.org

**SAN ANTONIO WOMEN'S CHAMBER OF COMMERCE**
600 HemisFair Plaza Way, Building 514
(210) 299-2636
www.sawomenschamber.org

**SOUTH SAN ANTONIO CHAMBER OF COMMERCE**
7902 Challenger Dr.
(210) 533-1600
www.southsachamber.org

## AREA SUPPORT GROUPS

**ALAMO AREA PARKINSON'S SUPPORT GROUP**
(210) 450-0551

**AL-ANON FAMILY GROUPS**
(210) 829-1392

**ALCOHOLICS ANONYMOUS**
(210) 828-6235

**BETTER BREATHERS CLUB**
(210) 826-4000

**BREAST CANCER HELPLINE**
(210) 692-9535

**CAREGIVERS INFORMATION AND FELLOWSHIP**
(210) 681-2975

**COMMUNITY BASED PREVENTION SERVICE (FAMILY VIOLENCE)**
(210) 733-8810

**DELTA SOCIETY PET GRIEF SUPPORT GROUP**
(210) 216-0920

**GRIEF SUPPORT GROUP (BRIDGES BEYOND GRIEF)**
(210) 497-8166

**HOPE HOSPICE COMMUNITY BEREAVEMENT PROGRAM**
(830) 625-7500

**LOW VISION SUPPORT GROUP**
(210) 334-1479

**MULTIPLE SCLEROSIS PEER SUPPORT (COMMON GROUND)**
(210) 286-7744

**SAN ANTONIO AREA WIDOWED PERSONS SERVICE**
(210) 754-9726

**SUBSTANCE ABUSE OUTPATIENT COUNSELING**
(210) 731-1320

## RESOURCES FOR RESEARCH

**DAUGHTERS OF THE REPUBLIC OF TEXAS RESEARCH LIBRARY**
The Alamo
300 Alamo Plaza
(210) 225-1071
www.drtl.org

**INSTITUTE OF TEXAN CULTURES**
801 E. Durango Blvd.
(210) 458- 2228
www.texancultures.utsa.edu

**SAN ANTONIO CENTRAL LIBRARY**
600 Soledad St.
(210) 207-2500
www.mysapl.org

**SAN ANTONIO CONSERVATION SOCIETY**
107 King William St.
(210) 224-6163
www.saconservation.org

# EDUCATION & CHILD CARE

San Antonio's educational heritage is as old as the city itself. A mission-based educational system was used by the founding Spanish as a necessary first step in colonizing the New World. Their plan called for Spanish missionaries to convert enough native people to establish Spanish Christianity in the region. Thus schools for the native inhabitants were of supreme importance, as education was the means to win the hearts and minds of the indigenous peoples. The friars who were first in charge of these mission schools were Franciscans from the competing colleges of Zacatecas and Queretaro in Mexico.

The first attempt to found a traditional school for San Antonio's settlers' sons in 1798 did not succeed, as there was little support for it. The boys it attempted to teach were mainly occupied, as was the town as a whole, with the more basic activities of survival on the frontier. In 1803 a future signer of the Texas Declaration of Independence, José Francisco Ruiz, was appointed schoolmaster, but his school did not last long either. Considering the city's strong Catholic heritage, it is no surprise that the city's first true educational institution, the Ursuline Academy for girls, was founded in 1851 by seven Ursuline nuns. There the Academy stayed until 1965, when new facilities were constructed on the city's northwest side. Its former campus, designed by San Antonio architect Francois Giraud, is now the site of the Southwest School of Art (SSA). The buildings, restored by the SSA, are now listed on the National Register of Historic Places.

Modern-day San Antonio now boasts five fully accredited universities, numerous seminaries, branch locations of several universities, an extensive community college system, 15 public school districts, several private schools and academies, and numerous preschools and child care centers.

## HIGHER EDUCATION

### OUR LADY OF THE LAKE UNIVERSITY

**411 SW 24th St.**
**(210) 434-6711, (800) 436-6558**
**www.ollusa.edu**

Another Catholic institution of higher education, Our Lady of the Lake was founded as a private school for girls in 1895. It was chartered by the state in 1919 and was opened to both men and women in 1969. The university's Old Main building, completed in 1895, has long been admired for its Victorian Gothic architecture, as has the Gothic Chapel (1923), designed by Leo M. J. Dielmann, which features stairs of Italian marble and stained-glass windows. Current enrollment of the university is 2,750 students. Our Lady of the Lake awards bachelor's degrees in some 33 areas of study and master's degrees in 14; it also offers 2 doctorates. It receives accolades for 2 of its programs, the Worden School of Social Service and the Harry Jersig Speech and Hearing Center. Its popular Weekend College and evening programs offer degrees in several areas.

**ST. MARY'S UNIVERSITY**
**1 Camino Santa Maria**
**(210) 436-3011, (800) FOR-STMU**
**www.stmarytx.edu**

This university traces its roots to St. Mary's Institute, established in San Antonio in 1852 by brothers of the Society of Mary. Recognized by the State of Texas in 1897, the institution, renamed St. Mary's College, grew rapidly after the turn of the century. It eventually was divided into 3 major schools: arts, sciences, and business. In 1927 it began operating as St. Mary's University.

St. Mary's University now has an enrollment of nearly 4,000 students and includes 5 schools: the School of Humanities and Social Sciences; the School of Science, Engineering, and Technology; the Bill Greehey School of Business; the School of Law; and the Graduate School. In addition to bachelor's degrees, master's degrees and doctorate degrees are also offered in some fields. St. Mary's law library is the largest legal information center in San Antonio.

**TRINITY UNIVERSITY**
**1 Trinity Place**
**(210) 999-7011, (800) TRINITY**
**www.trinity.edu**

Although Trinity traces its roots in Texas to 3 small Presbyterian institutions founded before the Civil War (making it one of the oldest universities in the state), the university itself was moved to San Antonio from Waxahachie in 1942 and to its current site in 1945. The striking campus skyline with its familiar bell tower can be seen from many areas of town. Architects O'Neil Ford and Bartlett Cocke designed the campus buildings using the revolutionary Youtz-Slick system of construction, which uses prefinished concrete floor slabs.

No longer a religious institution, Trinity now describes itself as a "professionally oriented liberal arts university." Its current student body of 2,600 consists mostly of undergraduate students. The university is consistently ranked as one of the top colleges in *US News & World Report.*

**i** **The University of Texas at San Antonio's independent student newspaper, *The Paisano,* is a weekly source for campus events.**

**UNIVERSITY OF TEXAS AT SAN ANTONIO**
**1 UTSA Circle (Main Campus)**
**(210) 458-4011**
**www.utsa.edu**

Part of the huge state university system, UTSA was established in 1973 and now has an enrollment of over 30,000 students. It offers 63 bachelor's, 49 master's, and 22 doctoral degrees. The main campus is located on the northwest side of the city; a smaller downtown campus was opened in 1997.

**UNIVERSITY OF TEXAS HEALTH SCIENCE CENTER**
**7703 Floyd Curl Dr.**
**(210) 567-7000**
**www.uthscsa.edu**

Another institution of higher learning located on San Antonio's northwest side, the University of Texas Health Science Center serves the city and South Texas. In addition to its main campus, it has campuses in Laredo and the Rio Grande Valley. More than 3,000 students a year train at the center, which is affiliated with more than 100 hospitals, clinics, and health care facilities in South Texas.

**UNIVERSITY OF THE INCARNATE WORD**
**4301 Broadway**
**(210) 829-6000, (800) 749-WORD**
**www.uiw.edu**
In 1884 San Antonio's first hospital, Santa Rosa Hospital, was founded by the Sisters of Charity of the Incarnate Word, a French order. The same order also founded a school on land bought from the Colonel George W. Brackenridge family. The university now has more than 7,000 students, many of whom are attracted by the strong nursing program here. The university offers degrees in some 70 subject areas. Its Adult Degree Completion Program is designed to make it easier for students to complete unfinished college degrees. Its other unique degree programs include music therapy and sports management.

## Community Colleges

The Alamo Community College District (210-485-0000; www.alamo.edu) has five separate campuses:

**NORTHEAST LAKEVIEW COLLEGE**
**1201 Kitty Hawk Rd., Universal City**
**(210) 486-5000**
**www.alamo.edu/nlc**
Located in Universal City, just northeast of San Antonio, Northeast Lakeview College is a 245-acre campus with 9 academic buildings. It enrolls more than 5,200 students working toward associate of arts, associate of science, associate of arts in teaching, or associate of applied science degrees.

**NORTHWEST VISTA COLLEGE**
**3535 N. Ellison Dr.**
**(210) 486-4000**
**www.alamo.edu/nvc**
This campus serves the city's northwest area. Students earn associate's degrees in the fields of business, government, humanities, fine arts, natural, physical, and social sciences as well as technical programs.

**PALO ALTO COLLEGE**
**1400 W. Villaret Blvd.**
**(210) 486-3000**
**www.alamo.edu/pac**
This campus, which opened in 1985, serves San Antonio's south side with more than 8,000 students enrolled in courses in agribusiness, aviation, engineering, social sciences, veterinary science, and industrial technology.

**ST. PHILLIPS COLLEGE**
**1801 Martin Luther King Dr.**
**(210) 486-2000**
**www.alamo.edu/spc**
St. Phillips College dates back to 1898, when it was founded as an Episcopal girls' school in La Villita. Now part of the Alamo Community College District, it offers courses on a variety of technical specialties via a nationally known program in computer-assisted instruction. The campus is located on the east side of downtown San Antonio.

**SAN ANTONIO COLLEGE**
**1300 San Pedro Ave.**
**(210) 486-0000**
**www.alamo.edu/sac**
With an enrollment of over 24,000, SAC is the largest institution in the city's community college system. It has both an Arts and Sciences division and a Professional and Technical Education division and offers classes both day and night. Telecourses and Internet courses are also available.

Also located in San Antonio are:

**BAPTIST UNIVERSITY OF THE AMERICAS**
**8019 S. PanAm Expy.**
**(210) 924-4338, (800) 721-1396**
**www.bua.edu**

**OBLATE SCHOOL OF THEOLOGY**
**285 Oblate Dr.**
**(210) 341-1366**
**www.ost.edu**

**TEXAS A&M UNIVERSITY—SAN ANTONIO**
**1450 Gillette Blvd.**
**(210) 932-6299**
**www.tamusa.tamus.edu**

**UNIVERSIDAD NACIONAL**
**Autónoma de Mexico**
**600 HemisFair Plaza Way**
**(210) 222-8626**
**www.unamsanantonio.unam.mx**

**WAYLAND BAPTIST UNIVERSITY**
**11550 I-35 North**
**(210) 826-7595**
**www.sa.wbu.edu**

**WEBSTER UNIVERSITY**
**(open to military and civilians)**
**www.webster.edu/sanantonio**

**CAMP BULLIS**
**Camp Bullis Training Site RR2**
**HQ Camp Bullis, Building 5000**
**(210) 226-3373**

**FORT SAM HOUSTON**
**2408 N. New Braunfels Ave., Suite 30**
**(210) 226-3373**

**LACKLAND AIR FORCE BASE**
**1550 Wurtsmith St.**
**(210) 674-0014**

## PUBLIC SCHOOLS

A wide range of school districts serves the city of San Antonio, including several that serve only students who reside on the many military bases located in San Antonio. Each district has an elected board and a superintendent, who is appointed. Each child must attend school in the district where his or her family resides. To enter 1st grade, a child must be 6 years old on or before September 1. Kindergarten is optional. Buses are provided to transport most children to and from school but do not cross district boundaries. Some schools, such as magnet schools or specialized schools, accept students from other districts.

Several local districts are noteworthy for their size or academic excellence. Northside Independent School District is the sixth-largest school district in Texas. North East Independent School District has been praised by several local publications as being a superior school district. East Central High School in the East Central district achieved "Recognized School" status with the Texas Education Agency due to its low dropout rates, high student test scores, and high attendance numbers. Collier Elementary in Harlandale Independent School District has been placed among the top 1 percent of elementary schools in the country by the US Department of Education.

To enroll your child in a San Antonio public school, contact your local school district. When you take your child to register, make sure that you bring your child's birth certificate, immunization records, Social Security number, and proof of residence.

## School Districts

### ALAMO HEIGHTS INDEPENDENT SCHOOL DISTRICT

**7101 Broadway**
**(210) 824-2483**
**www.ahisd.net**

In 1909 a two-room schoolhouse was built in a rural community, the area that is now known as Alamo Heights. The Alamo Heights Independent School District was officially created in 1923, with a total of 300 students.

In 1938 the athletic stadium was constructed by the Work Projects Administration, part of President Franklin D. Roosevelt's New Deal program to help pull the US out of the Great Depression. After World War II the community of Alamo Heights became a suburb of San Antonio. The district almost doubled in size in the few years following the war, thanks to the baby boom. The building that is today Alamo Heights High School was finished in 1950, but not before housing a number of different schools. Today's Alamo Heights Independent School District covers 9.4 square miles; contains 2 elementary schools, 1 junior high school, and 1 high school; and enrolls about 4,600 students, including kindergarten and pre-K students. The neighborhoods served by this school district are Alamo Heights, Terrell Hills, Olmos Park, and part of north San Antonio.

### EAST CENTRAL INDEPENDENT SCHOOL DISTRICT

**6634 New Sulphur Springs Rd.**
**(210) 648-7861**
**www.ecisd.net**

Serving more than 9,000 students, East Central Independent School District has 1 high school, 2 middle schools, 5 elementary schools, 2 intermediate schools, and an early childhood development center. East Central is affiliated with the East Central School Foundation Inc., a nonprofit organization that raises money to help promote public education programs in the district. Funds raised by the foundation go to computer software and equipment in the schools, alternative education programs, library materials, college scholarships for district students, and other programs that benefit the schools and students.

### EDGEWOOD INDEPENDENT SCHOOL DISTRICT

**5358 W. Commerce St.**
**(210) 444-4500**
**www.eisd.net**

With 15,000 students, Edgewood Independent School District is made up of 14 elementary schools and 8 secondary schools, including Wrenn Junior High, John F. Kennedy High School, Memorial High School, and a unique Fine Arts Academy. Students from district high schools can apply to enroll in the curriculum at the academy, which includes advanced classes in theater, music, video production, dance, and the visual arts.

### FORT SAM HOUSTON INDEPENDENT SCHOOL DISTRICT

**1902 Winans Rd., Fort Sam Houston**
**(210) 368-8741**
**www.fshisd.net**

Created in 1951, this school district serves the area around Fort Sam Houston Army Post in the northeast portion of the city. The student body includes 1,300 military dependents who live on the post. The school district is composed of 1 elementary school, 1 middle school, and Robert G. Cole High School.

**HARLANDALE INDEPENDENT SCHOOL DISTRICT**
**102 Genevieve St.**
**(210) 989-4300**
**www.harlandale.net**

There are 13 elementary schools, 4 middle schools, 2 high schools, 1 center for special needs students, and 2 alternate educational centers in the Harlandale Independent School District, which serves 14,000 students. The Harlandale district's Collier Elementary has been awarded Blue Ribbon status by the US Department of Education. This distinction placed Collier Elementary among the top 4 percent of elementary schools in the US. Harlandale ISD is affiliated with the Harlandale Education Foundation, whose aim is to ensure that every Harlandale district graduate receives at least $1,000 in financial aid for higher education at any type of institution.

**JUDSON INDEPENDENT SCHOOL DISTRICT**
**8012 Shin Oak Dr., Live Oak**
**(210) 945-5100**
**www.judsonisd.org**

Serving more than 22,000 students, Judson ISD is one of the area's fastest-growing school districts. As the fourth-largest district in Bexar County, it draws students from the communities of Converse, Kirby, and Selma, plus portions of Live Oak, San Antonio, Schertz, and Universal City. Judson, located in the northeastern sector of greater San Antonio, offers both a solid academic program and a wide variety of extracurricular activities.

**LACKLAND INDEPENDENT SCHOOL DISTRICT**
**2460 Kenly Ave., Lackland Air Force Base**
**(210) 357-5000**
**www.lacklandisd.net**

Created in 1953, this school district serves Lackland Air Force Base and the children who live on the base. The district consists of 1 elementary school and Stacy Junior-Senior High School, with a total of 900 students.

**NORTH EAST INDEPENDENT SCHOOL DISTRICT**
**8961 Tesoro Dr.**
**(210) 407-0000**
**www.neisd.net**

North East Independent School District encompasses 144 square miles of the San Antonio area. More than 63,000 students attend 44 elementary schools, 13 middle schools, 8 high schools, and 12 magnet school programs. North East School District has been praised as "one of the city's public-school gems" by the *San Antonio Express-News*. It has also been placed among the top 100 school districts in the country by *Money Magazine*. North East boasts a National Exemplary After-School Program at every elementary school and most middle schools through its Community Education Department.

**NORTHSIDE INDEPENDENT SCHOOL DISTRICT**
**5900 Evers Rd.**
**(210) 397-8500**
**www.nisd.net**

More than 94,000 students attend schools in the Northside Independent School District, whose boundaries encompass 355 square miles of the San Antonio area. If the enrollment count seems high to you, you're right. Northside is the fourth-largest independent school district in Texas. The area is growing at an astounding rate—over 3,000 new students arrive in Northside every year.

In addition to 15 traditional high schools the district also has 4 magnet high schools focusing on business careers, health careers, and communication arts, plus the Jay Science and Engineering Academy.

**i** Parents can learn the latest news from Northside Independent School District by listening to *Inside Northside Radio,* a half-hour, biweekly radio program available on the school district's website (www.nisd.net) or as a free subscription podcast.

### RANDOLPH FIELD INDEPENDENT SCHOOL DISTRICT

**Randolph Air Force Base, Universal City**
**(210) 357-2300**
**www.randolph-field.k12.tx.us**

This public school district serves 1,200 students, the children of military personnel living on Randolph Air Force Base. Randolph Field ISD is composed of 1 elementary school, 1 middle school, and 1 high school.

### SAN ANTONIO INDEPENDENT SCHOOL DISTRICT

**141 Lavaca St.**
**(210) 554-2200**
**www.saisd.net**

Established in 1899, San Antonio Independent School District is the 13th-largest school district in Texas. SAISD encompasses 79 square miles and serves 55,000 students. San Antonio ISD students come from the city and also the cities of Olmos Park and Balcones Heights and other parts of Bexar County. There are 95 schools in the district, including 52 elementary schools, 14 middle schools, 8 high schools, and 4 alternative schools. The ethnic makeup of San Antonio Independent School District's student body is as diverse as the city itself: 89.5 percent are of Hispanic origin, 7.4 percent are African American, and 2.7 percent are Caucasian. Fewer than 1 percent of the students are Asian or Pacific Islanders or American Indian. SAISD offers its students the chance to attend any of 13 magnet schools at the high school level. Each magnet school focuses on a particular area of study such as science, engineering, and technology; manufacturing; language immersion; or media production.

### SCHERTZ-CIBOLO-UNIVERSAL CITY INDEPENDENT SCHOOL DISTRICT

**1060 Elbel Rd., Schertz**
**(210) 945-6200**
**www.scuc.txed.net**

Located in a fast-growing 73 square-mile area on the city's northeast fringe, this district serves the communities of Schertz, Cibolo, Universal City, Selma, Converse, St. Hedwig, and Randolph Air Force Base. Its 12,000 students attend 7 elementary schools, 3 intermediate schools that house the district's 5th and 6th graders, 2 junior high schools, and 3 high schools. The district also holds a charter for an International Baccalaureate (IB) diploma program.

### SOUTH SAN ANTONIO INDEPENDENT SCHOOL DISTRICT

**5622 Ray Ellison Dr.**
**(210) 977-7000**
**www.southsanisd.net**

The South San Antonio Independent School District (locally referred to as "South San") has 1 high school, 4 middle schools, and 10 elementary schools and serves almost 10,000 students. This district offers several specialized programs, including an English as a second language (ESL) program and a special education program. South San Antonio ISD also has a department specializing in deaf education.

**i** Keep informed of all the area high school sports action as well as band and cheerleading events at www.sasports.com, which offers comprehensive online coverage for over 100 South Texas schools.

### SOUTHSIDE INDEPENDENT SCHOOL DISTRICT
**1460 Martinez Losoya Rd.**
**(210) 882-1600**
**www.southsideisd.org**

With over 5,000 students, this district includes, 4 elementary schools, an intermediate school, a middle school, and a high school. There is also an alternative education placement center. Special programs offered at Southside ISD include English as a second language (ESL), accelerated math and reading programs, and special education.

### SOUTHWEST INDEPENDENT SCHOOL DISTRICT
**11914 Dragon Lane**
**(210) 622-4300**
**www.swisd.net**

Southwest Independent School District contains 9 elementary schools, 3 middle schools, and 1 high school. The district covers a 115 square-mile area, is a mixture of urban, suburban, and rural areas in southwestern Bexar County, and educates 11,000 students.

## PRIVATE SCHOOLS & ACADEMIES

### THE CARVER ACADEMY
**217 Robinson Place**
**(210) 223-8885**
**www.carveracademy.org**

The Carver Academy opened just east of downtown in the fall of 2001 as the dream of David Robinson, retired center for the San Antonio Spurs. Robinson pledged $9 million of his own money to start this 501(c)(3) school, which is designed to serve elementary-age students from a culturally diverse community. The core curriculum focuses on excellence in reading and language arts, social studies, mathematics, science, technology, fine arts, athletics, and foreign languages, including German, Japanese, and Spanish.

### CATHOLIC SCHOOLS OF SAN ANTONIO
**Archdiocese of San Antonio**
**2718 W. Woodlawn Ave.**
**(210) 734-2620, ext. 232**
**www.sacatholicschools.org**

Given San Antonio's strong ties to the Catholic Church, it's not surprising that the city and the surrounding areas are home to numerous Catholic schools. The Archdiocese of San Antonio runs 30 elementary and 12 secondary schools. The schools are located within the city of San Antonio as well as in the nearby communities of Castroville, Converse, Del Rio, Floresville, Fredericksburg, Kerrville, New Braunfels, Seguin, Selma, and Uvalde. All of the schools are accredited through the Texas Catholic Conference Education Department. Particularly noteworthy among the schools are Incarnate Word, Antonian, Central, Saint Anthony's, and Providence.

**CORNERSTONE CHRISTIAN SCHOOLS**
**4802 Vance Jackson**
**(210) 979-6161, (210) 979-9203**
**www.sa-ccs.org**

Cornerstone Schools were organized as a ministry of San Antonio's huge Cornerstone Church. Located just outside Loop 1604 on the far north side, they include an elementary school, middle school, and high school. Among the electives offered to middle and high school students are music (chorus and band), Spanish, chapel, Bible studies, and athletics.

**KEYSTONE SCHOOL**
**119 E. Craig Place**
**(210) 735-4022**
**www.keystoneschool.org**

Keystone targets academically motivated and talented students in grades K through 12. Located in the historic Monte Vista neighborhood, it offers an accelerated curriculum, small classes, and experienced teachers. The campus includes a library, lab, theater, art studio, and athletic facilities.

**ST. MARY'S HALL**
**9401 Starcrest Dr.**
**(210) 483-9100**
**www.smhall.org**

Since 1879 this coeducational independent school, affiliated with the American Montessori Society and accredited by the Independent Schools Association of the Southwest, has offered day-school programs. Admission to the school is limited and selective, so the school recommends an early application. The program covers preschool through grade 12. The school offers a variety of special programs, including visual and performing arts and athletics, as well as a standard curriculum.

**SAN ANTONIO ACADEMY**
**117 E. French Place**
**(210) 733-7331**
**www.sa-academy.org**

San Antonio Academy accepts boys from pre-K through 8th grade. The interdenominational school aims to teach students values such as integrity, character, and spirituality, while providing a challenging curriculum. Classes at San Antonio Academy are small: There are 345 students and 37 full-time teachers, which means a 10-to-1 student-to-teacher ratio. The school is accredited by the Independent Schools Association of the Southwest.

**i** Texas students take the Texas Assessment of Knowledge and Skills (TAKS) test in each year during grades 3 to 11. It must be passed before high school graduation. The test includes sections on English language, math, science, and social studies.

**SAN ANTONIO CHRISTIAN SCHOOLS**
**19202 Redland Rd.**
**(210) 340-1864**
**www.sachristianschools.org**

Founded in 1968, SACS teaches 4-year-olds through 12th graders. Representing youngsters from more than 125 local churches, the students come from all ethnic, social, and economic backgrounds. One interesting facet of the SACS program is the long history of actively supporting missions. High schoolers have traveled on mission trips to the Dominican Republic, Haiti, Russia, and Africa.

**TEXAS MILITARY INSTITUTE**
**20955 W. Tejas Trail**
**(210) 698-7171**
**http://community.tmi-sa.org**

TMI provides day school for students in grades 6 through 12, and 5-day and 7-day Residential Life programs for youngsters in grades 9 through 12. Founded in 1893, it is the oldest Episcopal Church–sponsored college preparatory school in the Southwest. In addition to providing students with solid academics, TMI also boasts a nationally recognized Junior Reserve Officer Training Corps (JROTC). Other features include summer sports camps open to all students and summer school for TMI students.

**Parents of children with disabilities can call Any Baby Can (210-227-0170; www.anybabycansa.org) for assistance. The program helps the families of children who suffer from chronic illness or have special needs.**

**THE WINSTON SCHOOL SAN ANTONIO**
**8565 Ewing Halsell**
**(210) 616-6544**
**www.winston-sa.org**

This is an accredited, nonprofit, private school for children in grades K through 12 of average to superior intelligence who have learning differences. WSSA is geared to provide a college preparatory curriculum and is not an alternative curriculum for students whose primary disabilities are behavioral, emotional, or the result of limited intellectual potential.

## CHILD CARE CENTERS

Many San Antonio day-care centers offer kids—and their parents!—field trips, meals, and activities that are both fun and educational. There are many child care businesses in the San Antonio area, and we've been able to list only a few in this book. Parents can consult the San Antonio Yellow Pages to find the complete listing of centers in the city. We also strongly encourage parents to personally inspect the child care centers they are interested in and to interview the centers' personnel. There are also several child care referral services in San Antonio (usually free) to help parents select day care for their children. The Children Resources Division (210-246-5276) at 1222 N. Main Ave. and the Family Service Association of San Antonio (210-657-6278), which has several locations around San Antonio, can recommend child care services.

**BUTTONS-N-BOWS**
**9035 Huebner Rd.**
**(210) 690-6093**

Buttons-N-Bows has been in business for more than 25 years. This day-care and after-school program accepts infants through age 12. It aims to provide a Christian education to children attending both the day-care and after-school programs. The center is open from 6:30 a.m. to 6:30 p.m. Mon through Fri, and staff will pick up children from area schools.

**COUNTRY HOME LEARNING CENTER**
**Various locations**
**(210) 692-7205**
**www.countryhomelearningcenter.com**

These centers provide infants to 13-year-olds with unique day-care and after-school programs. Children who attend have the opportunity to learn dance, gymnastics, Spanish, computer literacy, and music and to ride horses. The classes here are very small, so each child receives individual attention. Kids have access to a computer lab, arts and crafts center, library, gymnasium, and Montessori centers. Visit the website for a list of locations.

**THE GODDARD SCHOOL**
**21785 Hardy Oak**
**(210) 494-2779**
**www.goddardschool.com**
Mom and Dad receive a daily activity report when picking up their little one at The Goddard School, which offers half- and full-day programs for infants, toddlers, pre-kindergarten, and kindergarten-age children. Art projects and computer games stimulate the minds of children who arrive at the child care center after school, while summertime means visits to area zoos and museums.

**KINDERCARE**
**Various locations**
**www.kindercare.com**
These centers offer both day-care and after-school programs. Kids attending KinderCare after school can be transported to and from schools in the area. The preschool program helps kids start reading at an early age. Most locations of KinderCare accept children from 6 weeks to 12 years, although some do not accept infants. All participants are served meals and snacks that are good for them. Visit the website for a list of locations.

**LA PETITE ACADEMY**
**Various locations**
**www.lapetite.com**
Full-day and half-day care and before- and after-school programs are offered at La Petite. For kids who attend school, transportation to and from school is available. Summer programs are also offered. Ages vary by location, as do opening and closing hours. La Petite Academy has 15 locations in the San Antonio area; check the Yellow Pages or the website for a complete list.

**LUV-N-CARE**
**Various locations**
**www.luvncarecenters.com**
These centers accept children from birth to age 13. Full- and part-time day care and before- and after-school programs are offered. Luv-N-Care also offers a summer camp program and a private kindergarten program. There is a swimming pool at each location, and extracurricular activities include piano, computer literacy, gymnastics, and dancing. Visit the website for a list of locations.

**A PLACE FOR KIDS CHRISTIAN LEARNING CENTER**
**6011 Grissom Rd.**
**(210) 680-5474**
**www.apkchristianlearningcenter.com**
Infants through preschool kids are welcome at this center, which offers Christian learning programs. Small classes ensure that every child gets individual attention. Instruction in areas as diverse as computers and gymnastics is provided. Full summer programs are available. A Place for Kids is open from 6:30 a.m. to 6:30 p.m.

**QUALITY KIDS CHILD CARE**
**5520 Eckhert Rd.**
**(210) 690-5050**
Located adjacent to the South Texas Medical Center, Quality Kids tends youngsters from infancy through age 12. Offering care from 6 a.m. to 6:30 p.m., it provides breakfast, field trips, and a large shaded playground for outdoor activities. Additionally, Quality Kids has a swimming pool (and certified lifeguard) on premises for swimming and swim lessons at no additional cost. Summer programs are available.

# HEALTH CARE & WELLNESS

**San Antonio's medical industry ranks among the best in Texas and in the Southwest, offering world-class training and treatment facilities. In fact, the industry serves as San Antonio's largest moneymaker, joining the booming tourism business and the steady military world as the city's top industries. A payroll topping $6.5 billion keeps 141,251 members of San Antonio's work force (one-sixth of the city's total work force) employed while more than $18.9 billion is added to the region's local economy thanks to the medical business. On the treatment end, San Antonio attracts patients from across the US and beyond, especially Mexico. And more than 40 countries regularly send physicians, dentists, and others in the medical field to the city for training.**

## EMERGENCY SERVICES

All the local public hospitals are equipped with emergency rooms. Major medical services can also be obtained there. For information on treatment facilities throughout the city, contact the Bexar County Medical Society, (210) 301-4368.

## SOUTH TEXAS MEDICAL CENTER

The area's largest concentration of health facilities is in the South Texas Medical Center. Located in the northwest portion of the city, this center spans more 900 acres and is home to 12 of the city's major hospitals as well as almost 80 clinics. The center includes the Audie Murphy Branch of the South Texas Veterans Health Care System, Christus Santa Rosa Medical Center, five hospitals in the Methodist Healthcare System, St. Luke's Baptist Hospital, University Hospital, and Warm Springs Rehabilitation Hospital. An estimated 26,000 employees work in the Medical Center, which operates with a combined budget of more than $2 billion. The University of Texas Health Science Center at San Antonio (UTHSCSA) is the core of the Medical Center, housing five professional medical schools covering both patient care and research. The schools award more than 50 degrees and professional certificates including doctor of medicine, doctor of dental surgery, and doctor of philosophy in nursing. The dental school is frequently cited as one of the country's best.

The center is also noted for its excellent cancer care and research facilities. The Cancer Therapy and Research Center, along with the UT Health Science Center, make up the San Antonio Cancer Institute, or SACI, which is noted for both its outpatient services and its research in the areas of breast cancer, cancer prevention, and molecular genetics.

Through the years, the South Texas Medical Center's resources have grown dramatically. A $50 million Children's Cancer Research Institute at UTHSCSA is just one addition.

San Antonio's military medical facilities also draw worldwide attention. Brooke Army Medical Center at Fort Sam Houston is one of the top burn hospitals in the world and also serves as a trauma center and a cancer center. Wilford Hall Medical Center is the largest medical facility of the US Air Force. In addition to medical and dental education, it provides a quarter of San Antonio's emergency medical care.

## HOSPITALS

### AUDIE L. MURPHY MEMORIAL VETERANS HOSPITAL

**7400 Merton Minter Blvd.**
**(210) 617-5300**
**www.southtexas.va.gov**

This 462-bed facility provides patient care, including geriatric care in its federally funded Geriatric Research, Education, and Clinic Center. The hospital is also home to one of the world's largest fungus-identification and -testing labs.

### BAPTIST MEDICAL CENTER

**111 Dallas St.**
**(210) 297-7000**
**www.baptisthealthsystem.com**

Baptist Medical Center is a 654-bed hospital located near the center of San Antonio, within walking distance of the River Walk. It offers complete cardiac care, a sophisticated level of peripheral vascular services, and maternal and newborn care, including a neonatal intensive care unit. Surgical and medical inpatient and outpatient care are offered here, as well as a large dialysis unit, gastrointestinal lab, an adult behavioral health center, emergency department, and other services of a general, acute care hospital. Its campus includes the Baptist Cancer Center, 2 medical office buildings connected by a climate-controlled walkway, and the Institute of Health Education. The communications center for San Antonio AirLife air medical transport system is located on the 6th floor of Baptist Medical Center.

In *US News & World Report*'s first-ever Best Hospitals metro area rankings in 2011, Baptist Health System was ranked as high-performing in more areas than any other San Antonio hospital. Baptist Health System hospitals were deemed high-performing in 9 adult specialties, including cancer; ear, nose, and throat; gastroenterology; geriatrics; gynecology; kidney disorders; neurology and neurosurgery; orthopedics; and pulmonology care.

### BROOKE ARMY MEDICAL CENTER—SAN ANTONIO MILITARY MEDICAL CENTER

**Fort Sam Houston**
**(210) 916-4141**
**http://sammc.amedd.army.mil**

This military center is housed in a 1.5 million-square-foot facility located at Fort Sam Houston. The 450-bed hospital is best known for its burn treatment and research, but it also provides primary care to more than 640,000 military personnel, both active duty and retired. The center also serves as a trauma center and a cancer research facility, conducting numerous research projects and anticancer drug trials.

**i** San Antonio has been a major center for military medicine since the first hospital was built at Fort Sam Houston in the late 1870s. Several of San Antonio's military bases have medical museums (see the Military chapter for details).

## CHRISTUS SANTA ROSA CHILDREN'S HOSPITAL (CSRCH)

**333 N. Santa Rosa St.**
**(210) 704-2011**
**www.christussantarosa.org**

Located in downtown San Antonio, CSRCH serves children from a 90-county area. The hospital is one of only a few children's hospitals in Texas, and was the first hospital in Texas entirely dedicated to the care of children. CSRCH is affiliated with the University of Texas Health Science Center at San Antonio and is recognized as a premier academic children's hospital. It is also a member of the Children's Hospital Association of Texas and the National Association of Children's Hospitals and Related Institutions. From neonatal intensive care to children's emergency services to titanium rib implants, CHRISTUS Santa Rosa provides innovative care specifically designed for children.

## CHRISTUS SANTA ROSA HOSPITAL—DOWNTOWN (CSRH)

**333 N. Santa Rosa St.**
**(210) 704-2011**
**www.christussantarosa.org**

Opened in 1869 as San Antonio's first private hospital, CSRH now has 2 locations, one in downtown San Antonio and one in the South Texas Medical Center. The centrally located downtown campus provides a full range of services for adults, including award-winning cardiac services, operating rooms, ICUs, and cardiac catheterization suites; a comprehensive cancer program in association with the Cancer Therapy and Research Center; complete obstetrical and newborn services, including the LifeCycles program; a wide range of inpatient and outpatient surgical services; a diabetes care program; a Dialysis Access Center; and 24-hour emergency services.

## CHRISTUS SANTA ROSA HOSPITAL—MEDICAL CENTER (CSRMC)

**2827 Babcock Rd.**
**(210) 705-6300**
**www.christussantarosa.org**

Licensed as part of CSRH and located in the South Texas Medical Center in northwest San Antonio, the hospital was established in 1986 and provides an array of specialty hospital services for adults. CSRMC is the site of the CHRISTUS Transplant Institute, which specializes in kidney, heart, and heart/lung transplantation. CSRMC also has particular strengths in cardiac services, orthopedic care and joint replacement, diabetes care/endocrinology, nephrology, and surgical services. The 24-hour emergency room was replaced in spring 2004 with a larger facility to allow more people to be served more efficiently. A full complement of physical rehabilitation services is also available at CSRMC with personalized inpatient and outpatient physical rehabilitation treatment provided for patients who have suffered stroke, spinal cord injuries, closed head injuries, neurological disorders, amputation, multiple trauma, and chronic pain.

## METHODIST AMBULATORY SURGERY HOSPITAL

**9150 Huebner Rd.**
**(210) 575-5000**
**www.sahealth.com**

Specializing in selective inpatient, outpatient, and day surgery, the Methodist Ambulatory Surgery Hospital offers 10 fully equipped operating rooms and 1 cystoscopy suite. This 37-bed facility offers patients the latest technology and many services usually associated with larger, full-service hospitals but on a smaller, more personalized scale.

**METHODIST CHILDREN'S HOSPITAL OF SOUTH TEXAS**
**7700 Floyd Curl Dr.**
**(210) 575-7000**
**www.sahealth.com**

Opened in October 1998, this 129-bed hospital features a 24-hour pediatric emergency room, pediatric and neonatal intensive care units, pediatric operating suites, children's imaging diagnostic services, and special outpatient clinics for children with complex diagnoses and chronic illnesses such as cystic fibrosis and brain tumors. The hospital houses San Antonio's largest private neonatal intensive care unit with 46 beds. A nurse triage line, Call-A-Nurse for Children (210-22-NURSE), operates 24 hours a day, 7 days a week, and provides free advice, in English or Spanish, from pediatric nurses.

**METHODIST HEART HOSPITAL**
**7700 Floyd Curl Dr.**
**(210) 575-6800**
**www.saheart.net**

Methodist Heart Hospital pioneered many firsts in cardiac care, including the first balloon angioplasty in the region in 1981, the region's first heart valve transplant, and the first live broadcast of a beating-heart bypass operation. Methodist Heart Hospital, like the Methodist Children's Hospital, is located on the same campus as Methodist Hospital, which is the cornerstone of the complex.

**METHODIST HOSPITAL**
**7700 Floyd Curl Dr.**
**(210) 575-4000**
**www.sahealth.com**

Methodist Hospital is San Antonio's largest private hospital. The facility opened in 1963 and today offers 683 beds. The flagship of the Methodist Healthcare System, the hospital has several specialty areas including blood and marrow stem cell transplants, oncology, cardiology, orthopedics, neurology, and women's services. Another unique facility is its Gamma Knife Center, opened in 1998. The first of its kind in South Texas, the center specializes in noninvasive radiological treatment of brain tumors and neurological disorders. More than 2,000 physicians practice at Methodist Hospital.

**METHODIST SPECIALTY AND TRANSPLANT HOSPITAL**
**8026 Floyd Curl Dr.**
**(210) 575-8110**
**www.sahealth.com**

This 379-bed facility has received widespread acclaim for its transplant programs, which include kidney, kidney/pancreas, heart, and liver. Specialty areas include inpatient and outpatient rehabilitation, behavioral health, and the latest treatments for cancer, impotency, incontinence, and gastroenteric disorders. The Methodist Cancer Center is also located within this hospital and offers specialized care for patients with all types of cancer. The facility also houses a program in which a specially trained team works with law enforcement officers to provide care for survivors of sexual assault. The hospital is the only one in San Antonio with 3 dedicated state-of-the-art surgical suites for laparoscopic surgeries.

**METHODIST TEXSAN HOSPITAL**
**6700 I-10 West**
**(210) 736-6700**
**www.methodisttexsanhospital.com**

Methodist Texsan Hospital (formerly Texsan Heart Hospital) is a 190,000-square-foot, 3-story hospital designed for 120 beds. Opened in early 2004, this facility has 4 operating suites, 4 cardiac catheterization labs, a 10-bed day patient area, and a cardiovascular and chest pain referral center/emergency department. Other features include a rooftop helipad and underground parking area. The hospital campus is located in central San Antonio inside Loop 410 (southwest corner of the I-10 and Loop 410 interchange).

**i** Each year over 10,000 babies are delivered at Methodist Hospital. The hospital's one-hour Peek-A-Boo tour offers expectant parents a look at various areas of the maternity ward, including the delivery room, the family waiting area, the second-floor newborn nursery, and the mother/baby unit.

**METROPOLITAN METHODIST HOSPITAL**
**1310 McCullough Ave.**
**(210) 208-2200**
**www.sahealth.com**

Located near downtown San Antonio, Metropolitan Methodist Hospital is a 339-bed acute care facility providing a complete range of health care services to San Antonio and the many neighborhoods and businesses that border its centralized location. Metropolitan Methodist Hospital offers mother and baby care, general medical and surgical care, neurosurgery, cardiac care, oncology, behavioral health, inpatient and outpatient rehabilitation, sleep disorders evaluation, and a 24-hour emergency department. It was among the first hospitals in the country to introduce a bar-coded electronic medication distribution method.

**NIX MEDICAL CENTER**
**414 Navarro St.**
**(210) 271-1800**
**www.nixhealth.com**

The central facility for the Nix Health Care System is the Nix Medical Center, a 24-story building in downtown San Antonio. Operating since 1930, the hospital (locally referred to as "the Nix") accommodates full medical, surgical, and geropsychiatric capabilities; outpatient and ancillary services; and acute care. The Heritage Center provides inpatient geropsychiatric care, and the Skilled Nursing Care service extends hospital care for patients who require skilled nursing but no longer need full hospital services.

**NORTH CENTRAL BAPTIST HOSPITAL**
**520 Madison Oak Dr.**
**(210) 297-4000**
**www.baptisthealthsystem.com**

This 126-bed hospital is a growing facility in a fast-growing area of the city. Home to the Baptist Regional Children's Center, North Central Baptist Hospital offers adult and pediatric emergency care, neurosciences, and maternal and newborn care. Also available are surgical and medical inpatient and outpatient care, a growing cardiac service, and other services of a general acute care hospital. Two medical office buildings are connected to the hospital by a climate-controlled walkway.

**NORTHEAST BAPTIST HOSPITAL**
**8811 Village Dr.**
**(210) 297-2000**
**www.baptisthealthsystem.com**

This 291-bed hospital in the northeast part of San Antonio launched a major building program in 2004 to add needed emergency and maternity beds. Northeast Baptist Hospital offers complete cardiac care, maternal and newborn care including a neonatal intensive care unit, surgical and medical inpatient and outpatient care, emergency department, and other services of a general acute care hospital.

**NORTHEAST METHODIST HOSPITAL**
**12412 Judson Rd.**
**(210) 757-7000**
**www.sahealth.com**

With 153 beds, Northeast Methodist Hospital is a full-service acute care facility convenient to those living in northeast San Antonio and neighboring areas. Northeast Methodist Hospital offers a 24-hour emergency room, cardiovascular services, oncology services, rehabilitation and physical therapy, the Breast Care Center, behavioral health care, and a Wellness Center.

**ST. LUKE'S BAPTIST HOSPITAL**
**7930 Floyd Curl Dr.**
**(210) 297-5000**
**www.baptisthealthsystem.com**

Located in the South Texas Medical Center, St. Luke's Baptist Hospital is a 291-bed facility. Its Women's Center offers all private rooms to new mothers and a neonatal intensive care unit. St. Luke's provides full orthopedic care for bones and joints and complete cardiac care. Also available are surgical and medical inpatient and outpatient care, geriatric behavioral health center, emergency department, and other services of a general acute care hospital.

**SOUTHEAST BAPTIST HOSPITAL**
**4214 E. Southcross Blvd.**
**(210) 297-3000**
**www.baptisthealthsystem.com**

Serving as the only hospital in the southeast quadrant of the city, the 181-bed Southeast Baptist Hospital is poised for tremendous expansion as this area prepares to welcome significant business and household growth. An international staff provides expertise in minimally invasive surgery, growing cardiac services, maternal and newborn care, surgical and medical inpatient and outpatient care, emergency department, and other services of a general acute care hospital.

**SOUTHWEST GENERAL HOSPITAL**
**7400 Barlite Blvd.**
**(210) 921-2000**
**www.swgeneralhospital.com**

Southwest General Hospital was started by a group of predominantly Hispanic physicians who believed a large number of people on the south side were unable to access health care because of deficiencies in San Antonio's infrastructure. The hospital opened in 1979 and continues today as a well-respected acute care facility with 289 licensed beds. Southwest houses BirthPlace, a state-of-the-art maternity center; the Wound Care Center; a skilled nursing facility; the Rehabcentre; and Southwest Imaging Center.

**UNIVERSITY HOSPITAL**
**4502 Medical Dr.**
**(210) 358-4000**
**www.universityhealthsystem.com**

The centerpiece for the South Texas Medical Center, University Hospital is the primary teaching hospital for the residency program at the University of Texas Health Science Center at San Antonio (UTHSCSA). A Level 1 trauma center, University is the home of many "firsts" for South Texas, including the first heart, heart-lung, and lung transplants and the first newborn heart transplant. This 604-bed facility is also noted for neonatology, pediatric cardiac surgery, rehabilitation services, fetal diagnostic services, and organ and bone marrow transplantation.

### WARM SPRINGS REHABILITATION HOSPITAL

**5101 Medical Dr.**
**(210) 616-0100, (800) 741-6321**
**www.warmsprings.org**

Warm Springs Rehabilitation Hospital uses an interdisciplinary team approach in both its inpatient and outpatient facilities that includes physical medicine and rehabilitation physicians, physical therapists, occupational therapists, speech pathologists, rehabilitation technicians, and rehabilitation nurses. These professionals combine their skills to provide both adults and children with comprehensive services for brain injury, spinal cord injury, orthopedic conditions, amputation, stroke, and neurological disorders. The hospital is located in the Medical Center, with clinics in southeast, northeast, northwest, and north-central San Antonio.

### WILFORD HALL AMBULATORY SURGICAL CENTER

**2200 Bergquist Dr., Lackland Air Force Base**
**(210) 292-7100**
**www.whmc.af.mil**

The largest medical center operated by the US Air Force, this facility serves as a primary-care facility, a trauma center, and an educational facility for physicians and dentists. More than 65 percent of the physicians in the US Air Force are trained at this facility, along with 85 percent of the force's dental specialists. Research projects are also conducted here in the areas of hyperbaric procedures, hypobaric procedures, bone-marrow transplant, and organ transplant.

## PUBLIC HEALTH CARE

Public health assistance is provided through the **San Antonio Metropolitan Health District** at 332 W. Commerce St. (210-207-8780; www.sanantonio.gov/health). This governmental agency promotes health care throughout Bexar County in areas including disease control, family health services, environmental health, and dental health. The district operates many public health clinics that offer a variety of services. Some provide walk-in immunizations, sexually transmitted disease diagnosis and treatment, substance-abuse treatment, administration of the Women, Infants, and Children Nutrition Program (WIC), and HIV testing and counseling. Not all services are available at all locations. Public clinics include:

### BUENA VISTA CLINIC

**2315 Buena Vista St.**
**(210) 225-0213**

### CALLAGHAN CLINIC

**4412 Callaghan Rd.**
**(210) 436-5042**

### DORIE MILLER CENTER

**2802 Martin Luther King Dr., No. 3**
**(210) 359-8882**

### ENVIRONMENTAL HEALTH WELLNESS CENTER

**911 Castroville Rd.**
**(210) 434-0077**

### FREDERICKSBURG CLINIC

**3600 Fredericksburg Rd.**
**(210) 738-3486**

### IMMUNIZATION CENTER

**345 W. Commerce St.**
**(210) 207-8894**

**KENWOOD CLINIC**
**302 Dora St.**
**(210) 644-8000**

**MARBACH CLINIC**
**7452 Military Dr.**
**(210) 645-4480**

**OLD HIGHWAY 90 CLINIC**
**911 Old Highway 90**
**(210) 644-8050**

**PECAN VALLEY CLINIC**
**802 Pecan Valley Dr.**
**(210) 337-7511**

**RITTIMAN CLINIC**
**1013 Rittiman Rd.**
**(210) 207-4750**

**SOUTH FLORES CLINIC**
**7902 S. Flores St.**
**(210) 644-8100**

**TUBERCULOSIS CLINIC**
**814 McCullough Ave.**
**(210) 207-8823**

**WEST END HEALTH CENTER**
**1226 NW 18th St.**
**(210) 644-8400**

**ZARZAMORA CLINIC**
**4503 S. Zarzamora St.**
**(210) 644-8600**

## MINOR EMERGENCY CLINICS

### Texas MedClinics

These privately owned clinics are open seven days a week from 8 a.m. to 11 p.m. to treat sprains, minor fractures, earaches, allergies, urinary tract infections, and other minor emergencies. Some locations are open Christmas and Thanksgiving.

**BLANCO CLINIC (NORTH-CENTRAL)**
**11811 Blanco Rd. at Parliament**
**(210) 341-5588**

**BROADWAY CLINIC (NORTH-CENTRAL)**
**1007 NE Loop 410**
**(210) 821-5598**

**EISENHAUER CLINIC (NORTHEAST)**
**7460 I-35 North**
**(210) 655-5529**

**INGRAM CLINIC (NORTHWEST)**
**6570 Ingram Rd.**
**(210) 520-5588**

**SOUTHEAST MILITARY DRIVE CLINIC (SOUTH-CENTRAL)**
**1111 SE Military Dr.**
**(210) 927-5580**

**WURZBACH CLINIC (NORTH-NORTHWEST)**
**9895 I-10 West at Wurzbach Road**
**(210) 696-5599**
**www.texasmedclinic.com**

## REFERRAL AGENCIES

**BEXAR COUNTY MEDICAL SOCIETY**
**6243 I -10 West, Suite 600**
**(210) 301-4391**
**www.bcms.org**
Need a doctor? If you're new in town and you don't know where to start, give this number a call for a referral in the specialty you seek.

**SAN ANTONIO DISTRICT DENTAL SOCIETY**
**3355 Cherry Ridge, #214**
**(210) 732-1264**
**www.sadds.org**
Like the medical society housed at the same address, this referral agency helps match

patients and doctors, in this case, dentists. The agency can help you find a dentist that meets your needs, whether that means one at a convenient location or one with a particular medical specialization.

## RESOURCES

**UNITED WAY OF SAN ANTONIO AND BEXAR COUNTY**
**700 S. Alamo St.**
**(210) 352-7000**
**www.unitedwaysatx.org**
This agency publishes *The Community Assistance Directory,* which lists nonprofit health, welfare, recreational, and educational resources for the community. You can obtain a copy of this publication by calling the office or ordering it by mail.

## SPECIALIZED HEALTH CARE PROGRAMS

### AIDS/HIV Care

The following facilities offer a wide range of services, including medical and dental care and referrals, psychiatric counseling and support groups, education and prevention programs, HIV testing, assistance with applications for governmental aid, legal assistance, referrals for rental and utility assistance, meals, and food pantries. Not every clinic offers all these services; call for details.

**ALAMO AREA RESOURCE CENTER**
**527 N. Leona St.**
**(210) 358-9995**
**www.aarcsa.com**

**ELLA AUSTIN HEALTH CENTER**
**1920 Burnet St.**
**(210) 434-0513**

**GAY AND LESBIAN COMMUNITY CENTER OF SAN ANTONIO**
**611 E. Myrtle St.**
**(866) 223-6106**

**HOPE, ACTION, CARE**
**132 W. Grayson St.**
**(210) 224-7330**
**www.hopeactioncare.org**

**SAN ANTONIO AIDS FOUNDATION (SAAF)**
**818 E. Grayson St.**
**(210) 225-4715**
**www.txsaaf.org**

**SOUTH TEXAS AIDS CENTER FOR FAMILIES AND CHILDREN**
**7271 Wurzbach Rd.**
**(210) 567-7400**

**TEXAS DEPARTMENT OF HEALTH**
**Public Health Region 8**
**7210 W. Olmos Dr.**
**(210) 821-5522**
**www.dshs.state.tx.us**

**UNIVERSITY HEALTH SYSTEM**
**4502 Medical Dr.**
**(210) 358-4000**
**www.universityhealthsystem.com**

### Mental Health

**CENTER FOR HEALTH CARE SERVICES**
**3031 I-10 West**
**(210) 731-1300**
**www.chcsbc.org**
This agency operates four mental-health programs covering substance abuse, mental retardation, mental health, and residential programs. Referrals are made on weekdays; for emergency referrals, call the Crisis Stabilization Unit at (210) 223-SAFE.

## Poison Center

### SOUTH TEXAS POISON CENTER
**(800) 222-1222**
**www.texaspoison.com**

Questions about poison control? Call the South Texas Poison Center for information on poisoning prevention and treatment for poisoning victims, animals included. They also deal with overdoses, snake bites, identification of pills, and toxic plants. The phone is answered daily around the clock, and assistance can be received in English, Spanish, or TDD for hearing-impaired callers. Interpreters are available for other languages.

## Therapeutic Programs

### CAMP CAMP
**2525 Ladd St.**
**(210) 671-5411**
**www.campcamp.org**

Camp CAMP (Children's Association for Maximum Potential) provides a wide range of recreational, rehabilitative, and respite services for severely disabled children and their families throughout the summer during 1-week residential camping sessions. Because CAMP serves children unable to attend other camps because of medical or physical conditions, medical personnel make up approximately 20 percent of the staff, with volunteer nurses and doctors assigned to each camp group.

### SADDLE LIGHT CENTER FOR THERAPEUTIC HORSEMANSHIP
**17560 Old Evans Rd., Selma**
**(210) 651-9574**
**www.thesaddlelightcenter.com**

The Saddle Light Center, located at the Retama Polo Park, provides equestrian therapy for children, teenagers, and adults with a wide range of disabilities, including neurological, orthopedic, learning, and emotional disabilities. The center is a member of the North American Riding for the Handicapped Association.

### THERAPEUTIC RECREATION PROGRAM
**San Antonio Parks and Recreation Program**
**1226 NW 18th St.**
**(210) 207-3018**
**www.sanantonio.gov/parksandrec**

Operating at the Garrett Community Center, the Therapeutic Recreation Program offers numerous activities, special events, and programs, including the BlazeSports Club for youth with physical disabilities. The program also offers wheelchair sports activities for adults through special events and cooperative efforts with other agencies.

### WARM SPRINGS REHABILITATION SYSTEM
**5101 Medical Dr.**
**(210) 616-0100**
**www.warmsprings.org**

Warm Springs Wheelchair Sports offers a surprisingly extensive slate of sports programs for teens and adults. Among the sports are archery, basketball, golf, hand cycling, hockey, scuba, and tennis. The football program often grabs public notice with the intense Spoke Bender Bowl, which is reputed to be as rough and physical as any sport can get.

# RETIREMENT

With its high standard of living, favorable cost of living when compared with many other cities its size, and good climate, San Antonio is considered one of Texas's top retirement spots. The San Antonio Chamber of Commerce estimates that retirees make up about 15 percent of the city's population. Many are active participants in the city's art scene, ecotourism, volunteerism, and employment worlds.

Many of San Antonio's retired residents live in the northwest portion of the city, at the entrance to the Hill Country. The northwest communities of Bandera and Kerrville are especially popular with active retirees who enjoy a small-town atmosphere. North of Austin, and about 90 minutes from San Antonio, Sun City Georgetown (www.delwebb.com) offers an extensive retirement community akin to Arizona and Florida's Sun City facilities.

## HOUSING

### Independent Living

**AIR FORCE VILLAGE I AND II**
**5100 John D. Ryan Blvd.**
**(800) 762-1122**
**www.airforcevillages.com**

The villages are designed for retired military officers and their spouses, with priority given to officers' widows and widowers in need of financial assistance. The villages give the residents access to continuing health care, as well as several conveniences.

**CHANDLER RETIREMENT APARTMENTS**
**137 W. French Place**
**(210) 737-5247**
**www.mmliving.org**

**THE MEADOWS RETIREMENT COMMUNITY**
**730 Babcock Rd.**
**(210) 737-1300**

Both the Chandler and the Meadows are part of Morningside Ministries, which also offers assisted living, nursing home, and home care. Independent living arrangements include cottages, apartments, or townhouse dwellings, all with optional services.

**THE MADISON ESTATES**
**8645 Fredericksburg Rd.**
**(210) 694-7000**
**www.holidaytouch.com**

The Madison provides a hot tub, billiard room, in-house beauty salon, pool, panic button, exercise room, and other amenities.

**TIMBERHILL VILLA**
**5050 Timberhill**
**(210) 684-3480**
**www.timberhillvilla.com**

Timberhill offers its residents the typical services, plus a few more—such as a travel agency—that you might not expect. Located in northwest San Antonio, Timberhill also offers covered parking for residents with vehicles.

**THE TOWERS ON PARK LANE**
**1 Towers Park Lane**
**(210) 822-8722, (800) 531-8496**
**www.thetowersonparklane.com**
The Towers on Park Lane offers high-end services that include a concierge, a pedestrian mall, elegant meals in the Gardenia Room, and a deli.

## Assisted Living

**BROOKDALE LIVING**
**Sterling House of Maltsberger**
**13303 Jones Maltsberger Rd.**
**(210) 561-9500**

**STERLING HOUSE AT THE MEDICAL CENTER**
**5996 Whitby Rd.**
**(210) 551-9500**

**STERLING HOUSE OF NEW BRAUNFELS**
**2457 Loop 337, New Braunfels**
**(830) 606-5300**

**CLARE BRIDGE MEMORY CARE**
**14595 Nacogdoches Rd.**
**(210) 653-6100**
**www.brookdaleliving.com**
Living at Alterra comes with several residential options, with different locations for assisted living and one that specializes in memory care. The Sterling Houses provides an intimate setting for those with limited mobility, as well as specialized programming to help residents maximize independence and quality of life. Clare Bridge Memory Care provides an environment that minimizes confusion and agitation.

**EMERITUS AT AMBER OAKS**
**4415 Rio D'Oro**
**(210) 653-3132**
**www.emeritus.com**
Amber Oaks is among the largest assisted-care facilities in San Antonio. It has a "comprehensive care plan" that regularly monitors care plans, and increases or decreases assistance as appropriate.

**INDEPENDENCE HILL AT STONE OAK**
**20450 Huebner Rd.**
**(210) 615-4000**
**www.independencehill.com**
Independence Hill is an assisted living community located north of Loop 1604. It is billed as providing "a loving and caring environment" complete with transportation, three daily meals, planned activities, and a wellness program.

# SENIOR RESOURCES

**CITY OF SAN ANTONIO ELDERLY AND DISABLED SERVICES**
**700 S. Zarzamora St., Suite 205**
**(210) 207-7172**
**www.unitedwaysatx.org/WOC/WOCC.html**
This department offers five services: a comprehensive nutrition program, supportive services for the elderly, a city homemaker program, a client-managed program, and a personal-attendant services program. Funded by the City of San Antonio General Fund, the Alamo Area Council of Governments, the Texas Department of Human Resources, and the Texas Rehabilitation Commission, the agency works to better

the lives of elderly and disabled persons in Bexar County. The Comprehensive Nutrition Program is available to citizens age 60 and older. Meals are served in a group setting to offer participants the opportunity to socialize. The program also offers transportation, recreation, health screenings, shopping assistance, and health and welfare counseling.

The Supportive Services for the Elderly Program offers door-to-door transportation for citizens age 60 and older to medical appointments, Social Security offices, food-stamp offices, and legal appointments as well as to the grocery store and bank. The service is free.

The Client-Managed Program provides assistance to adults who are permanently disabled. Along with personal care, the program offers meal preparation, home management, grocery shopping, companionship, and more. The Personal-Attendant Service is similar but is designed for disabled persons who are employed. The City Homemaker Program assists elderly citizens at home and also provides in-home attendant care.

**i** New San Antonio residents register to vote with the Bexar County Elections Department (203 W. Nueva St.; 210-335-VOTE; www.bexar.org/elections). There's a 30-day waiting period after registration before you can vote in a San Antonio election.

**DEPARTMENT OF AGING AND DISABILITY SERVICES (DADS)**
**Texas Department of Human Services**
**11307 Roszell St.**
**(210) 619-8148**
**www.dads.state.tx.us**

CCAD provides numerous services to allow aged and disabled persons to remain in their own homes. Among the services are adult foster care, housekeeping, family care, home-delivered meals, emergency response (via beepers), activities, family respite, and more.

**SOCIAL SECURITY ADMINISTRATION**
**Various locations**
**(800) 772-1213**
**www.socialsecurity.gov**
The Social Security Administration has several offices in San Antonio to assist residents with applying for benefits. The easiest way is to call the national toll-free number above (avoid calling on Monday: it's the busiest day).

## Additional Senior Resources

**ELDERWEB:TEXAS**
**www.elderweb.com**
ElderWeb:Texas is a user-friendly website that presents material ranging from legal issues to continuing care. From the main website, click on "regions," then scroll down to Texas.

**MORNINGSIDE MINISTRIES**
**700 Babcock Rd.**
**(210) 734-1000**
**www.morningsidemin.org**
Morningside Ministries, which operates multilevel facilities ranging from independent living to nursing home care, also offers a long list of resources on a referral website.

**SAN ANTONIO AARP INFORMATION CENTER**
**North Star Square**
**8507 N. McCullough Ave., Suite C-9**
**(210) 348-8684**
**www.aarp.org**

Volunteers at the San Antonio AARP Information Center can answer your questions and provide information about AARP. Driver safety classes and tax-aid assistance are also available at this location.

i A good source of information on senior living is the Seniors Resource Guide (www.seniorsresource guide.com). It provides information on health services (including in-home care), community resources and senior coalitions throughout the region.

**SAN ANTONIO COLLEGE**
**1300 San Pedro Ave.**
**(210) 785-6130**
**www.alamo.edu/sac/**
San Antonio College has a gerontology program, plus an Internet page that lists multiple sources of information that could be of interest to seniors.

**SAN ANTONIO OASIS**
**c/o Foley's Furniture Galleries**
**6161 NW Loop 410**
**(210) 647-2546**
**www.oasisnet.org/sanantonio**
San Antonio OASIS (Older Adult Service and Information System) offers opportunities for tutoring, volunteer work, programs on topics ranging from travel to fitness, and more.

**SAN ANTONIO PUBLIC LIBRARY**
**600 Soledad St.**
**(210) 207-2500**
**http://guides.mysapl.org/seniors**
The San Antonio Public Library has an Internet page for seniors that provides contact information for dozens of senior-oriented issues.

**TEXAS DEPARTMENT OF AGING AND DISABILITY SERVICES**
**701 W. 51st St., Austin**
**(512) 438-3011**
**www.dads.state.tx.us**
Texas Department of Aging offers an area list of Texas agencies on aging, plus information on recent legislation, health care, nursing homes, and an aging-related links page.

## SENIOR CENTERS

San Antonio is home to numerous senior centers that sponsor a host of programs—social activities, health screenings, transportation, meals, and even trips. Call the individual centers for details on hours (many are open weekdays only) and services. A partial list of centers follows.

**ACTIVITY CENTER FOR FRAIL AND ELDERLY (CENTRO DEL BARRIO)**
**123 Ascot Ave.**
**(210) 927-6883**

**BARSHOP JEWISH COMMUNITY CENTER**
**12500 NW Military Hwy.**
**(210) 302-6820**
**www.jccsanantonio.org**

**CASA HELOTES SENIOR CENTER**
**12070 Leslie Rd., Helotes**
**(210) 695-8510**
**www.esquaresecure.com**

**CHANDLER ESTATE IN LAUREL HEIGHTS SENIOR ACTIVITY CENTER**
**137 W. French Place**
**(210) 737-5196**
**www.mmliving.org**

## Close-up

### Winter Texans

Each year as winter's chill descends on the northern regions of the US, South Texas welcomes a flock of 1.3 million migrating "snowbirds," or winter Texans, eager to exchange snow shovels and sweaters for golf clubs and Bermuda shorts. Following is a small sample of the full menu of activities awaiting these seasonal Texans.

In the Rio Grande Valley community of **Harlingen,** visit the city's official bird, the Great Kiskadee, along with the other fine-feathered friends who call the 40-acre **Harlingen Thicket Bird Sanctuary** home. The city's Chamber of Commerce (311 E. Tyler St.; 800-531-7346; www.harlingen.com) offers a free birding guide and check-list. Across from the Municipal Auditorium, watch poetry in motion as 43 species of butterflies flit from flower to flower in the **Butterfly Garden,** located at 1204 Fair Park Blvd. Lovers of the great outdoors will also enjoy the **Arroyo Hike and Bike Trail,** a 2.1-mile trail that links together four city parks. Harlingen has been dubbed "The Antique Capital of the Valley," and that old McCoy cookie jar that used to sit on your mother's kitchen counter just might be found in of one of the many antiques stores that line Jackson Street. You can cruise down memory lane at the **Knapp Chevrolet Antique Car Museum** (US 83, Stuart Place Road exit), which houses a variety of blasts from the past, ranging from a 1929 Chevrolet to a 1957 Belair convertible. Military buffs will want to visit the **Iwo Jima Monument and Memorial Museum,** which is found on the campus of the Marine Military Academy near the airport.

While considered a magnet for vacationers due to its miles of beautiful beach, **South Padre Island** (800-OKPADRE; www.sopadre.com) offers more than just fun in the sun. The wetland habitat found at the four-acre **Laguna Madre Nature Trail** on the boardwalk behind the Convention Center and the **Laguna Atascosa National Wildlife Refuge** near the island are both paradise for birders. To acclimate yourself to the community, hop aboard **The Wave,** the island's trolley system.

Discover the origins of the two-year Mexican-American War during a ranger-led tour at **Palo Alto Battlefield National Historic Site** in **Brownsville** (800-626-2639; www.brownsville.org), which lies at the southern tip of the Rio Grande Valley. Nearby lies the city of **McAllen** (956-682-2871; www.mcallen.org), known as "The Square Dance Capital of the World," where more than 10,000 square dancers swing all winter to the voice of nationally known callers, and in early February people promenade to the annual **Texas Square Dance Jamboree.** The local Chamber of Commerce offers an extensive directory that lists dances as well as classes for the novice do-si-doer.

***Winter Texan Times*** (www.wintertexantimes.com)—a free publication distributed weekly each Thursday to RV parks and mobile homes in the Rio Grande Valley except during the months of October, November, and December, when delivery is every other week—keeps winter Texans informed of the latest events in the region.

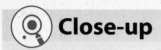

**CLAUDE BLACK COMMUNITY CENTER**
2805 E. Commerce St.
(210) 226-8561
www.sanantonio.gov

**COMANCHE PARK #2 SENIOR CENTER**
2600 Rigsby, Navajo Building
(210) 333-0414
http://bexar.tx.networkofcare.org

**COMMANDER'S HOUSE**
645 S. Main Ave.
(210) 224-1684
www.sanantonio.gov

**CHRIST THE KING SENIOR CENTER**
2610 Perez St.
(210) 434-3027
http://bexar.tx.networkofcare.org

**EL CARMEN SENIOR CENTER**
18555 Leal Rd.
(210) 626-2485

**ELLA AUSTIN COMMUNITY CENTER**
1023 N. Pine St.
(210) 224-2351
www.ellaaustin.org

**GOOD SAMARITAN CENTER**
1600 Saltillo St.
(210) 434-5531
www.goodsamaritancommunityservices.org

**GRANADA HOMES**
311 S. Saint Mary's St.
(210) 225-2645
www.granadahomes.net

**GREATER RANDOLPH AREA SENIOR PROGRAM**
250 Donalan, Converse
(210) 658-3578
www.grasp211.org

**HARLANDALE SENIOR CENTER**
115 W. Southcross Blvd.
(210) 924-4771

**HOLY FAMILY SENIOR CENTER**
152 Florencia Ave.
(210) 433-4265

**JARDIN DE SAINT JAMES NUTRITION CENTER**
420 Nunes St.
(210) 532-9239

**JEFFERSON AREA CO-OP**
201 Meredith Dr.
(210) 734-5016
www.serenityhomecaresa.com

**KENWOOD COMMUNITY CENTER**
305 Dora St.
(210) 732-1718
http://bexar.tx.networkofcare.org

**KIRBY SENIOR CENTER**
3211 Allen Sheppard Dr.
(210) 666-5124

**LEON VALLEY COMMUNITY CENTER**
6427 Evers Rd.
(210) 522-9966
www.leonvalleytexas.gov

**LION'S FIELD ADULT AND SENIOR CENTER**
2809 Broadway
(210) 826-9041
www.sanantonio.gov

**MADONNA NEIGHBORHOOD CENTER**
1906 Castroville Rd.
(210) 432-2374
www.uthscsa.edu

**MISSION SAN JOSE SENIOR CENTER**
6710 San Jose Dr.
(210) 923-8681
http://bexar.tx.networkofcare.org

**NEW MOUNT PLEASANT BAPTIST SENIOR CENTER**
1639 Hays St.
(210) 225-7907

**OUR LADY OF ANGELS SENIOR CENTER**
1224 Stonewall St.
(210) 923-6270
http://bexar.tx.networkofcare.org

**OUR LADY OF GUADALUPE CHURCH SENIOR CENTER**
1321 El Paso St.
(210) 223-5738
http://bexar.tx.networkofcare.org

**OUR LADY OF SORROWS SENIOR CENTER**
3107 N. St. Mary's St.
(210) 733-1247
www.sanantonio.gov

**PALACIO DEL SOL SENIOR CENTER**
400 N. Frio St.
(210) 224-0442

**PRESA COMMUNITY CENTER**
3721 S. Presa St.
(210) 532-5295
www.presa.org

**ROLLING OAKS BAPTIST CHURCH**
6401 Wenzel Rd.
(210) 590-4177
www.rollingoaksbaptistchurch.com

**ST. AGNES SENIOR CENTER**
804 Ruiz St.
(210) 223-1603

**ST. MARY MAGDALEN'S SENIOR CENTER**
1735 Clower St.
(210) 735-3700
http://stmm.info

**ST. MATTHEW'S CATHOLIC CHURCH SENIOR CENTER**
10703 Wurzbach Rd.
(210) 691-8947
www.stmatts.org

**ST. VINCENT DE PAUL SENIOR CENTER**
4222 SW Loop 410
(210) 670-1800
www.svdpusa.org

**SALVATION ARMY PEACOCK CENTER**
615 Peacock St.
(210) 733-0665
www.salvationarmysatx.org

**SOUTH SAN ANTONIO YWCA SENIOR CENTER**
503 Lovett Ave.
(210) 924-4691
www.ywca.org

## ALZHEIMER'S RESOURCES

**ALZHEIMER'S ASSOCIATION—SOUTH TEXAS CHAPTER**
7400 Louis Pasteur Dr., Suite 200
(210) 822-6449
www.alz.org/txstar
The association offers monthly support groups in both English and Spanish, counseling by telephone or in person to caregivers, a lending library of books and videos, and in-home tapes in English and Spanish.

## LIFETIME LEARNING

You're never too old to learn! Most school districts in San Antonio offer numerous learning opportunities for adults, senior citizens included. Some districts offer English as a second language (ESL) only, while others present a full slate of classes on intriguing subjects like computer proficiency, arts and crafts, tracing your ancestry, playing the dulcimer, line dancing, and more.

**INSTITUTE OF TEXAN CULTURES ACADEMY OF LEARNING IN RETIREMENT**
**8801 S. Bowie St.**
**(210) 458-2294**
**www.texancultures.utsa.edu**

**JUDSON INDEPENDENT SCHOOL DISTRICT**
**8012 Shin Oak Dr.**
**(210) 945-5100**
**www.judsonisd.org**

**NORTH EAST INDEPENDENT SCHOOL DISTRICT**
**8961 Tesoro Dr.**
**(210) 804-7000**
**www.neisd.net**

**NORTHSIDE INDEPENDENT SCHOOL DISTRICT**
**5900 Evers Rd.**
**(210) 397-8500**
**www.nisd.net**

**SAN ANTONIO COLLEGE SENIOR CITIZEN**
**Alamo Area Council of Governments**
**8700 Tesoro Dr., Suite 700**
**(210) 362-5200**
**www.alamoaging.org**

**SAN ANTONIO INDEPENDENT SCHOOL DISTRICT**
**237 W. Travis**
**(210) 354-0922**
**www.saisd.net**

## COMMUNITY ACTIVITIES

**SAN ANTONIO PARKS AND RECREATION DEPARTMENT SENIOR PROGRAMMING**
**Commander's House**
**645 S. Main Ave.**
**(210) 224-1684**
**www.sanantonio.gov/parksandrec**
Seniors age 50 and over can participate in community activities through the San Antonio Parks and Recreation Department. A range of activities are held at the Commander's House, a historic facility built in 1883 as the living quarters for the Commanding Officer of the Texas Arsenal. Classes here range from painting to guitar to ballroom dancing. Defensive-driving classes are offered on the last Mon and Tues of every other month. The facility also sponsors free blood-pressure checks once a month. For a minimal charge, participants at the center can purchase lunch every Tues, Wed, and Thurs.

**SAN ANTONIO PARKS AND RECREATION DEPARTMENT SENIOR PROGRAMMING**
**Lion's Field Adult and Senior Citizens Center**
**2809 Broadway**
**(210) 826-9041**
**www.sanantonio.gov/parksandrec**
Seniors can sign up for a variety of classes at this seniors' center; programs include ceramics, bridge, painting, exercise, and more. The Woodlawn Camera Club and the San Antonio Historic Association hold their regular meetings here as well. The center also operates a boutique featuring items made by center participants. The boutique is open Mon, Tues, Thurs, and Fri from 7:30 a.m. to 9 p.m., and Wed from 7:30 a.m. to 4 p.m. The center runs special events throughout the

year, including an annual Christmas arts and crafts sale.

## VOLUNTEER OPPORTUNITIES

**BEXAR COUNTY RETIRED SENIOR VOLUNTEER PROGRAM (RSVP)**
**1405 N. Main Ave., Suite 223**
**(210) 222-0301**
**www.seniorcorps.org**
Seniors looking for volunteer opportunities find plenty of options through the Retired Senior Volunteer Program, or RSVP.

**SAN ANTONIO PARKS AND RECREATION DEPARTMENT**
**(210) 207-8452**
**www.sanantonio.gov/parksandrec**
The Parks and Recreation Department offers a variety of volunteer opportunities: working with people with special needs, assisting participants in recreational education programs, working with others at community centers, and participating in park cleanups. Citizens can also help ensure the safety of the local parks by volunteering for the Park Watch program. For information, call (210) 207-8529.

**UNITED WAY OF SAN ANTONIO AND BEXAR COUNTY**
**700 S. Alamo St.**
**(210) 352-7000**
**www.unitedwaysatx.org**
The Volunteer Center at United Way of San Antonio and Bexar County offers participants a variety of opportunities, depending on their desires and their previous experience. The job bank (as well as the United Way website) lists volunteer openings, ranging from marketing assistants to clerical help to youth assistance.

## TRANSPORTATION

**VIA METROPOLITAN TRANSIT SERVICE**
**(210) 362-2020**
**www.viainfo.net**
San Antonio and Bexar County's public transportation system offers a wide range of buses that crisscross the region. Seniors age 62 and over qualify for VIA's Reduced Fare ID Card that allows you to pay half fare. Off-peak discounts for senior citizens and persons with disabilities are available weekdays from 9 a.m. to 3 p.m. and all day weekends, when you can ride for a mere 20 cents. Complimentary paratransit service is provided to individuals who have disabilities that prevent them from using fixed-route bus service. VIAtrans, the Americans with Disabilities Act's complimentary paratransit, is provided during the same hours of the day, same days per week, and within 0.75 mile of a fixed bus route. You can download an application for VIAtrans from www.viainfo.net/AccessibleService/VIATransApplication.pdf or call the Accessible Services Department at (210) 362-2140 or TTY (210) 362-2019.

## PUBLICATIONS

***NEW LIFESTYLES***
**(800) 869-9549**
**www.newlifestyles.com**
Published twice a year, this free guide to senior housing covers senior apartments, continuing-care retirement communities, retirement communities, assisted-living facilities, Alzheimer's care facilities, nursing and rehabilitation centers, home-care agencies, hospice-care agencies, and adult day-care centers.

# MEDIA

**Visitors to San Antonio who want to learn about the city should probably begin with something simple: turning on their radio or TV or reading a newspaper. The local media offer the quickest way to really get a feel for the Alamo City. Pick up a copy of the *San Antonio Express-News* or one of the smaller newspapers that focus on events and news in a particular area of town. Or tune in to a local TV or radio news program. In addition to helping visitors decide where to go and what to do, these media outlets offer great insight into how citizens of San Antonio conduct their day-to-day lives.**

## NEWSPAPERS & MAGAZINES

### Dailies

***SAN ANTONIO EXPRESS-NEWS***
**400 3rd St.**
**(210) 250-3000**
**www.mysanantonio.com**

In September 1865, only a few months after the end of the Civil War, August Siemering and H. Pollmar published the first issue of the weekly *San Antonio Express.* Daily publishing began in December 1866, with a subscription rate of $16 a year. Today this is San Antonio's main daily newspaper. The *San Antonio Express-News* covers weather, local events, business, and sports in addition to local and national news. Pick up a Friday issue for all of the information about what's happening in the Alamo City during the upcoming weekend.

### Other Newspapers & Magazines

***DAILY COMMERCIAL RECORDER***
**17400 Judson Rd.**
**(210) 250-2327**
**www.primetimenewspapers.com/dcr**

This newspaper is published weekdays (except legal holidays). The *Commercial Recorder* is a great source of public notices and public records taken from Bexar County courts, including court transactions, liens, and bankruptcies. The paper also publishes such business information as the granting of beer and wine permits, building permits, and sales tax permits. Copies of the *Daily Commercial Recorder* are available at several locations around the Bexar County Courthouse. Readers may also subscribe to the paper for $150 a year.

***LA PRENSA DE SAN ANTONIO***
**318 S. Flores St.**
**(210) 242-7900**
**www.laprensa.com**

*La Prensa de San Antonio* is San Antonio's only family-owned newspaper. Published in both Spanish and English, it comes out every Wed and Sun. La Prensa covers local and national news, business, entertainment, and sports. You can also check out *La Prensa*'s website, which offers access to the paper's archives.

***SAN ANTONIO BUSINESS JOURNAL***
**8200 I-10 West, Suite 820**
**(210) 341-3202**
**www.bizjournals.com/sanantonio**

As you might expect, the *San Antonio Business Journal* is a great place to find information on the San Antonio business scene. And much of the information in the print version of this weekly is also found on the *Journal*'s website. The website also allows readers to access nearly 40 other business papers. The online Web archive includes *Journal* articles from as far back as 1996.

***SAN ANTONIO CURRENT***
**1500 N. St. Mary's St.**
**(210) 227-0044**
**www.sacurrent.com**

The *Current* is San Antonio's free alternative newspaper, published weekly and distributed all over town. It covers the hipper element of the city and is particularly strong on local entertainment news. It often offers a different slant on local politics, and its classifieds can also make for interesting reading.

***SAN ANTONIO MAGAZINE***
**121 Interpark Blvd., Suite 407**
**(210) 268-1100**
**www.sanantoniomag.com**

Boasting over 100,000 readers, this lifestyle magazine covers trends, style, dining, travel and leisure, home and garden and events in San Antonio. *San Antonio Magazine* is published monthly.

**i** **When you arrive in town, locate a copy of the free *San Antonio Current*, which comes out every Thursday, for up-to-the-minute listings of the arts and entertainment scene.**

***SAN ANTONIO WOMAN***
**www.sawoman.com**

Published 6 times per year, this magazine features prominent San Antonio women as well as such subjects as food and dining, health, business, arts and culture, and more.

***YOUR SA SCENE***
**900 NE Loop 410**
**(210) 828-7424**
**www.scenepublications.com**

Published since 1999, this publication features lifestyle articles ranging from San Antonio's most expensive homes to Fiesta memories. Published biweekly.

## RADIO STATIONS

If you like Tejano and conjunto music, then you'll love San Antonio radio. Due to its cultural diversity and major Mexican influences, San Antonio's radio stations are filled with sounds from south of the border. Tejano music can be found on many radio dials in the San Antonio area. In fact, the Tejano sound is so popular here that there are several clubs around the city featuring music with a Latin beat. (See the Nightlife chapter for more information.) But whatever your taste in music, you're bound to find a local station that plays your favorite tunes.

Radio DJs are also a good source of inside information. Many have been working in San Antonio radio for more than a decade and know a great deal about local clubs, restaurants, and news. Change the frequency on the car radio often to get a variety of spins on the local scene.

## Christian

**KSLR AM 630**
**9601 McAllister Freeway**
**(210) 344-8481**
**www.kslr.com**
This station offers inspirational Christian talk radio. The lineup is varied, and every hour brings a new topic and host. The lineup changes on the weekends.

**KYFS FM 90.9**
**9330 Corporate Dr., Suite 808, Selma**
**(210) 651-9093**
**www.bbnradio.org**
Owned by the Bible Broadcasting Network of Charlotte, North Carolina, this 100,000-watt station covers San Antonio and surrounding South Texas with gospel-based programming around the clock. Highlights of the KYFS broadcast day include Dr. Chuck Swindoll, Dr. Donald Hubbard, and others, plus Sunday school and sermons on Sunday morning.

## Country

**Y100 FM**
**8122 Datapoint Dr., Suite 600**
**(210) 615-5400**
**www.y100fm.com**
If you've come to Texas for country music, then tune in to Y100 FM. And if you're looking for music news, then log on to the station's website, which has the latest entertainment headlines, listings for events in the San Antonio area, and local and national news and weather.

**KAJA FM 97**
**6222 NW I-10**
**(210) 736-9700, (800) 373-9700,**
**(210) 470-KJ97 (request line)**
**www.kj97.com**
KJ97 broadcasts Texas's favorite country music. Tune in to hear the latest country hits as well as the chart-toppers of yesteryear. The KJ97 website is a good source of country music news, events listings, contests, upcoming album information, and more.

**i** **San Antonio's current weather information is available 24 hours a day on National Weather Service radio station WXK67, at 162.5 MHz. If your regular AM radio cannot pick up the signal (it broadcasts at only 1,000 watts), you can purchase special weather alert radios at retailers such as Radio Shack.**

## Public Radio

**KPAC FM 88.3**
**8401 Datapoint Dr.**
**(210) 614-8977**
**www.tpr.org**
KPAC has been San Antonio's classical music source on FM since 1982, broadcasting musical programming 24 hours each day. The schedule includes live broadcasts of the Metropolitan Opera and recorded concerts of some of the world's finest symphony orchestras. Specialty programs include music for children, early music, and new CD releases.

**KSTX FM 89.1**
**8401 Datapoint Dr.**
**(210) 614-8977**
**www.tpr.org**
KSTX, KPAC's sister station, has a talk radio format, with most of its weekday programming produced by National Public Radio, including the popular news magazine *All Things Considered.* Tune in to KSTX on Saturday to hear live broadcasts of *A Prairie Home*

*Companion* and the local *Riverwalk Jazz,* which features the Jim Cullum Jazz Band broadcasting from Jim Cullum's Landing at the Hyatt, on San Antonio's River Walk, and from the Pearl Brewery.

## Retro

**KONO AM 860, KONO FM 101.1**
**8122 Datapoint Dr., Suite 600**
**(210) 615-5400, (210) 470-KONO (request line)**
**www.kono101.com**

Billing itself as the "Good Times Oldies" station, both KONO AM and KONO FM play music that is just that—good times oldies. The station's website features Internet audio, online radio, movie showtimes, music news, and concert tour information.

## Rock

**KISS FM 99.5**
**8122 Datapoint Dr., Suite 600**
**(210) 615-5400, (210) 470-KISS (request line)**
**www.kissrocks.com**

This rock radio station has many extra features to entice listeners to stay tuned. The station's website offers an event guide that keeps listeners up-to-date on current music events in San Antonio, including national tours.

**KZEP FM 104.5**
**427 9th St.**
**(210) 226-6444, (210) 470-5104 (request line)**
**www.kzep.com**

Tune in to KZEP for the greatest hits in classic rock music. The station also runs several contests, with prizes ranging from radio station collectibles to concert tickets. The station website has information on station DJs, rock news, and radio station contests.

## Talk

**KTSA AM 550**
**7800 I-10 West, Suite 300**
**(210) 340-1234, (210) 599-5555 (talk show call-in line)**
**www.ktsa.com**

This radio station began in 1922 as WCAR. Its name was changed to KTSA in 1927 when it was bought by Alamo Broadcast Company, and the company has changed hands several times since then. One of the highlights of KTSA history was a live interview with Orson Welles and H. G. Wells in 1939, one year after Orson Welles's broadcast of the author's *War of the Worlds*. In 1956 new owners introduced a "Top 40" format at KTSA, and in 1982 KTSA was the country's first AM station to broadcast in stereo. The station changed to all-talk radio in 1991 and has used that format since.

**WOAI AM 1200**
**6222 Northwest I-10**
**(210) 737-1200**
**www.woai.com**

This station has talk radio about a range of subjects and includes popular commentators such as Rush Limbaugh and Sean Hannity. WOAI's sister station, Ticket 760 (www.ticket760.com), is the local sports station, carrying live broadcasts of the San Antonio Spurs basketball games.

## Tejano

**KXTN 107.5**
**1777 NE Loop 410, Suite 400**
**(210) 470-5107**
**http://kxtn.com**

This station keeps listeners entertained with past and present Tejano hits the whole day through. The morning show features Jonny Ramirez with an array of jokes, interesting commentary, and music. The website includes live chats, contests, and entertainment.

## Classic Rock

**X 106.7 FM**
**8122 Datapoint Dr., Suite 600**
**(210) 615-5400**
**http://x1067fm.com**
Classic commercial-free rock is featured on this popular channel, which also offers many giveaways

## Television Stations

**KABB-TV FOX 29**
**4335 NW Loop 410**
**(210) 366-1129**
**www.foxsanantonio.com**
KABB-TV began in December 1987 as an independent station that was not affiliated with a national network. In 1995 KABB affiliated with the Fox Network.

**KENS 5 CHANNEL 5**
**5400 Fredericksburg Rd.**
**(210) 366-5000**
**www.kens5.com**
In 1950 George Stores formed the San Antonio Television Company, making San Antonio's KEYL the 99th TV station in the US. KEYL was changed to KENS 5 in 1955. The most advanced weather technology in South Texas is owned and operated by KENS 5, including Super Doppler, the most powerful radar of its kind in the San Antonio area. The station also has *Great Day SA*, a weekday local program featuring guests ranging from skydivers and African drum troupes to acupuncturists and face readers.

**KLRN CHANNEL 9**
**501 Broadway**
**(210) 270-9000**
**www.klrn.org**
PBS's San Antonio station KLRN provides daily programming that focuses on education for all ages. Through the day, most programs are aimed at preschool to grade-school children. In the evening, educational shows like *Frontline* and *Nova* are aired. KLRN-TV began broadcasting in 1962 and, until 1984, served both San Antonio and Austin through a transmitter in New Braunfels. Today, broadcasting from its 36,000-square-foot studio, KLRN offers local, regional, and national public broadcast shows.

**KSAT CHANNEL 12**
**1408 N. St. Mary's St.**
**(210) 351-1200**
**www.ksat.com**
This ABC affiliate station hit the airwaves in February 1957 as KONO TV, broadcasting the inauguration of President Eisenhower. When purchased in 1969, the station became KSAT Channel 12. The station has changed hands several times since 1969 and today is owned by Post-Newsweek, which bought KSAT in 1994. In 2003 the station earned a national award for crime prevention from the National Crime Prevention Council.

i San Antonio's cable television vendor is Time Warner Cable (8400 NE Loop 410, #200; 210-244-0500).

**KMYS CW 35**
**4335 NW Loop 410**
**(210) 366-1129**
**www.kmys.tv**
Formerly KRRT, Channel 35 is now KMYS, San Antonio's CW network station.

**KVDA TV 60**
**6234 San Pedro Ave.**
**(210) 568-0199**
**http://sanantonio.holaciudad.com/contenidos/telemundo.html**
This Spanish-language station is an affiliate of the Telemundo Television Network, The station transmits within a 60-mile radius of its San Antonio transmitter.

**UNIVISION KWEX 41**
**411 E. Durango Blvd.**
**(210) 227-4141**
**http://univision41.univision.com/**
Channel 41 is a Spanish-language station, the first commercially based Spanish-language TV station in the US.

**WOAI TV CHANNEL 4**
**1031 Navarro St.**
**(210) 226-4444**
**www.woai.com**
WOAI is San Antonio's NBC affiliate. In 2003 the station reverted to its original name, after operating for years as KMOL. WOAI is home to a local daytime entertainment program called *San Antonio Living,* which offers news, weather, entertainment headlines, education reports, and health updates. With live on-site broadcasts from around the city, Living host Leslie Bohl Jones delves into the many aspects of San Antonio and gives viewers a real feel for the city.

WOAI is one of the very few stations west of the Mississippi River whose call letters start with a W rather than a K. WOAI began in 1922 and so received "grandfather" status when federal government regulations mandated that all radio and television stations west of the Mississippi begin with K.

# INDEX

## T